Harness Overlays

Harness Overlays

Beat the Favorite

Bill Heller

Bonus Books, Inc., Chicago

02 01 00 99 98 5 4 3 2

Library of Congress Catalog Card Number: 92-75929

International Standard Book Number: 0-929387-97-X

Bonus Books, Inc.
160 East Illinois Street
Chicago, Illinois 60611

Printed in the United States of America

Race programs courtesy of the racetracks

To my brother, Orrin, and his lovely wife, Debbie

Contents

Acknowledgments

The biggest handicap in doing a book about handicapping is the immense amount of data required. No problem here. In a blanket photo-finish, it's hard to tell who finished first.

Dean Hoffman, Editor of *Hoof Beats Magazine* and Director of Publicity for the U.S. Trotting Association, has been a friend for years. He literally got this project rolling. In addition, he and his kind assistant, Corky Visminas, gave me access to mountains of data from 14 tracks across the country. Dean's input and enthusiasm are highly valued.

Millie Allen of Skip Carlson's Publicity Department at Saratoga provided countless charts and favors. Quickly.

At Yonkers Raceway, Director of Publicity Gary Sussman, a friend for 30 years and counting, provided important races used in the book as examples and helped set up interviews instantaneously. His assistant, Jason Frenchman, helped with the dirty work.

The Meadowlands' Ellen Harvey was just as helpful with races and obscure information I requested.

My friend Barry Ikler, a hopelessly addicted owner and fan of the sport, read the manuscript, checked my definitions and offered suggestions.

My proofreaders, Sue "Tuey" Milstein, Margaret Diggs and my wife, Anna, met tight deadlines.

Anna also helped with the charts and tables, and our 4-year-old son, Benjamin—a.k.a. Bubba—helped his Daddy with the printouts.

Definitions

(Parentheses show program symbols)

Blindswitch—With a horse directly in front of him, a horse racing two-wide is boxed in by a horse going three-wide. Or a horse three-wide is trapped by one racing four-wide. The blindswitch slows or kills the victim horse's momentum. Horses who were making a move on the outside only to get blindswitched are definitely worth following. Being at the track is an advantage. There, you can spot a horse who got blindswitched rather than relying on a horse's Past Performance Lines (PPs). Many times, it's impossible to decipher a blindswitch from the program.

Boxed In—A horse is unable to pull from the rail to the outside because another horse is directly alongside.

Break (x)—A horse loses the rhythm of his gait, making an abrupt stop during the race. This happens more with trotters than with pacers. A horse who breaks can still win the race once he recovers from his miscue. A horse who makes a break at the finish line is disqualified only if there is another horse within 1 length of him. That mistake is termed a lapped-on break.

Bute (b)—An equine painkiller similar to aspirin.

Claimed (c) or (z)—A horse purchased in a claiming race.

Claimer—A horse in a claiming race or the race itself.

Claiming Race—A race in which each horse can be purchased for a specified amount of money decided by the owner. The horse's ownership changes hands immediately after the race.

Cover—A horse racing on the outside with an outside horse directly in front of him. The first horse is giving cover to the second. The importance is twofold: 1) If the cover horse is first over (first on the outside), he's battling the wind—if any—while the second drafts in behind him; and, 2) if the cover horse is first over, he's battling the leader head to head while the second horse watches and waits. The fiercer the battle in front of him, the greater his chance of beating them both. Live cover means the horse in front of him continues to gain, allowing him to follow. Bad or dead cover means the horse in front didn't sustain his bid, thereby slowing the second horse's progress, usually forcing him to go three-wide to get around him.

Daily Double—A bet picking the winners of the first two races. Most tracks also have a Middle and/or Late Double. The principle is the same.

Disqualified (DQ)—A horse is taken down from his actual finish for interfering with another horse, making a lapped-on break, or gaining ground by galloping after a break.

Distanced (Dis)—Lost by more than 25 lengths.

Exacta—A bet picking the first two finishers in exact order; also called a perfecta.

Exacta Box—For two horses, it's playing them both 1-2 and 2-1 in order, the equivalent of a quiniella at twice the cost. A $2 exacta box costs $4. For three horses, it's $12 and covers all combinations. Boxing four horses costs $48 and so on.

Exacta Box Wheel—This covers every combination if your horse finishes first or second. A $2 exacta box wheel in an 8-horse field costs $28.

Exacta Wheel—Key a horse to win and play every other horse to finish second. In an 8-horse field, a $2 exacta wheel costs $14 to cover all seven horses for second. A horse can be wheeled for second at the same cost.

First Over—Moving first on the outside.

Flushing—A driver's strategy to get cover when his horse is moving up first over on the outside. As he advances, he gives the driver of the horse inside and in front of him an opportunity to pull, which ensures that driver that he won't be boxed in for the rest of the race. At the same time, this gives the first driver cover. Usually, a driver might try to flush one or two horses in front of him before he moves past them. Such decisions are made by two drivers in the matter of 1 or 2 seconds and greatly influence the result of the race.

Handicap—Figure a race.

Handicap Race (Hcap)—A race where post positions are assigned by a race secretary to balance the field. The best horses are assigned the outside posts; the weakest the inside ones.

Lasix (L)—An equine diuretic used for bleeders.

Late Closer (LC)—A series of races at a better level than most conditions but below stakes. Also termed Early Closer (EC) depending on eligibility requirements.

Leaving—Going for the lead at the start of the race.

Length—The length of a horse, which is equivalent to 1/5 of a second.

Light the Board—Finish in the money.

Maiden—A horse who hasn't won a pari-mutuel race.

Non-Winners (NW)—A race condition of Non-Winners of a specific number of races or amount of money. NW2 means Non-Winners of two races. NW $1,500L7 means Non-Winners of $1,500 in the last seven starts.

Parked—Racing on the outside, two, three or even more horses wide. On turns, parked horses are covering more ground than the horses inside them. Horses who race an entire mile on the outside at a 1/2-mile track travel a considerably longer distance. The shortest distance to the winner's circle is one traced immediately adjacent to the inner rail. A parked horse is identified in the program by a small circle superimposed next to his position during a race. Two circles mean the horse was three or more wide.

Pick 3—A bet picking the winners of three consecutive races.

Pick 4—A bet picking the winners of four straight races.

Pocket—Sitting second on the inside behind the leader. Generally, drivers don't pull the pocket, hoping that the leader can put away the challenge of the horse first over and give you an opportunity to get out. On the flip side, sitting in the pocket can prove fatal if the leader in front of you gets passed by one or more horses. The creation of the open stretch—a one-horse passing lane on the inside open to any horse other than the leader—has drastically changed the strategy for a horse in the pocket.

PPs—A horse's past performance lines in the program.

Qualifier (Qual)—A non-betting race for horses who have to beat a set time to be eligible to race, or a practice mile for a horse and/or driver.

Quiniclla—A bet picking the first two finishers in either order. Quiniellas pay roughly half as much as exactas, although there are sporadic differences high and low.

Second Over—Moving second on the outside.

Stakes—The highest level of races.

Third Over—Moving third on the outside.

Triple—A bet picking the first three horses in correct order; also called a trifecta.

Triple Box—Same principle as an exacta box: covering any combination of a specific number of horses. A $2 triple box of three horses costs $12. Include a fourth horse in the box and it now costs $48.

Triple Key/Part Wheel—Pick one horse to finish first, second or third and cover a specific number of other horses in the field to complete the triple. For an example, key the 6 to win and box four other horses to finish second and third. With $2 triples, the cost is $24. Add another horse to box under the 6, and the cost is $40. Horses can also be keyed to finish second or third.

Tuck—An opening on the rail taken by a horse on the outside to avoid being parked on a turn.

Universal Driver Rating (UDR)—A driver's percentage of firsts, seconds and thirds comparable to a baseball player's batting average. Anything over .300 is solid.

Wire to Wire—A horse leads from start to finish.

Winners Over (WO)—Winners with earnings over a specific amount of money. WO $10,000 means a horse must have won more than $10,000 to be eligible.

Beat the Favorite

CHAPTER 1

There are two kinds of harness racing bettors: the wealthy who can afford to wager thousands of dollars on a single race, and the rest of us. Let's deal with us.

There are no gimmicks here, no formulae and no meaningless guarantees. But there is a healthy dose of intelligent handicapping and betting ideas to make your trips to the track more profitable and more enjoyable.

To succeed in betting harness racing, it's imperative that we get value for our wagers. We do that by finding overlays, horses whose odds are higher than they should be, according to our handicapping. Underlays are the exact opposite: horses with odds lower than deemed reasonable. Underlays inherently create overlays.

We don't want to bet a 4-5 shot for a $3.60 payoff on a $2 bet. Heavy favorites are almost always underlays. But their highly-visible presence at harness tracks, especially ½-mile ones, produces overlays galore. And all kinds of value.

As hard as it is to believe, $1 bets—which should be available at every track for every race—can be a potent ally in wagers such as a Pick 4 or a triple. Betting single dollars to cover a large number of combinations can be surprisingly successful because it gives bettors leverage, a chance to extract value from those more difficult bets.

Handicapping should be fun. Handicapping a race, and seeing it unfold as predicted, produces a delicious thrill in addition to the payoff. It's even better if the winner is a harness overlay.

The novice fan might not understand that in pari-mutuel horse racing, bettors are trying to beat other bettors, not the track itself. Tracks take out a fixed percentage of the money bet, which is called the handle. The percentage remains constant, so it makes no difference if a winner pays $10 or $100. The bettors make the odds. If there's more correct win money wagered on Horse A in the first race than on Horse B in the second, A will pay less.

We want more.

We must identify fallible favorites. When do favorites lose at the tracks you frequent? Is it because of post position? The condition of the race? A wet track? A driver switch?

Harness Overlays operates from the same principles of its predecessor, *Overlay, Overlay*. Given: The more information you have, the better you'll handicap. That's why this book contains statistical analysis of more than 11,000 races throughout the country, and the strategy secrets of eight of the sport's best drivers.

In the beginning, you should develop a feel for the odds on the toteboard. Bettors get an initial indication of post time odds from the morning line, but morning lines are conservative and usually bound by a limited range, say a 3-1 favorite and longshots of 10-1 or 15-1. Actually, extremely few harness races have a 3-1 favorite. His odds will be much lower, say 3-5 to 5-2. Accordingly, nearly every race offers longshots of 20-1 to 50-1. More sophisticated bettors have a better feel for post-time odds, but it's easy to improve this skill. Simply write down the odds you expect 10 minutes before post time. Compare them with the final odds. Do it a few times and you'll develop a useful skill.

Here's how you'll use it. If you think the favorite should be 5-2 and he's 6-5 on the board, find the overlays he produces. One of them might be a horse you liked right from the start. If your handicapping came up with a horse who was the second choice on the morning line at 4-1, and he's now 6-1, go for it. If you identify a real contender who was 8-1 on the morning line and he's 15-1, go for it. In either scenario, you're getting value for your investment. Remember that value is the guiding principle. Get more for your money. Get higher odds than you expected. Never settle for significantly lower odds.

Don't fall into a trap. When you handicap the race and come up with a horse who opened up at 5-1 and is 6-5 a minute before post time, stay away! Even more important: don't get into a guessing game with yourself.

Don't decide to bet a 3-1 shot and then bet him at odds of 3-2. Don't rationalize this underlay by saying you'll bet more money to get a roughly equal profit. Sit out the race. Or bet another contender. There are healthier, more creative ways to bet favorites that you think will win.

Turn, Turn, Turn

In harness and thoroughbred racing, the number of turns a horse must negotiate is important. With thoroughbreds, especially 3-year-olds approaching the Kentucky Derby, there is considerable dialogue about whether or not a horse has gone two turns in a race so he'll be able to handle the two turns of the $1\frac{1}{4}$-mile Derby.

In harness racing, most tracks are $\frac{1}{2}$, $\frac{5}{8}$ or 1 mile. Respectively, a harnessbred must negotiate four, three or two turns to complete the standard 1 mile distance. An exception is Vernon Downs in central New York State, where horses race from a long chute on a $\frac{3}{4}$-mile track, dealing with just two turns for one mile.

Half-mile tracks are slower than $\frac{5}{8}$- and 1-mile ones because of more turns. This is reflected in comparative speed ratings listed in the track program.

Generally, trotters have more difficulty on $\frac{1}{2}$-mile tracks than pacers. Generally, physically larger pacers are better on bigger tracks.

Are the Races Fixed?

If that's your perspective, you should have given up a long time ago. Would you continue to play in a poker game if you believed the deck was marked? Of course not.

Harness racing has been tainted with this bad image for a long time. A driver controls his horse by two lines connected to a bit in the horse's mouth. That's how he steers him. Frequently, fans see a driver line-driving his horse in the stretch and misinterpret it as him pulling his horse back just as he's about to win.

There have been allegations of race-fixing in harness racing. There have been drivers and trainers suspended and banned from tracks. Unfortunately, such rare incidents devastate the sport's image. The most effective deterrent would be life-long bans for convicted race-fixers. As it is, judges at every track in the country try to ensure the product is pure.

Tips

Tips can drive you crazy, negating your handicapping completely. Most tips come from grooms, drivers, trainers or owners who are betting a horse heavily, most likely because he had a super training mile two or three days earlier. Tips can create the underlays we strive to find and bet against. Tip horses usually show up blatantly on the tote board. Before you throw out your own handicapping to hop aboard the "hot" horse, consider these two points: 1) If this so-called "inside information" got to you, how many hundreds of other bettors have the same scoop, and 2) where and when do you ever stop paying attention to tips? Win one, lose two? Win three, blow two? Avoiding tips makes the point irrelevant.

A Helping Hand

Selections in a newspaper, *Sports Eye*—a daily racing paper based in New York — or a tip sheet offer advice for a price. A small price, really, for a helping hand. But do we want one?

Newspaper handicappers usually attend the racetrack frequently, if not nightly. Their selections—which must be submitted the night before to make the next day's paper—are from a knowledgeable source, a person steeped with knowledge of her or his particular track. Yet even so, harnessbred handicappers in newspapers are correct anywhere from 25 to 40 percent of the time. Considering that the selections are done a day in advance without late scratches, driver switches and/or equipment changes, any percentage over 30 is a healthy one. But only if the selections are done by a handicapper whose name goes out daily with his selections. Occasionally, newspapers use anonymous handicappers with sobriquets such as Railbird, Clocker, Dan

Patch, etc. It's a despicable practice. Many times, a clerk in the sports department of the paper makes those selections with little or no knowledge of the sport. Other times, someone mixes up another person's picks for first, second and third with absolutely no thought.

Sports Eye does a magnificent job with its PPs, which have been used as programs at various tracks. But even their experts deal with reality. Hitting better than 35 percent is excellent. In thoroughbred racing, handicappers are glad to top 25 percent because of larger fields, changing distances and different track surfaces.

If you think those percentages are low, think about this. In newspapers, football handicappers do well if they top 50 percent of their picks with the spread. They only have to choose from two possibilities. Harness racing handicappers deal with eight to 10 possibilities in every race.

Regardless, glancing at a newspaper or *Sports Eye*'s selections can reveal information you failed to notice. That's helpful. It's not a source of gold. If you buy two different papers and/or *Sports Eye*, you'll have as many as five or six handicappers' selections. Many may agree on one race, yet invariably different handicappers come up with different winners. Sometimes right; sometimes wrong. That's the way it is. Use public handicappers if you like, or reach your own conclusions. If you enjoy the process of handicapping, check out someone else's suggestions after you make yours.

Now then, tip sheets. In a word: useless. They all advertise eight winners last night or a $400 exacta, but their authors do no better than newspaper handicappers. And just like them, they'll come up with different winners. If you find one handicapper on a tip sheet you think comes up with solid overlays, use him if you must. But relying on other people interferes with a handicapper's sense of closure. At the end of each race, you will know whether you were right or not. If you start blaming or celebrating someone else's picks, why handicap in the first place?

Go for it! Do it yourself!

Pinpointing the Vulnerable Favorite

If there are 50 ways to leave your lover, there are at least a dozen ways to leave the favorite:

- Overbet
- Chronic non-winner
- No excuse in losing last
- Perfect trip in winning last
- Poor post
- Negative driver switch
- A breaker
- Moving up in class
- Missed more than two weeks
- Different track condition
- Changed trainers
- Warmed up poorly

Roughly 30 to 45 percent of favorites win at harness tracks, and many of them are underlays. Horses that should be 2-1 go off at 4-5. A lukewarm favorite who should be 5-2 is 8-5. Having several winning favorites a night is easily understood. But there's a huge difference between a 3-1 favorite and one at even money (1-1). We're interested in the 55 to 70 percent of races won by horses who beat vulnerable favorites. These can be our overlays.

Harness racing at ½-mile tracks produces a near-fatal dose of short-priced winners. If you've got thousands of dollars to invest, fine. Go find the $3.60 winner.

Ideally, every track every night should contain at least a couple double-digit winners. We're not talking 99-1, rather 4-1. That's $10. Or 5-1: $12.

What's especially hard to take are evenings when chalk dominates totally, making it difficult, if not impossible, to make intelligent win bets at a fair value. When short prices get downright oppressive, betting becomes more difficult. Which one or two races out of 10 will an overbet favorite lose?

Here's how bad it gets from a 1992 sample of win prices:

- Balmoral, March 14 - 9 of 11 winners pay $5.20 or less.
- Buffalo, May 17 - All 11 pay $9 or less.
- Hawthorne, February 5 - 9 of 10 pay $9 or less.
- Hazel Park, May 6 - 10 of 11 pay $8.80 or less.
- Los Alamitos, February 1 - 7 of 12 pay $4.20 or less.
- Meadowlands, July 2 - 10 of 11 pay $7.20 or less.
- Meadows, June 13 - 12 of 13 pay $5.60 or less.
- Monticello, April 3 - 10 of 11 pay $7.40 or less.
- Northfield, July 16 - 9 straight pay $5.40 or less.
- Pompano Park, April 2 - 12 of 13 pay $8.20 or less.

- Saginaw, June 3 - 9 of 12 pay $6.20 or less.
- Saratoga, May 23 - All 11 pay $7.60 or less.
- Scioto Downs, June 23 - 8 of 9 pay $6 or less.
- Yonkers, May 8 - 9 of 11 pay $6 or less.

Get the picture?

Don't fret. There are winning overlays out there; they're just more difficult to find some nights. They are definitely worth the look.

Here are a dozen ways—incorporating important elements of handicapping—to cash in on overlays:

- Back class
- Needed a tightener
- Sign of life
- Lone speed
- Horse whom nobody believes
- Young and improving
- Moves inside
- Positive driver switch
- Poor trip in last
- Different track condition
- Warms up sharply
- Equipment change

We'll confine our overlays to horses who have a legitimate chance to win. Betting a horse that has no chance at 20-1 instead of 10-1 is useless.

Start at the Bottom

When evaluating a horse's Past Performance Lines (PPs), read from the bottom PP, the least recent, up to the top to see how the horse is coming into tonight's race, and to ensure you'll notice two or more horses who have faced each other previously.

Keep in mind the guiding rule: For every underlay, there are overlays. For every over-bet favorite, there are many overlays.

Here's a perfect example of a massive underlay creating overlays. This race illustrates three handicapping principles: 1) finding the vulnerable favorite; 2) avoiding horses who don't win, and 3) believing that young horses will improve in their first few starts—a reasonable assumption of progress.

Eight fillies and mares went to post at Saratoga, May 6, 1992, in a Non-Winners of 2 pari-mutuel races lifetime.

ONE MILE PACE
PURSE $1,600
WEDNESDAY, MAY 6, 1992
PICK THREE & EXACTA

FOURTH RACE

FILLIES & MARES
6 YEAR OLDS & UNDER
NON-WINNERS 2 PARI-MUTUEL RACES LIFETIME OR $1000 LAST 7 STARTS
ALSO ELIGIBLE: NON-WINNERS 1 PARI-MUTUEL RACE LIFETIME
TO DRAW INSIDE POST POSITIONS

WARM UP-BLACK

PROGRAM NUMBER | Date | Trk | Purse | Cd Class | Leaders Time Dis 1/4 1/2 3/4 | Winners Time | PP | 1/4 | 1/2 | 3/4 | Str | Fin | Ind 1/4 Time | Ind Time | Odds | Driver | Order Of Finish First Second Third | Temp

10-1 — 1 — BREEZY KNOLL SKIPI (NY) — YELLOW
b f 3 BrandNewFella-TwinklingImage-StrikingImage
Parks Breezy Knoll, Dekalb Jct, N.Y.
HENRY WESTBROOK JR (160) blk-or (10-0-0-0-.000) Tr—Henry Westbrook Jr (.000)
1992 5 0 0 2 $348 · 1991 4 0 0 0 $87 · Lifetime $435

Date	Trk	Purse	Cd Class	Dis 1/4 1/2 3/4	Time	PP	1/4	1/2	3/4	Str	Fin	Ind 1/4	Ind Time	Odds	Driver	Order Of Finish	Temp
4-24 92	Stga	1400	gd F&MNW1PMCD	1 30 3 102 2 133 4	204 4	4ix	8	8	8 7 3/4	8	8 dnf			63.00	HWstbrokJ	WilowyBauty,RacnginApri,NoPctr	47-0
4-3 92	Stga	1200	ft F&MNW1PMCD	1 30 101 4 134	206 2	3	3	3	2 1	3	3 3 1/2	32 4	207	12.40	HWstbrokJ	CroeCrkTcson,CranCas,BrzyKnlSkp	37-0
3-27 92	Stga	1200	sy F&MNW1PMCD	1 31 103 3 135 2	206 4	4	6	6	8 1/2	8	8 11 1/2	31 4	209	27.00	HWstbrokJ	PunkyLobel,DorsModi,CrusinCasi	42-0
3-20 92	Stga	1200	ft F&MNW1PMCD	1 30 101 2 132 4	207	2	4	4	4 1	4	3 1 1/2	33 3	208 2	13.50	HWstbrokJ	DntHtALdy,JclynsRvng,BrzyKnlSkp	33-0
3-13 92	Stga	1200	gd F&MNW1PMCD	1 31 1 103 2 135	205 3	4	5	5	5 4 1/2	5	5 15	32 1	208 3	49.50	HWstbrokJ	SzysShadow,CrusinCasi,MsRanbow	18-0
2-28 92	Stga		ft QUA	1 30 2 103 134 4	206 2	3	3	4	6 4 1/2	6	6 11 1/2	32 3	208 3	NB	HWstbrokJ	CasinoStrakr,WnthropeKd,FlaDor	25-0
7-23 9	Bnvl	925	gd 2YR EC	2 Dashes, 1 MILE IN 2:07.4 fin 4, 2:08.3 fin 6										NR	RGale		nr-0

2-1 — 2 — BARB BAKER — WHITE
b f 3 BakerField-Herbar'sAndrea-Cicero
Paul B. Rice, Thomas C. Greco & Sheryl A. Zabielski, NY
FRANK COPPOLA JR (150) ltbl-wh-br (53-7-7-6-.243) Tr—Paul Zabielski (.278)
Stga 2:07 1992 8 1 2 1 $1,940 · 1991 8 0 2 4 $4,121 · 3,2:07 Lifetime $6,061

Date	Trk	Purse	Cd Class	Dis 1/4 1/2 3/4	Time	PP	1/4	1/2	3/4	Str	Fin	Ind 1/4	Ind Time	Odds	Driver	Order Of Finish	Temp
4-29 92	Stga	1600	ft F&MNW2PMCD	1 30 1 102 1 133 3	204 3	5	5	5°	2° 1	1	2 hd	30 4	204 3	1.50	FCopolaJr	Abbeycrmbie,BarbBakr,DaringDram	63-0
4-24 92	Stga	1600	gd F&MNW2PMCD	1 30 102 1 134	204 4	3	3	4	4 5 1/2	3	2 ns	29 4	204 4	4.80	FCopolaJr	LJsWhey,BarbBaker,CroeCrkTucson	47-0
4-5 92	Stga	A 1500	ft NW2PMLTCD	1 29 2 101 132	202 1	3	3	3	4 2 3/4	3	4 5 1/2	31 2	204	17.00	FCopolaJr	BoldExplorer,Abycrombi,LJsWhey	48-0
3-27 92	Stga	1500	sy F&MNW2PMCD	1 30 1 103 134 3	206 4	6	6	6°	4° 2	4	4 4	31 3	207 3	9.50	GMattison	PaulasPrid,LJsWhey,StPadysPran	42-0
3-20 92	Stga		ft QUA	1 30 4 103 135	206	4	2	2	2 1 1/2	2	2 3/4	31	206 1	NB	GMattison	YoungBrandyWin,Barbakr,LoriLady	30-0
3-15 92	Stga	A 1500	ft NW2PMLTCD	1 29 2 102 1 133 1	203 3	5	1	1	3 3	7	7 dis			3.00	GMattison	GrandLgnd,BoldExplor,BoncastlHawk	21-0
3-6 92	Stga	1500	gd F&MNW2PMLT	1 30 2 102 2 133 2	204 1	6	6	6°	6° 3 1/2	5	3 6 1/2	31 3	205 3	2.80	FCopolaJr	TijuanaChef,HapyLadyJan,Barbakr	42-0

8-1 — 3 — REBER VALLEY MISS (NY) — PURPLE
b f 3 JacsueKermit-Romeo'sPromise-RomeoHanover
Eugene F. Cross, Willsboro, N.Y.
KIM CRAWFORD (155) red-blk-wh (34-7-6-4-.343) Tr—Eugene Cross (.250)
1992 13 0 0 0 $536 · West 2:12 2 1991 32 4 5 5 $4,736 · 2,2:12 2 Lifetime $5,272

Date	Trk	Purse	Cd Class	Dis 1/4 1/2 3/4	Time	PP	1/4	1/2	3/4	Str	Fin	Ind 1/4	Ind Time	Odds	Driver	Order Of Finish	Temp
5-1 92	Stga	1600	ft F&MNW2PMCD	1 29 4 104 3 135 4	206 2	3	2	2	2 1 1/2	3	4 5	31 2	207 2	17.90	KCrawford	CroeCrkTcsn,DntHtALady,WiwyBaty	58-0
4-24 92	Stga	1600	gd F&MNW2PMCD	1 30 102 1 134	204 4	4	4°	3°	5° 6	8	8 17 1/2	33 1	208 2	44.80	ECross	LJsWhey,BarbBaker,CroeCrkTucson	47-0
4-5 92	Stga	A 1200	ft NW1PMLTCD	1 30 3 101 2 133 3	204 3	8	7	7	6° 4	6	6 9 1/2	32 1	206 3	12.00	GMattison	WabbitTwouble,LivThDram,DarKly	48-0
3-29 92	Stga	A 1200	ft NW1PMLTCD	1 30 101 4 133 4	204 4	1	1	2	3 1 1/2	4	4 6 1/2	32	206	8.50	GMattison	BrmataPhil,BoncastlHawk,Baruck	54-0
3-20 92	Stga	1500	ft F&MNW2PMLT	1 30 102 3 133 4	203 4	4	5	5	5° 3	4	4 11 1/2	31 3	206	35.70	GMattison	SuzysShadow,LJsWhey,PacingTracy	33-0
3-13 92	Stga	1500	gd F&MNW2PMLT	1 31 3 105 135 3	207	1	2	2	4 2	3	4 7 1/2 dnf	31 2	207 2	14.80	ECross	Shandel,TCsTwiggy,HapyLadyJane	18-0
3-6 92	Stga	1500	gd F&MNW2PMLT	1 30 2 102 2 133 2	204 1	7	8	8	7° 5 1/2	7	7 12 1/2	32 1	206 3	61.30	ECross	TijuanaChef,HapyLadyJan,BrbBakr	42-0

6-1 — 4 — SONDANCE JEANNIE (NY) — BLACK
b m 4 SundanceSkipper-DarcyH-WiseWidower
James G. Wisnowski, Middlebury, Vt.
GLENN RAIA (135) red-white-gold (5-0-2-0-.222) Tr—Glenn Raia (.296)
1992 9 0 0 0 $120 · Stga 2:04 1991 5 1 0 0 $1,050 · 2,2:03 2 Lifetime $13,592

Date	Trk	Purse	Cd Class	Dis 1/4 1/2 3/4	Time	PP	1/4	1/2	3/4	Str	Fin	Ind 1/4	Ind Time	Odds	Driver	Order Of Finish	Temp
4-29 92	Stga	1500	ft FMNW1500L7	1 29 3 101 3 132	204 2	3	7	4°	4° 1 1/2	3	4 3/4	32 2	204 3	52.60	GRaia	HiLosGoddess,DarnysFily,Spooling	63-0
4-2 92	Stga	1500	ft NW1500L7CD	1 30 2 101 4 132 4	204 4	8	8	5°	4° 1 1/2	4	6 4	32 2	205 3	24.20	GRaia	WhosYourThunder,Spooling,Slybel	40-0
3-26 92	Stga	1500	sy NW1500L7CD	1 31 4 105 2 136 4	208 1	ex1	8x	8	8 dis	8	8 dis			3.10	FCopolaJr	BrndyLobl,CrispKash,CandySalwey	52-0
3-20 92	Stga		ft QUA	1 29 3 102 1 132 2	203	1	6	2°	1 2	1	4 4 1/2	31 3	204	NB	GRaia	FrnchKnight,PalasBgGy,RoyalDbin	30-0
3-12 92	Stga	1500	gd NW1500L7CD	1 29 3 101 4 132	204 1	3	9	9°	x9 dis	9	9 dis			11.50	FCopolaJr	NortheongRos,DarnysFly,HLosGods	27-0
2-28 92	Stga		ft QUA	1 31 2 104 1 136	207	6	7	7	7 9	7	6 8 1/2	31	208 4	NB	EVrloJr	FlywayFlash,SgnalHlHrb,TjanaChf	25-0
2-23 92	Stga	A 1500	gd NW1500L7CD	1 29 3 102 131 4	203 1	3	5	6	x7 dis	7	7 dis			11.00	EVrloJr	KystonTwist,EastfldDr,BrndNwJwl	34-0

4-1 — 5 — BELLE MOT — GREEN
b m 4 SmartestRemark-J.M.Rona-TarportCount
Norman Freinberg, Valatie, N.Y.
JORDAN MYERS (180) gray-grn-brown (10-1-0-1-.133) Tr—Jordon Myers (.222)
1992 1 0 0 0 $128 · 1991 13 0 0 2 $672 · 2,2:05 4 Lifetime $2,064

Date	Trk	Purse	Cd Class	Dis 1/4 1/2 3/4	Time	PP	1/4	1/2	3/4	Str	Fin	Ind 1/4	Ind Time	Odds	Driver	Order Of Finish	Temp
4-29 92	Stga	1600	ft F&MNW2PMCD	1 30 1 102 1 133 3	204 3	4	4	4	6° 3 1/2	5	4 1 1/2	30 3	204 4	22.40	JMyers	Abbeycrmbie,BarbBakr,DaringDram	63-0
4-24 92	Stga		gd QUA	1 29 3 100 3 131 1	202 2	4	3	3	3 4	3	4 4 1/2	31 2	203 2	NB	JMyers	FlywayFlsh,AngsHnvr,MchlsCraton	50-0
4-20 92	Stga		ft QUA	1 30 101 3 133	204 1	2	4	4	3 6 1/2	3	5 13 1/2	32 3	206 4	NB	JMyers	EarlPits,VwFromAbov,MsStrmMastr	50-0
11-22 91	Stga	1600	sy F&MNW2PMLT	1 31 4 104 3 136 1	208	4	5	4°	4°° 1/2	6	8 10 1/2	33 3	210	38.10	JMyers	ChrytsBaby,BonCstlDot,AlohaPar	45-0
11-8 91	Stga	1600	ft F&MNW2PMLT	1 30 2 102 132 4	204	6	6	6°	7° 5	6	6 11 1/2	32 2	206 1	28.20	JMyers	GnllHit,RuthiMagic,CalgaryBlChp	33-0
10-30 91	Stga	1600	ft F&MNW2PMLT	1 30 3 101 2 133	206 3	4x	8	8	8 dis	8	8 be dis			6.00	JMyers	HotRail,TCsTwiggy,CherryCola	48-0
10-25 91	Stga	1600	ft NW2PMLTCD	1 29 4 102 1 133 3	203 3	8	8	7	8 4 1/2	8	6 6 1/2	30 2	204 4	98.30	JMyers	Bradlypondchanty,Barsa,RthMagc	68-0

12-1 — 6 — SNOOKY K (NY) — RED
blk m 4 Jamuga-HelloChern-SayHello
Gregory C. Decker, NY & Linda A. Goldstein, Conn.
GREGORY DECKER (165) ltblu-red-white (5-1-0-1-.267) Tr—Gregory Decker (.333)
1992 11 0 0 1 $927 · Stga 2:04 1991 16 1 1 1 $1,965 · 3,2:04 Lifetime $5,179

Date	Trk	Purse	Cd Class	Dis 1/4 1/2 3/4	Time	PP	1/4	1/2	3/4	Str	Fin	Ind 1/4	Ind Time	Odds	Driver	Order Of Finish	Temp
4-29 92	Stga	1500	ft FMNW1500L7	1 29 3 101 3 132	204 2	1	3	5	5 2 1/2	6	5 2 1/2	32 2	204 4	20.00	GDecker	HiLosGoddess,DarnysFily,Spooling	63-0
4-24 92	Stga	1900	gd F&MNW3PMCD	1 30 1 101 3-133 3	203 3	4	4	4	6 4 1/2	6	4 7 1/2	30 3	205	40.00	GDecker	Highjacker,SisterSlop,MsRainbow	47-0
4-2 92	Stga	1500	ft NW1500L7CD	1 30 2 101 4 132 4	204 4	1	3	4	5 2 1/2	5	5 2 1/2	32	205 2	23.10	GDecker	WhosYourThunder,Spooling,Slybel	40-0
3-26 92	Stga	1500	sy NW1500L7CD	1 31 4 105 2 136 4	208 1	6	6	6	5° 3	5	5 6	32	209 2	38.10	GDecker	BrndyLobl,CrispKash,CandySalwey	52-0
3-19 92	Stga	1500	ft NW1500L7CD	1 29 3 100 4 131 4	203 1	5	5	5	5 3 1/2	6	5 6 1/2	32 1	204 3	105.90	GDecker	DenverDragon,WinSumPro,PamsCam	33-0
3-5 92	Stga	1500	gd NW1500L7CD	1 29 100 2 132 2	204 4	3	8	8	8 8 1/2	8	8 10 1/2	32 4	206 4	4.60	KCrawford	BrandNwJwl,DarnysFily,Rightsid	45-0
2-28 92	Stga	1900	sy F&MNW3PMCD	1 30 101 4 133	205 1	7	7	7	6 4	5	4 5 1/2	32 2	206 1	48.10	GDecker	Howdagoin,HotRail,Rightside	42-0

3-1 — 7 — L DEES GRAMMAROCKY — BROWN
b f 3 WaltonHanover-AccentHanover-Albatross
Charles Reed, Swansea, Ma.
PAUL MAGAN (180) green-gold (3-2-1-0-.852) Tr—Paul Magan (.778)
QPhld 2:04 1992 2 1 0 0 $924 · 1991 0 0 0 0 $00 · Q3,2:04 Lifetime $924

Date	Trk	Purse	Cd Class	Dis 1/4 1/2 3/4	Time	PP	1/4	1/2	3/4	Str	Fin	Ind 1/4	Ind Time	Odds	Driver	Order Of Finish	Temp
4-29 92	Stga	1400	ft F&MNW1PMCD	1 31 3 104 2 134 4	205 1	2	1	1	1 1/2	1	1 1 1/2	30 2	205 1	*1.00	PMagan	LDeGramarcky,BradashKm,ScotoFam	63-0
4-2 92	Phld	A 2800	ft MDNCDF-M	1 29 3 101 132 1	205	5	3i°°	2°	3 2 1/2	3 3	4 3	33	205 3	6.80	MLancastr	TwoAcs,WintrFrost,BunisMultiply	41-1
3-25 92	Phld		ft QUA	1 31 1 103 133 3	204	2	2	2	2 1 1/2	2 1 1/2	1 1/2	30 1	204	NB	MLancastr	LDeGrmarcky,ShnonSasy,DdgrHnvr	43-0
3-18 92	Phld		ft QUA	1 30 4 103 134 1	205 2	8	1°°	3	3 3	3 4 1/2	6 7 1/2	32	206 4	NB	MLancastr	VeraLobell,Lassie,DirectCouner	39-0
11-15 91	BB⅝		sy QUA	1 30 4 101 1 131 2	201 4	2	5	4°	3	3 7 5	3 4 3		210 2	NB	FOreilly	Cnecon,CldnrysRlph,LDeGrmaRck	42-0

12-1	**CHERRY COLA** (NY)					br m 4 Darson Hanover-Sugarpie-Songcan										1992 13 0 0 1			$1,063
						Cherry Hill Farm, Watervliet, N.Y.										Stga 2:05³ 1991 10 1 0 2			$1,064
8	MARK WHITCROFT (175) grn-wh-gold (7-1-0-0-.143)					Tr—Cheryl Whitcroft (.200)										3,2:05³ Lifetime			$2,127
	$4\text{-}29^{92}$	Stga	1600	ft F&MNW2PMCD	1	30^{1}	102^{1}	133^{3}	204^{3}	3	2	2	3^{2}	4	$5^{3}\frac{1}{2}$	31^{1} 205^{1} 14.30	MWhtcroft	Abbeycrmbie,BarbBakr,DaringDram	63-0
	$4\text{-}24^{92}$	Stga	1600	gdF&MNW2PMCD	1	30	102^{1}	134	204^{4}	6	7	7	$6^{\circ\circ}6\frac{1}{2}$	4	$4^{1}\frac{3}{4}$	31^{2} 206^{3} 58.70	MWhtcroft	LJsWhay,BarbBaker,CrossCrkTucson	47-0
	$4\text{-}3^{92}$	Stga	1500	ft F&MNW2PMCD	1	29^{4}	100^{1}	131^{3}	203^{1}	1	3	3	$3^{5}\frac{1}{2}$	4	$4^{13}\frac{3}{4}$	33 205^{4} 29.00	MWhtcroft	PnkyLobl,StPadysPrss,HapyLdyJan	37-0
	$3\text{-}20^{92}$	Stga	1500	ft F&MNW2PMLT	1	30	102^{3}	133^{4}	203^{4}	1	3	3°	$3^{\circ}1\frac{1}{2}$	5	$6^{17}\frac{1}{2}$	33^{1} 207^{2} 17.30	MWhtcroft	SuzysShadow,LJsWhay,PacingTracy	33-0
GRAY	$3\text{-}13^{92}$	Stga	1500	gdF&MNW2PMLT	1	31^{3}	105	135^{3}	207	8	8	6°	$3^{\circ}1\frac{1}{2}$	i4	5^{4p4}	32 207^{4} 30.60	MWhtcroft	Shandel,TCsTwiggy,HapyLadyJane	18-0
	$3\text{-}5^{92}$	Stga	1500	gdNW2PMLT	1	30^{2}	102^{2}	133^{2}	205	3	2	3	$4^{1}\frac{1}{2}$	7	$7^{8}\frac{1}{2}$	32^{4} 206^{3} 27.40	MWhtcroft	SandDart,FlywayFlash,HHThor	45-0
	$2\text{-}28^{92}$	Stga	1500	gdF&MNW2PMLT	1	29^{4}	101^{1}	132^{4}	204^{3}	3	3	3	$5^{2}\frac{1}{2}$	5	4^{13}	34 207^{1} 4.50	MWhtcroft	LaJazHot,DashrSwinsour,MadsonHi	42-0

The rail horse was Breezy Knoll Skipi, a maiden facing horses who had won one race. Breezy had won $435 lifetime from 9 starts, was dispatched at 50-1, and was easy to dismiss from the contenders.

The 3 horse, Reber Valley Miss, had done well as a 2-year-old at the fairs, winning $4,736, but her lifetime best was a 2:12.2 win, roughly eight to 10 seconds slower than the competition here. As a 3-year-old, Reber was out of the money in all 13 starts, winning just $536. Another throw-away.

Two important notes: 1) In harness racing, 2:12.2 means 2:12 and 2/5, not 2:12 and 2/10. Why? To make life more confusing. 2) The term pari-mutuel, which simply means there was wagering on the race, is important. Horses occasionally show up in a Non-Winners of 2 or in maiden races with victories at fairs in their PPs. If the races weren't pari-mutuel, they don't count in determining eligibility.

Each of the other six horses had last raced at Saratoga, April 29, in three different races.

The 4, Sondance Jeannie, and the 6, Snooky K., finished fourth by 3/4 of a length and fifth by 2 1/4, respectively, against Hi Los Goddess, who won in 2:04.2. If horses race in approximately the same final time, comparing their final quarter and final half is useful. For horses in a Non-Winners of 2, a final quarter of :30 and a final half in 1:00 are respectable on a 1/2-mile track.

Sondance got her last quarter in a dawdling :32.2 and her last half in 1:02.2 from the 3 post. The program provides her final quarter. Here's how we figure her last half. The time of the leader at the half was 1:01.3. Sondance was fourth on the outside, so we'll approximate her deficit there as 3 lengths, giving her a half-mile time of 1:02.1 (using 1 length = $\frac{1}{5}$ of a second). Since Sondance raced in 2:04.3, her final half was in 1:02.2.

Snooky went his last quarter in :32.2 and last half in 1:02.2 from the rail.

Their final quarter times were slow compared to the other horses in this race.

And they were chronic losers with records of 1-for-14 and 1-for-27 for the last two years. Avoid horses such as these, and maidens who have 10 or more starts without a win. They frequently find a way to lose.

One last consideration here: Sondance would go off at 7-2; the week before she'd been 52-1. A definite underlay.

The other common race featured the 2, Barb Baker, the 5, Belle Mot, and the 8, Cherry Cola. They'd finished second by a head, fourth by $1\frac{1}{4}$ and fifth by $3\frac{1}{2}$ to Abbeycrombie, who won in 2:04.3. Barb Baker got her last quarter in :30.4 and last half in 1:01.4 from the 5 post. Belle Mot closed in :30.3—1:02 from the 4 post. Cherry Cola went :31.1—1:02.4 from the 3 post. Cherry Cola, 1-for-23 the last two years, was another easy toss. So was Belle, who'd never finished better than third in 14 starts.

Barb Baker finished second by a nose two starts back, getting her last quarter in a sparkling :29.4. Her last half was 1:01.4.

We learned this by starting with her bottom PPs.

Previously, Barb Baker showed four ordinary efforts and one disaster: third by $6\frac{3}{4}$ at 5-2; seventh distanced at 3-1; fourth by 4 at 9-1 and fourth by $9\frac{1}{2}$ at 17-1. She then was second by a nose at 9-2; then second by a head at 3-2. She also showed a qualifier, when she was second. None of her other efforts concluded with a last half faster than 1:02. But Barb Baker is a deserved favorite moving in from the 5 post to the 2.

The only horse we haven't discussed is the 7, L Dees Grammarocky, who also raced on April 29, making only the second start of her career.

She'd raced in a qualifier as a 2-year-old in '91. She was third by 43 lengths in 2:10.2 on a sloppy track, and she didn't return to the races for four months, when she tried to qualify at Freehold. She drew the 8 post, made a strong early move, and tired, finishing sixth by $7\frac{1}{2}$ in 2:06.4.

She requalified a week later and went a much stronger mile, winning by half a length in 2:04 with a snappy last half in 1:00.3, including a final quarter of :30.1. Freehold's half-mile track is rated 2:02; Saratoga is at 2:02.1 in the comparative track speed ratings in the program.

L Dees made her pari-mutuel debut April 2 at Freehold. She was used hard early in an opening quarter of :29.3, and a first half in 1:01. Her PP line from the 5 post shows she was 3-wide and impeded as she moved up to second, parked out at the half. She tired, as she had every right to do from her troubled trip, finishing fourth by 3 at 6-1. Her last quarter was a crawling :33, completing a second half in 1:05.

Her only other start was her last, when she appeared in a maiden race at Saratoga April 29. She drew the 2 post and was bet down to even money. Off a 27-day layoff, she was a tremendous underlay at 1-1. But she won, wire-to-wire off a soft, easy first half in 1:04.2. She got her last quarter in :30.2, completing a last half in 1:00.4 while she increased her lead from half a length to 1¾. The point is that she wasn't in a furious drive to get that last half.

Let's summarize. Of the six contenders, all racing on the same night in their last starts, she had the fastest final quarter (:30.2) and the fastest last half (1:00.4) by far. She did it off slow fractions, but the fact remains that she won easily, and her final time of 2:05.1 was just ⅗ of a second slower than the best closer that night, Barb Baker, who raced in 2:04.3. Barb Baker finished second by a head in a driving finish.

Could L Dees have gone ⅗ of a second faster? She might have, if she'd been pressured instead of winning easily. But that's an assumption. The fact is her final ½-mile time was markedly faster.

Barb Baker was 1-for-16 lifetime and L Dees 1-for-2. Since we believe young, inexperienced horses will improve, we expect L Dees to step up off her easy win. Secondly, we have a severe distaste for chronic losers.

Barb Baker should have been the favorite because of her better post than L Dees, but they should have been close in odds. They weren't. Barb Baker was 2-5, a vulnerable favorite simply from her 1-for-16 record. Think about it: 1-for-16 lifetime and going off 2-5!

L Dees should have been 2-1 or lower off her easy score. She went off 5-1, got an early tuck fourth, and won by ¾ of a length in 2:04.2 to pay $13.00.

Barb Baker was second. That made her 1-for-17. And she didn't stop there. Her loss at Saratoga, October 7, 1992—still in a Non-Winners of 2—made her 1-for-33 lifetime. In four of her last seven starts, she'd gone off at 5-2 or lower, creating overlays every time.

Class

CHAPTER 2

A long, long time ago, harness racing was conducted with an easy-to-follow method of letter and number classification. From the bottom up—excluding maiden races, claimers and stakes—they were C-3, C-2, C-1; B-3, B-2, B-1; A-3, A-2, A-1, then Free-For-All or Open. Those were the good old nights.

The present conditional system can be incomprehensible to professional handicappers, let alone the public.

A race last May at The Meadowlands was for Non-Winners of $12,500 Last 7, OR Non-Winners of 4 races, OR Non-Winners of $125,000 lifetime, unless a horse won that $125,000 in 1991-92.

In a February race farther south in New Jersey at Freehold, the conditions were: Non-Winners of $250 per start in 1991-92 OR in last 10 starts, OR Non-Winners of $4,000 in 1991-92, OR Non-Winners of 4 pari-mutuel races lifetime.

Who brought a calculator?

Let's look at a race from Yonkers, February 19. The condition: Non-winners of $6,000 in Last 8 starts; Winners over $60,000 in 1991-92 ineligible.

Note the standard used at Yonkers is the last eight starts. At The Meadowlands, it was seven. Sometimes it's five.

10 PACE — $2 EXACTA

ONE MILE — NON-WINNERS OF $6,000 IN LAST 8 STARTS — PURSE $5,750
WARM-UP PINK — Winners over $80,000 in 1991-92 not eligible.

RED 1 FINESSE PLAYER (NY)

b g 7,by Nistross, High Finesse by High Ideal
Donna Young, East Windsor, N.J.
Tr.Bonnie DeVitis
Rejean Daigneault (135) Red-Blue
92 5 0 0 0 $1,514 — 91 18 7 2 2 $8,530 — 1:58.4 YR — Last 8 starts–$2,209 — 4 1:58.1 (1) — Lifetime $28,928

	2-8YR-5	1	gd	29^1	1.00^2	1.30^2	2.00^3	NW8000	5750	3	5	6	7^6	$7^7\frac{3}{4}$	5^7	2.02	9.10	(FilionHer)SirShannon,ChargeAndSend,SteppersOre	no lock
	2-1YR-1	1	fst	28^1	58^3	1.29^1	1.59^1	NW8000	5750	4	7	8°	$7^{8}\frac{3}{4}$	$7^9\frac{3}{4}$	4^{12}	2.01^3	3.00	(FilionHer)BigAndTough,LandmarkFella,Belmondc	4th over,stdy
	1-23Fhd-4	1	sly	29^1	59	1.29^1	2.00^2	NW400px	5800	3	7	7	8	$8^8\frac{1}{4}$	$4^7\frac{3}{4}$	2.02	31.80	(FilionHer)AdvancingN,PolarOrbit,GrandSlamPlay	
	1-16Fhd-1	1	gd	28	58^3	1.29^3	2.00^3	NW400px	5800	4	5	5	5°	$8^7\frac{1}{4}$	$5^5\frac{1}{2}$	2.01^3	13.90	(FilionHer)RoadFrontage,TylerGrant,AscendingDignity	
	1-4Fhd-3	1	sly	28^4	58^2	1.29^2	2.00^1	NW800px	7800	8	7	7	7	7^5	7^8	2.01^4	39.40	(FilionHer)Floored,SugarValleyLater,ManifestDestiny	
	12-27Fhd	1						NW400px	5800	8									scratched-sick
	12-20Fhd+5	1	fst	28	58^3	1.29^1	1.59^3	NW500px	6800	8	8	8	8	$7^4\frac{1}{4}$	$5^5\frac{3}{4}$	2.00^4	14.20	(DancerD)ManifestDestiny,ThornbirdHill,BigGinger	
8-1	12-7YR+5	1	fst	28^3	58	1.27^3	1.57^4	27000	7500	3	8	8	8^{11}	$8^8\frac{3}{4}$	$7^7\frac{3}{4}$	1.59^2	16.20	(AbbatielloC)CoventryClasc,SaveTheTgr,GdToSeymour	never close
	11-30YR+7	1	fst	29	59^2	1.29	1.58^3	NW8000	7000	4	5	6	5^6	$5^4\frac{1}{4}$	$5^4\frac{1}{2}$	1.59^2	21.40	(FilionHer)DelgatysGiftN,IdleFella,EverybodyWins	out final,mild

BLUE 2 POWER LINE

b g 5,by No Nukes, High Voltage by Meadow Skipper
C. Steinberg & E. & J. Levine, Seaford, N.Y.
Tr.Peter Stratton
Cedric Washington (145) Blue-Lt.Blue-Gold
92 5 0 1 1 $3,332 — 91 37 3 10 5 $21,653 — 1:58.4 YR — Last 8 starts–$4,272 — 4 1:58.4 — Lifetime $27,123

	2-6YR-1	1	fst	29^2	1.00^4	1.31^1	2.00^2	125/15000	5000	6x	6	6	6^5	$7^7\frac{1}{4}$	6^6	2.01^3	10.00	(MosherG)RunTheRisk,NationalHero,Weedy	impd.wd fnl,evn
	1-31YR-3	1	fst	28^2	59	1.29^4	2.00^3	NW4500	5000	5	6x	4	4^6	4^7	4^6	2.01^4	*1.00	(MarohnJ)TristanR,Beachmaster,IronstoneArtist	good recovery
	1-25YR-1	1	fst	28^2	59^3	1.29	1.59^2	W13501	8500	6	7	5°	$4^{\circ 2}\frac{1}{4}$	$3^2\frac{3}{4}$	$2^2\frac{1}{4}$	1.59^4	17.70	(MarohnJ)MostlyRhuten,PowerLine,SpikeLee	off wnnr's cvr
	1-17YR-5	1	fst	29^1	1.00	1.29^1	2.00^2	NW4000	4750	6	7	6°	$5^{\circ 8}\frac{3}{4}$	$4^4\frac{3}{4}$	$3^2\frac{1}{4}$	2.00^4	10.60	(MarohnJ)Preco,Justagranger,PowerLine	cover,mild
	1-10YR-4	1	fst	28^2	59^2	1.29^4	2.00^3	NW4000	4750	4	3	4	$6^3\frac{1}{4}$	5^5	$5^2\frac{3}{4}$	2.01^1	4.80	(MarohnJ)BabeRuth,Getty,ViewFromAbove	tucked,no rally
	12-27Fhd+5	1	fst	28^3	58^3	1.29	2.00^1	10000	5840	6	5°	3°	7°	$9^8\frac{3}{4}$	$9^8\frac{3}{4}$	2.02	9.10	(PierceR)VictoriousTime,CityBoss,AnchorO	
	12-11Fhd+5	1	fst	29^1	59^1	1.28^4	1.58^3	10000	4700	7	3°	5	5	$5^2\frac{3}{4}$	$4^1\frac{3}{4}$	1.59	39.70	(PierceR)GrobbelaarN,ChrisTom,Altab	
8-1	12-4Fhd-3	1	fst	29^4	1.00^1	1.30^3	2.01^3	10000	4700	4	4	4	5°	$4^3\frac{1}{4}$	$3^1\frac{1}{4}$	2.01^4	20.80	(ParkerH)BigBigBiggest,KeswaydinSkip,PowerLine	

WHITE 3 BOND STREET

b h 7,by Abercrombie, Ata Connie by Meadow Skipper
Harry Nisberg, Brooklyn, N.Y.
Tr.Jack Rice
Herve Filion (152) Red-Blue-White
92 2 0 0 0 $650 — 91 28 4 3 2 $55,615 — 1:52.4 M1 — Last 8 starts–$5,935 — 4 1:52.0 (1) T — Lifetime $550,432

	2-7M1-2	1	fst	29^1	58	1.27^1	1.55^2	NW8500	11000	7	9	9°	$9^{\circ 8}\frac{1}{4}$	$10^7\frac{1}{4}$	9^6	1.56^3	L5.70	(DavisE)Frankeejn,RampageHanover,CallMyLawyer	(L)ovr,no rally
	1-31M1-7	1	fst	28^1	57^1	1.26^4	1.55^3	NW8500	11000	3	6	7	$7^5\frac{3}{4}$	6^5	5^2	1.55^4	L10.20	(ManziC)Townsston,DaBeny,Nten	(L)sng,gradual
	1-18M1	1	fst	29^4	1.00^3	1.31^1	1.58^3	Qua		1	3	3	3^2	3^6	$3^7\frac{1}{4}$	2.00	Lnb	(LachanceM)AllDaTime,ShinyRascal,BondStreet	(L)3 hole,held
	11-18GS1+12	1	fst	27^1	56	1.26^1	1.54^1	NW10000	7500	2	5	5°	$3^{\circ 3}$	4^5	5^6	1.55^1	6.70	(McNicholM)Ironridge,SammyAlmahurst,Dictionary	uncvrd,gave way
	11-8GS1+13	1	fst	27^3	56^2	1.28^2	1.53^4	NW6750	4500	4	4	2	$4^{\circ 2}\frac{3}{4}$	$3^4\frac{1}{4}$	$3^8\frac{3}{4}$	1.55^1	4.70	(McNicholM)CaliforniaCam,Stylized,BondStreet	yld,shufl,mild
	10-12YR+8	1	fst	28^2	58	1.27^3	1.57^1	NW11000	10000	7	4	3°	$4^{\circ 1}\frac{3}{4}$	$7^3\frac{1}{4}$	$7^3\frac{1}{4}$	1.57^4	10.80	(CaseWJr)GrannysGarden,IroquoisBlueChip,BigDate	tck,chall,tired
	9-28GS1+10	1	fst	28	57^1	1.28^3	1.54^3	NW7500	5000	3	1°	1	1^{hd}	$1\frac{1}{4}$	$2\frac{1}{4}$	1.54^3	2.80	(PlutinoJ)JaDude,BondStreet,SammyAlmahurst	pressed gamely
6-2	9-21YR+10	1	fst	28	57^3	1.28^4	1.56^2	NW10000	9000	2	3	3°	$5^{\circ 3}\frac{1}{4}$	4^3	$4^2\frac{1}{4}$	1.56^4	3.80	(WingT)(dh)WightwrCnyn-PassamBgns,ChrisThndr	weak uncovered

GREEN 4 FRANKLAND A

b h 7,by Land Grant, Pete Cloud by Smoke Cloud N
Robert Gagliardi,Robert Sheehan, Manhasset, N.Y.
Tr.Robert Sheehan
James Marohn (115) Purple-White
92 5 0 0 0 $1,650 — 91 27 3 2 5 $8,125 — 1:58.3 YR — Last 8 starts–$4,400 — 6 1:58.3 — Lifetime $77,553

	2-8M1-1	1	fst	28^4	57^3	1.27^1	1.55^2	20000	8500	6	7	9	$9^{\circ 9}$	8^8	$6^7\frac{1}{4}$	1.56^4	L76.80	(FahyW)NiceTry,ExoticBet,CallMeBruce	(L)ot 3-4s,mild
	2-1M1-7	1	fst	27^4	57^2	1.27^3	1.56	20000	8500	6	6	6°	$5^{\circ 4}\frac{1}{4}$	$6^8\frac{3}{4}$	6^{11}	1.58^1	L17.80	(CampbellJo)InstrumentLnding,BrytanWndr,BallroMusc	(L)cover,empty
	1-25M1+0	1	fst	28^4	58^1	1.27	1.54^4	20000	8500	5	6	5°	$4^{\circ 1}\frac{1}{4}$	$4^3\frac{1}{4}$	$5^6\frac{3}{4}$	1.56	L33.50	(FahyW)TaxCreditN,Endoxo,CriticalMass	(L)winnr's cover
	1-18M1-11	1	fst	28^4	59^1	1.28^4	1.57^1	20000	8500	7	7	7	$7^{\circ\circ 8}\frac{3}{4}$	$5^5\frac{1}{4}$	$5^5\frac{1}{4}$	1.58^1	L42.20	(FahyW)InstrumentLanding,FriyasExtrsing,Abepen	(L)wide,Stnd
	1-4M1-3	1	gd	29^2	58^2	1.27^2	1.55^3	25000	10000	5	1	4	$4^{\circ 2}\frac{1}{4}$	6^4	5^{6}pl4	1.56^4	21.90	(FahyW)CoventryClassic,Walker,*CriticalMass	p.4,cover,empty
	12-28M1-5	1	fst	28^2	57	1.28^2	1.55^2	25000	10000	3	2	6	$6^{\circ 4}$	9^6	$7^3\frac{1}{4}$	1.56	26.10	(FahyW)GdToSymoure,CvntryClasc,MaGottaBret	shfld,no rally
	12-21M1	1	fst	29^1	59^4	1.29^2	1.57^2	Qua		1	2	3	3^3	$3^3\frac{1}{4}$	$6^5\frac{1}{4}$	1.58^2	nb	(SheehanR)TKsSkipper,NuclearFlash,Townston	gapping
4-1	11-30YR+7	1	fst	28^1	58^3	1.28^2	1.59^1	NW8100	7800	1	3	1	8^{12}	8^{15}	8dis	2.05^1	*.70	(MosherG)SaveTheTiger,ECsSuperStar,GoDutchGo	brushed,stopped

BLACK 5 LES HALL

b h 4,by Chipper Frost, Chipmans Starlite by Brown Star
Melvin Wayne Givens & George Hudson, Del.
Tr.Wayne Givens
Gary Mosher (160) Red-Green-White
2:00.3 DD ⅝ — 92 5 1 2 1 $5,360 — 91 9 0 0 1 $1,850 — Last 8 starts–$5,670 — 2 1:57.4 ⅝ — Lifetime $18,280

	2-8DD⅝	1	gd	27^4	58	1.28	1.59^4	Blue Hen	10000	9	5	6	$7^{\circ\circ}$	$3^2\frac{3}{4}$	2^{hd}	1.59^4	6.10	(GivensW)GrandGusto,LesHall,SpeakFrenchToMe	
	2-1DD⅝	1	fst	30	1.00^3	1.30	2.00^3	Blue Hen	3000	3	1	1	1	1^2	$1^2\frac{1}{4}$	2.00^3	2.40	(GivensW)LesHall,FoolOfGold,Bandeiva	
	1-25DD⅝	1	gd	28^3	59^4	1.29^2	1.59^4	Blue Hen	3000	8	1	1	1	2^{hd}	$3^3\frac{1}{4}$	2.00^2	24.30	(GreensO)UnfairAdvantage,QuillCaper,LesHall	
	1-18DD⅝	1	fst	30	1.00^3	1.31^4	2.02^1	Blue Hen	3000	7	1	1	1	$2^1\frac{1}{4}$	2^4	2.03	8.80	(GivensW)GrandGusto,LesHall,StarcroftWinner	
	1-11DD⅝	1	fst	28^3	1.00	1.29^2	2.00	Blue Hen	3000	7	4	4	6	$3^1\frac{1}{4}$	4^2	2.00^2	17.10	(GivensW)BigDean,SunnyAre,TrashToCash	
	12-28DD⅝	1	sly	28^3	1.00^1	1.31^2	2.03^4	NW1000	800	7	1°	1	2	5^{13}	5^{19}	2.07^3	*.80	(GivensW)ForrestRose,FunForBath,SteadyOtto	
	12-14DD⅝	1	gd	30^3	1.01^3	1.32^4	2.03^2	NW1250	800	2	1	2	3	2^1	$4^1\frac{1}{4}$	2.03^3	4.00	(GivensW)LeftyFrizzell,OhtobisGreat,MyGlory	
6-1	12-6DD⅝	1	fst	29	1.01	1.31^1	2.02	Qua		5	1°	1	1	1^1	3^2	2.02^1	nb	(GivensW)ScandiaPrincess,AngusMagnificently,LesHall	

YELLOW 6 RAPID SKIPPER

b h 7,by Scarlet Skipper, Sheri Hill by Hi Hill
S. & R. Lombardo, Ralph Auriemma, Dix Hills, N.Y.
Tr.Dan Daley
Dan Daley (162) Green-Gold-White
92 5 0 0 0 $725 — 91 34 3 4 2 $35,210 — 1:57.4 YR — Last 8 starts–$725 — 4 1:53.1 (1) — Lifetime $261,871

	2-8M1(A)-6	1	fst	28	58^2	1.28^1	1.56^3	NW8000	6500	7	6	1°	$1\frac{1}{2}$	2^{ns}	$5^8\frac{1}{4}$	1.58^1	29.40	(DaleyD)Harada,SoStated,MikeTomar	used,gave way
	2-2M1-8	1	fst	28^1	58^1	1.27^2	1.56^1	NW8000	6500	7	2	3x	8^{17}	8^{17}	8^{22}	2.00^3	54.50	(DaleyD)Trencher,Jate,TEsMac	tuck,broke
	1-27M1+1	1	fst	28^1	57^1	1.28^4	1.55^4	NW8000	6500	10	10	10	10^{11}	9^{10}	8^9	1.57^3	97.80	(DaleyD)SandlerHanover,Hapoca,MikeTomar	no moves
	1-18M1-11	1	fst	28^1	58^2	1.29^3	1.53^1	NW8500	8000	2	2	4°	$1^{\circ ns}$	$1\frac{3}{4}$	6^4	1.59	17.80	(DaleyD)KamasackBlueChip,ArnoldCrd,Whistlnd,Jim	lost cover,wknd
	1-11M1-2	1	fst	29^1	59^1	1.28^4	1.56^2	NW8500	8000	1	3	5	$4^3\frac{1}{4}$	$4^4\frac{1}{4}$	5^6	1.57^3	18.90	(DaleyD)Comedian,RalphsBoy,TEsMac	sat,little
	1-2M1	1	fst	29^3	59^2	1.29^3	1.58^2	Qua		3	2	2	$2^1\frac{1}{4}$	$2^1\frac{1}{4}$	2^{ns}	1.58^2	nb	(DaleyD)Stereotyped,RapidSkipper,SunseasR	pckd,good pace
	11-16YR+5	1	fst	30	1.00	1.28^4	1.57^3	NW8000	7000	4	4	6	$5^4\frac{3}{4}$	5^6	$6^8\frac{3}{4}$	1.59^2	37.80	(DaleyD)WightwrCanyon,BigBoldBarne,Stroland	tight quarters
6-1	11-9YR+4	1	fst	28	57^3	1.27^1	1.56^2	NW8000	7000	7	7	7°	$7^{\circ 7}\frac{1}{4}$	7^{11}	6^{18}	2.00	73.30	(DaleyD)Preston,PreciseVictory,DelgatysGiftN	little

ORANGE ‡LIVELY POWER — b h 4,by Big Power, Berdiola Hanover by Columbia George — Milton Letendre, Spencer, Mass.

7 — Gregory Annatoro (130) — Red-White — Tr.Milton Letendre

8-1

2:02.1 YR	92	4	1	0	0	$3,710
2:01.1 YR	91	25	3	3	4	$11,043
Last 8 starts—$4,714	3 2:01.1				Lifetime	$17,824

2-5YR-7	‡1	fst	29	1.00^{1}	1.30^{3}	2.00^{3}	NW8000	5750	4	4	2°	2°½	7^{11}	7^{11}	2.02^{4}	43.30	(WingT)PostOffice,Pasco,KentuckyImage	unc,chall,tired
1-29YR-5	‡1	fst	29^{1}	59^{2}	1.30	2.00^{1}	NW8000	5750	2	3	5	5^{3}	4^{3}¼	4^{6}	2.01^{2}	10.40	(AnnatoroG)SunseaR,StraightA,FiddlerBlueChip	sat in,even
1-22YR-3	‡1	fst	28^{4}	1.00^{2}	1.30^{2}	2.00^{3}	NW8000	5750	6	6	4°	4°2¼	5^{3}¾	6^{7}¼	2.02	10.50	(MarshJJr)SteppersRock,PostOffice,FiddlerBlueChip	cover,tired
1-7YR(A)-5	‡1	fst	28^{1}	58^{4}	1.32^{1}	2.02^{1}	NW4 3-4YO	6500	8	8	8°	8°°3¾	4^{1}¾	1no	2.02^{1}	55.50	(MarshJJr)LivelyPower,SpiralLee,DCsDignity	wide,driving
12-14Scr	‡1	sly	29	1.01	1.32	2.04^{3}	W301ps	1500	6	6	5°	4°	4	7^{6}¼	2.05^{4}	11.70	(AnnatoroG)LaneV,AndreSeelster,RaceMeScooter	
12-7Scr	‡1	sly	29^{4}	1.00^{4}	1.31	2.00^{1}	W301ps	1700	2	2	2	2	2	2^{1}	2.00[illegible]	11.00	(AnnatoroG)AndreSeelster,LivelyPower,[illegible]	
11-30Scr	‡1	gd	[illegible]	59^{4}	1.30^{1}	2.01	W301ps	1500	5	5	5°	5°°	2	2^{1}¼	2.01^{1}	15.30	(FitchL)AndreSeelster,LivelyPower,RaceMeScooter	
11-23Scr	‡1	fst	29^{2}	59^{4}	1.30^{4}	2.00^{4}	W301ps	1700	7	7	6°	5°°	3	3^{3}¼	2.01^{2}	15.20	(AnnatoroG)AndreSeelster,BranchbrookMoose,LivelyPower	

The 1, 6 and 7 horses all came out of the same condition in their last starts.

What of the four horses who didn't?

The 2 comes out of a $12,500/$15,000 claimer at Yonkers. The 3's last start was in a Non-Winners of $8,500 at The Meadowlands, but if you didn't know better, you would think the condition there covered eight starts. It didn't. The 4 horse was in a $20,000 claimer at The Meadowlands, and the 5 in a Late Closer, The Blue Hen, at Dover Downs in his last start.

The purses of the 2, 3, 4 and 5's last races were $5,000, $11,000, $8,500 and $10,000, respectively. Is that significant? Yes.

Here's a more detailed analysis of those four horses, and, as always, we start from the bottom PP and work up.

Following three races at Freehold in a $10,000 claimer, the 2 horse, Power Line, had raced in conditions at Yonkers: a Non-Winners of $4,000 twice; Winners of $13,501, and a Non-Winners of $4,500, before his last start in a claimer. Of those four races, his best was a second in the toughest one, Winners of $13,501. He fared poorly in the NW of $4,500 and in the $12,500/$15,000 claimer, but you can throw both races out because he suffered interference.

The 4 horse, Frankland A, was the shipper from the $20,000 claimer at The Meadowlands. At the bottom of his PPs, we discover that he has raced at Yonkers in a Non-Winners of $8,100, finishing distanced in eighth. This at least gives us a clue of how he compares to his competition tonight.

The 3 horse, Bond Street, is making a clear drop from Non-Winners of $8,500.

Les Hall, the 5 horse who's shipping in from Dover Downs, raced in the Blue Hen Series in his last five starts. He was fourth, second, third and first in four $3,000 legs of the series, and then second by a head in the $10,000 Final. Class-wise, it's impossible to tell the competition he faced there. But at the bottom, he showed conditional races, Non-Winners of $1,250 and Non-winners of $1,000 at Dover prior to entering the Blue Hen Series. Obviously, his races before the Blue Hen were against opponents much easier than his opponents tonight.

Is this definitive? No way, but it's the best we can do comparing PPs.

Bond Street jogged, paying $2.60. A good race to watch.

Determining class isn't an easy one-step process. Dividing a horse's earnings by his number of starts gives you average earnings per start, a useful barometer, but not an iron-clad indicator. There are frequent exceptions.

The $83,155 Jersey Cup Historic at The Meadowlands, June 27, 1992, attracted a field of 10 3-year-olds with 8 betting interests. Big Brat, Take It And Run and Tridium were coupled as a 3-horse entry.

6 MEADOWLANDS

PACE
ONE MILE
WARM UP COLOR-YELLOW
PURSE $83,155

EXACTA WAGERING

" JERSEY CUP "
3 YEAR OLD COLTS & GELDINGS
HISTORIC SERIES NO. 24

ASK FOR HORSE BY PROGRAM NUMBER — 140th RACING DAY SATURDAY, JUNE 27, 1992

7-2 TAKE IT AND RUN (M) — 1▲ — PP 3 RED
b c, 3, by Nihilator--Armbro Clever by Most Happy Fella — Tr.-Al Thomas Sr.-T.Haughton (.183)
Joseph J.Caloo & Joseph P.Moran, Mass. — M1 1:532 1992 11 4 2 2 $51,476
$64,244 - 3, 1:532 (1) Driver-TOM HAUGHTON 155 (grn-wht) (19-3-2-0-.216) BREEDER-JOSEPH J.CAICO,MASS. — M1 1:592 1991 7 2 2 0 $12,768

Date	Track Race #	Purse	Tk Cd	Type Class	Dist	1/4	1/2	3/4	Time	PP	1/4	1/2	3/4	Str	Finish	Lst 1/4	Time	Odds	Driver	First Second Third	Temp Allow
6-20	M1 3	15000	ft	3yr Opn	1	281	554	1252	153	2	3o1¼	1¹¼	1½	2¾	5³¼	281	1533	*.90	JPaviaJr	Deadlock,Tridium,InterLog	68-C
6-6	RcR% 10	92000	ft	3YR STK	1	28	582	1261	1543	5	6	4o2¼	1ohd	2hd	3¹¾	284	155	8.40	JPaviaJr	WstmHanovr,OckCombck,TakItandRn	80-C
5-29	M1 8	15000	ft	3yr Opn	1	273	55	1243	1532	7	89¼	8o8¼	5o4	44	1½	28	1532	12.30	THaughton	TakItandRn,KITThTranr,ShorPatrol	65-C
5-22	M1 9	15000	ft	3yr Opn	1	282	574	1254	1531	4	44½	74¾	65	65	42¾	27	1534	11.60	THaughton	SafetyKept,GammaRay,Pundit	85-C
5-2	PPk% 8	45400	ft	EC FINAL	1	274	571	126	154	5	6	64¼	5oo2¾	21	12	272	154	5.80	JPaviaJr	TakItandRn,IntrLog,ScardClods	76-C
4-25	PPk% 8	8000	ft	3YR EC	1	281	593	1272	1552	3	2	3¹½	32	32¼	4¹¾	28	1554	2.30	THaughton	IntrLog,ScardClouds,ShphrdBoy	77-C
4-18	PPk% 5	8000	ft	3YR EC	1	282	581	1264	1554	3	2	2¹¼	1o¼	11	2hd	29	1554	5.40	KOscarsson	Trdum,TakItandRn,MstangHanovr	76-C

7-2 TRIDIUM (M) — 1A▲ — PP 4 RED
br c, 3, by Jate Lobell--Turquoise by Bret Hanover — Tr.-Robert Bencal (.245)
North Street Stable,Englewood,N.J. — M1 1:543 1992 10 5 2 0 $39,710
$41,216 - 3, 1:543 (1) Driver-WILLIAM FAHY 160 (br-or) (700-79-75-69-.205) BREEDER-A B CUDDY STABLES LTD,ONT. — Lex1 1:563 1991 5 1 0 2 $1,506

Date	Track Race #	Purse	Tk Cd	Type Class	Dist	1/4	1/2	3/4	Time	PP	1/4	1/2	3/4	Str	Finish	Lst 1/4	Time	Odds	Driver	First Second Third	Temp Allow
6-20	M1 3	15000	ft	3yr Opn	1	281	554	1252	153	1	2¹½	34	42¼	3¹½	21	272	1531	7.90	WODonnell	Deadlock,Tridium,InterLog	68-C
6-6	RcR% 8	92000	ft	3YR STK	1	273	572	1251	154	3	3	3o¹½	1ohd	2¾	5⁵¼	294	155	8.70	JPaviaJr	RunThGauntlt,ExotcEarl,GameRay	80-C
5-27	M1 7	9000	ft	nw3 cd	1	28	571	1262	1543	5	12	1¼	1¼	1nk	2IP1	281	1543	*1.00	JoCampbell	Trdum,KatzHanovr,GanfPrst	58-C
5-16	VD% 9	26100	ft	H&H 3 STK	1	26	544	124	1534	7	1o	3	44	53	52½	292	1541	6.60	JeGregory	InstantAus,Mandri,ArmbroKhak	64-C
5-9	RcR% 10	236088	ft	3YR C STK	1	274	572	1254	1552	8	2o	3₂o2	77¾	77½	76½	291	1563	4.00	RWaples	NuclarTrox,AdmiralsGaly,Pundit	58-C
5-2	RcR% 10	29611	ft	3YR C STK	1	281	582	1264	1554	6	3	3³¼	2o½	2hd	11	29	1554	*2.70	RWaples	Tridium,Log,NuclearTerror	80-C
4-26	M1 11A	6500	ft	nw2 cd	1	282	563	1253	155	5	67	8o4¼	4o2¼	1¾	13¾	29	155	*.60	JoCampbell	Trdum,RdToThCrown,BransNBrawn	52-C

7-2 BIG BRAT (M) — 1B◆ — PP 6 RED
br c, 3, by Cam Fella--Spoiled Royal by Nistross — Tr.-Robert Bencal (.245)
North Street Stable,J.J.Caloo & R.J.Silverman, N.J., Mass. — Q M1 1:554 1992 5 0 0 0 $7,150
$363,021 - 2, 1:531 (1) Driver-JOHN CAMPBELL 155 (wht-mar-blue) (1294-236-157-157-.290) BREEDER-KENTUCKIANA FARMS,KY. — M1 1:531 1991 15 7 2 3 $355,871

Date	Track Race #	Purse	Tk Cd	Type Class	Dist	1/4	1/2	3/4	Time	PP	1/4	1/2	3/4	Str	Finish	Lst 1/4	Time	Odds	Driver	First Second Third	Temp Allow
6-19	M1 6	20000	gd	3yrC NJSS	1	273	561	1233	1524	4	78¾	7o4½	5o4¾	86	86	292	154	2.90	JoCampbell	IncrdblAus,AmrcanCosn,BgFnsh	66-C
6-13	GrR% 8	40000	ft	3YR STKE	1	274	57	124	1531	1	6	6	6	54¾	43		1534	19.60	SCondren	DirectFlght,NoTwistr,SaflyKpt	77-C
6-6	M1 9	38900	ft	3yrC NJSS	1	28	554	1232	1521	1	31¾	2o¾	1¹½	12	57¼	301	1533	2.40	JoCampbell	RockitLeRu,RoadRunrSpur,DrctFlO	74-C
5-23	M1 7	20000	ft	NJ Classic	1	273	56	1233	1521	1	45½	4o¹½	1o1	1¹½	97¾	301	1534	6.60	MLachance	Bilateral,CarlsbadCam,Gorbachv	85-C
5-15	M1 7	40100	ft	3yrC NJSS	1	283	564	126	1531	6	9o11¾	79¾	5o4¾	55	58½	28	1544	10.40	MLachance	WstmHanovr,DrctFlght,Largo	59-C
5-9	M1 2		ft	QUA	1	30	581	1264	1562	1	44	46	2o¼	13	13¾	27¾	1562	NB	MLachance	BigBrat,GnralCochran,Msintnsty	59-C
5-2	M1 2		ft	QUA	1	29	581	1282	1554	2	54¼	56	3o1½	2½	1ns	27	1554	NB	MLachance	BigBrat,RockitLeRu,Betrayed	68-C

5-2 LARGO — 2◆ — PP 1 BLUE
b c, 3, by Cam Fella--Ombre Rose by B.G's Bunny — Tr.-Robert Siegelman (.282)
Carmine Abbatiello Stb. Inc. & Jan R.Feldman, N.J. — M1 1:523 1992 19 5 2 5 $127,602
$132,958 - 3, 1:523 (1) Driver-CARMINE ABBATIELLO 145 (red-gold) (34-5-2-8-.258) BREEDER-CARMINE ABBATIELLO SB INC,etc. — M1 1:572 1991 5 1 0 1 $5,356

Date	Track Race #	Purse	Tk Cd	Type Class	Dist	1/4	1/2	3/4	Time	PP	1/4	1/2	3/4	Str	Finish	Lst 1/4	Time	Odds	Driver	First Second Third	Temp Allow
6-19	M1 7	100000	gd	3yrC NJSS	1	274	552	1231	1514	6	2¹¼	32¾	43	32¼	2¾	281	152	12.40	CAbbatiello	RocketLeRu,Largo,Bilateral	66-C
6-12	M1 2	38900	ft	3yrC NJSS	1	281	552	1224	1523	1	1¹½	42½	44½	45	1¾	29	1523	3.10	CAbbatiello	Largo,JCsSkiparoo,BombeSouffle	80-C
6-6	M1 11	39500	ft	3yrC NJSS	1	272	56	1243	1531	6	2¹¼	43½	43	53¾	41¾	282	1533	*1.10	CAbbatiello	StandTogthr,JovalKlan,CityNghts	74-C
5-30	M1 7	500000	ft	NJ Classic	1	272	543	122	1504	4	2¹¼	41½	42¾	44¾	45½	291	1514	42.00	CAbbatiello	WstmHnvr,CrlsbdCm,RnThGntlt	60-C
5-23	M1 3	20000	ft	NJ Classic	1	282	582	127	1534	7	21	2¹¼	2¹¼	2¹½	32¾	271	1542	12.10	CAbbatiello	WstmHanovr,AmrcanCousn,Largo	85-C
5-15	M1 7	40100	ft	3yrC NJSS	1	283	564	126	1531	8	2¹½	2¹¼	2¹¼	2¹¼	32	272	1533	35.60	CAbbatiello	WstmHanovr,DrctFlght,Largo	59-C
5-8	M1 10	15000	sy	3yr Opn	1	291	571	1261	1543	3	3¹½	32½	42¾	44¼	62¾	282	1551	3.80	CAbbatiello	LordWking,GamaRay,CarlsbadCam	50-C

20-1 FAKE LEFT — 3▲ — PP 2 WHITE
b c, 3, by Cam Fella--Madam Medusa by Albatross — Tr.-Larry Remmen St.-R.Remmen (.264)
Status Stables Inc,Brookline,Mass. — Shpl% 1:57 1992 5 1 0 1 $4,250
$36,859 - 2, 1:54 (1) Driver-MICKEY MC NICHOL 160 (blu-blk-wht) (768-77-79-70-.188) BREEDER-DREAMAIRE STABLE,N.J. — Lex1 1:54 1991 14 5 2 2 $32,609

Date	Track Race #	Purse	Tk Cd	Type Class	Dist	1/4	1/2	3/4	Time	PP	1/4	1/2	3/4	Str	Finish	Lst 1/4	Time	Odds	Driver	First Second Third	Temp Allow
6-21	Shpl% 13	2500	ft	3YR NJFS	1	284	58	127	157	7	4o	1	12	12	14¼	30	157	NB	RRemmen	FakeLeft,Skidamannkadoo,Bush	75-C
6-12	M1 2	38900	ft	3yrC NJSS	1	281	552	1224	1523	7	78¾	78	68¾	57	78	30	1541	21.50	RRemmen	Largo,JCsSkiparoo,BombeSouffle	80-C
5-30	M1 10	25000	ft	NJ Classic	1	274	55	1231	153	3	54½	54¾	6o4¾	46½	32¼	291	1532	23.20	RRemmen	ExoticEarl,Humstinger,FakeLeft	60-C
5-23	M1 6	20000	ft	NJ Classic	1	27	56	1241	1524	5	79	74¼	7o4	65	63¾	283	1533	33.40	RRemmen	Whatapact,Polanzo,RnThGantlt	85-C
5-15	M1 7	40100	ft	3yrC NJSS	1	283	564	126	1531	3	811½	1114	11o12	1011¼	812¾	272	1554	59.00	RRemmen	WstmHanovr,DrctFlght,Largo	59-C
5-5	Lex1 4		ft	QUA	1	294	591	1293	1581	5	1o	2	2¹¼	21	14¾	282	1581	NB	GShotty	FakeLeft,Imagic,ShannonCar	47-C
10-3	Lex1 5A	10250	ft	2YR LC	1	281	562	1253	154	3	1	2	1ohd	1¹¾	12¼	282	154	2.90	JPiccirano	FakeLeft,Log,CaviarWalkr	74-C

3-1 SHORE PATROL (M) — b c, 3, by Nihilator--Turn The Tide by Albatross
G.Mottram,K.Liebowitz,A.Mereon & L.Vernich, Ont.,N.J. — Tr.-Brad Mc Ninch St - T. Artandi (.247)
$528,524 - 2, 1:534 (1) Driver-JACK MOISEYEV 165 (blk-wh-go) (1307-246-162-147-.296) BREEDER-PRUB-ALMAHURST LP,KY — Q M1 1:55 1992 4 0 1 1 $24,500 / M1 1:534 1991 17 7 6 2 $504,024
4 · PP 5 · GREEN

6-13	GrR⅝ 4	40000	ft	3YR STKEL	1 284	587	126	1534	4	1o	1	1	1½	44		1543	2.05	JMoiseyev	Kingsbridg,ShosPrsr,SrvvorGolc	77-0
6-6	GrR⅝ 6	75000	sy	3YR C STK	1 274	563	126	1552	2	1o	2	3	37	210		1572	3.15	SCondren	CarlsbadCam,ShorPatrol,RichsEmpr	73-0
5-29	M1 8	15000	ft	3yr Opn	1 273	55	1243	1532	9	4o2½	1½	11	21	3½	29	1533	2.20	JMoiseyev	TakItandRn,KlThTranr,ShorPatro	65-0
5-22	M1 9	15000	ft	3yr Opn	1 282	574	1254	1531	6	67	5o3	4o3½	54½	52½	272	1534	1.80	JMoiseyev	SafelyKept,GammaRay,Pundit	85-0
5-16	M1 1		gd	QUA	1 291	57	1271	155	2	15	18	15	14½	13½	274	155	NB	JMoiseyev	ShorePatrol,Sleepwalk,Knowhow	58-2
5-9	M1 1		ft	QUA	1 301	582	128	1564	4	44	1½	2½	1½	14½	283	1564	NB	JMoiseyev	ShorPatrol,ArtLght,PlayByThRls	59-0
11-23	GSP1 10	584300	ft	2yr Ec	1 272	551	1233	1521	9	2o1½	31	33	32	24½	284	153	5.00	JMoiseyev	WstrnHanovr,ShorPatrol,LawtHanovr	54-1

5-1 COLE MUFFLER (M) — b c, 3, by Tyler B--Sandy's Sable by Race Time
R.Guida,Bonnie Castle Stbs.& Hunt Harness Horses Inc,Fla,N.Y — Tr.-Ken Seeber (.266)
$572,582 - 3, 1:542 (⅝) Driver-CATELLO MANZI 165 (wht-l blu-blu) (1074-132-128-131-.230) BREEDER-HANOVER SHOE FARMS INC,PA — RcR⅝ 1:542 1992 2 1 0 0 $48,000 / M1 1:542 1991 10 6 1 2 $524,582
5 · PP 7 · BLACK

6-13	GrR⅝ 6	40000	ft	3YR STKEL	1 273	573	1242	152	2	2	3	4	43½	56		1531	7.35	CManzi	CarlsbadCam,WarMyRng,WstrnHanovr	77-0
6-6	RcR⅝ 6	92000	ft	3YR STK	1 28	564	1252	1542	2	2	11	1nd	1½	1ns	29	1542	*.60	CManzi	ColeMuffler,Influntial,Funship	80-0
5-29	M1 3		ft	QUA	1 281	587	1272	1551	3	1½	1½	1½	13	17½	274	1551	NB	JoCampbell	ColeMuffler,Nosdrop,BornFamous	70-0
5-22	M1 2		ft	QUA	1 304	1002	1283	1571	3x	6o7½	2o1	2½	11	1½	282	1571	NB	JoCampbell	ColMufr,SantanaWnd,CactsFlowr	80-0
5-16	M1 5		gd	QUA	1 293	593	128	1561	2	32½	32½	25	26	29	29	158	NB	JoCampbell	LuckyCam,ColMufr,SantanaWind	58-2
11-9	GSP1 5		ft	QUA	1 292	593	1291	157	7	1½	1½	12½	14	14½	274	157	NB	RRemmen	ColMufr,KatzHanovr,Gardnrvonat	42-1
11-2	RcR⅝ 5	22838	ft	PRES ELIM	1 281	58	126	1543	8	4o	4o3½	4o2½	41½	710½	301	1563	*1.20	JoCampbell	WstrnHanovr,ShorPatrol,BoKnowsJat	52-0

15-1 FANNIE'S CHAMP — b c, 3, by On The Road Again--Lark Almahurst by Albatross
Realty Stables,Harrison,N.Y. — Tr.-Fred Grant (.142)
$42,400 - 3, 1:533 (¾) Driver-WILLIAM O' DONNELL 138 (wht-blu-or) (621-51-64-64-.174) BREEDER-ROAD RUNNER LP,N Y — VD¾ 1:533 1992 7 5 0 2 $29,130 / Sycs1 1:542 1991 9 2 1 3 $13,270
6 · PP 8 · YELLOW

6-19	M1 7		sy	QUA	1 301	592	1284	1574	7	78½	6o7½	610½	59½	35	28	1584	NB	WODonnell	BimanHanovr,NEOGrzy,FansChamp	63-3
5-25	VD¾ 6A	11550	ft	3YR NYSS	1 264	562	124	1533	5	6o	1o	1o1½	12½	12½	293	1533	*.70	WHennessey	FaniesChamp,Mandr,Subcompact	60-0
5-16	YR 4	8000	ft	3YR NYB LC	1 282	583	128	1581	9	7	5o	1	16	17		1581	*.20	JMarohn	FaniesChamp,Safront,Subcompact	51-0
5-8	M1 6	38900	sy	nw3 Lc	1 283	571	1253	1542	4	79½	7o8½	7o6½	66½	31	273	1543	*1.30	WODonnell	FalconsHonor,Tunrs,FanisChamp	50-0
5-1	M1 6	12500	ft	nw3 cd	1 29	581	1263	1541	6	67½	65½	6o3½	33½	31½	271	1543	*1.20	WODonnell	PrcarosMson,ForgnDgntary,FansChamp	55-0
4-17	M1 5	12500	gd	nw3 Lc	1 272	561	1264	155	8	810	86½	8oo4	32½	12	272	155	*1.60	WODonnell	FanisChamp,LosanaPrchas,Tlnrs	42-0
4-10	M1 4	12500	ft	nw3 Lc	1 283	564	1253	1543	5	8o7½	9o6½	10oo7½	42½	1dh	273	1543	*2.60	WODonnell	FansChamp(Dh)PrcarosMson,PrtyBoyFM	52-0

20-1 AMERICAN COUSIN — b c, 3, by Radiant Ruler--Plum Perfect by Nero
Robert D.Gregory & Ronald W.Gregory, Ont. — Tr.-Greg Gaskle (.241)
$28,869 - 3, 1:571 (1) Driver-JACK PARKER JR 140 (mar-l blu-wht) (72-5-4-7-.133) BREEDER-WILLIAM A BULMER,ILL — Lex1 1:571 1992 8 1 3 1 $20,490 / Mea⅝ 1:574 1991 12 2 2 0 $8,379
7 · PP 9 · PINK

6-19	M1 6	20000	gd	3yrC NJSS	1 273	561	1233	1524	1	12½	1½	2½	1½	2½	291	153	6.40	JParkerJr	IncrdblAus,AmrcanCosn,BigFnsh	66-0
6-12	M1 6	38900	ft	3yrC NJSS	1 273	56	1241	1524	1	44½	3o2½	2o1	3½	52½	284	1531	12.20	JParkerJr	ExoticEar,Bilateral,BigFinsh	80-0
6-8	M1 5	39500	ft	3yrC NJSS	1 274	562	1244	1523	9	32½	32½	33	32½	31½	272	1524	26.50	JParkerJr	DrctFight,KlThTranr,AmrcanCosn	74-0
5-30	M1 7	500000	ft	NJ Classic	1 272	543	122	1504	6	8o7½	87½	86½	713½	715	302	1534	48.70	RWaples	WstrnHnvr,CrlsbdCm,RnThGnt	60-0
5-23	M1 3	20000	ft	NJ Classic	1 282	582	127	1534	1	32½	42½	53	54	22½	263	1541	31.40	JoCampbell	WstrnHanovr,AmrcanCousn,Largo	85-0
5-15	M1 8	40100	ft	3yrC NJSS	1 282	562	1242	1533	2	44½	76½	76½	76	54½	284	1542	58.50	WFahy	Bilatral,RoadRnrSpr,PatrolMs	59-0
5-2	Lex1 9	2500	sy	NW1275L4CD	1 273	563	127	1571	4	5	4o	4o4½	43	16	292	1571	2.40	GGaskle	AmrcanCousin,OpnHat,TonsofPac	63-0

4-1 QUICK COMEBACK (M) — b c, 3, by Big Towner--Sarcastick by Slapstick
John L.Confort Jr.,New York,N.Y. — Tr.-Gerry Nelson St - R Waples (.144)
$57,430 - 3, 1:513 (1) Driver-RON WAPLES 150 (blue-gold) (45-6-4-6-.227) BREEDER-ROBERT A.TUCKER,N.J — M1 1:513 1992 7 3 2 0 $43,749 / Mea⅝ 1:562 1991 5 2 1 0 $13,681
8 · PP 10 · GRAY

6-13	Mea⅝ 4	17699	ft	3YO C PASS	1 274	572	1261	1544	4	1	1	1½	1½	1½	283	1544	*.30	RWaples	QckCombck,Atatonc,KystonRansom	80-0
6-6	RcR⅝ 10	92000	ft	3YR STK	1 28	587	1261	1543	7	1	11	2nd	1nd	2½	283	1544	8.00	RWaples	WstrnHanovr,QckCombck,TakItandRn	80-0
5-23	M1 2	15000	ft	nw4 cd	1 271	542	1222	1513	4	1½	12½	1½	12½	13½	291	1513	34.80	RWaples	QckCombck,ColFlyngFla,Camarac	85-0
5-9	RcR⅝ 6	4500	ft	3-4YR OPEN	1 282	582	1273	1571	5	1	2½	2½	3½	2ns	292	1571	5.60	RWaples	ExoticEar,QuckCombck,SothrnG	58-0
5-2	RcR⅝ 8	29511	ft	3YR C STK	1 282	592	127	1561	5	1	22	3½	4½	52	291	1563	13.40	RWaples	AdmralsGaly,RnThGantt,TylrsB	80-0
4-18	PPk⅝ 4	5500	ft	NW3700L6CD	1 274	56	1261	1552	8	7o	4o3½	5o2½	47½	69	303	1571	*1.60	RWaples	PowerSwipe,TalbotBandt,Kinzua	76-0
4-11	PPk⅝ 11	3600	sy	NW3FMNW4	1 283	592	129	1582	4	1	11	11	12½	15	292	1582	2.70	RWaples	QckCombck,NotAOr,HadsHorsman	76-0

TRACKMAN'S SELECTIONS: 2-8-4 (M) DENOTES MEADOWLANDS PACE ELIGIBLE HD NO. 1, 1A & 1B NORTH STREET STABLE AND J. CAICO OWNED ENTRY

In stakes races, class is a crucial factor. Belying the odds, the four standouts were clearly Cole Muffler, Shore Patrol, Big Brat and Largo.

Largo, the 2 horse starting from the rail, was the leading '92 money winner of the field with $127,602, though it's worth noting that he had 19 starts—8 to 17 more than every other horse. As a 2-year-old, Largo had won 1 of 5 races and just $5,356. He obviously did well as a 3-year-old, but the fact of the matter is he won just 1 of his last 7 races, and had not been tested outside of The Meadowlands. Several other horses here had been. Largo's last race was superb—he finished second by 3/4 of a length in 1:52 in the $100,000 New Jersey Sire Stakes—but he wasn't facing just New Jersey-breds this night.

Big Brat had been just awful in five starts as a 3-year-old despite the fact that three of them were from the rail. As a 2-year-old, he'd won seven of 15, been in the money in 12 of them, and bankrolled $355,871. He was clearly in poor form. About the only way you could bet him was by liking his two entrymates, Tridium and Take It And Run. We didn't.

Cole Muffler had been awesome at 2, going 6-1-2 (6 wins, 1 second, 2 thirds) in 10 starts and making $524,582. His only off-the-board performance was in the Presidential, when he was seventh by 10¼ lengths from the 8 post to the outstanding pacer Western Hanover. Shore Patrol was second.

In his 3-year-old debut, Cole Muffler was gigantic, gutting out a nose victory in the Terrapin Stakes at Rosecroft. In a separate division won by Western Hanover, Quick Comeback was second by 1¼, half a length in front of Take It And Run.

Cole Muffler's and Shore Patrol's last starts were in the eliminations of the $1 million North American Cup at Greenwood (Can.)—each horse skipped a week afterwards. Big Brat had also been in an elimination.

The three were in separate divisions. From the rail, Big Brat finished fourth by 3 to Direct Flight. Cole Muffler finished fifth by 6 out of the 2 hole to Carlsbad Cam. Shore Patrol used the 4 post to finish fourth to Kingsbridge. Their respective times were 1:53.4, 1:53.1 and 1:54.3.

Safe to say that the three were similarly mediocre, although Shore Patrol had the slowest time.

Shore Patrol's 2-year-old season was impressive, going 7-6-2 in 17 starts and earning $504,024. Shore Patrol began his 3-year-old season finishing fifth by 2¾ and third by ¾ of a length in two 3-year-old Open races at The Meadowlands. On a sloppy track at Greenwood, he finished second by 10 to Carlsbad Cam in the Burlington. He then was fourth in the Northern American Cup eliminations.

Of these four horses with a decided class edge, Largo went off at 3-2, Shore Patrol 6-1, Cole Muffler at 5-1 and Big Brat at 6-1 as part of the three-horse entry. Shore Patrol's odds were higher than in all his PPs. He won and paid $14.60.

Back Class

Back class refers to a horse's positive performances at a higher level. Back class can be measured in claimers or top stakes. An obvious example is a $4,000 claimer who had won twice at that level; moved up to a $6,000 claimer; lost two or three races, and was dropped back to $4,000. He's proven that he has enough class to win a $4,000 claimer, which is all you care about in tonight's $4,000 claiming race.

Many times, back class shows in a horse's PPs, and is easy to find.

Here's a race which also mixes our penchant for recognizing and eliminating horses who rarely win, and one of our basics: the bigger the underlay, the bigger the overlay.

A field of eight contested the fourth race at Saratoga, June 6, 1992, for 5-year-olds and under who were Non-Winners of 2 pari-mutuel races lifetime.

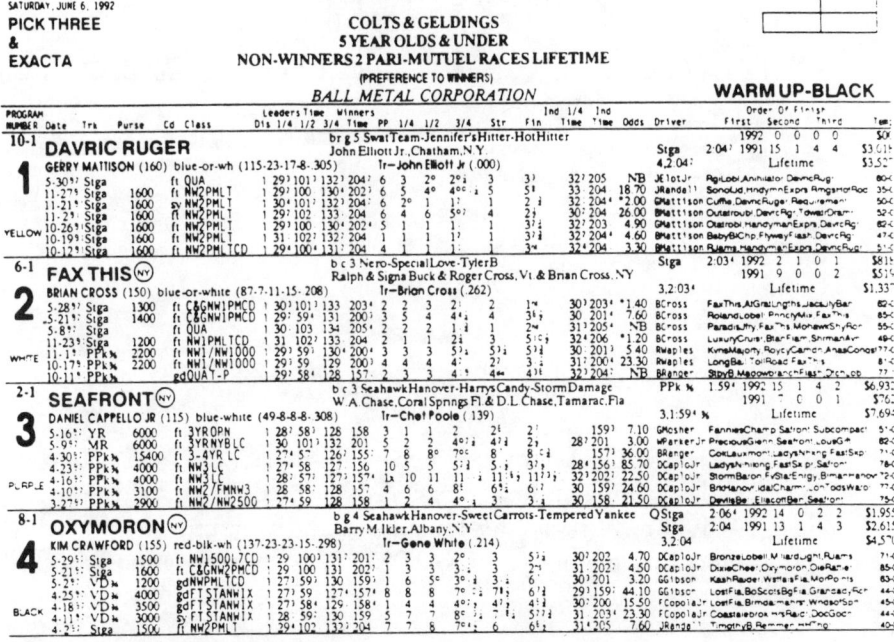

ONE MILE PACE
PURSE $1,500
SATURDAY, JUNE 6, 1992
PICK THREE & EXACTA

FOURTH RACE

COLTS & GELDINGS
5 YEAR OLDS & UNDER
NON-WINNERS 2 PARI-MUTUEL RACES LIFETIME
(PREFERENCE TO WINNERS)
BALL METAL CORPORATION

WARM UP-BLACK

10-1 — 1 — DAVRIC RUGER (YELLOW)
br g 5 SwatTeam-Jennifer'sHitter-HotHitter — John Elliott Jr., Chatham, N.Y.
GERRY MATTISON (160) blue-or-wh (115-23-17-8-.305) — Tr—John Elliott Jr (.000)
Stga 2:04^{2} — 1992 0 0 0 0 $0 — 1991 15 1 4 4 $3,01 — 4,2:04 Lifetime $3,52

Date	Trk	Purse	Cd	Class	Dis	1/4	1/2	3/4	Time	PP	1/4	1/2	3/4	Str	Fin	Ind 1/4 Time	Ind Time	Odds	Driver	Order Of Finish (First Second Third)	Temp
5-30 92	Stga		ft	QUA	1	29^{3}	101^{3}	132^{3}	204^{2}	6	3	2°	2°	3	3	32^{2}	205	NB	JElotJr	RgiLobl,Anihilator,DavncRug	60
11-27 91	Stga	1600	ft	NW2PMLT	1	29^{2}	100	130^{4}	202^{3}	6	5	4°	4°°	5	5	33	204	18.70	JRandall	SonoLid,HndymnExprs,RmgsHotRoc	35
11-21 91	Stga	1600	sy	NW2PMLT	1	30^{4}	101^{2}	132^{3}	204	6	2°	1	1	1	2	32	204^{4}	*2.00	GMattison	Cuffie,DavncRuger,Requirement	50
11-2 91	Stga	1600	ft	NW2PMLT	1	29^{2}	102	133	204	6	4	6	5°	4	2	30	204	26.00	BMattison	Outatroubl,DavcRgr,TowarDram	52
10-26 91	Stga	1600	ft	NW2PMLT	1	29^{3}	100	130^{4}	202^{4}	5	1	1	1	1	3	32^{2}	203	4.90	GMattison	Oatrobl,HandymanExprs,DavcRg	62
10-19 91	Stga	1600	ft	NW2PMLT	1	31	102^{2}	132^{2}	204	1	1	1	1	1	3	32^{2}	204^{4}	4.60	BMattison	BabyBiChp,FlywayFlash,DavcRg	47
10-12 91	Stga	1600	ft	NW2PMLTCD	1	29^{4}	100^{4}	131^{2}	204	4	1	1	1	1	3	32^{4}	204	3.30	BMattison	RJams,HandymanExprs,DavncRug	51

6-1 — 2 — FAX THIS (NY) (WHITE)
b c 3 Nero-SpecialLove-TylerB — Ralph & Signa Buck & Roger Cross, Vt. & Brian Cross, NY
BRIAN CROSS (150) blue-or-white (87-7-11-15-.208) — Tr—Brian Cross (.262)
Stga 2:03^{4} — 1992 2 1 0 1 $815 — 1991 9 0 0 2 $519 — 3,2:03^{4} Lifetime $1,33

Date	Trk	Purse	Cd	Class	Dis	1/4	1/2	3/4	Time	PP	1/4	1/2	3/4	Str	Fin	Ind 1/4 Time	Ind Time	Odds	Driver	Order Of Finish (First Second Third)	Temp
5-28 92	Stga	1300	ft	C&GNW1PMCD	1	30^{3}	101^{3}	133	203^{4}	2	2	3	2	2	1	30^{3}	203^{4}	*1.40	BCross	FaxThis,AtGratLngths,JacsJyBar	62
5-21 92	Stga	1400	ft	C&GNW1PMCD	1	29^{2}	59^{4}	131	200^{3}	3	5	4	4	4	3	30	201^{4}	7.60	BCross	RolandLobel,PnnclyMix,FaxThis	85
5-8 92	Stga		ft	QUA	1	30	103	134	205^{4}	2	2	2	1	1	2	31^{3}	205^{4}	NB	BCross	Paradisjfty,FaxThs,MohawkShyRor	55
11-23 91	Stga	1200	ft	NW1PMLTCD	1	31	102^{2}	133	204	2	1	1	2	3	5	32^{4}	206	*1.20	BCross	LuxuryCruisr,BlarFlam,ShrmanAvr	49
11-1 91	PPk	2200	ft	NW1/NW1000	1	29^{3}	59^{3}	130^{4}	200^{4}	3	3	3	5	5	5	30	201^{3}	5.40	RWaples	KvnsMajorty,RoycyCamdn,AnasConost	77
10-17 91	PPk	2200	ft	NW1/NW1000	1	29^{3}	59	129	200^{3}	4	4	4	4	2	3	31^{2}	200^{4}	23.30	RWaples	LongBal,TollRoad,FaxThis	8
10-11 91	PPk		gd	QUAT-P	1	29^{2}	58^{4}	128	157	2	3	3	4	4	4	32^{3}	204	NB	BRanger	StbyB,MeadowbranchFlash,DrchJob	77

2-1 — 3 — SEAFRONT (NY) (PURPLE)
b c 3 SeahawkHanover-HarrysCandy-StormDamage — W.A. Chase, Coral Springs Fl. & D.L. Chase, Tamarac, Fla
DANIEL CAPPELLO JR (115) blue-white (49-8-8-8-.308) — Tr—Chet Poole (.139)
PPk 1:59^{4} — 1992 15 1 4 2 $6,93 — 1991 7 0 0 1 $76 — 3,1:59^{4} Lifetime $7,69

Date	Trk	Purse	Cd	Class	Dis	1/4	1/2	3/4	Time	PP	1/4	1/2	3/4	Str	Fin	Ind 1/4 Time	Ind Time	Odds	Driver	Order Of Finish (First Second Third)	Temp
5-16 92	YR	6000	ft	3YROPN	1	28^{2}	58^{3}	128	158	3	1	1	2	2	2		159^{3}	7.10	GMosher	FanniesChamp,Safront,Subcompact	5
5-9 92	MR	6000	ft	3YRNYBLC	1	30	101^{3}	132	201	5	2	2	4°	4	2	28^{2}	201	3.00	WParkerJr	PreciousGlenn,Seafront,LousGift	62
4-30 92	PPk	15400	ft	3-4YR LC	1	27^{4}	57	126^{2}	155	7	8	8°	7°°	8	8		157^{3}	36.00	BRanger	ColLauxmont,LadysNhtng,FastSxp	71
4-23 92	PPk	4000	ft	NW3LC	1	27^{4}	58	127	156	10	5	5	5	5	3	28^{4}	156^{3}	85.70	DCaploJr	LadysNhtng,FastSxpr,Safront	78
4-16 92	PPk	4000	ft	NW3LC	1	28^{2}	57	127^{3}	157^{4}	1x	10	11	11	11	11	32^{3}	202^{2}	22.50	DCaploJr	StormBaron,FvStarEngy,BrmanHanov	72
4-10 92	PPk	3100	ft	NW2/FMNW3	1	28	58	128	157	4	6	6	8	6	6	30	159^{2}	24.60	DCaploJr	BndHanov,IdalCharm,LonTodsWard	77
3-27 92	PPk	2900	ft	NW2/NW2500	1	27^{4}	59	128	158	1	2	4	4°	3	3	30	158	21.50	DCaploJr	DevilsBet,EllacottBen,Seafront	75

8-1 — 4 — OXYMORON (NY) (BLACK)
b g 4 SeahawkHanover-SweetCarrots-TemperedYankee — Barry M. Ikler, Albany, N.Y.
KIM CRAWFORD (155) red-blk-wh (137-23-23-15-.298) — Tr—Gene White (.214)
QStga 2:06^{4} — 1992 14 0 2 2 $1,95 — Stga 2:04 — 1991 13 1 4 3 $2,61 — 3,2:04 Lifetime $4,57

Date	Trk	Purse	Cd	Class	Dis	1/4	1/2	3/4	Time	PP	1/4	1/2	3/4	Str	Fin	Ind 1/4 Time	Ind Time	Odds	Driver	Order Of Finish (First Second Third)	Temp
5-29 92	Stga	1500	ft	NW1500L7CD	1	29	100^{3}	131^{2}	201^{2}	2	3	3	2°	3	5	30^{2}	202	4.70	DCaploJr	BronzeLobell,MillardUght,RJams	71
5-21 92	Stga	1600	ft	C&GNW2PMCD	1	29	100	131	202^{2}	1	3	3	3	3	2	31	202^{2}	4.50	DCaploJr	DixieCheer,Oxymoron,OleRattle	85
5-2 92	VD	1200	gd	NWPMLTCD	1	27^{3}	59^{3}	130	159^{3}	1	6	5°	3°	3	6	30^{3}	201	3.20	GGibson	KashRaider,WstfalsFla,MorPoints	63
4-25 92	VD	4000	gd	FT STANWIX	1	27^{3}	59	127^{4}	157^{4}	8	8	8	7°	7	6	29^{3}	159^{2}	44.10	GGibson	LostFla,BoScotsBgFla,Grandady	44
4-18 92	VD	3500	gd	FT STANWIX	1	27^{3}	58^{4}	129	158^{4}	1	4	4	4°	4	4	30^{2}	200	15.50	FCopolaJr	LostFla,Brmdalmanr,WndsorSpr	45
4-11 92	VD	3000	sy	FT STANWIX	1	28	59^{2}	130	159	5	7	7	8°	7	5	31	203^{4}	23.30	FCopolaJr	Coastalebrook,HrsRaid,DocGodr	44
4-2 92	Stga	1500	ft	NW2PMLT	1	29^{4}	102	132^{3}	204	7	7	8	7°	6	6	31^{4}	205	7.60	JRandall	TimothyB,Remmer,HHTng	40

3-1 **FASTER THAN TIME** — br g 4 CuckooClock-JefsHumidity-WhataBaron — QStga 2:03 1992 2 0 0 1 $26

5 — Alan Gene Mattison,Hinsdale,N.H — Stga 2:03 1991 5 1 2 2 $1,485

BRUCE MATTISON (165) bl-or-wh (85-7-12-6-.184) — Tr—Clyde Mattison (.296) — Q4,2:03 Lifetime $1,745

GREEN

5-30	Stga	1500	ft	C&GNW2PMCD	1	28	59	130	200	6	6	5	5°	4	3	30	201	13.30	BMattison	SnstBly,BrysClanSwp,FastrThanTm 65-C
5-21	Stga	1600	ft	C&GNW2PMCD	1	29	100	131	202	6	4	4	2°	2	5	31	202	2.20	BMattison	DixieCheer,Oxymoron,OleRattler 85-C
5-15	Stga		ft	QUA	1	29	100	132	203	6	1	1	1	1	1	31	203	NB	BMattison	FstrThnTm,WntrrpsKd,GldCrdMgan 55-C
9-5	Rutln	600	gd	NW2PMLT	1	32	103	134	206	2	2°	4	4	2	2		206	*1.50	CMattison	JacsuBax,FastrThanTim,NoSnSpot nr-C
7-29	Stga	1500	ft	NW2PMLT	1	29	100	130	201	7	4	4°	4°	3	3	31	202	2.00	BMattison	StopMakngSns,Zphanah,FastrThanTm 72-C
7-20	Stga	1500	ft	NW2PMLT	1	30	59	130	200	2	4	5	5	5	2	30	201	6.50	BMattison	TimelyLeade,FastrThanTim,Ire 93-C
7-14	Stga A	1500	ft	NW2PMLT	1	30	102	132	203	6	5	5°	3°	4	3	31	203	3.50	BMattison	SnsalCnclon,DonsBRbon,FstrThnTm 75-C

4-1 **BRYS CLEAN SWEEP** (NY) — b c 3 TucsonHanover-MissyMarkos-FloridaPro — 1992 10 0 1 1 $1,01

6 — Neil B.Gold,Chatham,N.Y. — Sycs 1 1:57 1991 14 2 6 2 $34,20

CHARLES PULVER (185) blk-white-green (3-0-1-1-.296) — Tr—Charles Pulver (.178) — 2,1:57 1 Lifetime $35,224

RED

5-30	Stga	1500	ft	C&GNW2PMCD	1	28	59	130	200	2	1	1	1	2	2	30	200	4.80	CPulver	SnstBly,BrysClanSwp,FastrThanTm 65-C
5-23	Stga	1600	ft	C&GNW2PMLT	1	29	100	129	159	6	7	4	4°	3	x3x	29	200	36.30	CPulver	WarenPace,SunstBly,BrysClanSwp 88-C
5-16	Stga	1600	ft	C&GNW2PMLT	1	30	102	133	203	8	7	5°	4°	4	8	31	205	10.50	KCrawford	Pallor,BermataFn,SkeetShot 80-C
5-8	Stga		ft	QUA	1	29	102	133	204	5	5	5°	2°	2	2	30	204	NB	KCrawford	LadybgCoins,BrysClanSwp,OlRat 55-C
5-5	YR	4500	ft	3-4YRNW2CD	1	28	58	129	159	4	2	2°	3°	8	8		205	38.80	JMarshJr	PckofThWk,RockngRandy,SdsMystry 52-C
4-7	YR A	4500	ft	3-4YRNW2CD	1	28	59	129	159	1	2	3	4	7	8		204	8.10	JMarshJr	SpkAlmanrst,YorMothrsBoy,NvadaPlats 58-C
3-17	YR	4500	ft	3-4YRNW2CD	1	28	58	129	158	2	3	3	3°	3	5		201	14.40	LDuit	LJoeyAussie,MightyTuf,ToughSic 34-C

10-1 **MISTER THINGY** — b h 4 Bret'sChamp-LittleBayAlice-RaceTime — 1992 14 0 2 2 $3,585

7 — Robert J.Naginewicz,Chicopee,Mass — QStga 2:05 1991 14 1 1 4 $2,849

ROBERT NAGINEWICZ (155) white-red (2-0-0-1-.167) — Tr—Robert Naginewicz (.167) — Q3,2:05 Lifetime $6,434

BROWN

5-28	Stga	1500	ft	C&GNW2PMCD	1	29	101	130	200	1	2	3	3	3	3	30	201	3.50	RNagnwcz	RoindLobi,DashExprs,MstrThng 62-C
5-16	MR	1350	gd	NW800L6CD	1	31	102	133	203	3	1	2	3°°	2	2	30	203	3.70	RNagnwcz	TaresBst,MstrThngy,RuningDar 52-C
5-8	MR	1300	ft	NW2PMLTCD	1	31	102	133	202	4ix	7	7	7	6	6	29	204	*.60	RNagnwcz	PasngRmrk,ChmpagnRcks,AmicnF 54-C
4-26	MR A	1600	ft	12500CLCD	1	29	58	130	202	8	8	8	8	8	8	34	207	38.90	RNagnwcz	WingsHanovr,LusPrd,OpostonParty 45-C
4-18	MR	1570	sy	NW1000L6CD	1	29	100	132	204	8	9	9	9°°	7	4	31	206	29.20	RNagnwcz	GVFireball,SweetSd,DeborahA 40-C
4-7	MR	1360	ft	NW2PMLTCD	1	30	100	132	202	9	6	7	8	5	4	30	204	7.30	RNagnwcz	OpostonParty,Lcky Andrw,FrdsMrEd 58-C
3-31	YR A	4500	ft	3-4YRNW2CD	1	28	59	129	159	5	5	5	5°	4	3		201	82.00	RNagnwcz	PrincAlmond,Lovshack,MstrThng 48-C

12-1 **BRIDGE VIEW** — b c 3 Escort-Ms.Advocate-GeneAbbe — 1992 10 0 2 1 $1,2

8 — A.Wasserman,A.Scanio,L.Insalaco & J.Pappalardo,NY — GSP 1 1:57 1991 4 1 0 1 $2,00

JOHN STARK JR (145) red-wh-lblu (101-34-8-17-.437) — Tr—George Walters (.327) — 2,1:57 1 Lifetime $3,2

GRAY

5-30	Stga	1500	ft	C&GNW2PMCD	1	28	59	130	200	4	5	6°	3	3	4	30	201	7.10	JRandall	SnstBly,BrysClanSwp,FastrThanTm 65-C
5-21	Stga	1600	ft	C&GNW2PMCD	1	29	100	131	202	7	7	7	7°°	5	4	31	202	11.60	JRandall	DixieCheer,Oxymoron,OleRattle 85-C
5-9	Stga	1600	ft	C&GNW2PMCD	1	29	101	131	202	1	2	2	3	4	2	31	202	5.50	JRandall	EastCoastKd,BrdgVw,ToghTrading 70-C
5-3	VD	1700	ft	NW2PMLT	1	28	58	127	159	3	2°	2°	3°	6	7	34	202	7.10	CPeterson	DaylonBold,StarofTucson,BdBnd 59-C
4-18	VD	1700	gd	NW2PMLTCD	1	28	58	129	200	7	3°	1°	1	1	2	31	200	12.70	JRandall	ClascPrfction,BrdgVw,PlacdNoMr 45-C
4-10	VD	1700	ft	NW2PMLTCD	1	28	58	129	200	9	9	9	7	7	3	31	202	9.30	GGibson	SunsetVera,WidieWabit,Brdgvw 45-C
4-3	Stga		ft	QUA	1	30	102	132	203	4	6	6	5	5	4	31	205	NB	DMarshall	JacsuKmit,AvonBrz,MyradsKnyio 32-C

Horse by horse in post position order:

1. Davric Ruger—A tough horse to like even from the rail. The 5-year-old is making his first start since November 27 off a single qualifier. His 1991 record was 1-for-15, although he was in the money eight other times. His lifetime earnings of $3,527 is another serious knock. Pass.

2. Fax This—This 3-year-old was 0-for-9 last year, but has raced well in his two '92 starts, a third and a win in two maiden races. As

the 7-5 favorite in his last start, he won by a neck in 2:03.4 off a :30.3 final quarter and a 1:01.4 final half. Maybe.

3. Seafront—He's an obvious favorite off impressive races at Pompano Park, Monticello and Yonkers in much better company. He was a close third, then sixth by 12 lengths at Pompano in Non-Winners of 2. Then in a Late Closer series there, he was a distant 11th after a break, then third by 2½ while pacing his final quarter in :28.4 and the mile in 1:56.3. In the $15,400 final of the Late Closer—we discern it's the final because the legs of the series had $4,000 purses—he was eighth by 10¾ lengths, though he paced in 1:57.3.

In one start at Monticello, again in a Late Closer, he finished second by half a length in 2:01 after pacing his final quarter in :28.2 and his second half in roughly :59. The last quarter was especially impressive because Monticello's ½-mile track is slower than Pompano's ⅝.

Then in his last start, he raced in the 3-year-old Open at Yonkers chasing a runaway winner, Fannie's Champ. Seafront finished second by 7 lengths, trying the front end this time. He led at a :28.2 first quarter and a :58.3 first half. The race went in 1:58.1. Seafront's time was 1:59.3 with a second half in 1:01.

The purses he competed for in his PPs dwarf those of his rivals tonight.

Right about now, we go back to our evaluation of 'Maybe' for Fax This and change it to 'No Way.' We will also be more discriminating as we examine the other five horses here. Seafront is the obvious favorite.

Oh, almost forgot. His lifetime record was 1-for-22 and his lifetime earnings were just $7,694. And he hadn't raced in three weeks.

4. Oxymoron—Tough to recommend at 1-for-27 lifetime, but two starts back in this class, he was second by a nose, beating two of the four horses outside him tonight. Pass.

5. Faster Than Time—He finished fifth by 1¾ lengths behind Dixie's Cheer and Oxymoron two races back, but we must consider it was his first start—not including a qualifier—since last September, so he needed the race. In his last, he was third by 2¾, 1¼ lengths behind the place horse, Brys Clean Sweep, the 6 horse tonight. Faster's lifetime record is a healthy one: in seven starts, one win, two seconds

and three thirds, noted by 7 1-2-3. Normally, he'd be a contender at this level, but he's in too tough tonight. Pass.

6. Brys Clean Sweep—This is an interesting 3-year-old.

Five of his six PPs (excluding his qualifier) were dreadful: fifth, three straight eighths, and a third compromised by making a break. Regardless, his most recent race was a major improvement. Trying the front end in a Non-Winners of 2, he posted fractions of :28.4, :59.4 and 1:30 before tiring to finish second by a length and a half. The race went in 2:00.2. Brys got his last quarter in :30.3 and his final half in 1:00.3. In finishing second, he beat Faster Than Time and tonight's 8 horse, Bridge View.

Here's where class kicks in. Though his own win record was a weak 2-for-24 the last two years, his 2-year-old record was anything but weak. In 14 starts, he went 2-6-2 and earned a whopping $34,207. That was more than the lifetime earnings of every other horse he was facing tonight COMBINED.

Brys showed three poor races at Yonkers in Non-Winners of 2 with purses of $4,500, compared to the $6,000 purse Seafront went for in his last start there.

Sign of Life

Should a horse with bad PPs in a Non-Winners of 2 be able to beat another who finished second in the Three-Year-Old Open? Not usually. However, Brys had demonstrated a Sign of Life in his last race: that is, an indication that he's back on the way up, that his next race might be a win, and that, best of all, he may be an overlay.

Brys's Sign of Life had great meaning because he was the standout class horse in this field. Here's where form mixes with class. Whatever had caused his poor efforts might still be bothering him, but his last race suggests that he was returning to form. And his class had been good enough to amass $34,207 as a 2-year-old. Top contender.

7. Mister Thingy—Two good efforts in his last two starts, a second and a third, but 1-for-28 the last two years with earnings of $6,434. Also, he had inside posts, the 1 and 3, in his last two races and was moving outside to the 7 hole. Pass.

8. Bridge View—Competitive fourth trailing Brys by 1¼ lengths, but moves out from the 4 post to the 8 and is 1-for-14 lifetime with $3,277 on his card. Pass.

Now then, the odds. We thought Brys was a clear second favorite. But the final odds were: Davric 28-1, Fax This 11-1, Seafront 2-5, Oxymoron 5-1, Faster 8-1; Brys 10-1, Mister Thingy 47-1 and Bridge View 20-1.

2-5 on Seafront????

Here's a horse with a 1-for-22 lifetime record; shows a break in his PPs, and couldn't win in two tries in Non-Winners of 2 at Pompano, finishing a soundly-beaten sixth at 24-1 in the second one.

Yes, he subsequently performed better against much better competition. Then he was off three weeks. We're not saying he doesn't deserve to be a favorite. But is he vulnerable? Hell, yes!

2-5? We'd narrowed down the contenders to Seafront and Brys. Brys was going off the fourth favorite. Gigantic overlay.

Seafront tried going wire-to-wire and was pushed every step through torrid fractions. Brys came storming 4-wide on the final turn and won by 7 lengths to return $23.60. Faster rallied to finish second for an $84.20 exacta. Oxymoron was third as Seafront failed to light the board.

Really, 2-5?

Form

CHAPTER 3

You don't have to be a genius to understand form. The assumption is commonly made that a horse who ran well in his last start will maintain that form in his next start. And the one after that.

That's simplistic. Most horses don't maintain good or bad form for an entire season. Instead, they reach peaks, high and low. Peak performances can be sustained for one week or two months, but not the whole year. Consistency at a high level is the mark of distinction between good horses and great ones. Other horses are almost always headed in one direction, good or bad. That's why it's vital to read PPs from the bottom up. Doing this ensures you won't miss useful information—perhaps a race a month ago that three horses in tonight's race were in—and it will give you a handle on how each horse is coming up to this race, a solid indication whether a horse is heading up or down. Class considerations are useful here because it can define a horse's maximum level of performance. Brys Clean Sweep was a fine example in the last chapter.

Here's another:

SEVENTH YR. Saturday | OCT. 3- 1 Mile Pace. Open Handicap. Fillies & Mares. Purse $15,000. | **TRIPLE EXACTA**

A-1 POODLE PARTY • $273,723 3 1:56.4 (%) $2,083 — bl m 4,by Equitable, Toy Poodle by Most Happy Fella — 1:57.4 YR — 92 YR 31 3 5 3 $86,980 92 Tot 32 3 5 3 $86,980
Steve Jones, Montgomery, N.Y. Last 8 Sts $5,710 — 1:56.4 ScD% — 91 ★ 5 2 1 1 $18,840 91 Tot 28 6 5 5 •64,475
8-1 145 R.Schnittker 162 14-25-15 (.088) — W. Schnittker 142-13-22 13 (.082) Br.-OH James Michael, Bucyrus, Ohio — 90 YR 0 0 0 0 - 90 • 14 9 1 2★142,280
26 Sep 92 9YR gd85° 274 581 1.27 1.553 Opn Hcp FM 15000 3 69½ 78 64½ 54½ 58¾ SchnittkrR 292 30 282 293 1.572 +7 7w 6.20 ShaysPride^ns PrmRoyce5½ Dynamitendiamonds^ns Sat in even
18 Sep 92 9YR fst80° 274 571 1.26 1.552 Opn Hcp FM 15000 4 11½ 12 1hd 21 43½ SchnittkrR 274 292 284 30 1.56 +9 5w 2.20 PeasOfWork^ns DarkRoomLady1 BJsSpphre2 Spd,tired
11 Sep 92 10YR fst77° 273 554 1.252 1.553 Opn Hcp FM 15000 1 21 33½ 53½ 53¾ 41½ SchnittkrR 274 283 293 294 1.564 +9 3w 12.10 ClassySis^no DarkRoomLady1½ ShaysPride^nk Shf,traf even
05 Sep 92 5YR fst69° 264 554 1.26 1.562 Opn Hcp FM 15000 1 1hd 11½ 21 23 46 SchnittkrR 264 29 302 312 1.573 +12 5w 37.00 ClassySis5 DarkRoomLady1 LorrylandLady^nd Used 2x tired
29 Aug 92 8YR fst70° 281 584 1.271 1.563 Opn Hcp FM 15000 1 21½ 21½ 32½ 34½ 67½ SchnittkrR 28 303 283 302 1.58 +9 4w 21.80 LibHanover3 PeasOfWork^nd LorrylandLady2½ Yield,pit tired
15 Aug 92 3YR gd84° 274 582 1.272 1.553 Opn Hcp FM 17000 2 67½ 64½ 78½ 711 720 SchnittkrR 291 30 292 31 1.593 +8 7w 34.70 LibHanover1½ KrwJam3 PeasOfWork^nk Sluggish
08 Aug 92 9YR fst69° 28 563 1.251 1.561 Opn Hcp FM 17000 2 1hd 55½ 78½ 78½ 78½ WingT 28 294 283 302 1.564 +13 2w 11.40 ToyleeHanover½ PeasOfWork2½ LibHanover½ Yld,shuf tired
01 Aug 92 10YR fst72° 27 564 1.262 1.552 Opn Hcp FM 17000 2 32½ 42½ 67½ 54½ 45½ SchnittkrR 272 294 294 292 1.562 +9 4w 14.50 ToyleeHanover^ns LibHanover3 PeasOfWork2 Sat in mid late
25 July 92 3YR fst73° 273 572 1.261 1.552 Opn Hcp 17000 6 812 86½ 86½ 78½ 65 MorrillJJr 30 284 283 29 1.562 +9 4w 19.20 Mafi^nd MissIntensity1 ToyleeHanover1 No factor

B-2 CRIMSONS SISTER $156,321 3 1:56.0 (1) ★ $6,393 — b f 3,by J Js Biltmore, Bye Bye Jane by Bye Bye Max — 1:56.0 Sy1 — 92 YR 10 3 2 1 •105,981 92 Tot 21 4 5 3 •134,263
Charles Weidel & Global Stables, Inc., N.Y. Last 8 Sts $116,213 — 2:01.4 Sy1 — 91 YR 1 0 1 0 $7,500 91 Tot 9 2 5 1 $22,058
8-1 140 R.Cormier 10-1-2-0 (.100) — R. Cormier 10-1-2-0 (.100) +Br.-NY — 90 YR 0 0 0 0 - 90 Tot 0 0 0 0 -
26 Sep 92 9YR gd85° 274 581 1.27 1.553 Opn Hcp FM 15000 5 811 8°8½ 8°°8 87½ 714 CormierR 30 293 283 301 1.582 +7 7w 8.80 ShaysPride^ns PrmRoyce5½ Dynamitendiamonds^ns Little
19 Sep 92 5YR fst62° 281 573 1.26 1.552 NYSS 200000 4 33 3°1½ 2°1½ 22½ 22 CormierR 284 291 281 293 1.554 +8 6w 10.60 QuickComeonovr2 CrmsonsSister3 UnBelDx3½ Unc,second best
11 Sep 92 1YR fst77° 272 581 1.273 1.57 NW9000FM 7000 4 56½ 5°4½ 4°2½ 44½ 55½ CormierR 284 301 291 30 1.581 +9 3w 11.50 JJsBridget3½ SwingingMorgan1 BJsSapphire1 Cover in little
05 Sep 92 2YR fst69° 28 583 1.274 1.571 NYSS 95452 4 12 12 12 12 13½ CormierR 28 303 291 292 1.571 +12 5w *1.80 CrmsonsSister3½ IndianaJons3 WitsendsMissy^ns Unprss whp,safe
29 Aug 92 Btv fst62° 29 591 1.283 1.584 NYSS 25450 6 3 2 2° 22 21½ CormierR 1.59 5.00 QuickComeonover CrimsonsSister BJsEnn
21 Aug 92 VD fst W3001FM 3300 Scratched-sick
14 Aug 92 Sy1 fst66° 281 58 1.262 1.56 NYSS 23550 7 3 3 1 13 13½ CormierR 1.56 11.80 CrimsonsSister SeafoodDelight BJsEnn
07 Aug 92 Stg fst80° 281 58 1.272 1.583 NYSS 18624 7x 8 8 8 8 8dis CormierR 22.00 QuickComeonover SeafoodDelight SuccessRd
31 July 92 10YR sly NW9000FM 8000 4 Scratched-sick

C-3 DYNAMITENDIAMONDS $23,587 4 1:57.3 $822 — b m 4,by Albatross, Hope Hanover by Armbro Nesbit — 1:57.3 YR — 92 • 10 5 3 1 $19,265 92 Tot 24 5 3 2 $19,735
Frank Valloni, Jr., Katonah, N.Y. Last 8 Sts $17,515 — 2:02.4 KD% — 91 YR 0 0 0 0 - 91 Tot 21 3 6 1 $3,852
10-1 143 T.Wing 289 24 37 35 (.089) — S. Fava 79-23-10-6 (.295) Br.-PA Hanover Shoe Farms Inc., Hanover, Pa. — 90 YR 0 0 0 0 - 90 Tot 0 0 0 0 -
26 Sep 92 9YR gd85° 274 581 1.27 1.553 Opn Hcp FM 15000 1 44½ 43½ 43 44 35½ MarohnJ 283 301 284 29 1.563 +7 7w 8.70 ShaysPride^ns PrmRoyce5½ Dynamitendiamonds^ns Out late,pace
14 Sep 92 10YR fst63° 28 583 1.284 1.573 NW4 FM 5500 5 22 21½ 21½ 21½ 11 CaseWJr 282 302 301 283 1.573 +7 4w *.90 Dynmtndmnds1 SeafdDlght6 McMssRbyBck2½ Tck,pld,up late
06 Sep 92 9YR fst68° 281 591 1.282 1.58 NW4 FM 8050 4 11½ 11½ 11½ 12 13½ CaseWJr 281 31 291 293 1.58 +6 4w 1.80 Dynamitendiamonds3½ BeMine2½ ColoredBow2 Spd,driving
24 Aug 92 9YR fst78° 283 59 1.284 1.593 NW5 FM 8000 6 69 3°3½ 3x°°2 32 ix2x1 CaseWJr 302 291 293 303 1.594 +6 4w 2.20 *AmzngFddlr *Dynamitendmnds *ColordBw Dq,p 2 bthrd 2x
17 Aug 92 10YR sly66° 29 1.001 1.301 2.001 NW4 FM 5500 7 34 2°½ 11 12¾ 14 CaseWJr 294 302 30 30 2.001 +0 1w 3.10 Dynmtndmnds4 AmzngFddlr^ns McMsRbyBck½ Tuck,brush,safe
10 Aug 92 9YR fst75° 283 591 1.304 1.594 NW3 FM 5000 3 1hd 11½ 11½ 13 13 CaseWJr 283 303 313 29 1.594 +10 4w *.80 Dynamitendmnds3 PureSlide2 Pennstrmhvn3½ 1-4 move,easy
02 Aug 92 10YR fst74° 29 1.001 1.293 1.593 NW3 FM 5500 6 11½ 11½ 11 1x1½ x2x1 CaseWJr 29 311 292 301 1.594 +5 4w *1.20 PaulesPride *Jagalong *ColtsGaitTrace Dq,p 4 trd,brk
26 July 92 8YR sly66° 282 592 1.291 2.001 NW3 FM 5500 5 35 3°2½ 3°2 11½ 13¾ CaseWJr 292 303 293 303 2.001 -2 3w 5.80 Dynamitendiamonds3¾ TwoAces4½ SuccessRd3½ Tck,cvr wd,easy
14 July 92 5YR fst66° 28 572 1.274 1.583 10000FM NW2K 3500 3 55 2°1½ 1°hd 11½ 2nk CaseWJr 29 283 301 304 1.583 +9 6w *1.10 BelleairBluffs^nk Dynamitendmnds7 IndianRebel4½ Chall,top,tired

D-4 PEAS OF WORK $104,141 4 1:55.2 $1,878 — b m 5,by Jamuga, Happy Tigress by Nansemond — 1:55.2 YR — 92 YR 17 2 3 3 $36,230 92 Tot 22 3 5 4 $41,320
Orange County Paint Mfg., Inc., Middletown, N.Y. Last 8 Sts $22,280 — 1:56.2 YR — 91 • 12 4 4 2 •33,260 91 ★ 34 9 8 5 $47,922
6-1 150 J.Morrill,Jr. 253-39-34-28 (.154) — L. Frenette 35-5-2-5 (.143) +Br.-NY H. Sturgis,Jr., K. & R. Sturgis, N.Y. — 90 ★ 3 3 0 0 $7,250 90 ★ 13 11 1 0 $14,889
26 Sep 92 9YR gd85° 274 581 1.27 1.553 Opn Hcp FM 15000 7 32½ 3°2 3°1½ 32½ 45½ FilionHer 281 302 284 292 1.564 +7 7w 8.50 ShaysPride^ns PrmRoyce5½ Dynamitendiamonds^ns Weak unc,little
18 Sep 92 9YR fst80° 274 571 1.26 1.552 Opn Hcp FM 15000 5 67½ 4°3½ 4°2 31 1ns ParkerWJr 292 283 282 29 1.552 +9 5w 8.80 PeasOfWork^ns DarkRoomLady1 BJsSpphre2 Cvr,wide,drvg
11 Sep 92 10YR fst77° 273 554 1.252 1.553 Opn Hcp FM 15000 5 68½ 5°8½ 4°3 42¾ 51½ LancasterM 284 282 284 30 1.56 +9 3w 28.70 ClassySis^no DarkRoomLady1½ ShaysPride^nk Cover,no rally
05 Sep 92 5YR fst69° 264 554 1.26 1.562 Opn Hcp FM 15000 6 68½ 6°4½ 5°3½ 66½ 56 LancasterM 28 283 30 31 1.573 +12 5w 14.10 ClassySis5 DarkRoomLady1 LorrylandLady^nd 3d ov,wide trd
29 Aug 92 8YR fst70° 281 584 1.271 1.563 Opn Hcp FM 15000 3 45½ 3°1½ 2°1½ 22 23 LancasterM 291 294 282 294 1.571 +9 4w 3.30 LibHanover3 PeasOfWork^nd LorrylandLady2½ Mild chall,held
15 Aug 92 3YR gd84° 274 582 1.272 1.553 Opn Hcp FM 17000 4 45½ 3°1½ 2°1 33 34½ LancasterM 29 293 29 284 1.562 +8 7w 10.80 LibHanover1½ KrwJam3 PeasOfWork^nk Long unc,held
08 Aug 92 9YR fst69° 28 563 1.251 1.561 Opn Hcp FM 17000 5 88½ 6°8½ 4°2½ 52½ 2½ LancasterM 291 284 274 292 1.551 +13 2w 12.50 ToyleeHanover½ PeasOfWork2½ LibHanover½ Gd flow fast
01 Aug 92 10YR fst72° 27 564 1.262 1.552 Opn Hcp FM 17000 3 44 74 8°4½ 44¾ 32½ LancasterM 274 294 293 284 1.56 +9 4w 14.30 ToyleeHanover^ns LibHanover3 PeasOfWork2 Long wide,pace
25 July 92 3YR fst73° 273 572 1.261 1.552 Opn Hcp 17000 5 710 7°8½ 6°4 64 52 LancasterM 293 29 282 284 1.554 +9 4w 19.00 Mafi^nd MissIntensity1 ToyleeHanover1 3rd over mild

E-5 LOLA JEAN $101,496 5 1:53.4 (1) $1,741 — b m 5,by Good To See You, Monticello Abbe by Gene Abbe — 1:53.4 M1 — 92 YR 2 0 0 1 $1,150 92 Tot 27 6 3 3 $47,020
Anthony Odierno & Royal Stable, N.Y. & N.J. Last 8 Sts $16,400 — 1:55.1 Spk7/8 — 91 YR 0 0 0 0 - 91 • 19 5 5 2 $40,442
6-1 150 D.Dancer 385-49-44-60 (.127) — R. Fils 51-8-7-8 (.176) Br.-OH Donald S. McKee, Ohio — 90 YR 0 0 0 0 - 90 Tot 19 4 5 2 $14,034
19 Sep 92 5Fhd fst74° 273 573 1.27 1.554 W15001FM 9500 7 9 9 9 95 99½ FisherRJr ⅞574 +7 5w 7.10 HundredKisses FunnyLadyN JabberMouth
11 Sep 92 6GS1 fst70° 282 574 1.262 1.534 Rancocas 15000 6x 3°1½ 31½ 64 55 55½ FisherRJr 284 291 280 273 1.544 +0 3w 7.10 GiveMeAnInch^nd ToyleeHanover1½ Specialty2 Rough leaving
05 Sep 92 5Fhd fst78° 274 563 1.261 1.553 W15001FM 9500 1 3 1 1 12½ 12½ FisherRJr 1.553 +6 4w *2.80 LolaJean FunnyLadyN DirectKitten
29 Aug 92 12Fhd fst78° 28 57 1.264 1.572 W15001FM 9500 8 5° 5° 5°° 63½ 4½ MoiseyevJ 1.572 +8 4w 4.70 Dianebcs CherbourgN SummerChild
22 Aug 92 9Fhd fst80° 281 563 1.254 1.552 W15001FM 9500 3 3° 2° 4 31½ 32½ MoiseyevJ 1.554 +10 4w *1.40 GiveMeAnInch Decale LolaJean
13 Aug 92 7M1 fst71° 274 553 1.243 1.541 25-30000FM 12000 5 78½ 75½ 53 53½ 2no MoiseyevJ 292 272 282 29 1.541 +12 2w 3.70 TarBaby^no LolaJean^nd QuickAndFresh½ Traffic,flying
06 Aug 92 11M1 fst73° 283 57 1.263 1.551 25-30000FM 12000 3 32½ 3°2½ 3°1½ 11½ 1½ MoiseyevJ 29 282 292 282 1.551 +6 1w 6.50 LolaJean½ Decale1½ Weentimer½ Unc,safe drive
23 July 92 11M1 gd83° 274 564 1.26 1.55 25-30000FM 12000 8 3°2½ 1½ 31½ 97½ 108½ MoiseyevJ 281 283 292 303 1.564 +5 2w *2.80 BddysGrl1½ Weentimer½ (dh)BtyMs-QckAndFrsh^ns Stopped
16 July 92 7M1 fst71° 28 56 1.253 1.551 25-30000FM 12000 8 65½ 6°5½ 4°2½ 3½ 31½ MoiseyevJ 29 28 29 292 1.552 +5 1w *2.10 QuickAndFresh½ ChestnutRoad1 LolaJean^ns Trip,hanging

F-6 SHAYS PRIDE $227,567 4 1:53.0 (1) $3,335 — ch m 4,by Niafirst, Yollee Joy by Storm Damage — 1:53.0 M1 — 92 YR 11 3 0 1 $27,090 92 • 27 11 4 2 $90,040
Ron Pifetsky, Fred Fialkow & George Anthony, N.Y. Last 8 Sts $19,750 — 1:56.0 M1 — 91 YR 0 0 0 0 - 91 Tot 10 2 2 0 $21,730
5-1 145 L.Ouellette 829-117-83-83 (.188) — J. Orlando 11-1-0-6 (.091) +Br.-NY Gordon D. Helsl, Ontario — 90 • 2 1 1 0 ★82,206 90 Tot 15 5 5 2 •115,797
26 Sep 92 9YR gd85° 274 581 1.27 1.553 Opn Hcp FM 15000 6 21½ 21½ 21½ 22 1no OuelletteL 28 302 284 282 1.553 +7 7w 3.20 ShaysPride^no PrmRoyce5½ Dynamitendiamonds^ns Tuck,pckt,game
11 Sep 92 10YR fst77° 273 554 1.252 1.553 Opn Hcp FM 15000 3 43½ 4°5 2°1½ 21 31½ WojcioR 281 283 284 301 1.554 +9 3w 7.50 ClassySis^no DarkRoomLady1½ ShaysPride^nk Unc,chall flat
05 Sep 92 5YR fst69° 264 554 1.26 1.562 Opn Hcp FM 15000 3 2°hd 21½ 42½ 58 68½ OuelletteL 264 291 302 311 1.573 +12 5w 10.20 ClassySis5 DarkRoomLady1 LorrylandLady^nd Tck,dr late,pc
29 Aug 92 8YR fst70° 281 584 1.271 1.563 Opn Hcp FM 15000 4x 714 6°4½ 7°8 714 720 CaseWJr 31 283 284 321 2.003 +9 4w 3.40 LibHanover3 PeasOfWork^nd LorrylandLady2½ Broke leaving
08 Aug 92 4M1 fst69° 281 554 1.251 1.54 NW12500FM 16000 3 43 11½ 11½ 1nk 23 MoiseyevJ 284 27 292 292 1.543 +5 0w 10.60 SlickFit3 ShaysPride1 KrwJam^no Brush,no match
01 Aug 92 10YR fst72° 27 564 1.262 1.552 Opn Hcp FM 17000 5 2°1½ 31½ 31½ 33¾ 58½ WojcioR 271 294 293 303 1.571 +9 4w 19.70 ToyleeHanover^ns LibHanover3 PeasOfWork2 Tuck,pckt,tired
24 July 92 10YR fst80° 282 583 1.283 1.57 Opt40000M 10000 1 11½ 11½ 1½ 11½ 1no WojcioR 282 301 30 282 1.57 +10 5w *.90 ShaysPride^no PrmRoyce1½ LibHanover1½ 1-4 mv,prss,drv
17 July 92 10YR fst71° 271 574 1.271 1.572 Prf Hcp FM 12000 x8 814 7°5½ log log 5no ParkerWJr 30 284 1.572 +9 4w *2.30 HaChaCha^no ClassicVance^no PrmRoyce^no Brush,flat late
12 July 92 10YR fst74° 273 57 1.262 1.554 Opn Hcp FM 18000 7 2°no 11½ 1no 2hd 54 CaseWJr 273 292 292 301 1.563 +5 6w 2.80 ToyleeHanover1 SeeLine1½ PoodleParty½ Parked,top wknd

G-7 TOYLEE HANOVER ★ $515,697 5 1:54.2 (1) $5,331 — b m 7,by Albatross, Talla Hanover by Best Of All — 1:54.3 YR — 92 ★ 26 14 1 6★147,190 92 ★ 30 15 2 7★159,940
Mountain Top Farm, Paoli, Pa. Last 8 Sts $36,810 — 1:56.2 YR — 91 YR 32 5 8 9 ★98,120 91 Tot 39 7 9 9★114,870
3-1 125 J.Marsh,Jr. 302-35-40-38 (.116) — L. Remmen 20-5-1-4 (.250) Br.-PA Hanover Shoe Farms Inc., Hanover, Pa. — 90 YR 5 1 0 2 •12,535 90 Tot 32 7 3 4 $107,790
18 Sep 92 11GS1 fst75° 284 564 1.252 1.533 W15001FM 12500 6 68½ 6°7½ 5°3½ 34¼ 35 RemmenR 30 281 274 283 1.543 +1 2w *.90 DandyPromise½ IAmTrouble4½ ToyleeHanover1½ Too far back
11 Sep 92 6GS1 fst70° 282 574 1.262 1.534 Rancocas 15000 3 54 53½ 3°1½ 3½ 2nd RemmenR 291 292 28 271 1.534 +0 3w *1.00 GiveMeAnInch^nd ToyleeHanover1½ Specialty2 Arm hung
15 Aug 92 3YR gd84° 274 582 1.272 1.553 Opn Hcp FM 17000 7 57½ 5°2½ 4°2½ 44½ 44½ MarshJJr 291 294 284 283 1.562 +8 7w *1.10 LibHanover1½ KrwJam3 PeasOfWork^no Cover,no lock
08 Aug 92 9YR fst69° 28 563 1.251 1.551 Opn Hcp FM 17000 8 7°8 4°5½ 3°1½ 3½ 1½ MarshJJr 291 282 274 294 1.551 +13 2w *1.20 ToyleeHanover½ PeasOfWork2½ LibHanover½ Pkd,wide drvng
01 Aug 92 10YR fst72° 27 564 1.262 1.552 Opn Hcp FM 17000 8 8°9½ 6°3½ 4°°1½ 21½ 1ns MarshJJr 284 284 29 284 1.552 +9 4w *1.10 ToyleeHanover^ns LibHanover3 PeasOfWork2 3d ovr,brsh drv
25 July 92 3YR fst73° 273 572 1.261 1.552 Opn Hcp 17000 8 57 3°3½ 2°½ 31½ 31 MarshJJr 29 29 281 292 1.553 +9 4w *.30 Mafi^nd MissIntensity1 ToyleeHanover1 Tck,uncvrd held
12 July 92 10YR fst74° 273 57 1.262 1.554 Opn Hcp FM 18000 8 5°4 3°1½ 2°no 1hd 11 DancerD 282 284 291 292 1.554 +5 6w *1.30 ToyleeHanover1 SeeLine1½ PoodleParty½ Huge effort
27 Jun 92 6YR fst68° 271 572 1.263 1.553 Opn Hcp FM 18000 6 45½ 3°2 2°ns 31½ 31 MarshJJr 281 293 284 291 1.554 +9 5w *.80 SaraLorenRd1 PoodleParty^nd ToyleeHanover½ Tuck,chall wknd
20 Jun 92 6YR fst66° 271 562 1.254 1.56 Opn Hcp FM 18000 7 7°5½ 7°5½ 5°8½ 54½ 53½ MarshJJr 282 291 292 294 1.564 +9 5w *.50 ShaysPride^ns PrmRoyce½ PeasOfWork^no Tough trip

H-8 HUNDRED KISSES b m 4,by Abercrombie, Dozen Kisses by Meadow Skipper ★1:52.4 M1 92 YR 1 0 0 0 $1,360 92 Tot 35 11 8 2 $115,565
$137,986 4 1:52.4 (1) $3,302 Christmas City Stable, Bethlehem, Pa. Last 8 Sts-$38,235 1:55.4 M1 91 YR 0 0 0 0 - 91 Tot 23 5 3 2 $22,401
4-1 135 W.Case,Jr. 730-190-138-80 (.280) J. Mullin 12-2-1-2 (.167) Br.-KY John & Linda Rock, Pa. 90 YR 0 0 0 0 - 90 Tot 0 0 0 0 -

26 Sep 92 8Fhd	gd66°	282	573	1.264	1.554	W15001FM	9500	8	2°	1	1	1½	11½	MoiseyevJ					1.554	+7	4w	*1.10	HundredKisses JabberMouth Decate	
19 Sep 92 5Fhd	fst74°	273	573	1.27	1.554	W15001FM	9500	8	1°	1	1	1½	11	MoiseyevJ					1.554	+7	5w	4.30	HundredKisses FunnyLadyN JabberMouth	
05 Sep 92 7Fhd	fst76°	282	584	1.274	1.563	Opn Hcp FM	12500	7	7	5°	4°	42	54½	MoiseyevJ					1.572	+6	4w	1.80	SaraLorenRd IAmTrouble YankeeCoEd	
29 Aug 92 1Fhd	fst78°	274	584	1.262	1.554	Opn Hcp FM	12500	7	7	5°	3°	32	1nk	MoiseyevJ					1.554	+8	4w	2.90	HundredKisses SaraLorenRd GiveMeAnInch	
22 Aug 92 1Fhd	fst80°	274	572	1.264	1.561	Opn Hcp FM	12500	8	8	8°	7°	72½	1½	MoiseyevJ					1.561	+10	4w	2.80	HndrdKisses SaraLrnRd (dh)IAmTrble-PrmRyce	
14 Aug 92 11Fhd	fst75°	291	593	1.29	1.58	Opn FM	12500	2	4	4°	3°°	2no	11½	MoiseyevJ					1.58	+6	5w	*.80	HundredKisses JoyousWish FranksHarem	
08 Aug 92 9YR	fst69°	28	563	1.251	1.551	Opn Hcp FM	17000	7	6°4½	3°3	2°no	2½	43¼	CaseWJr	284	287	28	303	1.554	+13	2w	1.50	ToyleeHanover½ PeasOfWork2½ LibHanover½	Tough trp [illegible]
01 Aug 92 15M1 ▶	fst72°	274	57	1.261	1.533	NW12500FM	18000	9	9[illegible]	9°7½	9°°8¼	42½	1½	MoiseyevJ	294	283	292	254	1.533	+7	3w	4.80	HundredKisses½ EverythingGoesns KwnJam1¼	Exploded home
24 July 92 7M1	fst83°	274	563	1.253	1.533	NW10000FM	15000	6	811	9°7½	78	7½	65½	MrshllJIII	30	281	283	28	1.544	+4	0w	*1.80	SlickFit1½ EverythingGoesns KwnJam2½	Never in [illegible]

Shays Pride's victory in the Open Filly Handicap Pace at Yonkers, September 26, 1992, apparently had no impact with bettors when she made her next start in the same class from the same post, October 3.

In her gutty nose victory from the 6 post, September 27, Shays Pride won in 1:55.3 as the 3-1 favorite, crushing four of her rivals (horses 1 through 4) tonight. In doing so, she posted an extremely fast first quarter (:28) and last quarter (:28.2).

Of the three horses she hadn't beaten the week before:

• The 5, Lola Jean, was moving up off finishing ninth. Dismissed at 24-1.

• The 7, Toylee Hanover, had dominated this division much of the summer. However, she couldn't keep doing that indefinitely, as she was continually hindered by an assigned outside post in this handicap race. She'd lost her last three races, and this night would not go off the favorite for the first time in 10 starts. Sent off at 5-2, she would not finish in the money.

• The role of heavy favorite at 4-5 went to the 8 horse, Hundred Kisses. She'd won five of her last six, three of them from the 8 post and one from the 7. But all were at Freehold. Her race tonight was against better. In her final start before shipping to Freehold, Hundred Kisses raced at Yonkers in the Open Filly and Mare Handicap, finishing fourth by 3¼ lengths from the 7 post. Toylee won that one.

Shays Pride, who showed losing two of three meetings with Toylee in her PPs, didn't have a race in common with Hundred Kisses. Regardless, there are indicators, once again in the bottom PPs.

On July 24 at The Meadowlands in a Non-Winners of $10,000, Hundred Kisses finished sixth by 5¾ lengths to Slick Fit. Shays Pride raced against Slick Fit August 8 at The Meadowlands in a Non-Winners of $12,500, and was second by 3 lengths.

Hundred Kisses came back the next week in a Non-Winners of $12,500 and won by 3/4 of a length.

Shays Pride was certainly competitive with Toylee and Hundred Kisses, and she was starting inside both of them.

How was Shays Pride coming into this race?

Of the five least recent PPs, she was first and second once, and fifth three times. Following her second place finish at The Meadowlands mentioned above, she was given three weeks off.

Then, in four races at Yonkers in the Open:

- August 29—Broke and finished seventh by 20 from the 4 post.
- September 5—Sixth by 6 1/4 from the 3 post.
- September 11—Third by 1 1/4 from the 6 post.
- September 26—First by a nose from the 6 post as the 3-1 favorite.

Her weekly improvement was obvious.

Shays Pride was dismissed at 6-1, won by 3 lengths in track-record time, and paid $15.40.

Layoffs

Befitting their endurance and strength, harnessbreds usually race weekly. When they miss a week, it may mean the horse just didn't draw into a race fitting his conditions. Or, it may indicate problems.

If a horse is scratched, the PPs list either 'sick' or 'lame' as the reason. Take your own risk with 'sick.' The horse's illness could have been minor, and he's ready to race up to his potential this night. Or the illness might have taken more out of him, and he'll need a race or two to regain his form. Unfortunately, with sickness scratches, there's no way of knowing the extent and effects. Horses who are scratched as 'lame' should be avoided. There are just too many unknown factors at work.

When there's a two-week gap between his last PP and tonight's race without a scratch, the reasons may be benign. One way of examining that possibility is to compare the horse with his opponents tonight. Do they show a similar gap in their PPs? If they do, it's likely that their race didn't fill, or that overcrowding at this condition made several horses miss a week. Another possibility is that trainers intermittently give their horses one or two weeks off to freshen them. See if the horse has a similar gap in his own PPs. Start at the bottom and move up, and note any similar gaps. If there's another, how did he race after that gap?

If a horse is off three or more weeks, stay away. Our goal is valuable overlays, wagers of value. Betting horses missing that much time is just too speculative unless a horse shows strong efforts following a similar layoff in his PPs.

Tighteners

Horses off three or more weeks usually need tighteners, that is, a race or two to get back to their level of performance before the vacation. The longer the layoff, the more likely the need of a tightener.

Don't bet a horse off four to eight weeks unless he shows a race back, even if it's a qualifier. Stay away from horses completely out of action in that time frame.

However, feel perfectly comfortable betting a horse who has shown one race back. Though it may not be a super effort, the tightener will allow a horse to step up in his next start.

This brings us to an important point. We believe that horses should, and normally do, tire slightly or moderately in their first race back following a substantial layoff. He will benefit from that race, hence the phrase, "He needed that race."

We touch again on the idea of horses moving up or down in one direction. A horse off a decent yet tiring first race back should be heading upward.

There's an aside here. What of the horse who wins or races extremely well in his first start after a layoff? There are two schools of thought: 1) The horse came back sharp and is ready for an even bigger effort in his start, or 2) the horse will 'bounce.' What that means is that the horse did too well in his first start; that he overextended himself when he wasn't yet back in shape, and that he'll pay the consequences in his next start. We'll take a position of neutrality regarding bounce, and use this guiding principle: If the horse won his first race back despite a difficult, demanding trip, he's more likely to come up short and bounce in his next start than a horse who won easily off an easy trip in his return.

Let's look at a couple of races.

ONE MILE PACE
PURSE $2,000
WEDNESDAY, MAY 6, 1992
TRIPLE & EXACTA

SIXTH RACE

FILLIES & MARES
NON-WINNERS $2000 LAST 7 STARTS
OR 4 PARI-MUTUEL RACES OR $6000 LIFETIME
ALSO ELIGIBLE OPTIONAL CLAIMING ALLOWANCE $6000

WARM UP-RED

Columns: Date, Trk, Purse, Cd, Class, Dis, Leaders Time 1/4, 1/2, 3/4, Winners Time, PP, 1/4, 1/2, 3/4, Str, Fin, Ind 1/4 Time, Ind Time, Odds, Driver, Order Of Finish (First, Second, Third), Temp

---

8-1 **HIGHJACKER** — b m 4 B.G'sBunny-AddieGirl-StrikeOut — Jane & Glen W.Petit,Lewis N.Y.
1 KIM CRAWFORD (155) red-blk-wh (34-7-6-4-.343) — Tr—Eugene Cross (.250)
Stga 2:03 1992 4 1 0 2 $1,382 / Stga 2:01 1991 13 3 2 0 $4,038 / 3,2:01 Lifetime $6,037
YELLOW

Date	Trk	Purse	Cd	Class	Dis	1/4	1/2	3/4	Time	PP	1/4	1/2	3/4	Str	Fin	Ind 1/4	Ind Time	Odds	Driver	Order Of Finish	Temp
5-1 92	Stga	2000	ft	NW2000L7	1	29	100	131	201	8	9	9	8	6	7	29	202	27.30	DMarshall	EastfieldDel,FastFitz,BronzLobl	58-0
4-24 92	Stga	1900	gd	F&MNW3PMCD	1	30	101	133	203	1	1	1	1	1	1	30	203	*1.90	KCrawford	Highjacker,SisterSkip,MsRainbow	47-0
4-3 92	Stga	1800	ft	F&MNW3PMCD	1	29	100	131	203	2	2	2	3	2	3	32	204	*1.00	KCrawford	Shotouthights,Shankh,Highjackr	37-0
3-27 92	Stga	1800	sy	F&MNW3PMCD	1	31	103	134	206	4	5	5°	4	4	3	32	207	6.10	KCrawford	EldoradoSu,BonCastlDot,Highjackr	42-0
3-20 92	Stga		ft	QUA	1	30	101	132	203	3	1	2	2	4	5	32	205	NB	ECross	GrameChoice,Jusant,BosinAround	30-0
11-8 91	Stga	3334	ft	LC	1	28	59	129	200	scr	sk				scr					YongBlorrobi,PromsLobl,JDsAlar	33-0

5-2 **STORM E CLARE** (NY) — br m 7 StormDamage-Aurland-MeadowSkipper — Clare L.Smith, Syracuse, N.Y.
2 JOHN STARK JR (145) red-wh-lblu (19-8-2-4-.550) — Tr—Scott Leickert (.951)
Stga 2:01 1992 13 4 2 5 $6,564 / Stga 2:00 1991 42 13 1 7 $12,085 / 4,1:58 Lifetime $35,083
7,200 WHITE

Date	Trk	Purse	Cd	Class	Dis	1/4	1/2	3/4	Time	PP	1/4	1/2	3/4	Str	Fin	Ind 1/4	Ind Time	Odds	Driver	Order Of Finish	Temp
4-29 92	Stga	2000	ft	6000CLOP	1	28	59	129	201	9	3	2°	2°	2	1ns	31	201	3.10	JStarkJr	StormEClar,NorthsongRos,SstrSkp	63-0
4-11 92	VD	3200	sy	F&MWOCD-2	1	27	58	130	202	5	3	3	3°	6	8	33	204	3.80	HOkuskoJr	BmOnThRoad,BritonsFlam,Britsholnd	44-0
4-2 92	Stga	2100	ft	6000CLOP	1	29	101	132	203	2	4°	3°	4°	7	7	31	204	1.90	HOkuskoJr	NorthsongRos,Howdagon,BritsHoland	40-0
3-26 92	Stga	2100	sy	6000CLOP	1	31	103	134	205	1	2	2	2	3	3	32	206	*1.30	HOkuskoJr	LaJazHot,NorthsongRos,StormEClar	52-0
3-19 92	Stga	2100	ft	6000CLOP	1	29	59	130	202	2	2°	1	1	1	1	32	202	*1.60	HOkuskoJr	StormEClare,RaceMeTara,PutaLump	33-0
3-12 92	Stga	2100	gd	6000CLOP	1	28	101	133	205	2	4	2°	2°	2	3	32	206	*.90	KCrawford	Tropcal,Shotothights,StormEClar	27-0

3-1 **NORTHSONG ROSE** (NY) — b m 7 WhiteysFella-BeforeDawn-KatByrd — Coming Through Stable, Pittsfield, Ma.
3 ASA COOPER JR (185) gray-wh-black (4-1-1-0-.389) — Tr—Asa Cooper Jr (.519)
Stga 2:02 1992 11 8 3 0 $7,100 / Stga 2:02 1991 31 5 8 5 $7,523 / 5,2:02 Lifetime $30,228
7,200 PURPLE

Date	Trk	Purse	Cd	Class	Dis	1/4	1/2	3/4	Time	PP	1/4	1/2	3/4	Str	Fin	Ind 1/4	Ind Time	Odds	Driver	Order Of Finish	Temp
4-29 92	Stga	2000	ft	6000CLOP	1	28	59	129	201	5	1	1	1ns	1	2ns	31	201	*1.40	ACooperJr	StormEClar,NorthsongRos,SstrSkp	63-0
4-24 92	Stga		gd	QUA	1	29	101	132	202	6	5	5	6	6	4	29	203	NB	ACooperJr	PausesBigGuy,CedarLove,FamFatal	50-0
4-2 92	Stga	2100	ft	6000CLOP	1	29	101	132	203	9	3	4	6	3	1	30	203	*1.10	DMarshall	NorthsngRos,Howdagon,BritsHoland	40-0
3-26 92	Stga	2100	sy	6000CLOP	1	31	103	134	205	2	1	1	1	1	2	31	205	2.00	DMarshall	LaJazHot,NrthsongRos,StormEClar	52-0
3-19 92	Stga	1500	ft	4000CLOP	1	30	101	132	202	5	5	2	2	2	1	30	202	2.40	DMarshall	NorthsongRos,BngalBlitz,TgrsTon	33-0
3-12 92	Stga	1500	gd	4000CLOP	1	29	101	132	204	6	6	3°	3	2	1	32	204	10.20	ACooperJr	NorthsongRos,DamysFly,HiLosGods	27-0

4-1 **RACE ME TARA** — b m 7 GGSkipper-PayAsYouGo-ValiantBret — D.J. Hardy, Foxboro, Ma. & R.J. Pasquantonio, Franklin, Ma.
4 JAMES HARDY (125) white-grn-ltblu (7-2-2-0-.444) — Tr—James Hardy (.444)
Stga 2:03 1992 10 3 2 0 $4,916 / Scar 2:02 1991 36 3 8 2 $7,690 / 5,2:01 Lifetime $39,170
7,200 BLACK

Date	Trk	Purse	Cd	Class	Dis	1/4	1/2	3/4	Time	PP	1/4	1/2	3/4	Str	Fin	Ind 1/4	Ind Time	Odds	Driver	Order Of Finish	Temp
4-24 92	Stga	2900	gd	F&MHC	1	29	100	130	200	2	4	7	7	6	6	30	201	24.00	JHardy	OverNAbove,AshCanWyn,Maxposs	47-0
3-26 92	Stga	2100	sy	6000CLOP	1	31	103	134	205	3	3	3	3°°	4	4	32	206	6.70	JHardy	LaJazHot,NrthsongRos,StormEClar	52-0
3-19 92	Stga	2100	ft	5000CLOP	1	29	59	130	202	6	7	7°	6°°	5	2	31	203	4.30	JHardy	StormEClare,RaceMeTara,PutaLump	33-0
3-12 92	Stga	2100	gd	6000CLOP	1	28	101	133	205	1	3	4	5	4	4	32	206	1.80	JHardy	Tropcal,Shotothights,StormEClar	27-0
3-5 92	Stga	2100	gd	6000CLOP	1	30	101	132	203	3	2	3	2°	2	1	30	203	*2.20	JHardy	RacMTara,Shotouthights,Tropca	45-0
2-28 92	Stga	2100	sy	6000CLOP	1	30	102	133	205	6	6	6°	6°°	6	5	32	206	3.50	JHardy	AnnaAnna,HiLosGodes,StormEClar	42-0

9-2 **FASHION AFFAIR** (NY) — b m 8 PreciousFella-Bret'sEdition-BretHanover — Jon F. Joan M. Andrews & Daniel F O'Connor, Greenwich NY
5 FRANK COPPOLA JR (150) ltbl-wh-br (53-7-7-6-.243) — Tr—Daniel O'Connor (.167)
QStga 2:03 1992 0 0 0 0 $00 / Stga 1:59 1991 32 6 5 8 $14,160 / 7,1:59 Lifetime $65,104
GREEN

Date	Trk	Purse	Cd	Class	Dis	1/4	1/2	3/4	Time	PP	1/4	1/2	3/4	Str	Fin	Ind 1/4	Ind Time	Odds	Driver	Order Of Finish	Temp
4-24 92	Stga		gd	QUA	1	31	101	132	203	2	3	3	3	2	1	30	203	NB	FCoppolaJr	FashionAfair,GmtsSong,BlackC	50-0
11-15 91	Stga	2700	ft	10000CLCD	1	28	59	130	201	4	6	6°	9°	9	9			2.90	FCoppolaJr	Asheran,Upstage,Tropica	49-0
11-8 91	Stga	3334	ft	LC	1	30	100	130	200	6	6	6	6	6	6	31	205	6.30	FCoppolaJr	GlamorousBltmor,HiLosGods,Rghtsc	33-0
10-25 91	Stga	2700	ft	10000CLCD	1	28	101	132	203	4	5	3°	2°	2	3	31	203	2.40	FCoppolaJr	FamFatal,BoScotsPpr,FashionAfa	68-0
10-19 91	Stga	2700	ft	10000CLCD	1	29	59	131	203	8	8	8	7°	6	2	31	203	15.20	FCoppolaJr	BoScotsPpr,FashonAfa,FamFata	47-0
10-12 91	Stga	2700	ft	10000CLCD	1	28	101	133	204	4	6	5°	4°	3	3	30	204	7.20	FCoppolaJr	BoScotsPpr,Tnpligu,FashonAfa	51-0

10-1 **SISTER-SKIP** (NY) — b m 4 SkipByNight-Chugalove-ByeByeByrd — John R.Leslie, Aubrey A. & Lynne M.Kraeger, NY
6 JOHN LESLIE (190) red-black-white (5-0-2-1-.289) — Tr—John Leslie (.289)
1992 4 0 1 1 $820 / Stga 2:03 1991 8 3 0 0 $2,695 / 3,2:03 Lifetime $3,515
RED

Date	Trk	Purse	Cd	Class	Dis	1/4	1/2	3/4	Time	PP	1/4	1/2	3/4	Str	Fin	Ind 1/4	Ind Time	Odds	Driver	Order Of Finish	Temp
4-29 92	Stga	2000	ft	FMNW2000L7	1	28	59	129	201	1	2	3	3	3im	3	31	201	1.80	JLeslie	StormEClar,NorthsongRos,SstrSkp	63-0
4-24 92	Stga	1900	gd	F&MNW3PMCD	1	30	101	133	203	5	5	5	3°	3	2	30	204	1.90	JLeslie	Highjacker,SisterSkip,MsRainbow	47-0
4-5 92	Stga	A 2100	ft	NW2000L7CD	1	29	100	131	202	3	5	7	8	7	5	31	203	76.40	JLeslie	DakotaSport,XprsLan,Fortwntytwo	48-0
3-27 92	Stga	2100	sy	NW2000L7CD	1	28	100	130	203	8	8	8	8	8	8	33	207	146.20	JLeslie	LittleOff,XpressLane,WitsndsCal	42-0
3-20 92	Stga		ft	QUA	1	31	103	134	206	6	2	2	3	4	3	32	207	NB	BCross	Remmen,PunkyLobell,SisterSkp	30-0
11-18 91	YR	3500	ft	FMNW1PMCD	1	29	100	130	202	7	4°	4	7°	5	5		203	6.30	JLeslie	GloryNell,SugarGoose,SuesGold	48-0

10-1 **WANGO TANGO** — b m 4 ArmbroCadet-H.T.Emily-HenryT.Adios — Robert E.Negus, Schenectady, N.Y.
7 SCOTT MONGEON (145) black-gold (3-0-1-2-.407) — Tr—Scott Mongeon (.407)
PPk ⅝ 1:58 1992 11 3 2 2 $4,568 / PPk ⅝ 1:59 1991 15 2 3 1 $4,959 / 4,1:58 ⅝ Lifetime $9,527
8,700 BROWN

Date	Trk	Purse	Cd	Class	Dis	1/4	1/2	3/4	Time	PP	1/4	1/2	3/4	Str	Fin	Ind 1/4	Ind Time	Odds	Driver	Order Of Finish	Temp
4-8 92	PPk⅝	2100	ft	4000CL	1	28	58	127	157	1	7	7	6°	4	4	31	159	5.50	GLewis	SpringLake,ImThChamp,VolcanoKid	76-0
3-18 92	PPk⅝	1900	ft	4000CL	1	28	59	128	159	7	9	9	8°	5	4	30	200	4.30	GLewis	Throttle,TownBum,JamBreaker	73-0
3-9 92	PPk⅝	1900	ft	4000CLFM	1	29	59	129	200	5	6	5	4°	2	1	30	200	*1.70	GLewis	WangoTango,MostDightfl,AnthalSocal	77-0
3-2 92	PPk⅝	1700	ft	5800CLCD	1	28	58	127	156	7	3°	1°	4	8	7		200	*1.10	PWrenn	ThonAlmahurst,Brunfr,DoltKand	78-0
2-17 92	PPk⅝	1700	ft	4000CLFM	1	28	59	128	158	9	1	1	1	1	3	30	158	2.60	PWrenn	FathrMyNet,MiBarbera,WangoTango	78-0
2-10 92	PPk⅝	1700	ft	4000CLFM	1	29	59	128	158	6	1°	1	1ns	1	2	30	158	*.70	PWrenn	MiBarbera,WangoTango,CIWthAKs	71-0

12-1 **BRENDY LOBELL** — b m 7 NoNukes-BeverlyAlmahurst-MeadowSkipper — Kent J.Taylor, Albany, N.Y.
8 THOMAS CODDINGTON (140) bl-go-wh (3-0-1-0-.185) — Tr—Thomas Coddington (.289)
Stga 2:02 1992 12 2 0 1 $2,179 / Fhld 2:00 1991 28 3 1 5 $8,029 / 4,1:58 1 Lifetime $33,924
GRAY

Date	Trk	Purse	Cd	Class	Dis	1/4	1/2	3/4	Time	PP	1/4	1/2	3/4	Str	Fin	Ind 1/4	Ind Time	Odds	Driver	Order Of Finish	Temp
4-29 92	Stga	2000	ft	FMNW2000L7	1	28	59	129	201	7	8	8	8	7	6	31	203	21.30	TCodngton	StormEClar,NorthsongRos,SstrSkp	63-0
4-5 92	Stga	A 2800	ft	F&MHC	1	29	100	131	201	2	3	4	4	5	6	30	202	14.60	JHartmann	AshCanWyn,YoungBlotroubl,Maxpos	48-0
4-2 92	Stga	1500	ft	NW1500L7CD	1	29	101	132	202	2	2	2	2°	1	1	29	202	*1.20	JHartmann	BrendyLobel,WinSumPro,HiLoeGods	40-0
3-26 92	Stga	1500	sy	4000CLOP	1	31	105	136	208	7	3	4	4°	3	1	31	208	3.80	JHartmann	BrndyLobl,CrispKash,CandySafwey	52-0
3-19 92	Stga	1300	ft	2500CLCDz	1	30	102	132	203	8	6	6°	5°°	5	5	32	205	2.10	RPugliese	TimelyPlay,ShiwayRom,ClvrTrick	33-0
3-12 92	Stga	1300	gd	2500CLCD	1	28	101	132	204	8	8	8	7°°	5	4	31	204	22.00	RPugliese	ShsGotPlnty,ManinThSut,PnRvrsA	27-0

8-1 **TROPICAL** br m 5 GoodToSeeYou-HeatsOn-LightningWave — Paul Rice, Vincent Struffolino Jr. & Thomas Greco, NY

9 DANIEL CAPPELLO JR (115) blue-white (4-0-0-2-.167) Tr—Paul Zabielski (.278)

7,200 BLUE

Stga	2:05^4	1992	12	1	1	4	\$3,287											
YR	2:00^2	1991	31	9	4	5	\$17,547											
4,2:00^2		Lifetime					\$35,188											

4-11^{92}	VD	3200	sy F&MWOCD-2	1	27^4	58^2	130^1	202^4	9	6	6	7^{o4}	7^6	5^{1}	32^3	203^4	13.60	FCopolaJr	BmOnThRoad,BntnsFlam,BrtsHoland 44-0
4-2^{92}	Stga	2100	ft 6000CLOP	1	29^1	101^1	132^2	203	4	1	1	1^1	1	4^3	31^1	203^3	7.00	JRandall	NorthsongRos,Howdagon,BrtsHoland 40-0
3-19^{92}	Stga	2100	ft 6000CLOP	1	29^1	59^3	130^3	202^3	5	3	3	5^4	6	6^6	32^2	204	3.20	GMattison	StormEClare,RaceMeTara,PutaLump 33-0
3-12^{92}	Stga	2100	gd6000CLOP	1	28^4	101^3	133^2	205^4	4	1	1	1^1	1	1^2	32^2	205^4	4.70	GMattison	Tropcal,Shotothights,StormEClar 27-0
3-5^{92}	Stga	2100	gd6000CLOP	1	30^2	101^3	132^1	203	9	6°	4°	3^{o2}	3	3^2	30^4	203^2	2.70	GMattison	RacMTara,Shotouthights,Tropcal 45-0
2-28^{92}	Stga	2100	sy 6000CLOP	1	30^4	102^4	133^2	205	3	3	2°	1^{o1}	2	3^1	31^4	205^1	2.20	GMattison	HHChessie,BretsHolland,Tropcal 42-0

A field of nine went to post in a conditional race May 6, 1992, at Saratoga. The race was for Non-Winners of \$2,000 the Last 7 starts, OR Non-Winners of 4 races lifetime, OR Non-Winners of \$6,000 lifetime, OR optional \$6,000 claimers.

Ain't conditional racing wonderful?

Race Me Tara, the 4 horse, showed a month gap in her last two starts, March 26 and April 24. She'd been close in recent races but hadn't beaten the 2 horse, Storm E. Clare.

On March 26, Storm E. Clare finished third by 6¼ lengths from the rail in similar company as the 6-5 favorite. Tara, 6-1 out of the 3 hole, finished fourth by the same margin, 6¼ lengths, meaning a nose behind Storm. This doesn't tell us Tara was better—heck, she shows losses to Storm four times in her PPs—but it did say she was close to her from a more difficult post in that race.

We don't know why Tara missed a month. When she returned to the races, she was placed in the Open Filly and Mare Handicap, a decided step up. Sent off at 24-1, Tara did nothing but sit, finishing sixth by 5¾ in a race which went 2:00.2 with a last half in 1:00.1. Tara was seventh at the half and seventh at the three-quarters by 3¾ lengths. She got her last quarter in :30.2 and an estimated last half in 1:00.2. We get her final half time by calculating that when she was seventh at the half, she trailed by at least the same margin she lost by: 5¾ lengths. That's an educated guess of how many lengths a horse who's seventh at the half is behind the leader. But we don't know if there are gaps between the horses in front of her. Horses usually are 1 to 1½ lengths behind the horse in front of them on the rail. If our assumption is 1 or 2 lengths too kind to Tara, that's fine. Make her last half in 1:00.3 or 1:00.4. Even so, she got that last half faster than any of

Storm's 6 PPs. Additionally, Tara's :30.2 final quarter is a minimum of 4 lengths (that's 4/5 of a second) faster.

Let's emphasize that we're not contending that Tara is better than Storm, but we do know she was just a nose off in their last meeting from a worse post. Tara had been idle, but came back against much better fillies and mares. She didn't race spectacularly in that start, but facing that level of competition and racing somewhat evenly was an excellent tightener, a race she needed from her layoff. She will improve from that race, and she is dropping down to her normal level.

Tara didn't deserve to be the favorite here, but she was a logical contender. Storm went off 9-5; Tara at 8-1. Tara beat Storm by a head and paid $19.80.

Let's head south to New Jersey.

Bilateral was a perfect example of a horse benefitting from a tightener when he raced in a leg of the New Faces, a Late Closer series at The Meadowlands, March 20, 1992.

8 MEADOWLANDS
PACE
ONE MILE
WARM UP COLOR-GRAY
PURSE $15,000
ASK FOR HORSE BY PROGRAM NUMBER

EXACTA AND FIRST HALF OF LATE DOUBLE
** NEW FACES **
3 YEAR OLD COLTS & GELDINGS
N/W 5 PM RACES OR $75000 LIFETIME THRU 11/1/91
L.C. EVENT NO. 3 2ND LEG
69th RACING DAY FRIDAY, MARCH 20, 1992

20-1 CHEERFUL FELLA — **1** — RED
b g, 3, by Brand New Fella--Keeping Time by Race Time — Tr.-James Despain (.146)
J.S.Padjen,D.R.Breeze & P.T.Sibler, Ohio — Q M^1 1:59^1 1992 4 1 0 1 $3,962
$56,016 - 2, 1:$56^2$ (1) Driver-CATELLO MANZI 165 (wht-l blu-blu) (523-70-67-62-.245) BREEDER-BLUE CHIP PARTNERS,N.Y. — M^1 1:56^2 1991 9 3 2 3 $52,054

Date	Track Race #	Purse	Tk.	Cd.Type Class	Dist.	1/4	1/2	3/4	Time	P.P.	1/4	1/2	3/4	Str	Finish	Lst. 1/4	Time	Odds	Driver	Order of Finish: First Second Third	Temp Abov
3-13	M^1 9	15000	ft	3yr nw5 Lc	1	28^3	59^4	130^1	157^4	9	7o8¾	7 5½	6o3¾	6 3½	4 2¾	27^1	158^1	33.70	WFahy	SiSahib,PerfectPlay,LordWiking	26-2
3-6	M^1 4	15000	ft	3 yr	1	29	56^4	125	154^1	9	9 12½	9 12½	9 9½	6 5½	6 4¾	28^2	155^1	58.70	WFahy	LrdWing,RichsEmpr,LndwodCntror	41-C
2-29	M^1 3		ft	QUA	1	28^4	100^4	133^1	200^3	10	1o¾	1 1½	1 1½	1 1	3 2¾	28	201^1	NB	WFahy	SpctrAlmahrst,PrvwLobl,ChrflFla	24-3
2-21	Fhld 6A	5100	ft	NW300PSCD	1	30^1	100^1	130^2	159^4	7	7	5o	1o½	2½	3 2½	29^4	200^1	*.50	WFahy	EsprsoCal,WildrLobl,ChrfulFla	45
2-8	Fhld 6A	4300	sy	NW250PSCD	1	29	100^1	130	159^2	2	1o	1	1¾	1 1	1½	29^2	159^2	*.30	WFahy	CheerfulFella,Promise,Provanch	35-C

12-1 LINDWOOD CENTURION — **2** — BLUE
b c, 3, by Laag--Early Reward by Falcon Almahurst — Tr.-Joe Caraluzzi (.167)
Marvin Manheimer,Springfield,N.J. — 1992 4 0 0 1 $1,800
$76,059 - 2, 1:$54^3$ (1) Driver-MICKEY MC NICHOL 160 (blu-blk-wht) (402-38-30-41-.170) BREEDER-LINDWOOD FARM,PA. — M^1 1:54^3 1991 10 4 1 1 $74,259

Date	Track Race #	Purse	Tk.	Cd.Type Class	Dist.	1/4	1/2	3/4	Time	P.P.	1/4	1/2	3/4	Str	Finish	Lst. 1/4	Time	Odds	Driver	Order of Finish: First Second Third	Temp Abov
3-13	M^1 4	15000	ft	3yr nw5 Lc	1	27^4	57^1	127^2	156	10	7o5	2o1½	2o¾	5 4	7 4	29^1	156^4	8.90	MMcNichol	RitchiesEmpire,Marko,Bilatera	26-2
3-6	M^1 4	15000	ft	3 yr	1	29	56^4	125	154^1	5	2 1	2 1½	2 2½	2 1½	3 2	29^1	154^3	8.10	MMcNichol	LrdWing,RichsEmpr,LndwodCntron	41-C
2-29	M^1 7	15000	ft	nw4 cd	1	28^1	57^4	127^3	155^3	5	7 6	9 5¾	9 7½	9 6¾	9 4½	27^2	156^2	13.80	MMcNichol	JtJocky,CalfornaCam,FalconsCrwn	18-3
2-22	M^1 4	16000	ft	nw13000L7	1	27^4	56^2	126^1	153^3	6	7 6	8 6¾	8 7	6 7½	6 7	27^2	155	25.30	MMcNichol	MntnHdaway,BrandoHnvr,NksTror	39-C
2-15	M^1 1		ft	QUA	1	29^4	59^1	129	157^1	6	2o½	2 1½	3 1½	4 1½	2 3½	28^2	157^4	NB	MMcNichol	JstnKn,LndwodCntron,PatrotMs	40

30-1 DAGGER (L) — **3** — WHITE
b c, 3, by Direct Scooter--National Princess by Sonsam — Tr.-Robert Stevenson (.246)
Connie & Allen Skolnick,East Rockaway,N.Y. — M^1 1:58 1992 7 1 0 3 $7,450
$11,407 - 3, 1:58 (1) Driver-WILLIAM O' DONNELL 138 (wht-blu-or) (309-20-30-33-.154) BREEDER-A M J STABLES INC & M.BARNETT — HP⅝ 2:00^2 1991 5 1 0 1 $3,957

Date	Track Race #	Purse	Tk.	Cd.Type Class	Dist.	1/4	1/2	3/4	Time	P.P.	1/4	1/2	3/4	Str	Finish	Lst. 1/4	Time	Odds	Driver	Order of Finish: First Second Third	Temp Abov
3-14	M^1 2	9000	ft	nw3 cd	1	28^1	57^3	126^3	155^3	4	6 11½	6 7½	5o4½	5 3½	3 1½	28^2	155^4	31.80L	MLachance	Tulleners,Pundit,Dagger	26-2
3-6	M^1 4	15000	ft	3 yr	1	29	56^4	125	154^1	3	5 5½	4o3½	3o2¾	9 10½	9 17	32^1	157^3	89.80L	MLachance	LrdWing,RichsEmpr,LndwodCntron	41-C
2-25	M^1 10	8125	gd	nw2 cd	1	29^3	59^2	129^2	157^4	6	6 6½	6 10½	4o2½	1½	3 4½	28^4	158^3	30.70L	JoCampbell	JCsSkiparoo,ScootinAlong,Dager	35-0
2-14	M^1 3	6500	ft	nw2 cd	1	28^3	58	127^1	155^4	9	10 12½	10 9½	9 7	7 7½	4 8½	28^4	157^2	25.10L	MLachance	Mandretti,Pundit,RoyalAce	35-1
2-7	M^1 5	6500	ft	nw2 cd	1	29^3	59^2	128	158	3	4 5	2o1	1o1	1 2	1ns	30	158	4.60L	MLachance	Dagger,RoyalAce,DriveMeCrazy	31

4-1 SLEEPWALK — **4** — GREEN
b c, 3, by Tyler B--In Slo Motion by Sonsam — Tr.-Marion Tolson St.- N.Sodano (.275)
Joseph A.Hurley & Joseph W.Benson,Wilmington,Del. — M^1 1:55^2 1992 6 2 3 0 $35,625
$39,405 - 3, 1:$55^2$ (1) Driver-MIKE LACHANCE 149 (red-blk-wht) (591-64-91-75-.236) BREEDER-18 CARROT STABLE & J.W.BENSON — GSP¹ 1:56 1991 3 2 0 1 $3,780

Date	Track Race #	Purse	Tk.	Cd.Type Class	Dist.	1/4	1/2	3/4	Time	P.P.	1/4	1/2	3/4	Str	Finish	Lst. 1/4	Time	Odds	Driver	Order of Finish: First Second Third	Temp Abov
3-13	M^1 4	15000	ft	3yr nw5 Lc	1	27^4	57^1	127^2	156	3	9 7½	7o4½	3oo1½	2 1½	5 2½	28^4	156^2	2.70	MLachance	RitchiesEmpire,Marko,Bilatera	28-2
3-7	M^1 1		sy	QUA	1	29^4	59^2	129^1	158^1	4	6 5½	6 6½	4o5½	4 3	1 2	28	158^1	NB	MLachance	Slpwalk,GrdnrRvnah,WatnOnTod	41-2
1-29	M^1 7	83000	ft	nw2 Lc	1	28^1	55^4	124^1	152^4	6	7 6¾	7 5½	5oo5½	2 2½	2 1½	27^4	153	11.70	MLachance	WeatherVane,Sleepwalk,BigSquar	40-0
1-22	M^1 7	10000	ft	nw2 Lc	1	29^1	58^3	127^3	155^3	5	5 4½	3o1½	1 1½	1¾	2nd	28	155^3	*.90	MLachance	PrcarousMson,Slpwalk,BBokl	32-1
1-15	M^1 11	10000	ft	nw2 Lc	1	29^1	57^2	126^2	155^2	6	8 7½	8o6	2o1	2nd	1 1	28^4	155^2	*.90	MLachance	Slepwalk,Pipnsong,GnomMansLand	21-2

20-1 ROAD RUNNER SPUR — **5** — BLACK
br c, 3, by No Nukes--Shy Dawn by Meadow Skipper — Tr.-Richard Stillings (.000)
Roy D.Davis,Meadow Lands,Pa. — Mea⅝ 1:57^3 1992 2 1 0 0 $1,500
$20,137 - 3, 1:$57^3$ (⅝) Driver-JOE SCHWIND 150 (wh-go-red) (190-21-19-21-.203) BREEDER-A M CUDDY STABLES LTD,ONT. — Mea⅝ 1:58^3 1991 13 3 1 3 $18,637

Date	Track Race #	Purse	Tk.	Cd.Type Class	Dist.	1/4	1/2	3/4	Time	P.P.	1/4	1/2	3/4	Str	Finish	Lst. 1/4	Time	Odds	Driver	Order of Finish: First Second Third	Temp Abov
3-13	M^1 9	15000	ft	3yr nw5 Lc	1	28^3	59^4	130^1	157^4	7	8o6½	9 8	9 7½	8 9	8 7½	27^3	159^1	18.90	WODonnell	SiSahib,PerfectPlay,LordWiking	26-2
3-7	Mea⅝ 6	3000	gd	3-4 CG EC	1	27^3	58^1	127^1	157^3	2	3	1	2 2	2½	1¾	30	157^3	*.40	RStillings	RoadRunrSpur,ContryTm,SatnStar	56-1
2-28	Mea⅝ 3		ft	QUA	1	29^2	100^1	129	159	3	3	2o	2 2	2 2	1 2	29^3	159	NB	DSnyder	RoadRunrSpur,KystonLcky,Staric	41-0
2-21	Mea⅝ 3		ft	QUA	1	30^2	101^1	130^1	159	5	1	1	1 15	1 20	1 24	28^4	159	NB	DSnyder	RoadRunrSpur,ItZaMonky,FirNks	40-0
10-6	Mea⅝ 4	2400	ft	NW2PMLT	1	28^1	58	128^3	158^3	2	3	1	1½	1 1	1 1¾	30	158^3	*1.00	RStillings	RoadRnrSpr,Sponsor,KystonDxt	48-0

30-1 BELL BUCKLE — **6** — YELLOW
b g, 3, by Lon Todd Hanover--Pleasant by Don Thorpe — Tr.-Andy Murphy (.048)
John M.& John Como Jr.,Towaco,N.J. — YR 1:57^3 1992 8 1 0 1 $9,075
$25,459 - 3, 1:$57^3$ Driver-DONALD DANCER 164 (blu-gold) (48-0-5-8-.113) BREEDER-L.L.& N.W.NELSON,TENN. — YR 1:58^3 1991 11 8 2 1 $16,384

Date	Track Race #	Purse	Tk.	Cd.Type Class	Dist.	1/4	1/2	3/4	Time	P.P.	1/4	1/2	3/4	Str	Finish	Lst. 1/4	Time	Odds	Driver	Order of Finish: First Second Third	Temp Abov
3-14	YR	15000	ft	OPN HDCP	1	28^4	57^1	127^2	157^2	7	1o	2o	8o5¾	8 6¾	7 10	30^4	159^2	41.50	DDancer	DavisCup,Lionheart,Ludicrous	29-C
2-29	YR 9	15000	ft	3-4YROPNHC	1	27^4	57^1	127^4	157	8	5o	3o	6o5¾	6 9¼	7 13	30^4	159^3	10.60	DDancer	Lionhart,ThatsDancng,PrfctPla	23-C
2-22	YR 5	12500	ft	3-4YR OPN	1	28^1	58^1	128	157^3	7	1o	1	1 1	1 1½	1½	29^3	157^3	*1.50	DDancer	BelBuckle,GodHand,ShadowChas	43-C
2-17	M^1 10A	12500	ft	nw3 Lc	1	28^4	56^2	125^3	153^4	12	9 7½	9o8	7o7	11 12½	11 13½	29^2	156^2	101.70	DDancer	DualAFortun,Camaradn,CamStrid	46-0
2-11	M^1 7	12500	ft	nw3 Lc	1	27^3	57^1	127^1	154^3	2	1o½	3 1½	6 4½	5 5½	5 5¾	27^4	155^4	35.40	DDancer	StylshCam,Camaradr,PrcarosMson	38-1

5-1 BILATERAL — **7** — PINK
b c, 3, by Laag--Kay Blue Chip by Most Happy Fella — Tr.-Gene Riegle (.111)
George Segal,Highland,Ill. — Orl¹ 1:59^4 1992 1 0 0 1 $1,800
$14,716 - 2, 1:56 (⅝) Driver-WILLIAM FAHY 160 (br-or) (387-41-40-34-.193) BREEDER-ALMAHURST BLOODSTOCK N,KY. — Mea⅝ 1:56 1991 7 2 1 1 $12,916

Date	Track Race #	Purse	Tk.	Cd.Type Class	Dist.	1/4	1/2	3/4	Time	P.P.	1/4	1/2	3/4	Str	Finish	Lst. 1/4	Time	Odds	Driver	Order of Finish: First Second Third	Temp Abov
3-13	M^1 4	15000	ft	3yr nw5 Lc	1	27^4	57^1	127^2	156	11	6 5	10 7	10 7	6 5	3¾	27^2	156^1	64.30	WFahy	RitchiesEmpire,Marko,Bilatera	26-2
3-7	M^1 3		sy	QUA	1	28^2	57^4	126^3	155	8	9 19	8 24¾	8dis	6dis	6 30		201	NB	JCampbell	NoTwistr,Stagmastr,BransNBrawn	41-2
2-28	Orl¹		ft	QUA	1	29^2	101	131	159^4	1	2	2	2	2o1	1nk		159^4	NB	BRiegle	Bilateral,SeibelSpur,Ihop	60-0
8-10	Mea⅝ 4A	21515	ft	2YO C STK	1	27^3	57^2	126^2	156	2	4	4o	3o3½	2 1	1 1¾	29	156	3.90	JoCampbell	Bilatral,OsbornsTownr,OnaFix	75-0
7-31	ScD⅝ 4	1800	ft	S-G MDN CD	1	28^2	59^2	129	158^1	9	2o	1 1¾	1 1	1 2½	1 3½	29^1	158^1	*.50	BRiegle	Bilateral,HalosDram,WhitHalMax	82-0

30-1 GOLDEN THREADS — **8** — GRAY
br c, 3, by Troublemaker--Ribbon Almahurst by Nistross — Tr.-Nick Colanero (.217)
Mary Lynn Bell,Fishers,Ind. — M^1 1:56^2 1992 5 2 0 0 $8,512
$13,834 - 3, 1:$56^2$ (1) Driver-RON PIERCE 138 (red-wht-blu) (450-50-55-70-.231) BREEDER-BRITTANY FARMS,KY. — ScD⅝ 1:58^1 1991 7 1 1 1 $5,322

Date	Track Race #	Purse	Tk.	Cd.Type Class	Dist.	1/4	1/2	3/4	Time	P.P.	1/4	1/2	3/4	Str	Finish	Lst. 1/4	Time	Odds	Driver	Order of Finish: First Second Third	Temp Abov
3-13	M^1 9	15000	ft	3yr nw5 Lc	1	28^3	59^4	130^1	157^4	1	2 1½	3 2½	5 3½	4 3	5 2¾	27^3	158^2	67.50	MMcNichol	SiSahib,PerfectPlay,LordWiking	26-2
3-6	M^1 4	15000	ft	3 yr	1	29	56^4	125	154^1	7	7 10	7 9½	7 7½	8 8¾	8 12½	30^1	156^3	38.90	CManzi	LrdWing,RichsEmpr,LndwodCntron	41-0
2-29	M^1 4	9000	ft	nw3 cd	1	27^4	57	128	156^3	9	5 5¾	5 5	4o2¾	3 1¾	5 4	29	157^2	21.90	MMcNichol	HuncanAir,TorontoBlChp,Tinrs	18-3
2-17	M^1 8A	8125	ft	nw2 cd	1	29^1	57^3	126^3	156^2	5	2o1	3 1¾	3 1½	2 1½	1nk	29^3	156^2	6.50	MMcNichol	GldnThrds,CrmnLobi,JansGlt	46-0
2-13	M^1 3	6500	gd	nw2 cd	1	29^4	59^3	129^2	158	1	2o¾	1 1½	1¾	1 1½	1ns	28^3	158	*.60	MMcNichol	GldnThrds,BrnDomnator,InrCty	29-2

5-2 **LORD WILLING** ch c, 3, by Energy Burner--Osborne's Miss by O's Mississipi Mud Tr.-Andrea Chadwick (.667)
Keo Poopat,Monroe,Mich. M1 1:541 1992 2 1 0 1 $9,300
9 ♦ $114,390 - 3, 1:541 (1) Driver-JACK MOISEYEV 165 (blk-wh-go) (645-129-78-64-.300) BREEDER-KEO POOPAT,MICH. HP⅝ 2:003 1991 18 12 1 1 $105,090
3-13 M1 9 15000 ft 3yr nw5 Lc 1 283 584 1301 1574 3 1½ 2½ 3½ 3½ 3½ 272 158 *.50 EDavis SiSahib,PerfectPlay,LordWiling 28-2
3-6 M1 4 15000 ft 3 yr 1 29 564 125 1541 8 811½ 810¾ 8o7½ 32½ 12 274 1541 15.30 EDavis LrdWlng,RichsEmpr,LndwodCntron 41-0
2-28 Nor 4 ft QUA 1 301 1022 132 2023 2 1 1 1 16 15½ 2023 NB TButler LordWiling,GodGam,PnrdgChrsy 38-0
10-8 HP⅝ 7 17500 ft 2YOCOLTS 1 294 1013 1303 2003 3 4 3o1½ 2o½ 2hd 1½ 294 2003 *.50 TButler LordWiling,MaxwlTSmart,TruCadt 68-0
PURPLE 9-27 HP⅝ 8 104338 ft 2YR C MISS 1 294 1022 132 2011 1 4 3o 2o 1hd 1nk 2011 *.40 TButler LordWiling,MaxwlTSmart,TruCadt 54-0

20-1 **PATRIOT MISSILE** b c, 3, by No Nukes--Panache Lobell by Bret Hanover Tr.-Robert Kolachik (.313)
Jacqueline & Theodore Gewertz & Robins Racing Stb., N.J,N.Y. M1 1:57 1992 3 2 0 0 $8,449
10 ▲ $8,449 - 3, 1:57 (1) Driver-EDDIE DAVIS 167 (wht-red) (347-37-34-36-.196) BREEDER-LANA LOBELL FMS OF NJ INC,N.J. Q Gty1 2:00 1991 1 0 0 0 $00
3-10 M1 8 8125 sy nw2 cd 1 294 584 1283 1573 6 33½ 32½ 1o½ 1½ 12½ 29 1573 *1.50 JoCampbell PatrotMsl,CarmnLobl,ScotnAlng 46-0
3-3 M1 11 8125 ft nw2 cd 1 282 581 1291 157 9 911½ 8o7½ 6o3½ 42 15 27 157 6.20 JoCampbell PatriotMisil,NovaPk,DrvMCrazy 35-1
2-20 M1 5 6500 ft nw2 cd 1 28 583 1273 156 4 45½ 4o3½ 2o½ 57½ 510 301 158 7.10 JoCampbell TurningCircl,Hrolator,Saucison 37-1
2-15 M1 1 ft QUA 1 294 591 129 1571 1 31½ 32½ 2o½ 1½ 36½ 292 1582 NB JoCampbell JstnKn,LndwodCntron,PatrotMs 40-1
Blue-Rd 2-8 M1 5 ft QUA 1 292 1012 1321 2002 7 717½ 6o½ 5o6½ 55½ 32½ 271 2004 NB JoCampbell EvningFla,Hrolator,PatrotMsl 33-2

20-1 **COCOMO SON** b c, 3, by Ralph Hanover--Nightowe by Strike Out Tr.-Brad Mc Ninch St. - T. Artandi (.402)
Mardon Stables & Richard J.Bartel, Ont., B.C. 1992 3 0 0 0 $784
11 ▲ $105,562 - 2, 1:58(⅝) Driver-RAY REMMEN 170 (wht-grn-go) (127-18-21-16-.276) BREEDER-DAVID C.HENDERSON,ONT. GrR⅝ 1:58 1991 8 3 1 1 $104,778
3-8 GrR⅝ 3 9800 ft NW4R20000L 1 28 573 1271 1572 6 3oo 1 1og 1½ 4½ 1573 7.20 NMcKnightJr KnightHanovr,BlackPyjamas,ConcordRoad 42-0
3-1 GrR⅝ 10 9800 ft NW4R20000L 1 29 1003 1292 159 7 8 8 86½ 86½ 75½ 292 200 6.25 NMcKnightJr ConcordRoad,WndsofPac,BarngHanovr 35-0
2-20 GrR⅝ 8 9800 ft NW5000L6CD 1 282 592 1282 1574 5 8 8 85½ 75½ 65½ 292 159 22.50 NMcKnightJr Cimmtsy,StonhosJohnboy,GoldnJazman 35-0
2-14 GrR⅝ 3 ft QUA 1 302 101 131 2014 1 3 3 32½ 43½ 22 304 2021 NB BWallace Rapidcam,CocomoSon,MdnghtRad 31-0
LT-BLUE 2-5 FlmD 1 ft QUA 1 301 1014 1321 2004 2 2 2 32 34½ 28 294 2022 NB BWallace RadarHanover,CocomoSon,AisFela 32-0

3-1 **RITCHIES EMPIRE** b c, 3, by Seahawk Hanover--Profit or Loss by Falcon Almahurst Tr.-Monte Geirod St.- W.Robinson (.618)
Cynthia J.Moore & Michelle M.Demetzky, N.J. M1 1:54 1992 5 3 2 0 $21,031
12 ♦ $41,875 - 3, 1:54 (1) Driver-JOHN CAMPBELL 155 (wht-mar-blue) (654-108-84-75-.275) BREEDER-MAC PACING STABLE &2,OHIO. GrR⅝ 1:573 1991 9 1 5 0 $20,844
3-13 M1 4 15000 ft 3yr nw5 Lc 1 274 571 1272 156 5 5o3½ 1½ 1½ 1½ 1½ 283 156 *.80 JoCampbell RitchiesEmpire,Marko,Bilateral 28-2
3-6 M1 4 15000 ft 3 yr 1 29 564 125 1541 4 1o1 1½ 12½ 1½ 22 293 1543 *.30 JMoiseyev LrdWlng,RichsEmpr,LndwodCntron 41-0
2-22 M1 2 9000 ft nw3 cd 1 274 572 1264 154 7 45½ 1½ 1½ 12½ 12½ 271 154 2.50 JMoiseyev RtchsEmpr,Cistrphba,FlcnsCrwn 39-0
2-12 M1 5 6500 ft nw2 cd 1 293 592 1284 1564 1 2½ 12 1½ 14 17 28 1564 *.30 JMoiseyev RitchiesEmpire,Hojo,LaserGun 20-2
RED-WHT 1-31 M1 2 8125 ft nw2 cd 1 291 582 1282 1564 10 6o3½ 1½ 1½ 11 22½ 284 1571 *.90 JMoiseyev Findango,RitchisEmpr,LValntno 35-1

TRACKMAN'S SELECTIONS: 9-12-4 COCOMO SON AND RITCHIES EMPIRE WILL START FROM THE SECOND TIER

Bilateral's first race back came after two qualifiers, neither super efforts: He won in 1:59.4, and then couldn't handle a sloppy track and was sixth by 30 lengths.

However, Bilateral's '92 pari-mutuel debut was phenomenal at 64-1 in a division of the New Faces a week ago. Starting from the disadvantageous second tier in post position 11, he got away sixth and then settled in 10th. At the three-quarters pole, he was 10th by 7 lengths. After racing wide on the final turn, he scorched a final quarter in :27.2 to finish third by 3/4 of a length to Ritchies Empire in 1:56.1. Marko beat him for a second by a neck. This is worth noting because, in an earlier division of the New Faces tonight, Marko ran a strong second.

But our focus was the 12 horse, Ritchies Empire.

While Bilateral was making his first start of the season from a bad post (11), March 13, Ritchies Empire was making his fifth start of the season from the 5 post. Two points: 1) Ritchies Empire had already raced himself into shape, and 2) there was a change in post position from that race, Bilateral being the 7 horse and Ritchies Empire operating from post 12 in the second tier tonight.

The 7 post in a 12-horse field is no bargain, but Ritchies Empire got the worst of the draw. In each of his previous five races, he'd been first by the half. Getting there this night would be quite a feat from the second tier.

The biggest factor in comparing Bilateral and Ritchies Empire is that Bilateral, though he did come up 3/4 of a length short, was certainly eligible to improve off that performance.

Ritchies Empire was a vulnerable favorite.

Another top contender was the 9 horse, Lord Willing. In a separate division of the New Faces the week before, Lord Willing left, conceded the lead, and found no racing room in the stretch, finishing third by 1 1/4 lengths. He got his last quarter in :27.2, just as Bilateral did the same night. But Lord Willing raced in 1:58. Bilateral went 1:56.1, the equivalent of 9 lengths faster.

There's another speed point to consider. As a 2-year-old, Bilateral posted a mark of 1:58.1 at Scioto Downs in Ohio, then a 1:56 mark winning the Arden Downs Stakes at The Meadows outside Pittsburgh, Pennsylvania. Both track are considerably slower, rated at 2:02 and 2:02.1, than The Meadowlands (1:58.3), marking those two races as strong. By comparison, Lord Willing won the $104,338 Michigan Sire Stakes as a 2-year-old by pacing a 2:01.1 mile, and followed it with a 2:00.3 victory at Hazel Park, which is rated at 2:03.

Lord Willing, Ritchies Empire and Bilateral went off at odds of 7-5, 3-1 and 5-1. Bilateral wasn't a gigantic overlay, but it was more than a fair price for a horse who could have been sent off as the favorite. In a frantic finish, Bilateral won by a nose.

The Horses That Nobody Believes

Once in a while, horses develop reputations among bettors. If a horse is bet down to 6-5 and loses, he nonetheless might be bet heavily again the next week, and even the week after if he finished close to the winner. Conversely, there are Rodney Dangerfield horses who get no respect. If a horse wins at 10-1 and remains in the same class, he still may go off at a generous price, say 4-1 to 6-1, because the majority of bettors thought his first win was a fluke. They may especially think that if the horse moves up in company following a win. Thus, sporadically, you'll be able to get an overlay on a horse moving up off a win. If a horse has back class or is young and improving, don't be intimidated if he isn't being bet heavily. Take advantage of the situation. Remember, take every edge you can. In this case, you got value for your investment. And you may win.

Consider J J's Rebel, a fine example of a horse who doesn't get due respect. J J's was sent off at 15-1 from the 10 post in a Non-Winners of 4 races OR Non-Winners of $125,000 lifetime at The Meadowlands, May 30, 1992.

6-1 **FUNSHIP** b c, 3, by Nihilator--Pleasure Jet by Abercrombie Tr.-Brad Mc Ninch St. - T. Artandi (.2
Arlene Traub,New York,N.Y. Q M^1 1:56^1 1992 1 0 0 0 $
$82,079 - 2, 1:54 (1) Driver-JOHN CAMPBELL 155 (whi-mar-blue) (1146-195-142-141-.280) BREEDER-WECO INVESTMENTS INC,KY,etc. M^1 1:54 1991 16 4 2 2 $82,0
7♦ PINK

5-23	M^1 2	15000	ft	nw4 cd	1 27^1	54^2	122^2	151^3	8	2o1½	3o4	5o4	66½	88½	30	153^1	27.20	JoCampbell	OckComback,CoIFlyngFla,Camarad	85
5-16	M^1 4		gd	QUA	1 30^1	59^2	128^2	156^1	1	15	13	12½	12½	11½	27^4	156^1	NB	JoCampbell	Funship,Ringleader,NEOGirzy	56
5-9	M^1 7		ft	QUA	1 29^4	59^1	129	156^3	2	11½	11½	11½	11½	2hd	27^3	156^3	NB	JoCampbell	ExclusivFlight,Funship,PJsiroc	59
11-16	GSP^1 4	20000	ft	2yr Ec	1 27^3	58^2	127^1	155	4	66½	76½	7o4½	65½	53½	27^3	155^4	17.80	JMorseyev	LawilHanovr,DgrAlmahrst,BoaFra	45
11-8	GSP^1 10	3500	ft	2yr	1 27^1	57	126^4	155	4	2o½	2½	21½	43½	57½	29^2	156^2	10.50	DDancer	AirAsault,ScotrsBoy,ScotrVsor	36
11-2	RcR⅝ 9	22838	ft	PRES ELIMK	1 27^3	57^4	125^3	155	3	6	86½	86½	85	64½	28^4	156	52.50	WODonnell	ShpsPrsr,AdmralsGaly,DgrAlmahrst	52
10-24	GSP^1 3	3500	ft	2yr C	1 27^4	57^3	127^3	155^2	5	59½	56½	4o2½	55½	54½	28^4	156^4	*.80	WODonnell	AmbroKong,RapAlnton,InstantAs	6

7-2 **COOL FLYING FELLA** b h, 4, by Long Fella--Carmela Hanover by Warm Breeze Tr.-Richard Macomber (.3
Ronald G.Verosel,Laurel Hollow,N.Y. M^1 1:52^4 1992 7 4 1 0 $43.7
$105,284 - 3, 1:52^1 (1) Driver-RON PIERCE 138 (red-wht-blu) (843-104-107-130-.245) BREEDER-UNIV FLORIDA FOUNDATION,FLA. M^1 1:52^1 1991 28 5 7 3 $48.6
8♦ GRAY

5-23	M^1 2	15000	ft	nw4 cd	1 27^1	54^2	122^2	151^3	5	89½	9o8½	8o6	45½	23½	28^3	152^1	2.70	RPierce	OckComback,CoIFlyngFla,Camarad	85
5-16	M^1 10	15000	ft	nw4 cd	1 27^4	56^3	125^1	152^4	4	66	64½	5o4	3½	1nk	26^4	152^4	8.60	RPierce	CoIFlyngFla,HnryLtsgo,NoTwstr	54
5-9	M^1 8	15000	ft	nw4 cd	1 27^3	55	123^4	152^4	5	87½	96½	86½	54½	42½	28^1	153^2	31.10	RPierce	PrladwnBy,ThrForThRoad,JdgRyan	60
5-2	M^1 2		ft	QUA	1 29	58^1	128^2	155^4	6	912	913½	810½	814½	715	28^2	158^4	NB	RPierce	BigBrat,RocketLeRu,Betrayed	66
4-17	PPk⅝ 8		ft	QUA	1 30^2	59^3	129^3	158^1	4	2	21½	21½	2½	12	28^2	158^1	NB	RMacomber	CoIFlyngFla,NancyOmaha,ExcincAgan	75
4-7	PPk⅝ 7		ft	QUA	1 29^2	59^4	128^4	158	6	4o	44½	4o4½	45½	45½	29^2	159	NB	RMacomber	HotrodFalcon,RanaDiablo,ThBrid	72
2-29	PPk⅝ 8	42500	ft	3YR&UP LC	1 29	58	126^3	155^1	1	3o	11	1hd	11	1ns	28^3	155^1	e*.60	WHennessey	CoIFlyngFela,ScorLauxmont,RnR	73

12-1 **JUDGE RYAN** br g, 4, by Forrest Skipper--Odontos Belle by Nero Tr.-Earl Cruise (.32
Mishkin-Morgan Stable,Irvington,N.Y. M^1 1:53^2 1992 14 3 3 2 $33.8
$98,273 - 4, 1:53^2 (1) Driver-JOE SCHWIND 150 (wh-go-red) (360-33-36-42-.186) BREEDER-AMORIELLO STABLE,N.J.,etc. M^1 1:54 1991 20 3 3 2 $28,8
9♦ PURPLE

5-16	M^1 10	15000	ft	nw4 cd	1 27^4	56^3	125^1	152^4	1	21½	32½	11½	1½	75Pl6	28^3	153^4	9.40	JoCampbell	CoIFlyngFla,HnryLtsgo,NoTwstr	54
5-9	M^1 8	15000	ft	nw4 cd	1 27^3	55	123^4	152^4	3	11½	21½	21½	21½	31	29	153	7.60	EDavis	PrladwnBy,ThrForThRoad,JdgRyan	60
5-2	M^1 10	15000	ft	nw4 cd	1 28^3	57	125^2	153^2	3	11½	21½	21½	21	12	27^3	153^2	11.50	JoCampbell	JudgeRyan,Camaradene,WhirlVane	75
4-25	M^1 11	15000	ft	nw4 cd	1 28^1	56	124^4	153^4	4	64½	4o4½	4o2½	54	63½	29^2	154^3	3.10	WODonnell	..linrs,Camaradn,CaliforniaCam	42
4-18	M^1 9	15000	gd	nw4 cd	1 29	57^1	125^3	154^3	3	43½	65	6o3½	53½	21½	28^3	154^4	7.70	WODonnell	ClimaCam,JdgRyan,PsngChampon	42
4-11	M^1 8	15000	ft	nw4 cd	1 29^3	57^2	126^4	155^1	5	2½	33	3o2½	21½	21	28^1	155^2	17.70	WODonnell	Camaradene,JudgeRyan,BondSir	45
3-28	M^1 2	15000	ft	nw4 cd	1 28^1	58^1	128^2	156^3	9	911½	911½	99	99	85	27^2	157^3	11.20	WODonnell	Camaradn,FalconsCrown,NoTwstr	32

10-1 **JJ'S REBEL** br g, 5, by Direct Scooter--Ravens Dream by Raven Hanover Tr.-Arthur Foster (.25
Arty L.Foster,Cordova,Md. M^1 1:52^2 1992 18 3 2 2 $25.8
$93,360 - 5, 1:52^2 (1) Driver-CATELLO MANZI 165 (wht-l blu-blu) (924-112-111-114-.229) BREEDER-J.J.& M.J.J.CIGNETTO,PA. RcR⅝ 1:55^4 1991 21 5 3 3 $13,8
10♦ Blue-Rd

5-23	M^1 4	16000	ft	nw12750L7	1 28^1	55^2	124^1	152^2	3	53	65½	43½	52½	1¾	27^3	152^2	28.70	CManzi	JJsRebel,Spctacl,PatsFlagship	85
5-16	M^1 5	17000	ft	nw16000L7	1 27^3	56^1	124	151^3	4	57½	65½	64½	75½	53½	27^2	152^1	33.20	BWebster	TKsSkpr,ShognHnvr,PatsFlagshp	54
5-9	M^1 12	16000	ft	nw13500L7	1 27^4	55^3	123^4	152^2	9	32½	54½	65½	65	53dq8	28^1	153	43.90	BWebster	DgntyofMan,SandKy,ShognHanovr	60
5-2	M^1 9	17000	ft	nw13750L7	1 27^4	56^1	124^3	152^3	3	45½	44	4o2½	44	32½	28	153	34.60	BWebster	DgntyofMan,SmartAly,JJsRebel	75
4-25	M^1 4	11000	ft	nw8500L7cd	1 27^4	57^4	127^1	154^4	1	33	32½	32½	32	21½	27^2	155	8.80	EDavis	Pianist,JJsRebel,DrawingBoard	42
4-11	RcR⅝ 9	4800	ft	WO4000L6CD	1 29	59^1	128	157	6	7	75	75½	711	69½	30	159	5.10	JMorand	StratOSpd,Landshark,GamthiCpr	72
4-3	M^1 3	11000	ft	nw8500L7cd	1 29^2	100^1	129^4	157^2	8	7o6½	7o5	8o6½	45½	53	27	158	9.90	EDavis	AMond,OrangSovrgn,SamyAlmahrst	34

TRACKMAN'S SELECTIONS: 1-8-3

Check out his 5 most recent races:

• April 25—Second by 1½ lengths at 8-1 from the rail in a Non-Winners of $8,500 Last 7.

• May 2—Third by 2¼ at 34-1 from the 3 post in a Non-Winners of $13,750 Last 7.

• May 9—Fifth by 3—but disqualified and placed eighth for causing interference—at 43-1 from the 9 post in a Non-Winners of $13,750 Last 7.

• May 16—Fifth by 3½ from the 4 post at 33-1 in a Non-Winners of $16,000 Last 7 when he had the misfortune of taking on one of the country's top pacers, T K's Skipper, who won in 1:51.3. To finish fifth, J J's paced his last quarter in :27.2 and last half in :55. Horses who finish miles that fast are usually in stakes—winning them.

• May 23—In a class drop to Non-Winners of $12,750 Last 7, he won by ¾ of a length from the 3 post, capping off a :56 final half with a :27.3 final quarter. At 28-1. He paid $59.40 to win.

Tonight, he was in a similar spot. Actually, the purse was for $1,000 less than his previous start.

With a perfect drive by Cat Manzi, finding a tuck early, he roared home to win again, paying $32.00. An overlay? Yes, a major one. When we talk about horses usually headed in one direction, up or down, it's obvious that J J's was reaching peak form. The 10 post is difficult, but doesn't justify 15-1.

Know what? Off those two victories, and racing in the exact same class the next week, he won by ¾ of a length, paying $18.00.

There's an old saying: "If you missed the wedding (when he won), don't go to his funeral (when he lost)." The time to catch J J's was his second and/or third win when he was a decided overlay, not when he finally got bet more the following two weeks and lost.

Here's a good overlay from the fifth race at Yonkers, May 30, 1992.

5 **PACE**

ONE MILE
WARM-UP
BLACK

PREFERRED HANDICAP
Post positions (1-4) drawn, (5-8) drawn.

RED **GRANNYS GARDEN (NY)**

b h 7,by Storm Damage, Granny Ginny by Meadow Skipper — 1:56.1 YR — 92 14 2 2 3 — $29,520
Ivanhoe Stables, Inc., Chicago, Ill. — 1:57.1 YR — 91 32 3 5 2 — $38,456
Dan Daley (162) — Green-Gold-White — Tr.B.W. Norris — Last 8 starts–$20.750 — 7 1:56.1 — Lifetime — $205,194

1	5-23YR+12	1	fst	27^1	55^4	1.25	1.53^2	Opn Hcp	25000	2	4	5	6°°3¾	6^5	5⁸¾	1.55	27.70	(MarohnJ)CenterStrip,ThorFashion,JustinKin	not in hunt
	5-16YR	1	sly	28^4	1.00	1.31^2	2.00^4	Qua		3	1	1	1^2	1^3	1^4¾	2.00^4	nb	(MarohnJ)GrannysGarden,OutrageousKid,MyCaddy	jogged
	3-28YR+2	1	fst	28	57^4	1.27^2	1.57	Opn Hcp	25000	4	5	5	6^5¾	6^4¾	6^4¾	1.58	18.50	(MarshJJr)TamsteyBluegrass,PilgrimsPatriot,JustinKin	sat in,no gap
	3-21YR+3	1	fst	28	57^4	1.27^2	1.56^1	Opn Hcp	25000	1	2	2	3^1½	4^2¼	3^1¼	1.56^2	20.80	(MarshJJr)CountKhan,JustinKin,GrannysGarden	yld,pkd,mid
	3-14YR+0	1	fst	27^3	57^1	1.28^3	1.55^3	Opn Hcp	25000	4	5	7	8^5	7^5	4^6	1.56^4	21.10	(MarshJJr)TulsaBlueChip,JustinKin,ThorFashion	svd grnd mid
	3-7YR+6	1	fst	26^4	55^4	1.26	1.55^2	Opn Hcp	25000	2	4	3	5^2¾	5^7¼	4^7¾	1.56^4	17.40	(MarshJJr)JustinKin,OaklandAvenue,Explode	sat in,no gap
	2-29YR-1	1	fst	28	58	1.27^3	1.56^2	Opn Hcp	25000	1	2	2	2^2	2^2¾	2^2¼	1.56^4	20.40	(MarshJJr)SunDamage,GrannysGarden,TulsaBluChip	yld,pocket,held
10-1	2-22YR+9	1	fst	27^3	57^3	1.27	1.56^1	WB001	12500	4	1	1	1^1¼	1^1	1^{nk}	1.56^1	11.70	(MarohnJ)GrannysGarden,WilcoxGeneral,TooneyBilly	mild prss,safe

BLUE **BRING EM (NY)**

b g 5,by On The Road Again, Smooth Millie by Smooth Fella — 1:57.2 YR — 92 14 3 1 2 — $36,115
Mark Lancaster & Rob Hules, Columbus, N.J. — 1:58.3 Fhd — 91 40 7 12 5 — $86,510
Mark Lancaster (180) — Blue-Gold — Tr.Steve Lancaster — Last 8 starts–$23,375 — 4 1:56.3 — Lifetime — $248,549

2	5-23YR+12	1	fst	27^1	55^4	1.25	1.53^2	Opn Hcp	25000	3x	7	7	7^{14}	7^{15}	7^{14}	1.56^1	30.50	(LancasterM)CenterStrip,ThorFashion,JustinKin	broke early
	5-16YR+3	1	fst	27^2	55^4	1.24^4	1.54^4	Opn Hcp	25000	3	6	6	7°4¼	6^4¼	4^2¼	1.55^1	12.80	(LancasterM)ThorFashion,Lionheart,IdleFella	inside,all out
	5-9YR+5	1	fst	27^1	56^3	1.26	1.56	Opn Hcp	25000	2	4	4°	4°1¾	4^3	6^6¼	1.56^1	29.10	(LancasterM)JustinKin,BlackstickSide,(dh)ThorFshn-SmilyFace	cover,gapped
	5-2YR	1						Opn Hcp	25000	4									scratched-sick
	4-25YR+5	1	fst	27^4	57	1.25^4	1.55^3	Opn Hcp	25000	3	6	8	7^4	6^4	5^3	1.56^1	8.00	(LancasterM)OaklandAve,TulsaBlueChip,ThorFashion	rail,beat weary
	4-18YR+4	1	sly	28^2	57^3	1.26^3	1.56^1	Opn Hcp	25000	3	6	7	8°6¼	6^4¼	2^2	1.56^3	26.30	(LancasterM)PilgrimsPatriot,BringEm,JustinKin	very wide,sod
	4-11YR+1	1	fst	28^3	58^1	1.28^3	1.57^3	Prf Hcp	15000	4	3	5	5°°2¼	2¼	1^1	1.57^3	16.80	(LancasterM)BringEm,Stylized,HumberTrail	4 wide strng
8-1	4-4YR+4	1	fst	28^2	58^2	1.27^2	1.57^2	WB001 Hcp	15000	5	5	5°	5°°3¼	4^1¾	1^{nk}dh	1.57^2	4.20	(LancasterM)(dh)PikaByDay-BringEm,MolliesFella	dh,late surge
	3-28YR-2	1	fst	27^4	58	1.28^4	1.57^4	Prf Hcp	15000	7	6	6°	5°°2¾	6^4	5^3¼	1.58^2	18.70	(LancasterM)YoursJinx,PikaByDay,MolliesFella	3rd ov,wd,fltr

WHITE **B JS ENCORE (NY)**

b g 4,by Skip By Night, Tatting Bret by Brets Star — 1:57.0 YR — 92 16 3 7 1 — $34,222
Brian & Jennifer Nixon, Centerport, N.Y. — 1:58.2 YR — 91 34 8 3 5 — $29,780
Luc Ouellette (145) — Red-Black-White — Tr.Hugh McIntosh — Last 8 starts–$25,500 — 4 1:57.0 — Lifetime — $77,243

3	5-23YR-12	1	fst	27^1	56^4	1.25^4	1.54^4	WB001 Hcp	15000	8	4	4°°	3°2¼	2^5	2^2¼	1.55^1	7.00	(OuelletteL)HHSteel,BJsEncore,OnCoveRoadAgain	tck,2d best
	5-16YR-3	1	fst	27^2	55^4	1.24^4	1.54^4	Opn Hcp	25000	5	7	7°	6°°3¼	8^5¾	8^3¾	1.55^2	9.50	(MarohnJ)ThorFashion,Lionheart,IdleFella	wide brkd
	5-9YR+5	1	fst	28^1	58	1.28^4	1.55^3	WB001 Hcp	15000	8	2	2	3^2	3^2¾	2^3¼	1.56^1	17.50	(FilionHer)IdleFella,BJsEncore,PikaByDay	tck,pocket,held
	5-2YR+10	1	fst	27^2	57^1	1.28^2	1.54^2	Opn Hcp	25000	2	4	4	5^2¾	4^4¾	3^2	1.54^4	30.70	(MarohnJ)AmbroHerman,PilgrimsPatriot,BJsEncore	sat in,gd late
	4-25YR+5	1	fst	27^2	58^2	1.27^4	1.57	Opn 3-4YO	15000	2	1°	1	1½	1^1½	1^{nk}	1.57	*1.70	(OuelletteL)BJsEncore,MichaelsRevenge,FritzKiss	speed,driving
	4-11YR-1	1	fst	28^2	59	1.27^4	1.58^1	Opn 3-4YO	15000	2	2	1	1no	1no	2no	1.58^1	7.80	(MarohnJ)LesHall,BJsEncore,Ludicrous	rlk,prss,caught
	4-4YR+4	1	fst	28	58^2	1.27^2	1.57^2	Opn 3-5YO	15000	7	7	7°	7^6¼	7^5	7^4¼	1.58^1	5.50	(CaseWJr)InTrust,HumberTrail,Lionheart	flattened late
4-1	3-28YR+2	1	fst	28^1	58^3	1.28^1	1.57^3	Opn 3-4YO	15000	5	5	2°	2°no	2no	2^{nk}	1.57^3	10.70	(OuelletteL)Claustrophobia,BJsEncore,LesHall	chll,outgamed

GREEN **KEV TYLER**

b g 6,by Tyler B, Taffy Almahurst by Bret Hanover — 2:01.0 Fhd Q — 92 0 0 0 0
Rocklin Stables, Paradise, Pa. — 1:55.3 YR — 91 17 2 4 3 — $48,450
Richard Wojcio (150) — Blue-White-Yellow — Tr.Eric McEwan — Last 8 starts–$18.450 — 4 1:54.2 (1) — Lifetime — $168,796

4	5-20Fhd	1	fst	29^2	1.00^3	1.31^2	2.01	Qua		6	1°	1	1	1^5	1^5¼	2.01	nb	(WojcioR)KevTyler,GrandSlamPlay,WeePrinceN	
	5-8Fhd	1	sly	30^1	1.01^3	1.31^3	2.03	Qua		2	4	1	1	1^2¾	1^2¼	2.03	nb	(WojcioR)KevTyler,HorseSoldierA,SedonaStar	
	4-21SG1	1	fst	29^4	1.00^2	1.30	1.59	Qua		3	1	1	1	1^1	4^1¼	1.59^1	nb	(McEwanE)EWEasyMoney,Pennant,Delamar	
	8-24Fhd-9	1	fst	27^3	57^1	1.26^2	1.55	PrFm	15000	5	8	8	8	8dis	8dis	2.01^2	49.70	(WojcioR)AlertMove,TilWeMeetAgain,Cameleor	
	8-3YR-7	1	fst	27^1	56^4	1.25^3	1.54^4	Opn Hcp	22500	6	7	7	7°6	7^6¼	7^6¾	1.56^1	22.90	(WojcioR)Resonator,BretTheThird,DeloneyBluegrass	no rally
	7-27YR-7	1	fst	27^1	58	1.26^4	1.55^4	Opn Hcp	22500	3	2	2	3^1½	3^1½	2^2	1.56^1	8.80	(WojcioR)Resonator,KevTyler,SeeTheUSA	yld,pckt,held
	7-14YR-2	1	fst	27^2	56^3	1.26^2	1.54^1	Opn Hcp	24750	6	2°	3°	3°1½	7^8½	8^{20}	1.58^1	14.10	(WojcioR)AmbroHerman,Resonator,(dh)PacificO-DrpOff	parked,faded
8-1	7-6YR-2	1	sly	29	58^1	1.27	1.55^3	Opn Hcp	22500	2	3	5	3°2	2^1	3^2¾	1.56^1	17.40	(WojcioR)Resonator,OaklandAvenue,KevTyler	chall,brkd

BLACK	IDLE FELLA (NY)							b h 5,by Brand New Fella, White Idol by Runnymede Chuck									1:55.3 YR	92 18 5 1 3	$31,702
	Normand Fluet (150)						Gold-Black-White	J. Omboni, J. Omboni, Jr., N.Y.									1:56.1 YR	91 44 4 6 7	$49,743
5								Tr.Joseph Omboni,Jr.								Last 8 starts-$26,012	5 1:55.3	Lifetime	$124,070
	5-16YR-3	1	fst	272	554	1.244	1.544 Opn Hcp	25000	4	1°	1	1½	1¾	32	1.551	3.70	(OuelletteL)ThorFashion,Lionheart,IdleFella		spd,press brec
	5-9YR-5	1	fst	281	58	1.264	1.553 WB001 Hcp	15000	1	1	1	11	1½	1¾	1.553	4.50	(OuelletteL)IdleFella,BJsEncore,PksByDay		speed strong
	5-2YR-10	1	fst	272	564	1.253	1.544 Prf Hcp	15000	7	7	6°	6⁸½	6⁸	6⁸¾	1.56	10.90	(OuelletteL)HumberTrail,SmileyFace,PksByDay		no rally
	4-25YR-5	1	fst	272	572	1.264	1.561 Prf Hcp	15000	6	6	6°	6°4¼	5³½	42	1.563	13.80	(OuelletteL)AmbroHerman,CenterStrip,SmileyFace		belated pace
	4-18YR-4	1	gd	272	564	1.27	1.573 WB001	12500	4	1°	1	1¼	1¼	1no	1.573	6.00	(OuelletteL)IdleFella,MollesFella,ScootHerb		speed,all out
	4-13YR-4	1	fst	292	581	1.28	1.573 NW8000	7500	6	4	4	2°½	1¼	1¼	1.573	19.20	(OuelletteL)IdleFella,Wow,OnCoveRoadAgain		tck,brush,drvng
	4-4YR-4	1	fst	282	574	1.272	1.573 NW6000	5750	3	1	1	1¾	1½	1½	1.573	*2.10	(OuelletteL)IdleFella,NiddB,CinderDar		hard prss,drvng
5-1	3-28YR-2	1	fst	284	591	1.291	1.593 NW6000	5750	7	2°	1	1½	1½	22	2.00	9.50	(OuelletteL)ANutterButter,IdleFella,RapidSkipper		speed,no match

YELLOW	TWINKLE JOHN N							b g 8,by Transport Chip, Twinkle Estelle by Main Star									1:54.3 YR	92 15 6 2 0	$43,200
	James Marohn (115)						Purple-White	Brett Pelling & Richard Norman, Allentown, N.J.									1:56.2 M1	91 13 2 2 1	$14,525
6								Tr.Brett Pelling								Last 8 starts-$27,350	8 1:54.3	Lifetime	$105,975
	5-23YR-12	1	fst	274	574	1.27	1.564 Opt27000	9500	4	5	5°	2°hd	1½	13	1.564	*.20	(MarohnJ)TwinkleJohnN,PickOfTheWeek,Generama		sharp
	5-9YR-5	1	fst	271	562	1.254	1.552 Prf Hcp	12500	7	7	6°	3°°1¾	21	12	1.552	*1.50	(MarohnJ)TwinkleJohnN,Koch,SupergluBluegrass		3rd ov,wd,solid
	5-2YR-10	1	fst	272	564	1.262	1.543 WB001 Hcp	12500	5	5	3°	2°hd	13	17	1.543	3.20	(MarohnJ)TwinkleJohnN,Koch,TimberJack		chall,drew away
	4-25YR-5	1	fst	273	563	1.263	1.571 WB001	12500	6	7	7°°	5°°1¾	42	4½	1.572	2.70	(MarohnJ)MollesFella,GlobalAssault,SeaTheUSA		wide 2x,no kick
	4-18YR-4	1	gd	272	564	1.27	1.573 WB001	12500	2	4	4°	4°2¾	32	4hd	1.573	*1.80	(MarohnJ)IdleFella,MollesFella,ScootHerb		unc,late gain
	4-11YR-1	1	fst	273	572	1.263	1.57 WB001	12500	7	7	6	78	6⁵¼	6⁴½	1.574	41.30	(MarohnJ)AmbroHerman,Candrel,SeaTheUSA		ins,no rally
	3-16YR-0	1	fst	271	58	1.274	1.561 Opt27000	7500	6	6	6°	6°°5	47	4⁶¾	1.573	3.70	(MarohnJr)YouraJinx,DelgatysGiftN,FourSeventeen		tired wide even
3-1	3-7YR-6	1	fst	274	573	1.263	1.563 WB001 Hcp	15000	1	2	3	4½	3½	1¾	1.563	9.70	(MarohnJ)TwinkleJohnN,MollesFella,QuiteATan		pkt,ins,solid

ORANGE	H H STEEL							b g 5,by Cam Fella, Speed Heiress by Olympic Hanover									1:54.4 YR	92 20 3 4 6	$30,101
	Gino Palazzolo (165)						Green-Red-White	O. & J. Palazzolo, Colts Neck, N.J.									1:56.4 YR	91 27 2 4 3	$12,903
7								Tr.Gino Palazzolo								Last 8 starts-$16,690	3 1:54.2 (1)	Lifetime	$77,992
	5-23YR-12	1	fst	271	564	1.254	1.544 WB001 Hcp	15000	7	2	2°	1°1¼	15	1²¼	1.544	9.80	(PalazzoloG)HHSteel,BJsEncore,OnCoveRoadAgain		easy score
	5-16YR-3	1	fst	274	582	1.27	1.564 WB001 Hcp	15000	3	2	2	3²¾	45	3³¾	1.563	3.50	(PalazzoloG)Candrel,BigArrow,HHSteel		aim for 2d,mild
	5-9YR-5	1	fst	271	562	1.254	1.552 Prf Hcp	12500	4	3°	2°	1½	11	4³¼	1.56	6.20	(PalazzoloG)TwinkleJohnN,Koch,SupergluBluegrass		pkd 3/4s,brec
	5-2Fhd-9	1	fst	274	57	1.264	1.56 W15001	11000	x1	7	7°	5°	3³¼	3³¼	1.563	6.90	(PalazzoloG)ScottishStage,GypsysCaper,HHSteel		
	4-25Fhd-6	1	fst	291	591	1.282	1.571 W15001	11000	1	1	1	1	11	2nk	1.571	2.30	(PalazzoloG)PacificDream,HHSteel,PerfectPlay		
	4-18Fhd-5	1	fst	273	552	1.251	1.564 NW600ps	8000	5	1°°	1	1	11	3½	1.57	10.50	(PalazzoloG)ComplexFlicker,NoEncumbrance,HHSteel		
	4-11Fhd-3	1	fst	292	584	1.282	1.582 NW600ps	8000	6	4°	4°	2°	2¾	3¼	1.583	33.10	(PalazzoloG)URCagey,EarthStorm,HHSteel		
6-1	4-4Fhd-7	1	fst	272	572	1.273	1.572 NW600ps	8000	5	8	9	8°	6⁵¾	5⁴¼	1.581	36.80	(PalazzoloG)Koch,FurtherNotice,NoEncumbrance		

GREY	FULLA POTHOLES (NY)							ch g 4,by On The Road Again, Bye Fulla by Fulla Napoleon									1:56.2 YR	92 11 3 0 1	$17,625
	Michael Kimelman (135)						Blue-Gold	Anthony & Sheila Lowbeer, Ossining, N.Y.									1:53.0 Sy1	91 15 6 4 2	$75,572
8								Tr.Jean Berube								Last 8 starts-$16,750	3 1:53.0 (1)	Lifetime	$119,596
	5-23YR-12	1	fst	284	582	1.264	1.554 Opn 3-4YO	15000	5	5	4°	3°°¾	2nk	1¾	1.554	2.90	(KimelmanM)FullaPotholes,Lionheart,PerfectPlay		long wd,urged
	5-9YR-5	1	fst	27	564	1.263	1.56 Opn 3-4YO	17500	6	5°	3°	1°1	11	3¹¾	1.562	3.10	(KimelmanM)PerfectPlay,OnCvRdAgain,FullaPotholes		game try,brec
	5-4YR-7	1	fst	282	563	1.262	1.552 NW8000	9500	5	3	4°	1°1¼	17	1⁹½	1.552	3.60	(KimelmanM)FullaPotholes,SeawayNavigator,Shipwreckd		tck,wd top,easy
	4-27YR-5	1	fst	283	583	1.273	1.563 NW8000	9500	7	6	3°	2°1½	3²½	6⁴¾	1.573	5.70	(KimelmanM)Wavelength,SeawayNavigator,PunchDoctor		long unc trd
	4-18Fhd-5	1	fst	282	572	1.261	1.55 Opn	13000	4	5	5°	5°	5⁴½	5⁴¾	1.56	15.10	(KimelmanM)YouraJinx,CountryBeau,JABedford		
	4-11MR	1	sly	284	582	1.292	1.582 NW3100	2620	4	5°	4°	1	1⁷½	117	1.582	*2.00	(KimelmanM)FullaPotholes,PowerLine,ByeByeGoodbye		
	4-4PcD	1	fst	281	584	1.273	1.561 Inv Hcp	5500	6	6	6°	5°	8⁹¼	4⁶¾	1.573	10.60	(KimelmanM)BiscuitsBoy,WellsfordLadN,KeystoneGunner		
6-1	3-28PcD	1	fst	301	1.01	1.301	1.593 Inv Hcp	5500	3	4	4°	2°	65	7⁶¼	2.004	3.50	(KimelmanM)HelensPartner,WitsendsJack,BiscuitsBoy		

This Preferred Handicap also illustrates that a horse missing one week is not a major concern.

Of great interest here are B J's Encore and Idle Fella. They'd faced each other May 16 in the $25,000 Open Handicap at Yonkers. Idle Fella was sent off at 7-2 from the 4 post; B J's was 9-1 from the 5 post.

Idle Fella tried going wire-to-wire, setting unbelievably fast fractions for a ½-mile track: :27.2, :55.4 and 1:24.4. Pressed most of the second half, he tired late, finishing third by 2 lengths in the 1:54.4 mile.

B J's did little while racing wide, finishing eighth, though he only lost by 3½ lengths. It was the second straight week Idle Fella beat him.

While Idle Fella took the next week off, B J's dropped into a $15,000 Handicap at Yonkers. He put in a strong effort from the 8 post, got a tuck fourth, rallied three-wide and finished second by 2¼ lengths to H H Steel, whom he was facing again tonight out of the 7 post.

Now tonight's odds: B J's 7-5, Idle Fella 5-1. Think about this: In a race just two weeks back, Idle Fella was a much shorter price than B J's and beat him by a length and a half. Yes, there is a shift in post position tonight, but, given Idle Fella's early speed, not a significant one with B J's from the 3 and Idle Fella from the 5. And yes, B J's had put in a strong race since that start. But 7-5? Absurd. The bigger the underlay, the greater the overlay. In this race, the overlays were substantial. H H Steel went off at 10-1 from the 7 post. The 8 horse, Fulla Potholes—a lovely name as he's by On The Road Again out of the mare Bye Fulla—went off at 19-1 though he showed two wins and a third in his last three starts.

A definite underlay was the 6, Twinkle John N, at 2-1. He'd won three straight but was moving up in company, farther outside in post position, and had been beaten by a head by Idle Fella back on April 18.

Idle Fella won and paid $13.20. B J's was second.

Strategy I — The Meadowlands

CHAPTER 4

Leave? Pull now? Go first over, or try to flush cover? Fan wide at the top of the stretch, or test your patience sitting on the rail?

These and other instantaneous decisions made by eight to 10 drivers every race are complicated by the inexact responses of their horses, who are traveling as fast as 35 miles per hour.

Jumble the decisions, string them together over the two-minute span of a single race, and strategy is born.

"You can make an atrocious move staying in, then you get an opening and you look like a genius," John Campbell says.

More often than not—better make that a lot more often—Campbell, Mike Lachance, Catello "Cat" Manzi and Billy O'Donnell make enough right decisions to win.

In 1991, Hall of Famer Campbell became the first driver to earn more than $100 million in his career. The 37-year-old native of London, Ontario, has led North America in seasonal earnings eight times. His career UDR (Universal Driver Rating) is .319.

Campbell has emerged as a quiet, sincere spokesman for the sport. Among the champions he's driven are the brilliant trotters Mack Lobell and Peace Corps and the filly pacer Miss Easy.

Manzi, a schoolmate of the author in Liberty, New York—10 miles from Monticello Raceway—struggled in his initial years at The Meadowlands, then blossomed. His win totals from 1985 to '89 were 103, 124, 264, 432 and 687, when he was second in the nation. On June 20, 1992, Manzi picked up a catch drive on Horse of the Year Artsplace at The Meadowlands and won easily in 1:49.2, the fastest race mile ever.

Manzi's large racing family includes his dad Al, brother Steve, cousin Eddie Lohmeyer and cousin John Manzi, Director of Public Relations at Monticello and immediate past President of the United States Harness Writers Association.

Lachance, the 42-year-old son of a cattle farmer in St. Augustine, Quebec, followed his brothers Gilles, Pierre and Andre into racing.

He led North America in wins four straight seasons, 1984-87, and began 1992 ranked third in career wins and fourth in career earnings, with a .306 UDR.

Lachance drove 1989 Horse of the Year Matt's Scooter, whose 1:48.2 time trial, September 23, 1989, was the fastest harness mile ever recorded. He also drove Gordie Jeff and BJ Scoot.

Hall of Famer O'Donnell, known as Billy O and/or the Magic Man, considered a career in plumbing. Seriously.

In a remarkable eight-year run, 1981-89, he was first four times and second four times in earnings. He is third in all-time earnings.

O'Donnell, 48, was born in Spring Hill, Nova Scotia, and spent his formative racing years in New England, where he prospered as Jim Doherty's second trainer.

O'Donnell's '85 season was memorable as he piloted Horse of the Year Nihilator and Trotter of the Year Prakas.

Campbell, Manzi, Lachance and O'Donnell dominate at The Meadowlands' 1-mile track. But how? Their gifted hands are a given. So, too, is the stock they drive at the country's premier race meet. The variables are their decisions as the race unfolds. Their strength is their ability to get their horses into a position where they can win—their strategy.

Obviously, drivers' decisions depend on the quality of the horse. Yet while horses' abilities vary, key tactical decisions are constant. Every race. Every night. Every week.

Here's how some of them are made.

Pre-Race

How much time do you spend handicapping?

"Not enough time," Lachance says. "I should. It's very important to sit down and look at the program. Sometimes I look the night before. I'll look at a program 15 to 20 minutes at the track."

Manzi also doesn't spend much time: "I don't really handicap. I know the horse. Generally, I go from that. I used to study, but it's different now. I'll often leave Freehold (where he races daily in the afternoon) for The Meadowlands and not know what horses I have in some nights."

Campbell says, "At The Meadowlands, I'll look at the program the night before. I'll glance over it again the next night before my first drive, then three to four minutes again each race before I go out."

O'Donnell says, "It's a mind over matter situation. It's like speed reading. When I go in the paddock, I can read a race in 5 seconds. I get the next night's program. I go into the locker room and look at it 15 to 25 minutes. I like to do that before I start driving that night."

How big a plus is it to be familiar with rival horses and rival drivers?

"It's a tremendous help to know the horses, know the drivers, know the trainers," O'Donnell says.

Manzi agrees: "I drive against the same guys all the time. I know their strategies a little. I know their abilities."

Campbell says, "Drivers' styles have a lot to do with your decisions. You're not always right. You make an educated guess on what you expect.

"I'm out there practically every race. If a horse races at The Meadowlands two times, I know him. It's an edge for all of us who drive a lot. If I see a horse I know, it helps me make decisions."

Lachance says, "I think it's important, but not as important as on a ½-mile track. On a ½-mile track, there's only so many moves you can make. On a 1-mile track, you don't know what other drivers are going to do. There are a thousand strategies you can have."

Leaving

Ten-horse fields makes leaving more difficult. Do you shop for a hole or go on?

"It's different at The Meadowlands than at a ½-mile track," Lachance says. "Even if you spend half a day looking at the program, you don't know what's going to happen behind the gate. You have to pick up things as they happen."

Manzi says, "Finding a hole is not the most important thing. A hole can sometimes be the worst place you can be, to drop in fourth or fifth. At the half, you'll be last because everybody is on the move."

Campbell bases hole shopping on "how much we're going. If we're in the featured pace and they're going to the quarter in :29, you better go to the top. If they're going :27 in an overnight, you can look for a tuck, but you better decide pretty quick because the hole won't be there long."

What are the merits of dangling (staying outside waiting for cover)? Do you search for cover immediately?

"When you're trying to decide on the pace, you hang for a while because you want to see what's happening," Manzi says. "But you can't wait forever."

Lachance labels it "fishing. You just see what's going to happen."

Campbell calls it "riding out. Quite often, I will dangle. Especially at The Meadowlands, you don't want to get caught up in a speed duel. You can wait for a quarter of a mile and go look for cover."

O'Donnell says, "Finding cover is very important. Most of the time, it's difficult."

When do you commit to making the lead no matter what? When do you take back?

"A lot of times, you decide when the gate leaves," O'Donnell says. "Say you've got the 5 horse and the 4 and 3 don't leave. You have to step on the gas and go. I'll pull back usually if there are two or more inside of me leaving, especially with the new (staggered) gate. The staggered starting gate is very difficult. It's like a six-pack of beer: It makes you more confident than you really should be."

Campbell says, "If you're leaving and you want to make the front, you want to go no more than two-wide before the first turn. If you're leaving and it looks like you're going to be more than two-wide before the turn, you're in trouble."

Manzi says the commitment to make the top "is sometimes made as the gate leaves. You have to be aware of the pace. If you feel the pace is too quick, you have to conserve the horse."

Lachance says, "I pull back when I feel the pace is going too fast and I see it's going to take forever to get to the front."

Is going wire-to-wire more difficult on a track with constant action?

"You better have a pretty good horse," O'Donnell says. "My preference is getting to the front by being the last one to get there. In the spring, speed doesn't hold up as well as in the summer."

Campbell says, "Most horses that go wire-to-wire are dropping in class. Front-end speed holds up better than it used to since they changed the surface of the track several years ago."

Lachance says, "It's difficult. It's tough to get a tough first quarter and then keep it going. But if you get an easy first quarter, you can do it."

Manzi notes the difference between a front-end attempt at The Meadowlands' 1-mile track compared to Freehold's 1/2-mile one: "At Freehold, you can conserve your horse a little by slowing down on the turn. At The Meadowlands, you don't have that luxury."

Will you park a horse after making the lead?

O'Donnell thinks it can be a suicidal decision: "If you park a guy at The Meadowlands, there's another guy right behind him."

How about getting parked? If you leave twice and get hung each time, will that affect a decision to leave a third time the same night?

"No, because I always try to do what I have to do," Lachance says. "Sometimes it's going to turn against me, but it's not going to keep happening."

Manzi says, "I think it does affect you. It's a game of confidence. When things are going good, you drive better. Horses know if you're confident or not. There's one thing you can't hide from a horse. That is your confidence."

O'Donnell offers a similar assessment: "Confidence is a big part of it. If you just come in for one drive a night, it's different. Being here all the time is a big edge. When I drive eight horses, if I screw up one or two times, I can go out, win a race, then forget about it."

Campbell says, "You have to take the races one at a time."

What about letting go and re-taking?

"If it's a horse that has enough speed to take you down to the half, but you feel he can't carry it enough to win, you let him go and re-take," Campbell says. "It's kind of an unwritten rule. If a guy lets you go, you're supposed to let him take back. Some guys don't. If you let him go and he doesn't let you re-take, if he's going to park you, both horses are in trouble. The horse has to have a break (rest) somewhere in there."

Lachance says, "Nobody wants to stay behind a 40-1 longshot if he's got the favorite. Top drivers know that if you let them get the lead, you'll take back."

Manzi says, "Usually a guy lets you take back." But O'Donnell notes, "It's not as common as it used to be. There are always more horses coming. If you let one go, you might get shuffled (back). You're taking a big chance."

Mid-Race

When do you pull?

"Let's say you're in the hole and you see a horse coming on the outside," Campbell says. "If he's a live horse, there are two ways to look at it: 1) Don't go out and he can box you in, or 2) pull and go and you give him a perfect trip second-over. It's a double-edged sword."

Manzi counters, "Watch the driver in front of you to see if there's any sign of him urging his horse. It's not a good idea to be looking back too much."

Lachance says, "It's a tough question. Nobody wants to be first-over. You try to get cover, but if you're sitting fourth or fifth going to the half, you have to pull."

O'Donnell says, "You wait as long as you can. The fresher you keep your horse, the farther he'll go."

Being in the outside flow allows drivers to avoid "The Meadowlands Shuffle," when a good position on the rail early in the race becomes the worst place to be as horse after horse roars past on the outside. If two, three or more of the outside flow horses make the lead, the driver of the boxed-in horse has lost too many lengths to recover. Your opinion?

"It's almost impossible to avoid the shuffle," O'Donnell says. "It's really hard. It'll happen once every 15 drives. You just sit there and take it like a man, and hope it doesn't happen again."

Campbell knows the feeling: "First at the quarter and last at the three-quarters, that's the shuffle. There's no way you can tell when it's going to happen. Instinct plays a big part. You learn a lot about your opponents."

Manzi says, "Sometimes the flow isn't a flow. You get to a certain point and it stops."

Lachance labels the outside flow as "very important. You have 10 horses in the race. Everybody wants to be second-over. You just have to go with the flow." About the shuffle, he says, "There's no way to know. It's part of racing."

Flushing cover is a subtle process, requiring drivers to identify one or two horses they want to follow on the outside, then allowing those drivers time to pull to the outside in front of them. How does it work?

"It's very important to get the right horse you're flushing," O'Donnell says. "Say you're sitting sixth and the horse sitting fourth is 4-5, and the horse sitting fifth is 30-1. You want to rush up there as fast as you can to keep the 30-1 shot at the rail and still flush the 4-5 horse."

But that's only part of the problem. How long do you wait for a horse to pull, and is it always best to flush cover?

"Sometimes, horses have trouble stopping and starting," O'Donnell says. "A lot of horses have different gears. Going first-over lets them do it on their own."

Campbell says, "If I have a real competitive horse and I'm moving well, I won't stop for cover."

Of the times he does stop, he says, "Obviously, you don't want to be waiting long for cover. Second-over is where you want to be. You might rush up past a few horses, then wait. You'll wait on a guy longer at the quarter than the five-eighths. Very few horses race better without cover. Even the ones that appear to race better without it would race better with cover if the cover's going fast enough."

Lachance says, "You can flush cover, but you can't wait too long. You can't wait there forever. There are some horses who race better without cover, horses who are grinders. But those are few."

Manzi says, "If you know the horse in front of you, you wait for cover, but you can't wait too long. Nobody sits and waits for cover long."

The Finish

Heading around the final turn approaching The Meadowlands' 990-foot-long stretch is always an adventure because there are so many horses capable of winning at that point. True?

"That's why The Meadowlands is so much tougher," O'Donnell says. "At other tracks, there are only three horses that belong in a given class. At The Meadowlands, there are seven."

Manzi adds, "There are a great number of live horses at the top of the stretch. Everybody's in a position where he can win."

Finding the best position isn't easy. Can you avoid blindswitches and/or escape from them?

"Getting out of a blindswitch is a matter of luck," Campbell says. "That's something that racing luck decides."

O'Donnell says, "Blindswitches are tough. Normally, you get only one chance to decide whether or not to go three-wide. You either pull or sit in and hope a hole opens up a little bit later. It's a decision you have to live by."

What goes into a decision to go three-wide?

"To go three-wide on the turn at The Meadowlands is tough," Lachance says. "Not too many go three-wide and are around to talk about it at the wire."

Campbell says, "If your horse feels strong and you're right up with your cover, you wait and follow him. As soon as the leader starts to get away from the first-over horse, you have to go three-wide. You watch the first-over. If he's live, you stay right on his helmet."

Manzi says, "You don't want to go three-wide too early, but if you've got a lot of horse, you just go."

O'Donnell tries to gauge the horse in front of him: "You go three-wide when you think the horse you're following isn't going to take you any farther. You can feel him coming back to you. Usually, that driver is trying to do something to keep his horse going."

If going three-wide can be poor strategy, how wise is it to fan four-wide or five-wide at the top of the lane?

Lachance says many times the driver doesn't have a choice: "It's not always up to you. Some horses, when they get tired, bear out. Sometimes you have to fan five-wide, six-wide or seven-wide."

O'Donnell says, "You don't want to fan wide if you can help it. But say there are three horses in the outer tier. You get a chain reaction if first-over is all done. Second-over goes three-wide, but has a mediocre horse. Third-over has to go four-wide. You have to fan wide."

Other times, you have to sit cool on the rail and hope an opening appears. Is this an exercise in patience?

"Staying patient is one of the hardest things to do at The Meadowlands," Campbell says. "I fan out too wide many times, three- or four-wide. It's one thing I do too much. I think everyone does. Your horse feels strong. You don't wait for the guy in front of you. But if you're three-wide with cover and go four-wide, it's hard to do. You lose so much ground when you're that wide."

Manzi says, "Being patient isn't difficult at all if you have enough horse."

Doesn't staying inside through the stretch raise the risk of never getting out?

"You can stay in with horses you know," O'Donnell says. "Sometimes you have to stay in. Other times, when you're a short price, you have to go out. People bet a lot of money. They want a roll for their money. They've got to get a chance."

Openings through the stretch may be too narrow or can disappear in two or three seconds. When do you go for it?
Campbell says, "If you're sitting third on the rail, the guy in the 2 hole has a tendency to go to his outside. Horses drift one way or the other when they're tired. If you see part of an opening, sometimes you take a shot, go in, and it'll open up. But any time you go up the rail, you risk getting shut off."

Manzi says, "That's just a decision you have to make. Sometimes you start through a hole and you can't get through. You have to grab a hold and pull back."

Lachance cautions, "When you're trying to go between horses, you have to make sure you have enough room before you go in. It's dangerous."

Are some horses reluctant to pass others on the inside?
O'Donnell says it's worth considering: "Yup, it does happen. It's just the way they're trained, I guess. When you train three colts at the same time, you train them moving up on the outside."

Campbell says, "Very few horses won't pass on the inside, especially on a mile track. On a ½-mile track, it's harder because the stretch is shorter. It takes a little while for a horse in front of you to bear out. It's natural for a horse to bear in on the turn and out on the straightaway."

Nearing the finish line, drivers frequently go to the whip. But the whip's effectiveness is being questioned more and more.
"I think the less you use it, the better off you are," Manzi says. "If you're working hard and doing the best you can, and somebody hits you with a whip, are you going to do better? Horses don't respond to getting beaten. They react to being scared. You hit once or twice and that's it."

Lachance says, "I like to use a whip, but at The Meadowlands, a driver should use the whip less. I do it less myself. It's nearly a quarter-mile stretch. If you hit him at the top of the stretch, it's too early. You have to line-drive more. I'm line-driving more than ever. If you want to get the job done, you have to use your hands more than the whip."

Campbell sees two sides of the issue: "The whip is used too much here, but our fans want us to use whips. You try not to use it when you can. Most horses don't go forward that much when you hit them. You try to hit the sulky or the saddle number or wheel disk. They'll respond to that noise. There are some horses who absolutely won't go unless you get into them real hard, and you're out there to win races."

O'Donnell says, "Seventy-five percent of the whipping is for the public and 25 percent for the horse. It depends entirely on the horse. Say you're moving like hell, you give him one slap. If he doesn't respond, then hit the wheel disk."

Where's the best spot to be at The Meadowlands?

O'Donnell: "Second-over. You can go wide. You've got the whole track in front of you."

Manzi: "In front. Second-over isn't always second-over. It can turn into first-over."

Lachance: "Second-over."

Campbell: "Everybody wants to be second-over at The Meadowlands. If you can be second-over, and first-over takes you right to the leader, you can't ask for anything more. The horse has to do the rest from that point."

And the worst spot?

Campbell: "Fourth- or fifth-over with no live cover."

O'Donnell: "Fifth on the rail at the three-quarters."

Manzi: "Being last at any point."

Lachance: "The 3 hole going to the half."

Speed

CHAPTER 5

Speed is almost always thought of in the context of early speed—the ability of a horse to leave, make the lead early, and attempt to go wire-to-wire. Usually, horses who consistently leave are easy to spot in their PPs: a string of 1's—and maybe a couple of 2's—at the first quarter call from bottom to top.

If there are two or more speed horses in a race, their respective first quarter fractions are crucial. Is one fast enough to make the lead? Or will there be a suicidal early speed duel?

Frequently, there is a more germane consideration: Is there a horse in the race who figures to be the lone speed?

The eighth race at Los Alamitos, March 21, 1992, featured a cast of 12 in a $6,000 claiming race.

2nd Half $2 Twin Tri
1 MILE PACE

$2 EXACTA
8th Race

CLAIMING. Purse $3,800. Claiming price $6,000. (Non-winners in last 6 starts). Allowed price: Amanda's Cadet, Rusty's Boy, $7,500.

LOS ALAMITOS MEDICAL CENTER

1 4-1 Red

Driver—TIM MAIER (97-16-19-8-.301). Trainer—D Maier (.325). Green, Orange and White

Supreme Fashion N (L)

B. h. 6, by Enterprise(F)—Sparkle Bret, by Knowing Bret
Own.—[illegible]—William [illegible]—Denise Maier, Cal
Br.—J W Hunter (NZ)
1:55^2, LA, '91 — No Record, '92 — 1:55^2, LA Lifetime

Lifetime— $22,801

1992	9	0	1	4	$2,560
1991	28	3	4	3	$15,[illegible]

Date-Trk	Temp/Dist		¼	½	¾	Fin	Odds		¼	½	¾	str	Fin	Driver PP	Cond/Purse	Final ¼	Time	First 3 Finishers	Comments
14Mar92-8LA	54	1	:29^3	:59^4	1:29	1:57^{2}ft	2½	LB	2^2	2^2	3^3	4 7¾	4 11¼	TMaier 4	C6000 Nw6 3000	:30	1:59^3	HappyPtronN,MightyBuster,KotrTobrukN	Outfinished 10
7Mar92-3LA	55	1	:29^3	1:00^3	1:30^1	2:01^{2}gd	3½	L	2 1½	2½	1 1½	1 1½	3^n	TMaier 3	C6000 Nw6 2500	:32^2	2:02^3	PortBuoyN,GandrooN,SuprmFshonN	Big move, hung 9
28Feb92-9LA	63	1	:30	:59^1	1:28^3	1:58^{4}ft	3	L	5 6½	4 4 ½o	2 ½o	2^{nk}	2^{nk}	T Maier 6	6000 2500	:30	1:58^4	IllicitAffr,SuprmFshonN,KotrTobrukN	Short lead str 8
20Feb92-6LA	55	1	:28^4	:59	1:29^1	1:58^{2}gd	*1	L	3^2	1 1½	[illegible]	[illegible]	3 1½	T Maier 1	6000 3000	:30^2	1:59^3	[illegible],PrinceJon,SuprmFshonN	Under pressure 11
14Feb92-8LA	52	1	:28^1	:59^4	1:29^1	1:58^{2}gd	20	L	1½o	3 3½	5^4	5 5¾	7 4¾	T Maier 9	6000 4000	:29^3	1:59^3	LadshipHoover,HappyTimeBoy,Quando-Quando	Wide early 10
7Feb92-12LA	55	1	:29	1:01^4	1:32	2:01^{3}gd	2½	L	6^{11}	6 7½o	5 5½o	5 7½	6 4½	T Maier 6	6000 3000	:29^3	2:02^4	HappyTimeBoy,NobleAlanN,[illegible]Tornado	Road trouble 6
1Feb92-5LA	54	1	:29^2	:58	1:28^3	1:58^{1}ft	4½	L	7^{11}	7^{12}	8 8½o	5 9½	3^1	T Maier 6	6000 3000	:28^2	1:59^2	MstrHolmsdN,HrmRuls,SprmFshonN	Closedwell late 7
25Jan92-10LA	62	1	:28^2	:59^4	1:30^2	1:59^{2}gd	5½	L	8^{14}	9 9½o	8 8½o	6^7	3^3	T Maier 6	6000 4500	:28^2	2:00	MstrHlmsdN,MghtyBstr,SprmFshnN	Closedwell late 10
24Jan92-6LA	60	1	:29^3	1:00^4	1:31	2:00^{3}gd	2½	L	2 1½	1 1½	1 1½	1½	4 2½	T Maier 2	6000 3000	:30	2:01	[illegible],MstrHlmsdN,MghtyBstr	Fought gamel; 8

Driver—RANDY EDMONDS (21-1-2-1-.116). Trainer—R Edmonds (.122). Gold-Black-White Lifetime— $19,741

2 6-1 White

Amanda's Cadet

B. g. 4, by Armbro Cadet—Sleek Amanda, by Charter Captain 1992 7 0 0 0 $582
Own.—Verna J Edmonds, Battle Creek, Mich 1991 28 4 1 4 $12,580
Br.—Edmonds Stables (Mich) 1:594, HP, '91 No Record, '92 1:594, HP Lifetime

14Mar92-6LA 55 1 :28 :573 1:28 1:591ft 28 79½ 88 63 31½ 52½ REdds2 Cd6000 Nw6 3000 :31 1:593 Midnight Sun, Calloway, Gundaroo N Clear late 11
7Mar92-1LA 55 1 :293 1:01 1:312 2:013gd 15 714 77o 76½o 54 44 REdds6 Cd6000 Nw6 2500 :30 2:022 TkngWht'sLeft,OhtobQuick,MstrMov 3wide last turn 7
25Feb92-6LA 58 1 :28 :574 1:27 1:571ft 91 1114 1112 1112 914 77½ R Edmonds8 6000 3000 :292 1:593 MnrtTorndo,ChlmrkFrdom,$PrtByN Passedtiredone: 12
22Feb92-2LA 62 1⅛ :301 1:01 2:02 2:304ft 17 611 611x 717be 725 724½ R Edmonds6 6000 2500 — 2:353 Land Force N, Rodelle N, Big Valley Costly break 7
5Feb92-7LA 55 1 :304 1:04 1:344 2:052sy 13 46½ 46½ 33x 614 6dis R Edmonds2 6000 2500 — 2:103 Entremettew, Gotabegusty, PacenClyde Heavy going 8
30Jan92-6LA 63 1 :273 :574 1:292 2:00 gd 8 816 811o o62½o 38½ 48½ R Edmonds7 6000 2500 :313 2:013 Entremttlr,MidnghtSun,ChlmrkFrdom Rough gaited 9
25Jan92-13LA 54 1 :293 1:00 1:30 1:584gd 50 714 712 77½ 717 714½ REdnds6 Nw2200 L6 5000 :301 2:013 GlenburnStarN,Syrtin'tsopete,ScotsWhHeN No factor 7
28Dec91-Nor 35 1 :282 :583 1:284 2:001gd 18 8 8 7o 68 612 R Edmonds8 15000 6300 — 2:023 Ballet Music, Anchor B Two, Orvieto N 9
21Dec91-Nor 35 1 :281 :583 1:28 2:00 gd 21 6 6 6o 52 41½ R Edmonds4 15000 4500 — 2:001 Papa's David G, Come On Todd, Sad To See You 9

Driver—STEVE WARRINGTON (195-42-36-21-.353). Trainer—R Tondreau (.830). Gray-Red-White Lifetime— $7,870

3 20-1 Blue

Rifleman *CB* (L)

Br. rig. 8, by Solid Fuel—Miss Deecee Ton, by Airliner 1992 3 0 0 0
Own.—John Prescott, Oceanside, Cal 1991 12 0 1 2 $952
Br.—Golden West Stables (Cal) No Record, '91 No Record, '92 1:572, LA Lifetime

14Mar92-6LA 55 1 :28 :573 1:28 1:591ft 48 LB 33½o 45o o97½o 1111 1111½ SWrrnt7 Cd6000 Nw6 3000 :32 2:012 Midnight Sun, Calloway, Gundaroo N Parked mile 11
6Mar92-9LA 53 1 :29 :592 1:283 1:574gd 78 LB 59 68½ 916 9dis 9dis S Warrington3 10000 5000 — 2:042 Crown The King A, Cam Hill, Top Liner N Off form 9
28Feb92-8LA 62 1 :272 :573 1:264 1:562ft 91 LB 55½ 78 1112 1121 1123½ F Sherren2 12000 6300 :314 2:01 Quiet As A Mouse,Danforth,BuyMeBack Needed start 11
21Feb92-LA 63 1 :293 :594 1:282 1:583gd 11½ 25 38½ 212 310 J Prescott5 Qua :301 2:003 HighlandWalkA,SmoothBayN,Riflemn Good tightener 7
23May91-7LA 64 1 :283 :582 1:291 1:583ft 17 LB 21½ x9 9dis 9dis 9dis J Anderson7 6000 1700 — — MisterSprksN,RynThomsN,JovesBond Scattered field 9
16May91-6LA 61 1 :282 :593 1:302 1:593ft 9½ LB 32½ 33 43 34 34½ M DiFrancoJr2 6000 1700 :293 2:002 Two Oceans, Battering Ram, Rifleman Never left rail 8
11May91-13LA 64 1 :29 1:003 1:31 1:583ft 10 LB 43 43½ x53½o 8dis 8dis M DiFrancoJr4 6000 1700 — — StarKingdomN,FlashBromacN,ReataJck Costly break 8
7May91-10LA 82 1 :274 :572 1:283 2:003ft 8 LB 78½ 86½ 74½ 86 85½ MDiFrancoJr10 6000 3400 :272 2:013 Certain Style N, Sky Friar, WindDriven Saved ground 12
30Apr91-6LA 60 1 :293 1:01 1:302 2:004ft 5½ LB 21½ 21½ 21½ 22 43½ M DiFrancoJr2 6000 1700 :304 2:012 Kittiwake LobeN,Manistique,CertainStyleN No excuse 7

Driver—JOE ANDERSON (183-21-28-11-.347). Trainer—M Silva (.800). Blue, White and Gold Lifetime— $73,863

4 8-1 Brown Green

Ready N Able *CB* (L)

Blk. g. 7, by Majestic Skipper—Voodoo Child, by Thorpe Hanover 1992 5 0 0 0
Own.—Mark A Silva, Buena Park, Cal 1991 43 3 6 5 $6,317
Br.—MaryBeatrice&WilliamMeyer (Cal) 1:582, PCD, '91 No Record, '92 1:552, LA Lifetime

11Mar92-6LA 55 1 :291 :594 1:29 2:003ft 59 LB 42o 33o 67½o 1215 1014½ M Silva6 6000 3000 :33 2:032 Pacen Clyde, ZippingAlong,HallviewSprit Wide early 12
28Feb92-6LA 65 1 :283 :582 1:281 1:582ft 63 LB 32½o 23o 87½ 1116 1117½ M Silva3 6000 3000 :321 2:024 Brittany Son, Leave The Bar,MidnightSun Tough trip 12
20Feb92-6LA 55 1 :284 :59 1:291 1:582gd 73 LB 54½o 65½ 109½ 1013 1115½ M Silva8 6000 3000 :313 2:022 Main TopicN,PrinceJon,SupremeFashionN Tough trip 11
15Feb92-8LA 55 1 :294 :594 1:30 2:011gd 16 L x1014 10dis 10dis 10dis 10dis M Silva2 6000 3000 — — Lord Moss N,OhtobeQuick,LandForceN Rough gaited 10
5Feb92-2LA 60 1 :283 1:004 1:322 2:042sy 5½ LB 714 611o x823 — — M Silva4 6000 2500 — — LndForceN,SubleJohn,GmblingKingN On move, broke 8
31Jan92-LA 60 1 :292 1:002 1:302 1:59 gd 13 13 11½ 23 59 M Silva5 Qua :302 2:004 Handiboy N, Garritross N, BHDominator Needed race 7
30Nov91-PcD 63 1 :28 :581 1:28 2:001ft 2 L 4 1 1 11½ 2nk M Silva7 Nw1350 L6 1800 :321 2:001 Union Fella, Ready N able, Rebecca Raven 10
27Nov91-PcD 32 1 :284 :583 1:291 2:011ft *6-5 L 3o 1 1 1nk 12½ M Silva4 Nw1350 L6 1520 :32 2:011 Ready N Able, Reata Buckwheat, Manson 10
20Nov91-PcD 64 1 :284 :574 1:272 1:584ft *2½ L 2o 1 1 11½ 21½ M King1 Nw1350 L6 1800 :314 1:581 Sweet Sid, Ready N Able, Sunset Sam 10

Driver—MARC AUBIN (211-23-24-32-.222). Trainer—M Aubin (.310). Blue-Red-White Lifetime— $78,103

5 9-2 Black

Sly Agent N — Bute, but no Lasix

B. g. 8, by Sapling(F)—Sly Dancer, by Sly Yankee 1992 5 0 0 0
Own.—Ernie G & Lily M Gomer, Upland, Cal 1991 30 4 4 1 $20,073
Br.—M J Bradford (NZ) 1:551, LA, '91 No Record, '92 1:551, LA Lifetime

14Mar92-6LA 55 1 :28 :573 1:28 1:591ft 3½ B 12½ 12 1hd 1hd 62½ MAubn1 Cd6000 Nw6 3000 :313 1:593 Midnight Sun, Calloway, Gundaroo N Blistering pace 11
4Mar92-LA 60 1 :294 1:004 1:313 2:013ft 13 13½ 1½ 1½ 1½ M Aubin1 Qua :30 2:013 Sly Agent N, Bestoranam N, GorsieStreetN Held safe 5
6Feb92-Haw 19 1 :291 :592 1:292 1:592ft 53 L 1 1 2 816 817½ M Aubin8 12000 5000 — 2:03 Pals Dancer, My Papa N, Good N Loyal 9
31Jan92-Haw 32 1 :293 1:00 1:30 1:593ft 29 L 2 4 7 9dis 9dis M Aubin1 12000 6700 — 2:051 Woodie Wright, Rafer N, Siouxland Reward 9
22Jan92-Haw 30 1 :29 :594 1:294 2:001sy 90 L 1 1 3 916 917 M Aubin7 10000 H 6000 — 2:033 Commander Van, Be Jewelled, C U Ater 9
15Jan92-Haw 9 1 :303 1:004 1:313 2:01 gd 22 L 1 2 4 9dis 9dis M Aubin3 10000 5600 — 2:072 Foxie Winner, Happy Mindale, Frank Henry N 9
7Jan92-Haw 34 1 :291 :594 1:31 2:002ft L 1 1 1 12 13½ M Aubin8 Qua :292 2:002 Sly Agent N, Little Strikes, Walts Rorty 9
19Oct91-7May 42 1 :284 :59 1:292 2:001ft 13 L 2o 2o 8o 812 813½ D Knox5 10000 6000 — 2:03 Ohlmstead, Commander Van, Little Buckeroo N 9
11Oct91-9May 61 1 :273 :57 1:274 1:591ft 15 L 2hdo 11o 2½ 44 64½ D Knox4 Nw4000 L6 6000 :323 2:003 Glenburn Star N, Ptr Li, Ravin Ruhr 8

Driver—ROBERT ROSEN (80-11-13-16-.264). Trainer—R Rosen (.280). Blue, Black and Gold Lifetime— $36,710

6 20-1 Yellow

Nojestic N (LF)

B. g. 6, by Majestic Chance—Noble Gay, by Bachelor Star(F) 1992 6 0 0 0 $175
Own.—Roslyn John & Jacqueline Levenson, San Jacinto, Cal 1991 15 6 1 1 $16,740
Br.—C C J Walker Estate (NZ) 1:581, LA, '91 No Record, '92 1:594, Sac Lifetime

14Mar92-8LA 54 1 :293 :594 1:29 1:572ft 25 B 78 98o o78½o 912 9dis RRosn11 Cd6000 Nw6 3000 — 2:024 HppyPtronN,MightyBustr,KolrTobrkN 3 wide backstr 10
7Mar92-1LA 55 1 :293 1:01 1:312 2:013gd 5½ B 34½ 33½ 32o 78 713½ TMaier1 Cd6000 Nw6 2500 :329 2:041 TkngWht'sLft,OhtobQuck,MstrMov Parked-no cover 7
28Feb92-7LA 55 1 :283 :583 1:291 1:582ft 5½ 813 88½o 84½o 88½ 814½ T Maier7 6000 2500 :324 2:024 Leave The Bar,RollOnBoogie,MidnightSun No excuse 9
5Feb92-5LA 58 1 :30 1:013 1:322 2:05 sy 13 52½o 11½ 12½ 12 45 T Maier8 6000 2500 :333 2:06 Mount Hutt, Shipps Course, PrinceJon Gave way late 8
31Jan92-1LA 65 1 :291 :594 1:293 1:594gd 2 1nko 11½ 11½ 1nk 77½ T Maier8 6000 2500 :313 2:011 LandForceN,DustyLaneHwk,PcenClyde Gave way late 8
24Jan92-8LA 57 1 :293 1:01 1:293 1:59 gd 2 B x48 11½ 24½x 9dis 9dis T Maier1 10000 5000 — — YankeeSkip,LandslipHanover,YarramaN Rank at start 9
17Jan92-Dmr 60 1 :303 1:022 1:323 2:013ft 3 22½ 21 1nk 1½ T Maier3 Qua :304 2:013 Nojestic N, Man Around Town, Joliette Sharp effort 5
7Jly91-8LA 77 1 :27 :583 1:281 1:58 ft *2 B 44½ 11½ 1hd 11½ 31½ J Anderson1 6000 2000 :301 1:581 Midnight Son, Kittiwake Lobell,NojesticN Faded late 8
23Jun91-4LA 75 1 :282 :58 1:28 1:58 ft *9-5 B 77½x 63½o 42½x 78 722½ J Anderson6 6000 2000 :34 2:022 RynThomsN,TyphoonGrz,IntrpdForc Broke, recoverd 9

Driver—ROSS CROGHAN (180-45-25-29-.382). Trainer—T Jacobson (.885). Blue-Black-White Lifetime— $39,140

7 6-1 Brown Gray

Zipping Along *CB* (L)

Br. g. 6, by Jambanger—Zody's B B, by Native Vic 1992 8 2 2 1 $6,182
Own.—James Lackey, Garden Grove, Cal 1991 9 1 1 2 $3,300
Br.—Isabel R Trapp (Cal) 2:001, CLO, '91 2:02, CLO, '92 1:563, LA Lifetime

11Mar92-6LA 55 1 :291 :594 1:29 2:003ft 5½ L 64½o 12 13 12 2nk J Lackey12 6000 3000 :313 2:003 Pacen Clyde, Zipping Along, Hallview Sprit Tuff loss 12
4Mar92-8LA 55 1 :29 :59 1:294 2:002ft 18 L 1214 1114 1110½ 99½ 99½ J Lackey8 6000 3000 :304 2:021 Big Valley, Main Topic N, SuableJohn Closedwell late 12
18Feb92-8Clo 41 1 :29 :594 1:302 2:012ft 3 3 1o 1nk 32 R Therres2 10000 4200 :312 2:014 Township Nugget, Sky Fortune Teller,ZippingAlong 9
6Feb92-6Clo 50 1 :301 1:012 1:31 2:012ft 15 5 6o 4o 44½ 48½ R Therres5 6000 3000 — 2:022 Tiger Pilot, Rooster Run, Patsys Bunny NW 9
25Jan92-6Clo 52 1 :32 1:022 1:323 2:03 gd 7½ 42½ 53½ 32 21½ 22½ S Shimo3 6000 3000 :304 2:033 Mandonny, Zipping Along, Hec With Walley 9
18Jan92-6Clo 41 1 :291 :594 1:301 2:011ft 4½ 711 32o 30o 810 813 S Shimo6 6000 3000 :331 2:034 P(3)Rooster Run, Mandonny, J R Jimmy 9
11Jan92-5Clo 43 1 :301 1:00 1:304 2:02 gd 2½ 31½ 11½ 11 12 12½ J Lackey8 6000 3000 :311 2:02 Zipping Along, Hec With Walley, Captain Cavalla N 9
1Jan92-3Clo 46 1 :282 1:001 1:294 2:002gd 43 43o 1nko 121 14 J Lackey [illegible] 6000 7400 — 2:003 Zipping Along, Mr Fabulous, Royal Supreme 9

8 10-1 Orange

Driver—DON MONKMAN JR (38-4-1-4-.156). Trainer—R Siaiams (.094). Red and Black Lifetime—$32,076

Gotabegusty CB (L) Br. g. 6, by Donell—Woman, by Dunne Hanover 1992 8 0 1 1 $1,4

Own.—Henry O'Shea, Santa Ana, Cal 1991 36 3 6 6 $11,5

Br.—Dorothy & Robert Bastian (Cal) 1:58, LA, '91 No Record, '92 1:584, SAC Lifetime

14Mar92-6LA	56	1	:28	:573	1:28	1:591ft	14	LB	811	79o	3nko	53	42¼	RSleth5	Cd6000 Nw6 3000	:313	1:593	Midnight Sun, Calloway, Gundaroo N	Rough trip
4Mar92-6LA	55	1	:29	:59	1:294	2:002ft	17	LB	1012o	98½o	o97½o	77¾	710¾	R Sleeth7	6000 3000	:312	2:022	Big Valley, Main Topic N, SaubleJohn	3wide last turn
22Feb92-2LA	62	1⅛	:301	1:01	2:02	2:304ft	9	LB	33	34¼	34¼	34¼	43¼	J Lackey1	6000 2500	—	2:312	Land Force N, Rodelle N, Big Valley	Winner too tuff
15Feb92-10LA	55	1	:283	1:00	1:301	2:002gd	11	LB	711	68o	48½o	49	59¾	T Kerr4	6000 3000	:304	2:022	HillviewSpirit,ChelemrkFreedom,BigVlley	Outfinished
8Feb92-6LA	59	1	:28	:583	1:291	1:594gd	4¾	LB	45¼	31¾	1½	44¼	811	T Kerr3	6000 3000	:314	2:01	Entremtllur,OktobQuick,MidnightSun	Big move, hung
5Feb92-7LA	56	1	:304	1:04	1:344	2:052sy	*¾	LB	12	12	1½	1nk	22¼	J Lackey4	6000 2500	:311	2:054	Entremetteur, Gotabegusty, Pacen Clyde	2nd best
31Jan92-1LA	66	1	:291	:594	1:293	1:594gd	4¼	LB	2nk	21½	32	31im	89¾	J Lackey1	6000 2500	:313	2:012	Land Force N, Dusty Lane Hawk,PacenClyde	Blocked
24Jan92-13LA	52	1	:291	1:00	1:301	2:004gd	4	LB	44¼	21o	1hdo	11	37	J Lackey3	6000 2500	:32	2:021	DustyLneHwk,MinTopicN,Gotbgusty	Parked-no cover
28Dec91-5Clo	48	1	:294	1:013	1:32	2:031gd	24		7	7	6	44	32	G A Abbott6	8000 3000	—	2:033	Lordover N, Clover Duke, Gotabegusty	

9 15-1 Brown

Driver—ROBERT SLEETH (55-8-5-6-.250). Trainer—D De John (.085). Purple and White Lifetime—$21,672

Sardar CB (L) B. g. 7, by Solid Fuel—Stonegate Danish, by Bret's Star 1992 4 0 0 0 $1(

Own.—Gilberto Herrera, Sacramento, Cal 1991 15 5 0 1 $8,4

Br.—Thomas&Claudia Westbrook (Cal) 1:57, LA, '91 No Record, '92 1:57, LA Lifetime

7Mar92-1LA	56	1	:293	1:01	1:312	2:013gd	3¼	LB	12¼	11¾	11¾	11¾	55¼	JAndrs7	Cd6000 Nw6 2500	:311	2:023	ThingWht'sLeft,OktobeQuick,MstrMov	Gave way late
26Feb92-6LA	65	1	:283	:582	1:281	1:582ft	27	LB	54¼	54o	34o	710	911¼	R Reeser10	6000 3000	:314	2:003	BrittnySun,LeveTheBr,MidnightSun	Parked-no cover
14Feb92-8LA	52	1	:281	:584	1:291	1:582gd	58	B	68½o	78¾	109	1014	1019¾	T Kerr4	8000 4500	:311	2:021	LndslipHnover,HppyTimeBoy,Qundo-Qundo	Out of it
25Jan92-10LA	62	1	:282	:594	1:302	1:592gd	43	LB	1010	1014	109¾	1014	918¾	T Ratchford7	8000 4500	:31	2:03	MistrHolmsdlN,MightyBustr,SuprmFshonN	No factor
23Jan92-LA	70	1	:311	1:022	1:332	2:042gd			5	510	33½o	24	34	T Ratchford8	Qua	:31	2:051	All In Good Time, C Speeder, Sardar	Used twice
6Jan91-10LA	66	1	:274	:571	1:27	1:564ft	9	LB	32¼	42¼	63	53	32¼	J Anderson10	8000 5200	:294	1:571	Mister Sparks N, Entremetteur, Sardar	Saved ground
31May91-7LA	62	1	:271	:553	1:253	1:554ft	14	LB	53¼	46	44o	819	8dis	M Aubin3	12000 3900	—	2:064	Exposition,SlyAgntN,SomthingAwsom	Shuffled back
23May91-5LA	64	1	:28	:573	1:28	1:564ft	5¼	LB	54½o	64	43¼	59¼	511¾	J Anderson9	10000 3300	:302	1:59	PasadenaPhantom,MikesBoy,MrcsBoy	Rough gaited
4May91-LA	75	1	:31	1:013	1:314	2:012ft			22	32¼	33	42¼	45	D Dejohn3	Qua	:30	2:022	Zobadias N, Cadiz N, BH Freedom	2nd over

10 6-1 Red/white

Driver—KEITH CLARK (52-5-4-3-.158). Trainer—K Clark (.172). Green and Gold Lifetime—$20,938

Roll On Boogie (L) B. g. 5, by Bogart—Greta, by Doctor Andy 1992 8 0 2 0 $1,5

Own.—Keith Clark (lessee), Calgary, Alta 1991 34 8 5 5 $17,7

Br.—Bill M Nielsen (Man-C) 1:581, CLG, '91 No Record, '92 1:581, CLG Lifetime

14Mar92-8LA	54	1	:293	:594	1:29	1:572ft	11	L	810	87¾	89½o	612	511¾	KClark5	Cd6000 Nw6 3000	:29	1:593	HppyPtronN,MightyBustr,KotrTobrukN	Road trouble
7Mar92-3LA	55	1	:293	1:003	1:301	2:012gd	2¼	L	32¼	1½	23¼	58	721	KClark2	Cd6000 Nw6 2500	:343	2:054	PortBuoyN,GundrooN,SupremeFshionN	Dueled, tired
29Feb92-6LA	58	1	:28	:574	1:27	1:571ft	11	L	916o	87o	65½o	69	54¼	K Clark8	6000 3000	:30	1:58	MinertTorndo,ChelemrkFrdom,‡PortBuoyN	Post hurt
20Feb92-7LA	56	1	:283	:583	1:291	1:593ft	40	L	57	58	53½o	53¼	2¾	K Clark9	6000 2500	:30	1:593	Leave The Bar,RollOnBoogie,MidnightSun	3 wide 3/4s
25Jan92-7Clg	30	1	:29	1:004	1:293	2:00 ft	5¾		78	74¼	86¼	78¾	68	B Clark7	5000 2400	:301	2:011	Call Your Bluff, Micks Storm, Igetthepicture	
18Jan92-5Clg	58	1	:281	:583	1:282	1:592ft	18		610	610	79	77¾	67¾	B Clark3	7000 2800	:303	2:004	Dynamo Wind, Laser Star, Time For Ralph	
10Jan92-10Clg	41	1	:283	:59	1:284	1:591ft	5		43	33	32o	611	613	B Clark1	6000 2600	:323	2:014	Dynamo Wind, In The Ditch, Nolan Ryan	
3Jan92-7Clg	27	1	:30	1:014	1:312	2:013ft	8		22	22¼	32	43	21	B Clark2	7000 2000	:30	2:014	Nile Captain, Roll On Boogie, Champagne Notice	
27Dec91-7Clg	43	1	:291	1:003	1:291	1:59 ft	16		35	53¼	67	511	310	B Clark2	7000 2800	:302	2:01	Pentax, Shyloh Goona, Roll On Boogie	

11 15-1 Blue/White

Driver—GABRIELE BERNAT (5-0-0-1-.066). Trainer—T Jacobson (.085). Maroon, Blue and White Lifetime—$120,283

Sky Explosive (L) Br. g. 8, by Tyrant—Keystone Whirlwind, by Keystone Ore 1992 1 0 0 0

Own.—Gabriele Bernat, Garden Grove, Cal 1991 9 0 1 0 $1,23

Br.—Sky West Farms (Alta) No Record, '91 No Record, '92 1:571, CLG Lifetime

14Mar92-6LA	56	1	:28	:573	1:28	1:591ft	70	LB	913	911	78	64	75¾	JLckey6	Cd6000 Nw6 3000	:311	2:001	Midnight Sun, Calloway, Gundaroo N	Appeared short
4Mar92-LA	60	1	:294	1:004	1:313	2:013ft			36	35	53	53	54¼	J Lackey2	Qua	:303	2:023	SlyAgentN,BestormN,GoisieStreetN	Good tightener
25Apr91-7LA	56	1	:283	:583	1:282	1:591ft	31	LB	11	2½o	43¼	89¼	811¾	G Bernat5	6000 1700	:322	2:012	GainingControl,ShahmanN,Mnistique	Burned up early
18Apr91-5LA	53	1	:293	:594	1:293	1:592ft	9¼	L	69¼	67½	77½	65	89¼	G Bernat6	6000 1700	:293	2:003	Hot Charger, Manistique, Rifleman	Saved ground
13Apr91-LA	70	1	:30	1:002	1:31	2:011ft			34	47	49	37	311½	G Bernat4	Qua	:304	2:032	KeystoneCousinN,GoldRun,SkyExplosiv	Under wraps
22Feb91-6Clo	46	1	:292	:591	1:31	2:004ft	*1		11	11	23¼	710	8dis	B Davis2	Nw1500 L6 2700	—	2:054	Bionic Raider N, Nazko Ambush, Game of Chance	
15Feb91-5Clo	58	1	:30	1:001	1:32	2:04 gd	6¾		711	711o	57o	77	64¾	B Davis6	Nw1500 L6 2700	:313	2:05	Sealover Hanover, Loose Buck, Bionic Raider N	
9Feb91-6Clo	59	1	:293	1:00	1:303	2:013ft	6¼		79	78	74	53¼	41¾	B Davis8	Nw1500 L6 2700	:30	2:02	Golden Kid, Tenor Hanover, Sealover Hanover	
2Feb91-7Clo	57	1	:284	:59	1:314	2:062gd	7¾		32	32	o1½o	32	2nk	B Davis8	Nw2300 L6 3400	:343	2:062	Bradner Garcon, Sky Explosive, Maintain Your Cool	

12 15-1 Up Blu/Yellow

Driver—TODD RATCHFORD (127-4-10-12-.106). Trainer—D Thornton (.122). Maroon, Gray and Black Lifetime—$5,305

Rusty's Boy CB B. g. 4, by Nimble Almahurst—Speedlane, by Tamerlane 1992 6 0 0 1 $4(

Own.—Eugene Thornton & Steve Takatama, Cal 1991 17 2 2 3 $4,81

Br.—E Thornton & S Takatama (Cal) 2:004, LA, '91 No Record, '92 2:004, LA Lifetime

12Mar92-10LA	52	1	:291	:59	1:273	1:581ft	75		711	68½o	712o	910	917	TRatchford6	Nw2r 3r 4500	:313	2:013	Riselittlehell,JimminAlmhurst,PAWrZone	Outfinished
4Mar92-10LA	53	1	:281	:574	1:272	1:59 ft	35		1014	1012	88o	810	98¼	TRatchford3	Nw2r 3r 4500	:311	2:001	Donna'sRowdy,EasyPlay,Riselittlehell	3wide last turn
26Feb92-3LA	66	1	:29	:58	1:282	1:591ft	12		77½	78¾	86½o	75¼	63¾	TRatchford4	Nw2r 3r 3000	:301	1:594	Vacationing,RoyalCavalloN,IndinScoutN	Road trouble
20Feb92-8LA	56	1	:292	:591	1:294	2:01 gd	43		811	68¾	64½o	53im	31¼	TRtcfrd6	Nw2r Mdn 4500	:302	2:011	Easy Play, Dundee's Curt, Rusty's Boy	Forced wide
13Feb92-8LA	55	1	:291	1:003	1:31	1:594gd	19		44¼	64¼	75	55¾	711½	RKblr2	Nw2r Mdn 4500	:301	2:02	Vacationing, Torme, Zaca Creek	Saved ground
8Feb92-5LA	59	1	:29	1:001	1:304	2:001gd	22	B	712	78¾	88½o	89¾	79¾	R Kuebler6	Nw2 Cd 3000	:30	2:02	Mariah's Mitzvah, Vacationing,AllThatRythm	4th over
31Jan92-LA	67	1	:304	1:021	1:32	2:002gd			812	714	·714o	610	623	R Kuebler6	Qua	:302	2:051	All That Rythm, Sintama, Some Me	Needed race
14Jly91-8LA	79	1	:282	:571	1:28	1:581ft	21		78¾	712	811	813	816¾	J Anderson4	Nw3 Cd 2200	:311	2:012	Mini Series, Billy Casino N,WarmWeather	Dull effort
10Jly91-9LA	67	1	:292	1:012	1:311	2:004ft	5	B	54¼	56	78¼	99¼	94¼	J Anderson2	Nw3 Cd 2200	:291	2:013	PGA Pro, Chuckie Joey, Billy CasinoN	Shuffled back

MEDICATION—SUPREME FASHION N(LASIX, BUTE), RIFLEMAN(LASIX, BUTE), READY N ABLE(LASIX, BUTE), SLY AGENT N(BUTE), NOJESTIC N(LASIX, BUTE), ZIPPING ALONG(LASIX), GOTABEGUSTY(LASIX, BUTE), SARDAR(LASIX, BUTE), ROLL ON BOOGIE(LASIX), SKY EXPLOSIVE(LASIX).

'LF)— FIRST TIME LASIX MEDICATION. UNCOUPLED—ZIPPING ALONG & SKY EXPLOSIVE. SECOND TIER—ROLL ON BOOGIE, SKY EXPLOSIVE & RUSTYS BO'

To begin our analysis of early speed, we immediately toss out the 10, 11 and 12 horses, who start in the second tier behind the 1, 2 and 3, respectively, at this 1-mile track. It's kind of tough making the lead with another horse in front of you.

Excluding the 5 horse, Sly Agent N, these were the number of times the nine other horses raced on the lead in their PPs, in post position order: Supreme Fashion N, 1-9; Amanda's Cadet, 0-9; Rifleman, 1-9; Ready N Able, 1-9; Nojestic N, 1-9; Zipping Along, 0-9; Gotabegusty, 1-9, and Sardar, 1-9.

The Rifleman and Ready N Able raced on the lead only in separate qualifiers. Supreme Fashion N's lone race on the lead—five starts back—was accomplished off a :28.1 first quarter while being parked. He yielded the lead in a :58.4 half, dropping back to third. Nojestic's lone race on the lead was with fractions of :29.1 and :59.4 on a track labeled "good." Just like Supreme Fashion N, Nojestic had not cleared the lead before the first quarter.

Gotabegutsy tried the front end on a sloppy track, posting fractions of :30.4 and 1:04. Sardar tried going wire-to-wire in his last start. He tired to fifth despite soft fractions of :29.3, 1:01 and 1:31.2 on a track rated "good."

This takes us to Sly Agent N.

A case can be made for him in many ways: class—he was the leading money-winner of this group last year; form—a definite Sign of Life in his last start, and drugs—he'd been racing on the diuretic Lasix at Hawthorne in Chicago, but raced much better in his last start without Lasix at Los Alamitos, and he was not using it tonight. Lasix is discussed further in the next chapter.

Sly's strongest attribute, though, was speed. He jumps off the page as the lone speed. Always check a race to see if there's one such horse in a race and handicap accordingly.

Sly Agent N was the type of horse with PPs at the quarter-pole of all 1's and 2's. Excluding two qualifiers (he made the lead in both), he had seven races, four on the lead with opening quarters of :29.1, :30.3, :29 and :28, and half miles in :59.4, 1:00.4, :58.4 and :57.3, respectively.

In two of his other three races, he bid for the lead but was parked out second in fractions of :27.3-:57, and :28.4-:59.

His lone race not on the lead was a horrible performance in the pocket, one of his many poor races at Hawthorne. Something was definitely wrong with Sly in his last four races there as he was crushed consistently.

His connections shipped him to California, where he qualified wire-to-wire in 2:01.3. Off that effort, he zoomed to the lead in :28 and :57.3. He led to the head of the stretch past a three-quarters in 1:28, then tired to finish sixth. But he was beaten by just 2½ lengths. After the first quarter he had led by 2½ lengths against four of the horses he was facing again tonight.

Yet another worthy note: He'd been bet down to 7-2 in his California debut as he dropped significantly in class from $12,000 claimers in Chicago.

Off a month layoff, this 9-year-old could only benefit from his first race back. With the lack of speed to challenge him tonight, he should have been a solid favorite. Instead, he went off at 3-1. A big overlay? No. However, there are times we'll bet a horse at 3-1 when we think we are getting value, that is, when we think a horse should be at much lower odds, say 3-2 or 8-5 here.

Sly made the lead easily, went wire-to-wire and paid $8.40.

The sixth race at Saratoga, October 1, 1992, cried for a closer.

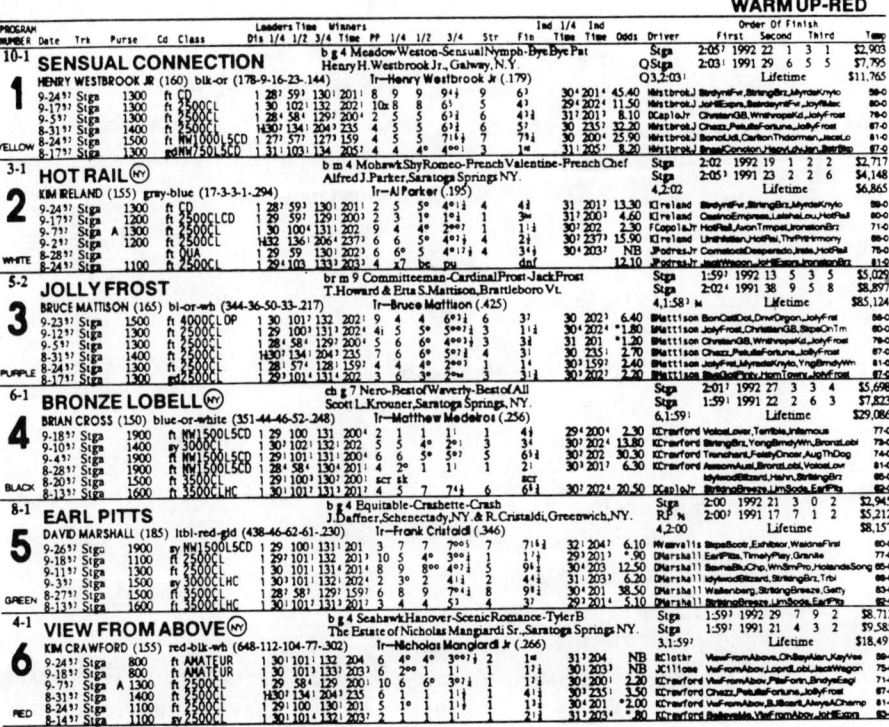

ONE MILE PACE
PURSE $1,500
THURSDAY, OCTOBER 1, 1992
TRIPLE & EXACTA

SIXTH RACE

THE AUTUMN GOLD PACING SERIES - 1ST LEG

WARM UP-RED

10-1 — 1 — SENSUAL CONNECTION (YELLOW)
b g 4 MeadowWeston-SensualNymph-ByeBye Pat
Henry H. Westbrook Jr., Galway, N.Y.
HENRY WESTBROOK JR (160) blk-or (178-9-16-23-.144) Tr—Henry Westbrook Jr (.179)
Stga 2:05^2 1992 22 1 3 1 $2,903
QStga 2:03^1 1991 29 6 5 5 $7,795
Q3,2:03^1 Lifetime $11,765

Date	Trk	Purse	Cd	Class	Dis	1/4	1/2	3/4	Time	PP	1/4	1/2	3/4	Str	Fin	Ind 1/4 Time	Ind Time	Odds	Driver	Order Of Finish (First, Second, Third)	Temp
9-24^92	Stga	1300	ft	CD	1	28^2	59^3	130^1	201^1	8	9	9	9^4¼	9	6^3	30^4	201^4	45.40	HWstbrokJ	BirdyntFvr,StringBrz,MyrdsKnyto	59-0
9-17^92	Stga	1300	ft	2500CL	1	30	102^1	132	202^1	10x	8	8	6^5	5	4^3	29^4	202^4	11.50	HWstbrokJ	JoHillExprs,BstrdaynFvr,JoyMac	80-0
9-5^92	Stga	1300	ft	2500CL	1	28^4	58^4	129^2	200^4	2	5	5	6^3½	6	4^3¾	31^2	201^3	8.10	DCaploJr	ChrstenGB,WnthropeKd,JolyFrost	78-0
8-31^92	Stga	1400	ft	2500CL	H	30^2	134^1	204^3	235	4	5	5	6^3½	6	5^2	30	235^2	32.20	HWstbrokJ	Chezz,PetullsFortune,JollyFrost	87-0
8-24^92	Stga	1500	ft	NW1000L5CD	1	27^2	57^2	127^3	159	4	5	5	7^16¾	7	7^9¾	30	200^4	25.90	HWstbrokJ	BonoUdi,CarltonThdorman,JacaLo	81-0
8-17^92	Stga	1300	gd	NW750L5CD	1	31^1	103^1	134	205^2	4	4	4°	4^oo1	3	1^ns	31^1	205^2	8.20	HWstbrokJ	[illegible]	87-0

3-1 — 2 — HOT RAIL (NY) (WHITE)
b m 4 MohawkShyRomeo-French Valentine-French Chef
Alfred J. Parker, Saratoga Springs NY.
KIM IRELAND (155) gray-blue (17-3-3-1-.294) Tr—Al Parker (.195)
Stga 2:02 1992 19 1 2 2 $2,717
Stga 2:05^3 1991 23 2 2 6 $4,148
4,2:02 Lifetime $6,865

Date	Trk	Purse	Cd	Class	Dis	1/4	1/2	3/4	Time	PP	1/4	1/2	3/4	Str	Fin	Ind 1/4 Time	Ind Time	Odds	Driver	Order Of Finish (First, Second, Third)	Temp
9-24^92	Stga	1300	ft	CD	1	28^2	59^3	130^1	201^1	2	5	5°	4^o1½	4	4½	31	201^2	13.30	KIreland	BirdyntFvr,StringBrz,MyrdsKnyto	59-0
9-17^92	Stga	1200	ft	2500CLCD	1	29	59^2	129^1	200^3	2	3	1°	1^o½	1	3^ns	31^2	200^3	4.60	KIreland	CasinoEmpress,LatshaLou,HotRail	80-0
9-7^92	Stga A	1300	ft	2500CL	1	30	100^4	131^1	202	9	4	4°	2^oo2	1	1^1½	30^2	202	2.30	FCopolaJr	HotRail,AvonTrmpet,IronstonBrz	71-0
9-2^92	Stga	1200	ft	2500CL	H	32	136^1	206^4	237^3	6	6	5°	4^o2¾	4	2½	30^2	237^3	15.90	KIreland	Unthrstan,HotRai,ThrPrtHrmony	80-0
8-28^92	Stga		ft	QUA	1	29	59	130^1	202^3	6	6°	5	4^o12¾	4	3^4½	30^4	203^2	NB	JPodresJr	ComstockDesperado,Irsta,HotRail	75-0
8-24^92	Stga	1100	ft	2500CL	1	29^4	103	133^3	203^3	4	x7	be	pu		dnf			12.10	JPodresJr	JackWagon,JoHillExprs,IronstonBrz	81-0

5-2 — 3 — JOLLY FROST (PURPLE)
br m 9 Committeeman-CardinalFrost-JackFrost
T.Howard & Etta S.Mattison, Brattleboro Vt.
BRUCE MATTISON (165) bl-or-wh (344-36-50-33-.217) Tr—Bruce Mattison (.425)
Stga 1:59^2 1992 13 5 3 5 $5,029
Stga 2:02^4 1991 38 9 5 8 $8,897
4,1:58^3 M Lifetime $85,124

Date	Trk	Purse	Cd	Class	Dis	1/4	1/2	3/4	Time	PP	1/4	1/2	3/4	Str	Fin	Ind 1/4 Time	Ind Time	Odds	Driver	Order Of Finish (First, Second, Third)	Temp
9-23^92	Stga	1500	ft	4000CLOP	1	30	101^2	132	202^1	9	4	4	6^o3½	6	3^2	30	202^3	6.40	BMattison	BonCatDol,DrwrOrgon,JolyFrst	58-0
9-12^92	Stga	1300	ft	2500CL	1	29	100^3	131^3	202^4	4i	5	5°	5^oo2½	3	1^1½	30^4	202^4	*1.80	BMattison	JolyFrost,ChristianGB,StpsOnTm	80-0
9-5^92	Stga	1300	ft	2500CL	1	28^4	58^4	129^2	200^4	5	6	6°	4^oo3½	3	3¾	31	201	*1.20	BMattison	ChrstenGB,WnthropeKd,JolyFrost	78-0
8-31^92	Stga	1400	ft	2500CL	H	30^2	134^1	204^3	235	7	6	6°	5^o2½	4	3^1	30	235^1	2.70	BMattison	Chezz,PetullsFortune,JollyFrost	87-0
8-24^92	Stga	1300	ft	2500CL	1	28^1	57^4	128^1	159^2	4	4	4°	2^oo1	1	1^4	30^3	159^2	2.40	BMattison	JolyFrst,MyrdsKnyto,YngBrndyWn	81-0
8-17^92	Stga	1300	gd	2500CL	1	29^2	101^4	131^4	202	3	6	3°	2^ons	3	3^1½	30^3	202^2	2.20	BMattison	[illegible],HomTowny,JolyFrost	87-0

6-1 — 4 — BRONZE LOBELL (NY) (BLACK)
ch g 7 Nero-BestofWaverly-BestofAll
Scott L.Krouner, Saratoga Springs, NY.
BRIAN CROSS (150) blue-or-white (351-44-46-52-.248) Tr—Matthew Medeiros (.256)
Stga 2:01^2 1992 27 3 3 4 $5,698
Stga 1:59^1 1991 22 2 6 3 $7,823
6,1:59^1 Lifetime $29,086

Date	Trk	Purse	Cd	Class	Dis	1/4	1/2	3/4	Time	PP	1/4	1/2	3/4	Str	Fin	Ind 1/4 Time	Ind Time	Odds	Driver	Order Of Finish (First, Second, Third)	Temp
9-18^92	Stga	1900	ft	NW1500L5CD	1	29	100	131	200^4	2	1	1	1^1	1	4½	29^4	200^4	2.30	KCrawford	VoicelLover,Terrible,Infamous	77-0
9-10^92	Stga	1400	sy	3000CL	1	30^2	102^1	132^1	202	5	5	4°	2^o1	3	3^4	30^2	202^4	13.80	KCrawford	StringBrz,YongBrndyWn,BronzLobl	79-0
9-4^92	Stga	1900	ft	NW1500L5CD	1	29^1	101^1	131^1	200^4	6	6	5°	5^o2	5	6^5¾	30^2	202	30.30	KCrawford	Trenchant,FeistyOnoer,AugThDog	74-0
8-28^92	Stga	1900	ft	NW1500L5CD	1	28^4	58^4	130^4	201^1	4	2°	1	1^1	1	2^1	30^3	201^2	6.30	KCrawford	AwsomAusl,BronzLobl,VoicelLovr	81-0
8-20^92	Stga	1500	ft	3500CL	1	29^1	100^3	130^2	200^1	scr	sk				SCR					IdylwodBlizard,Hahn,StringBrz	65-0
8-13^92	Stga	1600	ft	3500CLHC	1	30^1	101^2	131^3	201^2	4	5	7	7^4½	6	6^5¾	30^2	202^4	20.50	DCaploJr	StrikingBreeze,UmSoda,EarlPts	62-0

8-1 — 5 — EARL PITTS (GREEN)
b g 4 Equitable-Crashette-Crash
J.Daffner, Schenectady, NY. & R. Cristaldi, Greenwich, NY.
DAVID MARSHALL (185) ltbl-red-gld (438-46-62-61-.230) Tr—Frank Cristaldi (.346)
Stga 2:00 1992 21 3 0 2 $2,945
RP ⅝ 2:00^2 1991 17 7 1 2 $5,212
4,2:00 Lifetime $8,157

Date	Trk	Purse	Cd	Class	Dis	1/4	1/2	3/4	Time	PP	1/4	1/2	3/4	Str	Fin	Ind 1/4 Time	Ind Time	Odds	Driver	Order Of Finish (First, Second, Third)	Temp
9-26^92	Stga	1900	sy	NW1500L5CD	1	29	100^1	131^1	201	3	7	7	7^oo5	7	7^16¾	32^1	204^2	6.10	HWasvalls	StpsBootr,Exhibitor,WaldnsFirst	60-0
9-18^92	Stga	1100	ft	2500CL	1	29^2	101^1	132	201^3	10	5	4°	3^oo½	1	1^2¼	29^3	201^3	*.90	DMarshall	EarlPtts,TimelyPlay,Granite	77-0
9-11^92	Stga	1300	ft	2500CL	1	30	101^1	131^4	201^4	8	9	8^oo	4^o2½	5	9^6½	30^4	203	12.50	DMarshall	SwnaBluChp,WnSmPro,HolandsSong	65-0
9-3^92	Stga	1500	sy	3000CLHC	1	30^3	101^1	132^1	202^4	2	3°	2	4^1½	2	4^4½	31^1	203^3	6.20	DMarshall	IdylwodBlizard,StrkngBrz,Trbl	68-0
8-27^92	Stga	1500	ft	3500CL	1	28^2	58^2	129^2	159^2	6	8	9	7^o4½	8	9^8½	30^4	201	38.50	DMarshall	Wallenberg,StrikingBreeze,Getty	83-0
8-13^92	Stga	1600	ft	3500CLHC	1	30^1	101^2	131^3	201^2	3	4	4	5^3	4	3^2	29^3	201^4	5.10	DMarshall	StrikingBreeze,UmSoda,EarlPts	62-0

4-1 — 6 — VIEW FROM ABOVE (NY) (RED)
b g 4 SeahawkHanover-ScenicRomance-TylerB
The Estate of Nicholas Mangiardi Sr., Saratoga Springs NY.
KIM CRAWFORD (155) red-blk-wh (648-112-104-77-.302) Tr—Nicholas Mangiardi Jr (.266)
Stga 1:59^3 1992 29 7 9 2 $8,712
Stga 1:59^2 1991 21 4 3 2 $9,585
3,1:59^2 Lifetime $18,491

Date	Trk	Purse	Cd	Class	Dis	1/4	1/2	3/4	Time	PP	1/4	1/2	3/4	Str	Fin	Ind 1/4 Time	Ind Time	Odds	Driver	Order Of Finish (First, Second, Third)	Temp
9-24^92	Stga	800	ft	AMATEUR	1	30^1	101^1	132	204	6	4°	4°	3^oo2½	2	1^ns	31^3	204	NB	RClothr	ViewFromAbove,OhSayAlan,KayVee	89-0
9-18^92	Stga	800	ft	AMATEUR	1	30	101^3	133^2	203^3	6	2^oo	1	1^1	1	1^2½	30^1	203^3	NB	JCillone	VwFromAbov,LoprdLobl,JackWagon	75-0
9-7^92	Stga A	1300	ft	2500CL	1	29	58^4	129	200^1	10	6	6°	3^o2½	1	1^2½	30^4	200^1	2.20	KCrawford	VwFromAbov,PlsForn,BndysEagl	71-0
8-31^92	Stga	1400	ft	2500CL	H	30^2	134^1	204^3	235	6	1	1	1^1½	1	4^1½	30^3	235^1	3.50	KCrawford	Chezz,PetullsFortune,JollyFrost	87-0
8-24^92	Stga	1100	ft	2500CL	1	29^1	100	130^1	201	5	1°	1	1^1½	1	1^3½	30^4	201	*2.00	KCrawford	VwFromAbov,BJBoard,AlwysAChamp	81-0
8-14^92	Stga	1100	sy	2500CL	1	30^1	101^4	132^1	203^2	2	1	1	1^1	1	2^1½	31^3	203^4	*.80	KCrawford	Bellevable,VwFromAbov,JoHillExprs	83-0

12-1	**PETULI'S FORTUNE**				b h 7 FortuneTeller-LacyJane-OilBurner											PPk ⅝	1:58^1 1992 22 5 5 2			$6,715
					T.M.Rooney, R.E.Dufresne & E.S.Thompson, Vt.											PPk ⅝	1:56 1991 17 5 2 2			$9,693
7	TODD ROONEY (155) grn-go-wh (27-3-9-1-.309)				Tr—Todd Rooney (.312)											6,1:56 ⅝	Lifetime			$70,301
	9-24^{92}	Stga		1300	ft CD	1 28^7	59^3	130^1	201^1	3	6	6°	6° 7½	6	9^4	31^2 202	4.80	TRooney	StrdyntFvr,StringBrz,MyrdeKnyto	89-0
	9-7^{92}	Stga	A	1300	ft 2500CL	1 29	58^4	129	200^1	4	2°	1°	1 1½	2	2 7½	31^3 200^3	•1.20	TRooney	ViewFromAbov,PtlsFortn,BndysEagl	71-0
	8-31^{92}	Stga		1400	ft 2500CL	H30^2	134^1	204^3	235	5	2	2	2 1½	2	2ns	30^1 235	6.60	TRooney	Chazz,PetulisFortune,JollyFrost	67-0
	8-24^{92}	Stga		1300	ft 2500CL	1 28^1	57^4	128^1	159^2	7	6	6	6 6½	8	7 3½	31^4 201^1	11.60	TRooney	JollyFrst,MyradeKnyto,YngBrndyWn	81-0
	8-14^{92}	Stga		1300	sy 2500CL	1 29^3	102	132^2	203^1	5	2	2	3 1½	2	2 1½	30^4 203^2	•1.10	TRooney	JoyfMac,PtlsFortn,YongBrandyWn	83-0
BROWN	8-3^{92}	Stga		1300	ft 2500CL	1 27^1	57^2	128^2	159^4	7	4	4	2° ½	1	1½	31^1 159^4	10.50	TRooney	PetulisFortune,Dongwey,Irate	80-0
8-1	**YOUNG BRANDY WINE**				b g 6 Charo'sSkipper-ArmbroBabs-SteadyStar											Stga	2:00^4 1992 22 4 4 3			$4,931
					Bruce Hamilton,Albany NY.											Stga	2:00^2 1991 31 10 6 3			$10,527
8	MARK WHITCROFT (175) grn-wh-gold (95-6-7-12-.146)				Tr—Scott Hamilton (.381)											5,2:00^2	Lifetime			$22,427
	9-25^{92}	Stga		1300	ft CD	1 28^3	59^4	130^3	201^1	6	1°	1	1 1	1	2 1½	31 201^3	4.10	JStarkJr	ShesGotPlnty,YngBrndyWn,LshaLo	58-0
	9-18^{92}	VDM		1400	ft 3000CL	1 27	58^4	129	200^2	6	1°	1	2 1½	2½	5 5½	32^1 201^2	•1.60	JGregory	StringsBet,BabyBn,TrorUnleshd	78-0
	9-10^{92}	Stga		1400	sy 3000CL	1 30^2	102^1	132^1	202	1	1	1	1 1	1	2ns	29^4 202	4.10	MWhtcroft	StringBrz,YongBrandyWn,BronzLobl	73-0
	8-31^{92}	Stga		1100	ft 2500CL	1 30	59^4	130^3	201^3	5	3°	1°	1 1	1	1 2	31 201^3	•1.00	JStarkJr	YngBrndyWn,WhosYrThdr,ImetnBrz	67-0
	8-24^{92}	Stga		1300	ft 2500CL	1 28^1	57^4	128^1	159^2	3	2°	2°	3° 2½	4	3 4	31^2 200^1	3.60	JStarkJr	JollyFrst,MyrdeKnyto,YngBrandyWn	81-0
GRAY	8-14^{92}	Stga		1300	sy 2500CL	1 29^3	102	132^2	203^1	2	3	3°	2° 1½	3	3 3	31^1 203^4	3.30	DMarshall	JoyfMac,PtlsFortn,YongBrandyWn	83-0
12-1	**LIME SODA**				b g 8 LimeTime-J.M.Tanya-AdiosRonnie											Stga	2:00 1992 25 4 4 2			$4,572
					G.W.Maring, F.J.Criscione & S.A.Giuliano, NY.											Stga	2:00^1 1991 41 4 2 12			$6,834
9	FRANK COPPOLA JR (150) ltbl-wh-br (712-126-101-103-.304)				Tr—Salvatore Giuliano (.105)											5,1:59^1 M	Lifetime			$39,091
	9-24^{92}	Stga		1300	ft CD	1 28^2	59^3	130^1	201^1	7	8	8	8 3½	7	8 4	31^1 202	19.30	BMattison	StrdyntFvr,StringBrz,MyrdeKnyto	59-0
	9-10^{92}	Stga		1400	sy 3000CL	1 30^2	102^1	132^1	202	7	7	7	7 3½	7	7 16	31^1 205^1	30.00	GKamal	StringBrz,YongBrndyWn,BronzLobl	73-0
	9-3^{92}	Stga		1500	sy 3000CLHC	1 30^3	101^1	132^1	202^4	1	2	3	2° ½	4	8 8	32 204^2	4.20	GKamal	IdylwoodBlizzard,StrikingBrz,Trbl	88-0
	8-27^{92}	Stga		1500	ft 3500CL	1 28^2	58^2	129^2	159^2	9	5	4°	2° 1	3	6 6	31 200^3	6.30	GKamal	Wallenberg,StrikingBreeze,Getty	83-0
	8-13^{92}	Stga		1600	ft 3500CLHC	1 30^1	101^2	131^3	201^2	5	3	3°	2° ½	1	2 1½	29^4 201^3	10.00	GKamal	StrikingBreeze,LimSoda,EarlPits	82-0
BLUE	8-6^{92}	Stga		1100	ft 2500CL	1 28^4	100^1	129^3	200	2	4	2°	1° 1	1	1 1½	30^2 200	2.40	GKamal	LimSoda,Chairman,FlatironCofine	80-0

In this unusual series for bottom-level claimers—$2,500-$3,000—Bronze Lobell, View From Above, Young Brandywine and, to a lesser extent, Petuli's Fortune, showed early speed from the 4, 6, 8 and 7 posts, respectively. Young Brandywine appeared to be the quickest leaver, but he had the 8 post and was certainly going to be pushed early by one, two or three of the other speed horses inside of him.

That meant a closer had to win. The leading candidates were Hot Rail from the 2 post, Jolly Frost from the 3, and Earl Pitts from the 5.

Hot Rail was 1-for-19 in '92 and 3-for-42 the last two years. He'd go off at 7-2. Pass.

Jolly Frost was clearly the one to beat, dropping down from a third-place finish in a $4,000 claimer. He'd been first twice and third four times in his last six races. He'd go off at 7-2, a modest overlay.

Earl Pitts also made a legitimate drop from a conditional race, Non-Winners of $1,500 Last 5, where he was seventh by 16¾ lengths from the 7 post, on a sloppy track.

Let's check out his PPs:

- August 13—$3,500 claimer—Third by 2 at 5-1 from the 3 post.
- August 27—$3,500 claimer—Ninth by 8¼ at 38-1 from the 6 post.

- September 3—$3,000 claimer—Fourth by 4¼ at 6-1 from the 2 post. On a sloppy track.
- September 11—$2,500 claimer—Ninth by 6¼ at 12-1 from the 8 post.
- September 18—$2,500 claimer—First by 7½ at 4-5 from the 10 post.
- September 26—NW $1,500 Last 5—As described above: a distant seventh at 6-1 from the 3 post. On a sloppy track.

What have we got from these PPs?

Two were on sloppy tracks. Two others were in higher company. The PPs with the most relevance to tonight's race are the two races in $2,500 company on a fast track: a forgivable poor finish from the 8 post, and a 7½-length win at 4-5. He'd go off at 9-2, benefit from a prolonged battle for the lead, and win, paying $11.60.

Trips and Ships

CHAPTER 6

Trip handicapping, a term in vogue lately, has been cited by thoroughbred handicappers as though it were a breakthrough. Harness handicappers know better. They've used trip handicapping 10 races a night for years.

For a variety of reasons, harness handicapping offers exceedingly detailed trip analysis for those who want to spend the time. Unlike thoroughbreds, harnessbreds race almost exclusively at the same distance, 1 mile, and on the same surface, dirt, rather than dirt and turf. Routinely, there are the same number of starters, eight or 10 depending on the size of the track. They also routinely race once a week, many times on the same night. That's important because there is no substitute for seeing races live—on-track or off—rather than handicapping solely from the program.

If you like to hit the track Saturday nights, you'll probably see many of the horses who raced the previous Saturday, many times in the same class with mostly the same opponents. Watching races, live or via replays, gives you a strong sense of the dynamics of the race: which horses were boxed in with no chance; which got used hard going first-over; which frontrunner had soft fractions and which had fast demanding ones under pressure; which had a poor post and was given a soft, unaggressive trip; which needed a tightener and got one.

Excuses are cheap. Our task is identifying the legitimate ones.

In any eight-horse race on a ½-mile track, anywhere from one to four will have a good trip, meaning the race's dynamics unfolded in their favor. Let's say four did. Only one wins, obviously. The other three who had good trips weren't good enough to take advantage. The other four in the field with poor trips had, realistically, little or no opportunity to win.

These are observations we carry into each of the eight horses' next starts. Taking notes or just watching replays will do nothing but help. The more time you put in, the better you'll handicap.

Many good and bad trips stand out. Examples:

• You bet the 3 horse who doesn't leave and is fifth at the quarter pole. Another horse moves up on the outside, followed by a second horse on the outside. The 3 never gets a chance to pull out, remaining boxed in the rest of the way. Bad trip? No trip. The horse had no chance of winning. Unless the horse needed a tightener, disregard this trip.

• You bet the 6 horse, who races from off the pace. He pulls out on the paddock turn—the second of four turns on a ½-mile track—and tries to flush another horse for cover. There are no takers, so he must continue his move forward by going first over and engaging the leader. But, with no pressure from a horse on the outside, the leader was allowed to set a slow pace, let's say 1:02.3 for horses who normally would go a half in 1:00. The leader uses the soft first half to roar home in :59 flat. Your 6 can't keep up on the outside and tires, finishing fourth. The trip? A highly difficult one. The dynamics of the race went against him: first-over with no cover; extremely slow first half, and a rocket-fast second half. Evaluate the 6's trip as a hard one, and do likewise for the horses that were behind him. They may be capable of a :59 second half, but to gain on the leader they'd have to go :58 or faster to make up lengths. Actually, a horse in that type of situation may become an overlay in his next start. Say we bet the 7 horse who was last going to the half, seventh at the three-quarters, and fourth at the finish, beaten by three lengths. He was six lengths behind the leader at the half and made up three lengths. Since the leader went the last half in :59, the 7 got his last half in a sparkling :58.2. Then add in the factor that he raced on the outside most of the second half. If he went three- or four-wide doing so, the more impressive the performance. When this horse races again, many bettors may evaluate his last start as a poor one. He deserves better. While reaching this conclusion, you'll get better: better odds. An overlay.

• Another race. You bet the 1 horse, a frontrunner, who gets no pressure early in his race. He sets slow or moderate fractions, yet doesn't last in the stretch and loses, finishing second by a neck. The trip? Excellent. The effort? Horrible. If a speed horse from the best post can't win off slow fractions and no pressure, how will he do when things don't go his way? Avoid him; he may be an underlay after finishing a close second.

Analysis of each horse's PPs makes it possible to get a feel of how tonight's race will develop. We're not talking clairvoyance here, rather reasonable opinions on how a race sets up—its dynamics. Much of it is common sense: Does a frontrunner have one or two early speed horses to outquick? Are any of the favorites compromised by a bad post position or a bad driver switch? Did a come-from-behind horse have virtually no chance in his last start because of the fractions of the race?

Then there are tougher questions. If a horse is likely to sit in mid-pack for the first half mile or so, is he likely to get live (good) cover from a contender in front of him? Could he, in turn, be good cover for a contender behind him? This doesn't mean you'll know exactly who's going to go first and second over every race, but considering the possibilities can't hurt.

Some horses are grinders. They don't have a quick burst of speed, but they can gradually wear down horses in front of them. This type of horse is more likely to do well going first over. Other horses have one strong kick. Are they going to be compromised by a bad post, which could force them three- or four-wide on the final turn? Driver evaluations figure here, too. Most important, if a late-run horse needs a good trip to win, then you want to have an aggressive driver who won't sit the rail for long, perhaps too long. If there's a driver switch on this type of horse, note if it's substantial, good or bad.

Great Trips

Casino Empress was the 4 horse in a $2,500 claimer for fillies and mares at Saratoga, September 17, 1992.

ONE MILE PACE
PURSE $1,200
THURSDAY, SEPTEMBER 17, 1997
FIRST HALF MID DOUBLE
&
EXACTA

SEVENTH RACE

FILLIES & MARES
CLAIMING ALLOWANCE $2500

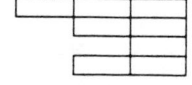

WARM UP-BROWN

10-1 SNOOKY K (NY) — 1
blk m 4 Jamuga-HelloCherri-SayHello
Gregory C.Decker, NY & Linda A.Goldstein, Conn.
GREGORY DECKER (165) ltblu-red-white (41-3-2-7-.157) Tr—Gregory Decker (.211)
Stga 2:03^1 1992 28 1 1 3 $2,690
Stga 2:04 1991 16 1 1 1 $1,965
4,2:03^1 Lifetime $6,942
3,625 YELLOW

Date	Trk	Purse	Cd	Class	Dis	1/4	1/2	3/4	Winners Time	PP	1/4	1/2	3/4	Str	Fin	Ind 1/4 Time	Ind Time	Odds	Driver	Order Of Finish: First, Second, Third	Temp
9-9^{97}	Stga	1300	ft	2500CL	1	30	102	132^4	203^3	5	5	6°	6°^{7}½	4	4½	30^3	203^4	59.50	GDecker	FlyingGravel,Irat,Ulnthfatien	77-0
9-5^{97}	Stga	1300	ft	2500CL	1	28^4	58^4	129^2	200^4	6	7	7	7°^{4}½	7	5^{5}½	31^3	202	37.50	GDecker	ChristianGB,WnthropeKd,JollyFrost	78-0
8-31^{97}	Stga	1400	ft	2500CL	1H	30^2	134^1	204^3	235	x2	7	7	7dis	7	7dis			25.20	GDecker	Chezz,PetulleFortune,JollyFrost	67-0
8-24^{97}	Stga	1100	ft	2500CL	1	30^3	102	132^1	203^1	4	1	1	1^1	1	1^{2}½	31	203^1	2.40	GDecker	SnookyK,DownwynLloyd,GrantsSong	81-0
8-14^{97}	Stga	1100	sy	2500CL	1	30^1	101^4	132^1	203^2	8	3	4	3^2	3x	x4x^{11}½	33	205^3	27.80	GDecker	BelieveMe,ViewFromAbov,JoHiExprs	63-0
8-10^{97}	Stga	1100	ft	2500CL	1	29	59	130^2	202^1	5	2°	2°	2°^{1}	2	4^{2}½	32	202^3	3.30	GDecker	KayV,IronstonBrz,ThrPartHarmony	77-0
8-5^{97}	Stga	1100	ft	2500CL	1	29^1	100^2	130^4	202^1	6	5	7	6°^{5}½	4	3^{5}½	31^2	203^1	10.40	GDecker	BadBadDad,ThrPartHarmony,SnookyK	72-0

9-2 HOT RAIL (NY) — 2
b m 4 MohawkShyRomeo-French Valentine-French Chef
Alfred J.Parker,Saratoga Springs NY.
KIM IRELAND (155) gray-blue (12-2-3-0-.306) Tr—Al Parker (.199)
Stga 2:02 1992 17 1 2 1 $2,469
Stga 2:05^3 1991 23 2 2 6 $4,148
4,2:02 Lifetime $6,617
3,625 WHITE

Date	Trk	Purse	Cd	Class	Dis	1/4	1/2	3/4	Winners Time	PP	1/4	1/2	3/4	Str	Fin	Ind 1/4 Time	Ind Time	Odds	Driver	Order Of Finish: First, Second, Third	Temp
9-7^{97}	Stga	A 1300	ft	2500CL	1	30	100^4	131^1	202	9	4	4°	2°°^{2}	1	1^{1}½	30^2	202	2.30	FCopolaJr	HotRail,AvonTrmpet,IronstonBrz	71-0
9-2^{97}	Stga	1200	ft	2500CL	1H	32	136^1	206^4	237^3	6	6	5°	4°^{2}½	4	2½	30^2	237^3	15.90	KIreland	Ulnthfatien,HotRail,ThrPrtHrmony	88-0
8-28^{97}	Stga		ft	QUA	1	29	59	130^1	202^3	6	6°	5	4°^{12}½	4	3^{4}½	30^4	203^2	NB	JPodresJr	ComstockDesperado,Irate,HotRail	75-0
8-24^{97}	Stga	1100	ft	2500CL	1	29^4	103	133^3	203^3	4	x7	be	pu		dnf			12.10	JPodresJr	JackWagon,JoHiExprs,IronstonBrz	81-0
8-15^{97}	Stga		gd	QUA	1	30^1	101^3	132^2	202^3	3	2	2	2^5	2	2^{4}½	30	203^2	NB	JPodresJr	JimsJet,HotRail,RomigeFlight	60-0
8-12^{97}	Stga		ft	QUA	1	32	103	132^4	203	7	6x	7	7dis	7	7dis			NB	JPodresJr	YoungBillotroubie,HillRulr,AllVies	67-0
7-29^{97}	Stga	1300	ft	2500CL	1	29^2	101	130^3	201^1	scr	lm				scr					WinSumPro,WhosYourThundr,Rghted	88-0

3-1 KAY VEE (NY) — 3
b m 8 Holland-SocialDirector-Calcaneus
Patricia O'Brien, Saratoga Springs, N.Y.
BRUCE MATTISON (165) bl-or-wh (317-33-47-29-.217) Tr—John Nazarian (.364)
Stga 2:02^1 1992 15 2 3 1 $2,430
Stga 2:02^1 1991 24 1 2 3 $1,930
7,2:02^1 Lifetime $22,377
3,000 PURPLE

Date	Trk	Purse	Cd	Class	Dis	1/4	1/2	3/4	Winners Time	PP	1/4	1/2	3/4	Str	Fin	Ind 1/4 Time	Ind Time	Odds	Driver	Order Of Finish: First, Second, Third	Temp
9-5^{97}	Stga	1200	ft	2500CL	1	29^2	100^2	130^3	202	5	5	5°	4^2	4	2ns	31	202	4.30	BMattison	SatrdaynitFvr,KayV,WhosYorThndr	78-0
8-25^{97}	Stga	1300	sy	2500CL	1	29^2	101^1	131^2	203^4	9	5	5	5^{4}½	4	6^{3}½	32^2	204^3	4.80	BMattison	Chezz,Donaway,Rightside	75-0
8-20^{97}	Stga	1300	ft	2500CL	1	29	101	132^1	202^4	10	6	6°	4°^{1}½	2	1^3	30^2	202^4	7.20	BMattison	KayVee,LeopardLobel,ChristianGB	65-0
8-10^{97}	Stga	1100	ft	2500CL	1	29	59	130^2	202^1	6	7	7	5°^{2}½	5	1^{1}½	31^2	202^1	8.00	BMattison	KayV,IronstonBrz,ThrPartHarmony	77-0
8-4^{97}	Stga	1100	ft	2500CL	1	29	59^2	130^4	203^1	3	5	6	8°^{5}	7	3^{2}½	32	203^4	26.30	BMattison	TheRightPrice,MagicArtist,KayVe	69-0
7-16^{97}	Stga	1250	ft	2500CL	1	29	100	130^3	201^2	1	2	3	3^4	4	6^{8}½	31^3	203	13.60	BMattison	FullaDor,LeopardLobel,SaltAgain	77-0
7-9^{97}	Stga	1100	ft	2500CL	1	31	102^2	133^3	204^4	1	2	1	1½	2	2½	31^2	205	1.90	BMattison	HirryTear,KayV,WindyNotchRhulr+	78-0

8-1 CASINO EMPRESS (NY) — 4
b m 6 Niatross-Native Empress-Adios Vic
Charles E.& Joan C.Henderson,Lebanon,Conn.
JOHN CROSS (120) bl-or-wh (19-1-0-3-.105) Tr—John Cross (.085)
Stga 2:02 1992 7 2 0 0 $1,036
VD ½ 1:59^4 1991 24 2 1 3 $3,562
5,1:59^4 ½ Lifetime $6,657
3,000 BLACK

Date	Trk	Purse	Cd	Class	Dis	1/4	1/2	3/4	Winners Time	PP	1/4	1/2	3/4	Str	Fin	Ind 1/4 Time	Ind Time	Odds	Driver	Order Of Finish: First, Second, Third	Temp
9-11^{97}	Stga	1100	ft	2500CL	1	29^3	100^4	130^2	202	1	2	3	3^1	3	1½	31^2	202	*2.10	JCross	CasinoEmpress,Praiseworthy,BilMat	65-0
9-5^{97}	Stga	1300	ft	2500CL	1	28^4	58^4	129^2	200^4	7	8	8	8^{5}½	8	8^{7}½	31^3	202^1	80.20	JCross	ChristanGB,WnthropeKd,JollyFrost	78-0
8-28^{97}	Stga	1300	ft	2500CL	1	28^3	59^1	130^2	202	1	1	3	4^{1}½	4	5^{6}½	32^4	203^2	8.20	JCross	WinSumPro,CindrKat,WinthropeKd	81-0
8-14^{97}	Stga	1300	sy	2500CL	1	29^3	102	132^2	203^1	6	8	8	7°^{5}½	7	5^{7}½	31^1	204^3	18.30	JCross	JoyfMac,PtlsFortn,YongBrandyWn	63-0
8-8^{97}	Skow	750	ft	NW500CD	1	31	102	132^1	202^4	8	8°	7	6^{4}½	6	6^4	30^3	203^3	22.30	SMacKnz	SumPilot,MolysView,MightyFrand	74-0
7-18^{97}	Bang	600	ft	NW50PSCD	1	31	102	132^2	204	6	2°	1	1^5	1	1^4	31^3	204	*.80	SMacKnz	CasinoEmpress,ColaCowboy,JtSldpr	80-0
7-11^{97}	Bang	700	ft	NW75PSCD	1	29	101^1	132	202^3	3	5	7	7^{3}½	6	4^3	30^3	203^1	9.10	SMacKnz	Aaherah,SwftAnfa,GateTime	72-0

12-1 SHOOTOUTTHELIGHTS — 5
b f 3 AllwinSteady-Carola Lobell-Airliner
Lee W.Denman, David M.Pepin & James L.MacIntyre, NY.
RAYMOND TREMBLAY (170) bl-wh-go (95-13-7-20-.248) Tr—Paul Onyon (.307)
Stga 2:03^1 1992 20 4 3 1 $5,247
VD ½ 2:01^1 1991 6 1 0 0 $820
2,2:01^1 ½ Lifetime $6,067
4,250 GREEN

Date	Trk	Purse	Cd	Class	Dis	1/4	1/2	3/4	Winners Time	PP	1/4	1/2	3/4	Str	Fin	Ind 1/4 Time	Ind Time	Odds	Driver	Order Of Finish: First, Second, Third	Temp
9-4^{97}	Stga		gd	QUA	1	29	59^4	130^4	202^3	8	2	2	4^{5}½	5	5^{19}	33^4	206^2	NB	DCaplolJr	FlyngGrvl,Shimrc,Jad,CharlFxtrt	64-0
8-12^{97}	Stga		ft	QUA	1	32	103	132^4	203	8	7	6	6^{23}½	6	6dis			NB	DCaplolJr	YoungBillotroubie,HillRulr,AllVies	67-0
8-5^{97}	Stga	1300	ft	2500CLCD	1	29	59^3	130^2	201^2	scr	lm				scr					DaytonEclps,JollyFrst,DnvrDragon	72-0
7-29^{97}	Stga	1300	ft	2500CL	1	29^2	101	130^3	201^1	x7	8	8	8^{5}½	8	8^{14}½	32^1	204	9.70	DCaplolJr	WinSumPro,WhosYourThundr,Rghted	68-0
7-16^{97}	Stga	1450	ft	2500CL	1	28^3	59^3	130^3	202	1	2	1	1½	1	2½	31^2	202	*1.60	DCaplolJr	JollyFrost,Shtothghts,LckyMarvn	77-0
7-8^{97}	Stga	1450	ft	2500CL	1	29^3	101^4	131^2	201	7	3	4	4°^{1}½	4	6^{6}½	30^2	202^2	27.70	DCaplolJr	LeishaLou,Spitzad+,WinSumPro~	73-0
6-24^{97}	Stga	1300	gd	2500CLCD	1H	30^3	133	204	235^2	4	3	4	5^{2}½	3	1^1	31	235^2	9.50	DCaplolJr	Shotouthlights,WinSumPro,Rghted	69-0

4-1 LEISHA LOU — 6
b m 6 Insomniac-GardenState-Airliner
Rosalie A.Cristaldi,Greenwich,N.Y.
FRANK COPPOLA JR (150) ltbl-wh-br (650-114-95-99-.307) Tr—Frank Cristaldi (.337)
Stga 2:00^4 1992 28 7 5 2 $7,445
Stga 2:00^4 1991 35 11 5 4 $9,454
5,2:00^4 Lifetime $30,790
3,000 RED

Date	Trk	Purse	Cd	Class	Dis	1/4	1/2	3/4	Winners Time	PP	1/4	1/2	3/4	Str	Fin	Ind 1/4 Time	Ind Time	Odds	Driver	Order Of Finish: First, Second, Third	Temp
9-10^{97}	Stga	1400	sy	3000CL	1	30^2	102^1	132^1	202	6	6	6	4°^{2}½	4	5^{5}½	30^3	203^1	5.20	FCopolaJr	StringBrz,YongBrndyWn,BronzLobl	73-0
9-2^{97}	Stga	1500	ft	4000CL OP	1	30^2	102	131^4	202^1	9	2	3	3°^{1}	3	2ns	30^1	202^1	2.00	GMattison	DnvrDragon,LshaLou,NorthengRos	68-0
8-25^{97}	Stga	1900	sy	5000CL OP	1	29^2	100	130^3	201	4	7	6°	6°^{5}½	6	6^{10}½	31^3	203^1	3.00	GMattison	Tropical,StpAsidLadis,FamFatal	75-0
8-12^{97}	Stga	1900	ft	5000CL OP	1	28^2	58^1	129^2	159^3	4	3	3°	1°hd	2	5^5	31^1	200^3	*1.00	GMattison	DamysFlfy,SndayLov,SndancNancy	70-0
8-5^{97}	Stga	1900	ft	5000CL	1	29^2	101	131^3	201	3	1	1	1hd	1	2ns	29^2	201	*1.10	GMattison	HapyFidler,LshaLou,RuthiMagic	72-0
7-28^{97}	Stga	1500	ft	4000CL OP	1	29^2	100^2	130^3	200^4	1	2	2	2^2	2	1^{1}½	29^4	200^4	*1.10	GMattison	LeishaLou,SundayLove,BearBreath	74-0
7-21^{97}	Stga	1650	ft	4000CL OP	1	29^1	59^4	130^2	201^1	8	2°°	1	1½	1	1½	30^4	201^1	8.50	GMattison	LeishaLou,BKsJmyClar,Chcrbry	71-0

10-1 COLUMBIA JOON — 9
b m 8 IcarusLobell-ColumbiaMiss-Columbia George
J.P.Camerino, J.J.Shufon & R.J.Coccodrilli, NY.
BERT BELANGER (140) bl-wh-go (297-34-41-38-.234) Tr—Richard Ingils (.167)
QStga 2:03^1 1992 6 1 0 0 $550
Stga 2:00^2 1991 21 5 2 0 $5,411
7,2:00^2 Lifetime $45,700
3,000 BLUE

Date	Trk	Purse	Cd	Class	Dis	1/4	1/2	3/4	Winners Time	PP	1/4	1/2	3/4	Str	Fin	Ind 1/4 Time	Ind Time	Odds	Driver	Order Of Finish: First, Second, Third	Temp
9-11^{97}	Stga		ft	QUA	1	30	100^2	131^3	203^1	5	3°	1	1^{1}½	1	1^{2}½	31^3	203^1	NB	DCaplolJr	ColmbaJon,OnLastBlst,StrmEClar	60-0
8-20^{97}	Stga	1300	ft	2500CL	1	29	101	132^1	202^4	scr	sk				scr					KayVee,LeopardLobel,ChristianGB	65-0
8-12^{97}	Stga	1300	ft	2500CL	1	30^3	102^1	132^4	202^4	7	6	5°	5°^{2}½	5	6^{7}½	30^4	204^1	50.70	GMattison	MyradsKnylo,SaByBy,SatrdayntFvr	70-0
8-6^{97}	Stga	1300	ft	2500CL	1	28^4	59^4	130^4	201^1	6	6	x8	8^{10}	8	8^{15}½	31^3	204^2	21.40	GMattison	Chezz,MyradsKenylou,LopardLobl	80-0
7-22^{97}	Stga	1300	ft	2500CLCD	1	28^4	100^1	130^4	201	2	2	2	4^{1}½	6	6^{10}	32	203	*2.90	DCaplolJr	DnvrDragon,ThGratHlry,FnThankYo	72-0
7-14^{97}	Stga	1100	ft	2500CL	1	29^1	59^4	131^3	203^2	3	2	2	3^{1}½	3	1ns	31^3	203^2	*1.20	DCaplolJr	ClmbaJon,ThRghtPrc,FlatmCoins	79-0
7-8^{97}	Stga	1450	ft	2500CL	1	29^3	101^4	131^2	201	8	10	10	9^9	9	9^{14}½	30^4	204	21.20	PSlasser	LeishaLou,Spitzad+,WinSumPro~	73-0

5-2 **WIN SUM PRO** b m 5 Flatout-MissPronouncer-KennyHanover Stga $2{:}00^7$ 1992 24 6 5 2 $6,185
Christina I.Kane,Saratoga NY. Stga $1{:}59^7$ 1991 38 3 9 5 $19,129
10 DANIEL CAPPELLO JR (115) blue-white (357-49-63-62-.293) Tr—John Kane (.384) 3,1:59 % Lifetime $34,192
3,000 ORANGE

$9\text{-}11^{92}$	Stga	1300	ft	2500CL	1	30	101^1	131^4	201^4	2	1	1	1^1	1	2^1	30^1	202	*1.30	FCopolaJr SavnaBluChp,WnSmPro,HolandsSong 65-0
$9\text{-}5^{92}$	Stga	1300	ft	2500CL	1	28^4	58^4	129^7	200^4	8	3°	4°	$5^{o}3\frac{1}{2}$	5	6^5	32	202	7.40	FCopolaJr ChristanGB,WnthropeKd,JollyFrost 78-0
$8\text{-}28^{92}$	Stga	1300	ft	2500CL	1	28^3	59^1	130^7	202	6	5	4°	$3^{oo}1$	1	1^{ns}	31^7	202	2.10	FCopolaJr WinSumPro,CindrKat,WinthropeKd 81-0
$8\text{-}22^{92}$	Stga	1300	ft	2500CL	1	28^1	58^4	129	200^7	10	6	5°	$4^{o}3$	2	$1^7\frac{1}{4}$	30^4	200^7	13.00	FCopolaJr WinSumPro,CraigoMcgee,AvngrHill 74-0
$8\text{-}11^{92}$	Stga	1300	ft	2500CL	1	28^7	59^4	131^7	201^3	5	5	5	$6^{o}3\frac{1}{4}$	5	$4^5\frac{3}{4}$	31	203	4.40	FCopolaJr JollyFrst,WhosYorThndr,HolndsSng 75-0
$8\text{-}5^{92}$	Stga	1300	ft	2500CLCD	1	29	59^3	130^7	201^7	4	2°	2°	$2^{o}\frac{3}{4}$	3	4^7	31^1	201^4	1.80	FCopolaJr DaylonEclps,JollyFrst,DrvrDragon 72-0
$7\text{-}29^{92}$	Stga	1300	ft	2500CL	1	29^7	101	130^3	201^1	9	4	2°	2^{ohd}	2	$1^1\frac{1}{4}$	30^3	201^1	*1.60	FCopolaJr WinSumPro,WhosYourThundr,Rghted 66-0

Horses who have great trips shouldn't be penalized unless they fail to get the job done. Casino Empress got a great pocket trip from the rail in her last start, but she did win a $2,500 claimer by ¾ of a length as the 2-1 favorite.

Moving out to the 4 post was a minus. A tougher field of $2,500 claimers was a minus. Her 8-1 morning line was maybe a tad high, yet reasonable.

Her odds: 24-1 off a win as the 2-1 favorite in the same company.

Overlay? Gigantic. Did I have her? No way. If only I'd read this book first. . .

Poor Trips

Bad trips can be obvious. Witsend's Dale drew the 5 post in a Non-Winners of $1,500 Last 7 starts at Saratoga, July 2, 1992.

ONE MILE PACE
PURSE $1,500
THURSDAY, JULY 2, 1992
FIRST HALF MID DOUBLE
&
EXACTA

SEVENTH RACE

NON-WINNERS $1500 LAST 7 STARTS
INELIGIBLE: WINNERS OF $7500 IN 1992

WARM UP-BROWN

8-1 **HIGHJACKER** b m 4 B.G'sBunny-AddieGirl-StrikeOut Stga $2{:}03^3$ 1992 10 2 0 2 $2,342
Jane Petit, Lewis, N.Y. Stga $2{:}01^3$ 1991 13 3 2 0 $4,038
1 EUGENE CROSS (200) red-gold-white (8-1-0-0-.125) Tr—Eugene Cross (.125) $3{,}2{:}01^3$ Lifetime $6,997
YELLOW

Date	Trk	Purse	Cd	Class	Dis	Leaders Time 1/4	1/2	3/4	Winners Time	PP	1/4	1/2	3/4	Str	Fin	Ind 1/4 Time	Ind Time	Odds	Driver	Order Of Finish First Second Third	Temp
$6\text{-}24^{92}$	Stga	1800	gd	F&MNW3PMCD	1	29^1	59^4	130^7	201^1	7	5°	4°	$4^{o}7\frac{1}{2}$	6	$6^{12}\frac{1}{4}$	33^1	204	7.80	ECross	DarngDram,WlowyBaty,BrzyKnotNR	69-0
$6\text{-}17^{92}$	Stga	1600	ft	NW1500L7CD	1	30	135^1	204^7	235	8	2	2	2^1	1	1^7	30^1	235	16.60	ECross	Highjackr,AwsomAus,YongMrchant	79-0
$6\text{-}3^{92}$	Stga	1900	ft	NW2000L7CD	1	29	101^1	131^1	200	8	8	8	$7^{o}3$	7	$7^{rd}\frac{1}{2}$	30^1	202^1	59.60	ECross	ItsCavier,LitleOf,FindlyHanovr	77-0
$6\text{-}27^{92}$	Stga	1900	gd	FMNW2000L7	1	29^1	101	131^4	201^1	4	1	2	$3^1\frac{1}{4}$	3	$6^8\frac{1}{4}$	30^3	202^4	21.10	KCrawford	CalWthAKs,MsRainbow,Tnptqu	51-0
$5\text{-}13^{92}$	Stga	2000	ft	FMNW2000L7	1	28^7	59^3	129^7	159	4	5	5°	$5^{o}4\frac{1}{4}$	6	$7^{11}\frac{1}{2}$	31	201^1	5.80	KCrawford	WangoTango,MsRainbow,SisterSlup	79-0
$5\text{-}6^{92}$	Stga	2000	ft	FMNW2000L7	1	30	100^1	131	202^7	1	2	3	$3^1\frac{1}{4}$	3	$4^7\frac{1}{4}$	31^4	203	3.90	KCrawford	RacMTara,StormEClar,NorthrngRoe	56-0
$5\text{-}1^{92}$	Stga	2000	ft	NW2000L7	1	29^7	100^3	131^7	201^1	8	9	9	$8^5\frac{1}{4}$	6	$7^3\frac{1}{4}$	29^4	202^7	27.30	DMarshall	EastfieldDel,FastFritz,BronzLodi	58-0

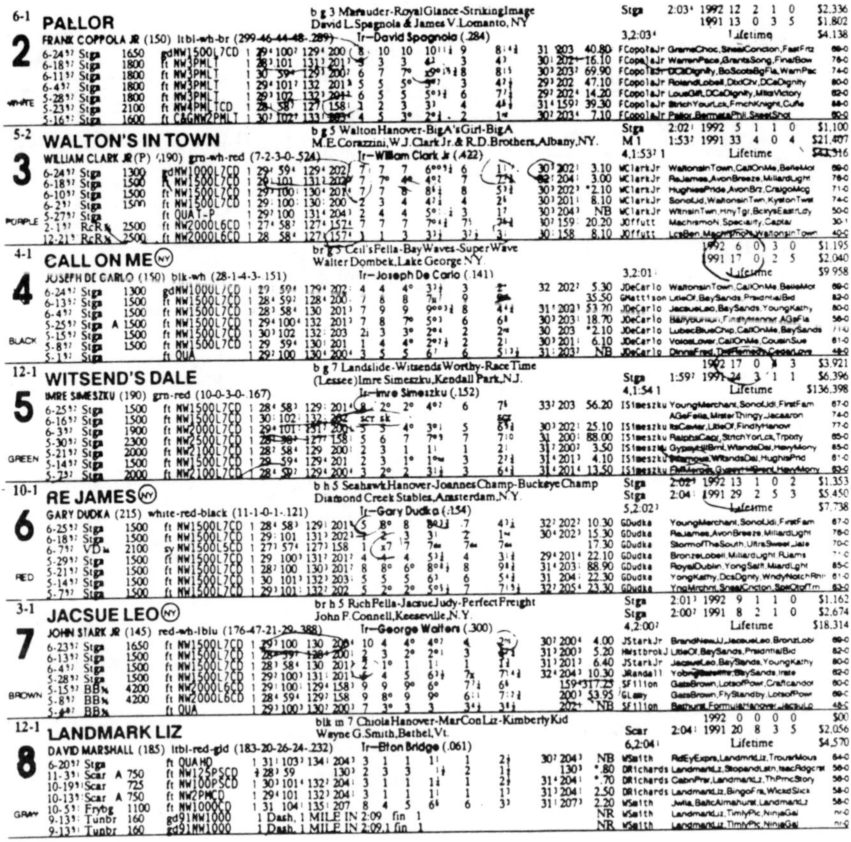

6-1 PALLOR
2 FRANK COPPOLA JR (150) ltbl-wh-br (299-46-44-48-.289)
b g 3 Marauder-RoyalGlance-StrikingImage
David L.Spagnola & James V.Lomanto, NY
Tr—David Spagnola (.284)
Stga 2:03⁴ 1992 12 2 1 0 $2,336
1991 13 0 3 5 $1,802
3,2:03⁴ Lifetime $4,138
6-24 Stga 1650 gd NW1500L7CD 1 29⁴ 100⁷ 129⁴ 200 8 10 10 10 9 8 31 203 40.80 FCopolaJr GrameChoc,SnealConcion,FastFrtz
6-18 Stga 1800 ft NW3PMLT 1 28³ 101 131³ 201³ 3 3 3 4 3 4³ 30¹ 202⁴ 16.10 FCopolaJr WarrenPace,GrantsSong,FinalBow
6-11 Stga 1800 ft NW3PMLT 1 30 59⁴ 129³ 200⁷ 6 7 7° 9° 8 8 30³ 203⁷ 69.90 FCopolaJr DCaDignity,BoScotsBgFla,WarnPac
6-4 Stga 1800 ft NW3PMLT 1 29⁴ 101⁷ 132 201³ 5 5 5° 5 3 4 29³ 202 47.10 FCopolaJr RolandLobell,DbdChr,DCaDignity
5-28 Stga 1800 ft NW3PMLT 1 29³ 102 132³ 201² 6 5 5 5 6 7 29⁷ 202⁴ 14.20 FCopolaJr LousGift,DCaDignity,MitaVictory
WHITE 5-23 Stga 2100 ft NW4PMLTCD 1 28 58⁷ 127 158¹ 1 2 3 3³ 4 4 31⁴ 159⁷ 39.30 FCopolaJr StrchYourLck,FrnchKnight,Cufe
5-16 Stga 1600 ft C&GNW2PMLT 1 30⁷ 102⁷ 133¹ 4 5 3° 2 2 1 30⁷ 203⁴ 7.10 FCopolaJr Pallor,BermetaPhil,SaeetShot

5-2 WALTON'S IN TOWN
3 WILLIAM CLARK JR(P) (190) grn-wh-red (7-2-3-0-.524)
b g 5 WaltonHanover-BigA'sGirl-BigA
M.E.Corazzini,W.J.Clark Jr.& R.D.Brothers,Albany,NY.
Tr—William Clark Jr (.422)
Stga 2:02¹ 1992 5 1 1 0 $1,100
M1 1:53⁷ 1991 33 4 0 4 $21,407
4,1:53⁷ 1 Lifetime $43,316
6-24 Stga 1300 gd NW1000L7CD 1 29 59⁴ 129⁴ 202 7 7 7 6° 6 1 30³ 202¹ 3.10 WClarkJr WaltonsInTown,CallOnMe,BelleMor
6-18 Stga 1500 ft NW1500L7CD 1 29 101 131² 202 7 7° 4° 4° 7 7 32¹ 204¹ 3.00 WClarkJr ReJames,AvonBreeze,MillardLght
6-10 Stga 1500 ft NW1500L7CD 1 29⁷ 100¹ 130⁴ 201 7 7 8 8 8 5 30³ 202⁷ *2.10 WClarkJr HughiesPride,AvonBrz,CraigoMog
6-2 Stga 1500 ft NW1500L7CD 1 29 100 130 200 2 3 4 4 4 2 30³ 201¹ 8.10 WClarkJr SonoUdi,WaltonsinTwn,KystonTwst
5-27 Stga ft QUAT-P 1 29⁷ 100 131⁴ 204³ 2 4 4 5° 3 1⁷ 30³ 204³ NB WClarkJr WltnsInTwn,HnyTgr,BckysEastrLdy
PURPLE 2-1 RcR 2500 ft NW2000L6CD 1 27⁴ 58⁷ 127⁴ 157⁴ 7 7 7 7 7 7 30⁷ 159 20.20 JOffutt MachismoN,Specialty,Captal
12-21 RcR 2500 ft NW2000L6CD 1 28 58⁴ 127 157⁴ 1 1 3 3 3 3 30 158 8.10 JOffutt LcsBen,MachismoN,WaltonsinTown

4-1 CALL ON ME (NY)
4 JOSEPH DE CARLO (150) blk-wh (28-1-4-3-.151)
br g 5 Ceil'sFella-BayWaves-SuperWave
Walter Dombek,Lake George NY.
Tr—Joseph De Carlo (.141)
1992 6 0 3 0 $1,195
1991 17 0 2 5 $2,040
3,2:01 Lifetime $9,958
6-24 Stga 1300 gd NW1000L7CD 1 29 59⁴ 129⁴ 202 4 4 4° 3 3 2 32 202⁷ 5.30 JDeCarlo WaltonsinTown,CallOnMe,BelleMor
6-13 Stga 1500 ft NW1500L7CD 1 28⁴ 59² 128⁴ 200 7 8 8 7 9 35.50 GMattison LittleOf,BaySands,PresidntialBid
6-4 Stga 1500 ft NW1500L7CD 1 28³ 58⁴ 130 201³ 7 9 9 9° 8 4 31⁴ 202³ 53.70 JDeCarlo JacsueLeo,BaySands,YoungKathy
5-25 Stga A 1500 ft NW1500L7CD 1 29⁴ 100⁴ 132 201³ 7 8 7° 5 6 6 30³ 203¹ 18.70 JDeCarlo Ballyounion,Finstymanor,AGeFla
5-15 Stga 1500 ft NW1500L7CD 1 30³ 102 132 203 2 3 3° 2 2 2 30 203 *2.10 JDeCarlo LubecBlueChip,CallOnMe,BaySands
BLACK 5-8 Stga 1500 ft NW1500L7CD 1 29 59⁴ 130¹ 201 1 4 4° 2 2 2 30³ 201¹ 6.10 JDeCarlo VoiceLover,CallOnMe,CousinSue
5-1 Stga ft QUA 1 29⁷ 100 130⁴ 200⁴ 3 5 5 6 6 5 31 203⁷ NB JDeCarlo DinnaFred,DeFlemeth,CedarLove

12-1 WITSEND'S DALE
5 IMRE SIMESZKU (190) grn-red (10-0-3-0-.167)
b g 7 Landslide-WitsendsWorthy-RaceTime
(Lessee)Imre Simeszku,Kendall Park,N.J.
Tr—Imre Simeszku (.152)
1992 17 0 1 3 $3,921
Stga 1:59⁷ 1991 24 3 1 1 $6,396
4,1:54 1 Lifetime $136,398
6-25 Stga 1500 ft NW1500L7CD 1 28⁴ 58³ 129 201⁴ 8 2° 2° 4° 6 7 33⁷ 203 56.20 ISimeszku YoungMerchant,SonoUdi,FirstFam
6-16 Stga 1500 ft NW1500L7CD 1 30 102 132 202 scr sk scr AGeFella,MisterThingy,Jacaaron
6-3 Stga 1900 ft NW2000L7CD 1 29⁴ 101 131⁷ 200 5 5 4° 3° 5 6 30³ 202¹ 25.10 ISimeszku ItsCavier,LittleOf,FindlyHanovr
5-30 Stga 2300 ft NW2500L7CD 1 28 58⁴ 127⁷ 158 5 6 7 7 7 7 31 200 88.00 ISimeszku RalphsCapr,StrchYorLck,Trpbdy
5-21 Stga 2000 ft NW2100L7CD 1 28⁷ 58⁴ 129 200 2 3 1 1 1 2 31⁷ 200⁷ 3.50 ISimeszku GypsyHillBrnl,WitsndsDal,HevyMony
GREEN 5-14 Stga 1500 ft NW1500L7CD 1 29 59⁴ 129⁴ 201 2 3 1° 1 3 2 31⁴ 201³ 4.10 ISimeszku Intamous,WitsndsDal,HughisPrid
5-7 Stga 2000 ft NW2100L7CD 1 28⁴ 59⁷ 129⁴ 200⁴ 3 2° 2 3 3 6 31⁴ 201⁴ 13.50 ISimeszku FMMercos,GypsyHillBrnl,HevyMony

10-1 RE JAMES (NY)
6 GARY DUDKA (215) white-red-black (11-1-0-1-.121)
b h 5 SeahawkHanover-JoannesChamp-BuckeyeChamp
Diamond Creek Stables,Amsterdam,N.Y.
Tr—Gary Dudka (.154)
Stga 2:02³ 1992 13 1 0 2 $1,353
Stga 2:04 1991 29 2 5 3 $5,450
5,2:02³ Lifetime $7,738
6-25 Stga 1500 ft NW1500L7CD 1 28⁴ 58³ 129 201 5 8° 8 8 7 4 32⁷ 202⁷ 10.30 GDudka YoungMerchant,SonoUdi,FirstFam
6-18 Stga 1500 ft NW1500L7CD 1 29 101 131³ 202³ 2 2 3 3 2 1 30⁴ 202³ 15.30 GDudka ReJames,AvonBreeze,MillardLight
6-7 VD 2100 sy NW1500L5CD 1 27³ 57⁴ 127³ 158 1 x7 7 7 7 7 17.30 GDudka StormofTheSouth,UltraSweet,Jale
5-29 Stga 1500 ft NW1500L7CD 1 29 100³ 131⁷ 201⁷ 4 4 4 5 4 3 29⁴ 201⁴ 22.10 GDudka BronzeLobell,MillardLight,RJams
RED 5-21 Stga 1500 ft NW1500L7CD 1 28⁷ 100 130³ 201⁷ 8 8° 6° 8° 8 9 31⁴ 203 88.90 GDudka RoyalDublin,YongSalt,MlardLght
5-14 Stga 1500 ft NW1500L7CD 1 30 101³ 132³ 203 5 5 5 6 6 5 31 204 22.30 GDudka YongKathy,DcsDgnty,WndyNotchRn
5-7 Stga 1500 ft NW1500L7CD 1 29³ 101 132⁷ 202 5 2° 2° 5° 7 7 32⁷ 205⁴ 23.30 GDudka YngMrchnt,SnealCncton,SpitOfTm

3-1 JACSUE LEO (NY)
7 JOHN STARK JR (145) red-wh-lblu (176-47-21-29-.388)
br h 5 RichFella-JacsueJudy-PerfectFreight
John F.Connell,Keeseville,N.Y.
Tr—George Walters (.300)
Stga 2:01³ 1992 9 1 1 0 $1,162
Stga 2:00⁷ 1991 8 2 1 0 $2,674
4,2:00⁷ Lifetime $18,314
6-23 Stga 1650 ft NW1500L7CD 1 29⁷ 100 130 200⁴ 10 4 4° 4° 4 2 30⁷ 200⁴ 4.00 JStarkJr BrandNewJJ,JacsueLeo,BronzLobl
6-13 Stga 1500 ft NW1500L7CD 1 28 59⁷ 128⁴ 200 2 3 2° 2° 3 31³ 200³ 5.20 HWstbrokJ LittleOf,BaySands,PresidntialBid
6-4 Stga 1500 ft NW1500L7CD 1 28³ 58⁴ 130 201 2 1° 1 1 1 1 31³ 201³ 6.40 JStarkJr JacsueLeo,BaySands,YoungKathy
5-28 Stga 1500 ft NW1500L7CD 1 29⁷ 100⁷ 131 201 4 4 5 6 7x 7 32⁴ 204³ 10.30 JRandall YoungSatellite,BaySands,Irate
BROWN 5-15 BB 4200 ft NW2000L6CD 1 29 100 129⁴ 158³ 9 9 9° 6° 7 6 159 317.25 SFillon GatsBrown,LotsofPowr,Craftcandor
5-8 BB 4200 ft NW2000L6CD 1 28⁴ 59⁴ 129⁷ 158 9 8° 9 9° 6 7 200³ 53.95 GLamy GatsBrown,FlyStandby,LotsofPowr
5-4 BB ft QUA 1 29³ 100³ 130⁷ 200³ 7 3° 3 3 3 3 202 NB SFillon Bathurst,FormulaHanover,JacsuLo

12-1 LANDMARK LIZ
8 DAVID MARSHALL (185) ltbl-red-gld (183-20-26-24-.232)
blk m 7 ChiolaHanover-MarConLiz-KimberlyKid
Wayne G.Smith,Bethel,Vt.
Tr—Elton Bridge (.061)
1992 0 0 0 0 $00
Scar 2:04 1991 20 8 3 5 $2,056
6,2:04 Lifetime $4,570
6-20 Stga ft QUAHD 1 31 103³ 134 204³ 3 1 1 1 1 2 30⁷ 204³ NB WSmith RdEyExprs,LandmrkLiz,TrouvrMous
11-3 Scar A 750 ft NW125PSCD 28³ 59 130³ 2 3 3 1 2 1 130³ *.80 DRichards LandmarkLz,StopandLstn,IsacRdgcrst
10-19 Scar 725 ft NW100PSCD 1 30³ 101⁴ 132⁷ 204 3 1 1 1 1 2 31⁴ 204 *.70 DRichards CabnPrsr,LandmarkLz,ThPrncStory
10-13 Scar A 750 ft NW2PMCD 1 29⁴ 101 132³ 204 3 1 1 1 1 1 31³ 204 2.50 DRichards LandmarkLz,BingoFra,WickdSlick
GRAY 10-5 Frybg 1100 ft NW1000CD 1 31 104 135 207 8 4 5 6 6 3 31 207³ 2.20 WSmith Jwlia,BalticAlmahurst,LandmarkLz
9-13 Tunbr 160 gd91NW1000 1 Dash, 1 MILE IN 2:09 fin 1 NR WSmith LandmarkLz,TimlyPic,NinjaGal
9-13 Tunbr 160 gd91NW1000 1 Dash, 1 MILE IN 2:09.1 fin 1 NR WSmith LandmarkLz,TimlyPic,NinjaGal

From the bottom of his PPs up, he was sixth, second twice, seventh and sixth before being scratched sick. His first race back 22 days later was his top PP, when he had the 8 post and was second on the outside at the quarter and at the half, fourth on the outside by 2 lengths at the three-quarters, and seventh by 6 lengths at odds of 56-1.

Any horse parked on the outside from the 8 hole on a ½-mile track has a bad trip. The faster the early fractions, the worse the trip. Witsend's were extremely fast for this class: :28.4 and :58.3. At the three-quarters in 1:29.1, he was two lengths back before tiring to finish seventh by six lengths. This race, his first in three weeks, would serve as a tightener. Moving inside from the 8 post to the 5 was another plus.

Witsend's Dale went off at 8-1. As bad as his trip was the previous week, his trip tonight was perfect: leaving, tucking in second, sitting the pocket and getting through on the inside to win. He paid $18.80, a moderate overlay.

Here's a major one:

Davis Cup was the 6 horse in a field of 8 at Yonkers, March 14, 1992, contesting the Open 3- & 4-Year-Old Pace.

7 **PACE** — ONE MILE — WARM-UP ORANGE

$3 TRIPLE — OPEN — 3 & 4-Year-Olds.

$2 EXACTA — PURSE $15,000

RED 1 — FULLA POTHOLES (NY)
ch g 4,by On The Road Again, Bye Fella by Fulla Napoleon — 1:53.8 Sy1 — 92 2 0 0 0 $875 — 91 15 6 4 2 $75,572
Anthony & Sheila Lowbeer, Ossining, N.Y.
Michael Kimelman (135) — Blue-Gold — Tr.Michael Kimelman — Last 8 starts-$33,814 — 3 1:53.0 (1) — Lifetime $102,846

3-7YR+6	1	fst	26^4	57^2	1.26^4	1.56	Opn 3-4YO	17500	1	3	4	5^{2}¼	8^{6}¼	5^{2}¾	1.56^3	2.90	(KimelmanM)NukesTerror ThorFashion Lionhear'	angle mid pace
2-29YR-1	1	fst	27^4	57^1	1.27^4	1.57	Opn 3-4YO	15000	5	7	7°	7^{oo}5¾	7^{11}	6^{11}	1.59^1	6.90	(KimelmanM)Lionheart ThatsDancing PerfectPlay	8w wide out
2-22M1	1	fst	29^2	59^1	1.28^4	1.57^4	Qua		6	6	5°	2^{o1}	2^{1}¾	2^{1}¾	1.58	nb	(KimelmanM)Chocole FullaPotholes GetAboutTowr	lost cover game
2-15M1	1	fst	29^4	59^1	1.29	1.57^1	Qua		8	1^{oo}	1	1ns	3^{1}¾	4^{10}	1.59^1	nb	(KimelmanM)JustinKin LindedCenturion PatriotMasse	used weakened
9-14YR+8	1	fst	27^4	56^2	1.25^4	2.03^1	NYSS	200000	4	1°	1	1xhd	acc	dnf		*1.00	(KimelmanM)"GloucstrCt "BlackGoldRd ionly2finishec	prss.brk lef
9-2VD^p	1	fst	25^3	53^4	1.23^1	1.54	NYSS	21650	2	3°	2°	1	1^{1}¾	2¾	1.54	*.70	(KimelmanM)SideLeader FullaPotholes KingGeorgeRoac	
8-25MR	1	fst	28	57^2	1.28	1.56^4	NYSS	38600	9	2	3	4	3^{2}¾	2^1	1.56	*1.40	(KimelmanM)StormanJesse FullaPotholes BlackGoldRoac	
8-1 8-18Sy1	1	fst	26^4	54^3	1.24^2	1.53	NYSS	30800	3	2°	4	5	3¾	1^1	1.53	*.90	(KimelmanM)FullaPotholes ForeignDignitary BlackGoldRoac	

BLUE 2 — LUDICROUS
b h 4,by Nihilator, Reel Hilarious by Shadow Wave — 1:57.4 YR — 92 10 1 1 0 $14,480 — 1:54.1 GS1 — 91 19 5 5 1 $80,370
The Black Bag Stable, Miller Place, N.Y.
Frank Popfinger (160) — Blue-Gold — Tr.Frank Popfinger — Last 8 starts-$9,530 — 3 1:54.1 (1) — Lifetime $86,520

3-7YR+6	1	fst	26^4	57^2	1.26^4	1.56	Opn 3-4YO	17500	6	2°	2	2^{1}¾	3^{1}¾	6^{2}¾	1.56^3	18.30	(PopfingerF)NukesTerror ThorFashion Lionhear'	tok pkt brec
2-29YR-1	1	fst	27^4	57^1	1.27^4	1.57	Opn 3-4YO	15000	6	2°	1	1¾	2no	5^{4}¾	1.57^4	16.70	(PopfingerF)Lionheart ThatsDancing PerfectPlay	pkd.prss brec
2-22YR+9	1	fst	29^4	59^3	1.28^1	1.57^2	Opn 3-4YO	17500	7	6	4°	4^{o1}¾	5^3	6^{4}¾	1.58^2	7.10	(PopfingerF)IroquoisBlueChip DatesDay Lionhear'	good cvr wknc
2-15YR-1	1	sly	29	59	1.28^2	1.57^4	Opn Hcp 4YO	15000	6	1	1	1^{2}¾	1^2	1^{3}¾	1.57^4	*1.30	(MarohnJ)Ludicrous DatesDay SpecialLeebroo	never ir doubt
2-8YR-5	1	gd	29^2	59^1	1.28^3	2.00	Opn 3-4YO	18000	6	6	2°	2^{ono}	2no	4^{1}¾	2.00^1	4.40	(MarohnJ)SpecialLeebrook PerfectPlay Lionhear'	horror trip trc
1-30M1-2	1	fst	28^1	56	1.25^2	1.54^1	Complex	15000	5	9°	9	8^{oo6}	8^{9}¾	7^{8}¾	1.55^4	12.30	(PopfingerF)FalconWhistle CubanFantasy *KnightLbl	no threat
1-23M1-17	1	sly	28^3	57^3	1.27^1	1.56^4	Complex	15000	3	2°	2	2^{1}¾	4^{2}¾	8^7	1.58^1	11.00	(PopfingerF)Pashu OSoBrave CubanFantasy	yield faded
5-1 1-16M1-7	1	fst	28^4	57^3	1.27^1	1.55^4	Complex	15000	5	5°	2°	2^{ono}	3^{2}¾	8^{9}¾	1.57^3	2.90	(PopfingerF)TwinAngel ThorFashion Youngphiladelphiar	parked faded

WHITE 3 — LES HALL
b h 4,by Chipper Frost, Chipmans Starlite by Brown Star — 1:57.2 YR — 92 8 2 4 1 $14,538 — 91 9 0 0 1 $1,050
Melvin Wayne Givens & George Hudson, Del.
Walter Case,Jr. (135) — Maroon-White — Tr.Wayne Givens — Last 8 starts-$14,538 — 4 1:57.2 — Lifetime $28,487

3-7YR+6	1	gd	27^3	57	1.27^3	1.57^2	Opn 3-4YO	12500	3	2	2	2^{1}¾	2^{1}¾	1no	1.57^2	5.70	(MosherG)LesHall Goodhearted DirectKiller	yld.pkt driving
3-2YR-3	1	fst	26^4	57^4	1.27^2	1.58^1	NW8000	7500	6	6	i5	4^{2}¾	3^{1}¾	2^{ns}	1.58^1	108.30	(MosherG)SaveTheTiger LesHall MichaelsRevenge	impd 1st missed
2-19YR-3	1	fst	29^4	1.01^1	1.31^1	2.01	NW6000	5750	5	2	2	2^{2}¾	2^3	2^{3}dh	2.01^3	6.40	(MosherG)BondStreet(dh)FinessePlayer-LesHal	dh tok hung ite
2-8DD^{+}	1	gd	27^4	58	1.28	1.59^4	Blue Her	10000	9	5	6	7^{oo}	3^{2}¾	2no	1.59^4	6.10	(GivensW)GrandGusto LesHall SpeakFrenchToMe	
2-1DD^{+}	1	fst	30	1.00^3	1.30	2.00^3	Blue Her	3000	3	1	1	1	1^2	1^{2}¾	2.00^3	2.40	(GivensW)LesHall FoolOfGold Bandeiva	
1-25DD^{+}	1	gd	28^3	59^4	1.29^2	1.59^4	Blue Her	3000	8	1	1	1	2no	3^{3}¾	2.00^2	24.30	(GreeneO)UnfairAdvantage QuillCaper LesHal	
1-18DD^{+}	1	fst	30	1.00^3	1.31^4	2.02^1	Blue Her	3000	7	1	1	1	2^{1}¾	2^4	2.03	8.80	(GivensW)GrandGusto LesHall StarcroftWinne	
6-1 1-11DD^{+}	1	fst	28^3	1.00	1.29^2	2.00	Blue Her	3000	7	4	4	6	3^{1}¾	4^2	2.00^2	17.10	(GivensW)BigDeen SunnyAre TrashToCash	

GREEN 4 — LIONHEART
b h 4,by No Nukes, Tessa by Albatross — 1:57.0 YR — 92 9 2 0 5 $25,470 — 1:58.4 YR — 91 20 9 1 2 $25,800
Jaisan Inc. & Myron Mintz, N.J.
Luc Ouellette (145) — Red-Black-White — Tr.Joseph Foley — Last 8 starts-$24,270 — 4 1:57.0 — Lifetime $51,510

3-7YR-6	1	fst	26^4	57^2	1.26^4	1.56	Opn 3-4YO	17500	5	6	6°	6^{oo2}¾	5^4	3^2	1.56^2	9.10	(OuelletteL)NukesTerror ThorFashion Lionhear'	8w wide mic
2-29YR-1	1	fst	27^4	57^1	1.27^4	1.57	Opn 3-4YO	15000	x1	3	4	3^2	3^{1}¾	1¾	1.57	7.00	(WaplesR)Lionheart ThatsDancing PerfectPlay	out final sokc
2-22YR+9	1	fst	29^4	59^3	1.28^1	1.57^2	Opn 3-4YC	17500	1	2	3	3^{1}¾	2^{1}¾	3¾	1.57^2	7.20	(WingT)IroquoisBlueChip DatesDay Lionhear'	yld pkt wknc
2-15YR-1	1	sly	29	59	1.28^2	1.57^4	Opn Hcp 4YO	15000	7	5	5	5^{5}¾	5^6	5^8	1.59^2	23.60	(WingT)Ludicrous DatesDay SpecialLeebroo	tok never close
2-8YR-5	1	gd	29^2	59^1	1.28^3	2.00	Opn 3-4YO	18000	7	7	8	8^{6}¾	6^{3}¾	3^{1}¾	2.00^1	28.50	(WingT)SpecialLeebrook PerfectPlay Lionhear'	wide good rally
2-1YR-1	1	fst	29	1.00^1	1.28^4	1.57	Opn Hcp	24000	1	3	4	5^4	5^{4}¾	5^{7}¾	1.58^2	34.50	(WingT)CovertAction CountKhan Cevertator	overmatched
1-25YR-1	1	fst	28	58	1.28	1.58^1	W800'	15000	1	1	1	1^{1}¾	1^{1}¾	1^{nc}	1.58^1	*1.20	(WingT)Lionheart MolliesFella HumberTrax	every pc drvng
3-1 1-15M1-3	1	fst	29^2	57^3	1.27^1	1.55^4	Trendsetter	10000	5	2°	2	3^{1}¾	2^{1}¾	3^{2}¾	1.56^1	2.40	(O DonnellW)PraiseKash SayItAndSo Lionhear'	yield no match

BLACK 5 — TRAVEL AGENT (NY)
ch h 4,by On The Road Again, Hurricane Cheer by Storm Damage — 2:02.1 YR Q — 92 7 0 2 0 $9,375 — 1:57.0 YR — 91 35 7 3 6 $39,741
Gary Mosher & J. Bottari, Oakland, Me
Gary Mosher (160) — Red-Green-White — Tr.Glenwood Boulier — Last 8 starts-$10,075 — 3 1:57.0 — Lifetime $49,371

3-7YR-6	1	fst	29	59	1.27^2	1.57^3	Opn 3-4YC	15000	7	7	8	8^{oo6}¾	8^{6}¾	7^{4}¾	1.58^2	15.00	(MosherG)Aggravate ChefTheJet FritzKiss	out fr it gar
2-29YR-1	1	fst	27^4	57^1	1.27^4	1.57	Opn 3-4YC	15000	2	4	6	5^{4}¾	4^{3}¾	4^{4}¾	1.57^4	2.50	(MosherG)Lionheart ThatsDancing PerfectPlay	sat in midly
2-22YR+9	1	fst	27^1	56^2	1.25^3	1.54^4	Opn 3-4YC	15000	1	2	2	2^2	2^{1}¾	2^{3}¾	1.55^2	*1.40	(MosherG)SunDamage TravelAgent ShanAlmahurst	yld pkt.2d bst
2-15YR-1	1	sly	29^1	1.00	1.29^3	1.59^1	Opn Hcp 4YO	12500	7	8	8^{oo}	5^{oo3}¾	5^{4}¾	5^6	2.00^2	6.50	(MosherG)Detante FirstCity NoblePavarott	long wide trc
2-8YR-5	1	gd	28^3	59^3	1.29^3	1.59^2	Opn 3-4YC	13500	3	2	1	1^{1}¾	1^{1}¾	2^{2}¾	1.59^4	*1.00	(MosherG)DatesDay TravelAgent HHFedera	tok 1 4 mi trc
2-1YR-1	1	fst	27^3	57^3	1.28	1.58^3	27'3300C	8500	3	4	5	5^5	5^4	5^{3}¾	1.59^1	8.40	(MosherG)BigDate TwinsJohnny TimberJack	mid finish
1-25YR-1	1	fst	29^1	1.00^1	1.29^3	1.59^2	NW1100C	10500	5	7	8	8^{o5}¾	8^6	8^{4}¾	2.00^1	7.30	(MosherG)YourAmo TooneyBay SeawayNavigator	not involved
10-1 1-17YR	1	fst	30^3	1.01^3	1.33	2.02^1	Qua		4	1	1	1^{1}¾	1^6	1^{7}¾	2.02^1	nb	(ToscanoA)TravelAgent Nescam PersuadableOx	jogged home

YELLOW **DAVIS CUP (NY)** — b g 4.by Temujin. Nouveaute by Brand New Fella — 1:57.2 YR — 92 10 5 2 1 $14,854
Lawrence Roman, Brookville, N.Y. — 2:02.4 MR — 91 14 5 5 1 $5,479
Richard Wojcio (150) — Blue-White-Yellow — Tr.Robert Bongiorno — Last 8 starts--$13,627 — 4 1:57.2 — Lifetime $20,333

6	3-7YR-6	1	fst	29	59	1:27^2	1:57^3	Opn 3-4YC	15000	8	8	6	6^{15}	7^5	5^3	1:58^1	2.00	(WojcioR)Aggravate ChefThauet FritzKiss	few wide str.
	2-29YR-1	1	fst	28^1	58^2	1:27^3	1:57^2	Opn 3-4YC	12500	5	6	6	2°°3	2^1	1^2	1:57^2	*1.40	(WojcioR)DavisCup ChefThauet Aggravate	big burs'
	2-22Fhd-10	1	fst	29^2	59^2	1:28^4	1:57^2	NW6000ps	8000	3	3	4	5	4^2	1^1	1:57^2	9.50	(WojcioR)DavisCup PomPomLobell Floorec	
	2-16MR(A)	1	gd	29^4	1:00^2	1:32^4	2:02^2	NW1850	1750	4	5	4^1	1	1^1	1^1	2:02^2	*.50	(ParkerWJr)DavisCup SmashingEscort Patocr	
	2-9MR(A)	1	gd	29^3	1:01	1:32^3	2:05	NW2200	2100	4	5	5°	4°	5^5	1^3	2:05	3.20	(TaggartJJr)DavisCup PreciousJJ AlbertonAceA	
	2-2MR(A)	1	fst	29^3	1:00^2	1:31^2	2:02^2	NW1900	1800	7	7	7	6°°	5^7	2^5	2:03^2	7.90	(TaggartJJr)AuburnsShadow DavisCup JustMavna	
	1-26MR(A)	1	fst	29^1	1:01^1	1:31^4	2:01^4	NW2200	2100	3	4	6°	5°°	5^4	3^4	2:02^3	8.80	(TaggartJJr)FoghornLeghorn Brice DavisCup	
4-1	1-19MR(A)	1	fst	29^3	1:01^2	1:33	2:04	NW2200	2100	3	5	5°	4°°	4x^3	7^{14}	2:06^4	13.90	(TaggartJJr)PreciousJJ Brice ScenicScooter	

ORANGE **BELL BUCKLE** — b g 3.by Lon Todd Hanover. Pleasant by Don Thorpe — 1:57.3 YR — 92 7 1 0 1 $9,075
John Como & John Como Jr., Towaco, N.J. — 1:58.3 YR — 91 11 8 2 1 $16,384
Donald Dancer (150) — Blue-Gold — Tr.Andy Murphy — Last 8 starts--$11,700 — 3 1:57.3 — Lifetime $25,459

7	2-29YR-1	1	fst	27^4	57^1	1:27^4	1:57	Opn 3-4YO	15000	8	5°	3°	6°°5	6^9	7^{13}	1:59^3	10.60	(DancerD)Lionheart ThatsDancing PerfectPun	pkd mid chi trc
	2-22YR-9	1	fst	28^1	58^1	1:28	1:57^3	Opn 3-4YC	12500	7	1°	1	1^1	1^1	1^1	1:57^3	*1.50	(DancerD)BellBuckle GoodHearted ShadowChase	speed driving
	2-17M1(A)-0	1	fst	28^4	56^2	1:25^3	1:53^4	Ean 10W	17500	12	9	9°	7°7	11^{12}	11^{13}	1:56^2	101.70	(DancerD)DialAFortune Camaradene CamSince	cover brec
	2-11M1-4	1	fst	27^3	57^1	1:27^1	1:54^3	Ean 16W	12500	2	1°	3	6^4	5^5	6^5	1:55^4	35.40	(DancerD)StylishCam Camaradene PrecariousMission	1/4 mi vid shr
	2-4M1-5	1	fst	28	57^1	1:27^4	1:56^4	Ean 16W	12500	7	5°	1	1^2	2^1	4^6	1:58	10.50	(DancerD)Environmentalist Stereotyped PipersSong	pnko press wknc
	1-22M1-3	1	fst	29^1	58^3	1:27^3	1:55^3	Trendsetter	10000	3	7	7°	4°3	4^3	4^{3}dh3	1:56^2	13.20	(DancerD)PrecariousMission Sleepwalk *BellBuckle	p 3 wnnrs cvr
	1-15M1-3	1	fst	28^4	57^2	1:27^1	1:55^3	Trendsetter	10000	8	3°	1	1^{ns}	3^2	6^{11}	1:57^4	*1.50	(DancerD)BigSquare StreakingStopper HerbertViola	pkd hvy prs trc
8-1	1-8M1	1						Trendsetter	10000	1									scratched-sck
	12-17YR-1	1	fst	27^1	58^4	1:29	1:59^1	NW3 2-4YC	5250	4	1	1	1^1	1^1	1^2	1:59^1	*.40	(DancerD)BellBuckle Gantry LittleRaptr	press early e:

GREY **GOOD HEARTED** — b g 4.by Direct Scooter. No Pushover by Precious Fella — 92 8 0 2 0 $7,325
Constance & Ronald Knigge, Roseland, N.J. — 1:55.2 GS1 — 91 17 5 5 1 $22,619
Mark Lancaster (180) — Blue-Gold — Tr.Ronald Knigge — Last 8 starts--$7,325 — 3 1:55.2 (1) — Lifetime $29,944

8	3-7YR-6	1	gd	27^3	57	1:27^3	1:57^2	Opn 3-4YO	12500	5	1°	1	1^1	1^1	2no	1:57^2	1.80	(OuelletteL)LesHall Goodhearted Directuer	rated caught
	2-29YR-1	1	fst	27^4	57^1	1:27^4	1:57	Opn 3-4YC	15000	3	6	5°	4°°4	8^{12}	8^{17}	2:00^2	34.90	(LancasterM)Lionheart ThatsDancing PerfectPun	cvr wide tired
	2-22YR-9	1	fst	28^1	58^1	1:28	1:57^3	Opn 3-4YC	12500	4	2	2	3^1	3^1	2^1	1:57	5.70	(LancasterM)BellBuckle GoodHearted ShadowChase	vid pkt at o:
	2-15M1-5	1	sly	29	58^1	1:27	1:56^4	NW3	9000	3	4	5	5°°3	5^5	5^8	1:58^2	10.50	(ParkerH)Claustrophobia HurricaneAlert Deadion	gapped cove
	2-4M1-5	1	fst	27^4	58	1:27^4	1:54^4	Ean 16W	12500	11	7	10	10°°8	9^{11}	8^{14}	1:57^3	17.00	(CampbellJo)StylishCam DialAFortune PrecariousMiss	off gate cac
	1-27M1-1	1	fst	28	56^1	1:25^2	1:55^2	Chil Factor	12500	1	5	3	1^1	2no	5^5	1:56^3	12.40	(ParkerH)LouisianaProse ForeignDignity PinoFres	stole away
	1-20M1-6	1	fst	28^2	57^2	1:27	1:56	Chil Factor	12500	1	4	1°	1^1	2^2	9^5	1:57	11.70	(WebsterB)FullThrottle RacyMasquerader ForeignDignity	usd prss locked
6-1	1-13M1-0	1	fst	29^1	58	1:27^2	1:55^2	Chil Factory	12500	9	8	6°	4°3	8^{11}	8^{16}	1:58^3	13.50	(ParkerH)DialAFortune RedOctober OurGiantCross	long unc weak

Page 15

Davis Cup, a late-running 4-year-old, had won three straight out of town before his last two starts at Yonkers. Both were in the same class as tonight.

From the 5 post, he won by two lengths as the 7-5 favorite. Seven days later, he was sent off at 2-1 from the disadvantageous 8 post. He rallied from seventh by 5 lengths at the top of the stretch to finish fifth by 3¼. The comment in *Sports Eye* was "Followed wide, steady."

It doesn't take a genius to figure out a come-from-behind horse out of post 8 at Yonkers is a perfect candidate for a bad trip. The optimum question is: How bad was that last trip?

Check out the fractions: The first half went in a slow :59. While Davis Cup's final time of 1:58.1 was 4/5 of a second slower than his win the previous week, he actually ran the same final half of :59.1. His final three-quarters were 4/5 of a second faster than in his win.

So his fifth out of the 8 hole wasn't bad at all. Moving inside to the 6 could do nothing but help. Yet from those two races at Yonkers, a win by two lengths at 7-5, and a fifth from the 8 post at 2-1, he went off at 5-1, winning and paying $13.20.

Shippers

Usually, the first step in evaluating shippers is determining the level of competition they've been facing.

But the absolute first step in evaluating shippers to or from New York is checking their drug dependency.

The two drugs in question are Lasix, a diuretic for bleeders, and bute, a pain-killer, frequently compared to aspirin, which is occasionally taken by humans.

New York is the only racing state in the country which prohibits all drugs 48 hours before post time. Most other states allow Lasix and bute. Lasix is the more important of the two.

The percentage of race horses who bleed—it's called EIPH for Exercise Induced Pulmonary Hemorrhaging—may be as high as 50. It's a controversial issue, complicated because flushing a horse's system may expunge other drugs, and because many believe that Lasix enhances a horse's performance.

We don't have to come to a philosophical conclusion. What's important is recognizing shippers going off the drug because they're racing in New York, or horses from New York using Lasix in other states for the first time. Frequently, a horse's first race with Lasix is an improved performance.

Our subject in the Open Handicap at Yonkers, June 27, 1992, is Letterkenny Lad N. A horse with an 'N' last in his name means the horse came from New Zealand.

PACE — ONE MILE — WARM-UP BLACK — **OPEN HANDICAP** — **$2 EXACTA** — PURSE $25,000

RED **IDLE FELLA (NY)** — b h 5,by Brand New Fella, White Idol by Runnymede Chuck — 1:55.3 YR '92 22 6 2 3 $42,952 — 1:56.1 YR '91 44 4 6 7 $49,743

Luc Ouellette (145) — Red-Black-White — J. Omboni, J. Omboni, Jr., N.Y. — Tr.Joseph Omboni,Jr. — Last 8 starts--$22 950 — 5 1:55.3 — Lifetime $135,320

1 — 10-1

6-20YR-9	1	fst	27^1	55^1	$1{:}24^2$	$1{:}53^2$	Opn Hcp	25000	3	4	4	3^{o2}¾	6^5	8^8¾	$1{:}54^4$	8.90	(Ouellette)	Camachine CenterStrp JustnKr	uncovered brea
6-13YR-10	1	fst	27^1	56^2	$1{:}24^2$	1:53	Opn Hcp	25000	6	7	7°	$7^{o}4$½	8^6	7^3½	$1{:}53^3$	14.30	(Ouellette)	JustnKr CenterStrp AmbroHermar	outrur
6-6YR-11	1	fst	27^4	57^2	$1{:}26^2$	$1{:}54^4$	W800' Hcp	15000	7	2°	1	1^1¾	1^2	2½	$1{:}54^4$	3.40	(Ouellette)	BringEm IdleFella GrannysGarden	speed caught
5-30YR-7	1	fst	28^1	58^1	$1{:}26^3$	1:56	Prf Hcp	15000	5	4	4	4^3	4^2	1^1	1:56	5.60	(Fluet)	IdleFella BJsEncore BringEm	improve just c
5-16YR-3	1	fst	27^2	55^4	$1{:}24^4$	$1{:}54^4$	Opn Hcp	25000	4	1°	1	1½	1^2¾	3^2	$1{:}55^1$	3.70	(Ouellette)	ThorFashion Lionheart IdleFella	spd,press brea
5-9YR-5	1	fst	28^1	58	$1{:}26^4$	$1{:}55^3$	W8001 Hcp	15000	1	1	1	1^1	1^1½	1^3¾	$1{:}55^3$	4.50	(Ouellette)	IdleFella BJsEncore PassByDay	speed strong
5-2YR-10	1	fst	27^2	56^4	$1{:}25^3$	$1{:}54^4$	Prf Hcp	15000	7	7	6°	6^6½	6^6	6^6¾	1:56	10.90	(Ouellette)	HumberTrail Smileyface PassByDay	no rally
4-25YR-5	1	fst	27^2	57^2	$1{:}26^4$	$1{:}56^1$	Prf Hcp	15000	6	6	6°	$6^{o}4$¾	5^3½	4^2	$1{:}56^3$	13.80	(Ouellette)	AmbroHermar CenterStrp Smileyface	belated pace

BLUE **SMILEY FACE** — b g 5,by Nihilator, Happy Sharon by Most Happy Fella — Smiley Face Stb. & Howard Taylor, N.Y. & Pa. — 1:54.4 YR 92 18 2 2 4 $34,650 — 1:53.2 VD ¾ 91 19 8 2 4 $97,180

2 Ray Schnittker (145) Brown-Gold — Tr.Warren Schnittker — Last 8 starts-$19,300 — 4 1:53.2 ¾ Lifetime $168,098

	6-20YR-9	1	fst	27	56^2	$1:25^4$	$1:54^4$	W800¹	15000	5	3	1	1^1¼	1^2	1^3	$1:54^4$	2.20	(OuelletteL)SmileyFace Improvisation GrannysGarder	top cruised
	6-13HP¾	1	fst	27^1	55^4	$1:24^2$	$1:54^3$	Inv	15000	2	2^2	2	3	3^2¼	3^1¼	$1:54^4$	15.90	(BoringC)BalancedAttack FabulousSmileyFace	
	6-6Mid	1	fst	28	57^1	$1:25^4$	1:55	Inv Hcp	15000	5	6	6	6	5^4¾	5^3¼	$1:55^3$	9.30	(MorrillJJr)OsbornesTowner KashinPrint SummicrestHappy	
	5-30YR-7	1	fst	27^3	58^3	$1:28^3$	$1:57^1$	W800¹ Hcp	15000	5	5	5^1	3^{o1}¼	4^1¼	4^2¼	$1:57^3$	2.60	(LancasterM)Lionheart PacificDream LordTylerHanover	good move fin
	5-16YR-3	1	fst	27^2	55^4	$1:24^4$	$1:54^4$	Opn Hcp	25000	6	8	8	$8^{oo}4$¾	7^5	7^3¼	$1:55^2$	13.80	(MorrillJJr)ThorFashion Lionheart IdleFella	8w wide brec
	5-9YR-5	1	fst	27^1	56^3	1:26	1:55	Opn Hcp	25000	3	1^1	1	1no	2^1¼	3^2¾dh	$1:55^3$	11.40	(SchnittkrR)JustinKin BlackstickSide (dh ThorFshn-SmlyFace	dr.prss brec
	5-2YR-10	1	fst	27^2	56^4	$1:25^3$	$1:54^4$	Prf Hcp	15000	4	1	1	1^1¾	1^1¼	2^1¼	1:55	6.90	(SchnittkrR)HumberTrail SmileyFace PassByDay	speed caught
8-1	4-25YR-5	1	fst	27^2	57^2	$1:26^4$	$1:56^1$	Prf Hcp	15000	1	2	3	3^2¼	3^2	3^2	$1:56^3$	6.50	(SchnittkrR)ArmbroHerman CenterStrip SmileyFace	yld pkt no gair

WHITE **CENTER STRIP (NY)** — b h 5,by On The Road Again,Little Stripper by Meadow Skipper — Letts Farm, Smithfield, R.I. — 1:53.2 YR 92 8 1 3 1 $31,750 — 1:54.4 PcD¾ 91 31 8 4 0 $84,890

3 Robert Tiabert (165) Blue-White-Red — Tr.Ronald Marshall — Last 8 starts-$31,750 — 5 1:53.2 Lifetime $457,610

	6-20YR-9	1	fst	27^1	55^1	$1:24^2$	$1:53^2$	Opn Hcp	25000	4	5	5^{oo}	$4^{oo}2$¼	2^1	2^{nk}	$1:53^2$	3.40	(TiabertR)Camachine CenterStrip JustinKin	just missed
	6-13YR-10	1	fst	27^1	56^2	$1:24^2$	1:53	Opn Hcp	25000	2	2	2	3^{o1}¼	3^2	2^{nk}	1:53	5.50	(TiabertR)JustinKin CenterStrip ArmbroHerman	trip.strong pce
	6-6YR-11	1	fst	27	54^3	1:24	$1:53^1$	Opn Hcp	25000	4	4	4	4^3¼	4^4¼	3^4¼	1:54	19.90	(TiabertR)ArmbroHerman ArcaneHanover CenterStrip	angled str mild
	5-30YR-7	1	fst	28^1	57^1	1:25	$1:53^3$	Opn Hcp	25000	4	5	4°	3^{o1}¼	3^1¾	7^8¾	$1:55^2$	9.00	(LancasterM)Cambest ArcaneHanover ArmbroHerman	lost cvr brec
	5-23YR-12	1	fst	27^1	55^4	1:25	$1:53^2$	Opn Hcp	25000	1	3	3	1^{hd}	1^1¼	1^1¾	$1:53^2$	10.90	(TiabertR)CenterStrip ThorFashion JustinKin	gritty mile
	5-16YR-3	1	fst	27^4	58^2	1:27	$1:55^4$	W8001 Hcp	15000	4	7	8	8^8¾	8^9¼	7^8¼	$1:57^2$	*1.80	(TiabertR)Candral BigArrow HHSteel	sat in wknd
	5-9YR-5	1	fst	28^1	58	$1:26^4$	$1:56^3$	W8001 Hcp	15000	7	8	7°	$7^{oo}4$¼	6^5¼	8^7	1:57	5.10	(TiabertR)IdleFella BusEncore PassByDay	4 wide little
4-1	4-25YR-5	1	fst	27^2	57^2	$1:26^4$	$1:56^1$	Prf Hcp	15000	2	4	2°	2^o¼	2¼	2^1	$1:56^2$	17.80	(TiabertR)ArmbroHerman CenterStrip SmileyFace	long unc game

GREEN **PILGRIMS PATRIOT (NY)** — b h 6,by Nistroos, Irene Almahurst by High Ideal — Lawrence Stein & Claire Speno, N.J. — 1:54.1 YR 92 20 3 3 4 $80,820 — 1:53.0 M1 91 28 6 6 6 $110,640

4 Walter Case,Jr. (135) Maroon-White — Tr.Jeffrey LaPoff — Last 8 starts-$33,750 — 5 1:53.0 (1) Lifetime $677,332

	6-20YR-9	1	fst	27^1	55^1	$1:24^2$	$1:53^2$	Opn Hcp	25000	5	6	6	7^4¾	7^6	7^8	1:55	*1.70	(CaseWJr)Camachine CenterStrip JustinKin	no moves
	6-13YR-10	1	fst	27^1	57	1:26	$1:54^1$	W800¹	17500	1	3	1	1^1	1^1	1^2¼	$1:54^1$	*.80	(CaseWJr)PilgrimsPatriot Camachine Improvisator	1/4 move easy
	6-6Gy¹	1	gd	28^3	58^4	1:29	1:57	Qua		7	4^1	1	1	1^1	1¾	1:57	nb	(MenzC)PilgrimsPatriot BigDate RomanticSup	
	5-9YR-5	1	fst	27^1	56^3	1:26	1:55	Opn Hcp	25000	7	6x	6^{oo}	$7^{o}4$¼	7^6¾	8^9¼	$1:56^4$	*1.50	(CaseWJr)JustinKin BlackstickSide (dh ThorFshn-SmlyFace	tck.unc.brk trd
	5-2YR-10	1	fst	27^2	57^1	$1:26^2$	$1:54^2$	Opn Hcp	25000	6	6	5^1	4^{oo1}¼	2^1¼	2^1	$1:54^3$	*.80	(CaseWJr)ArmbroHerman PilgrimsPatriot BusEncore	cvr wide solid
	4-25YR-5	1	fst	27^4	57	$1:25^4$	$1:55^3$	Opn Hcp	25000	8	5^1	2°	2^{o1}	5^3¾	7^8	$1:57^1$	*.90	(CaseWJr)OaklandAve TulsaBlueChip ThorFashion	pkd wd chll trd
	4-18YR-4	1	sly	28^2	57^3	$1:26^3$	$1:56^1$	Opn Hcp	25000	8	3^1	1^1	1^1¼	1^1¼	1^2	$1:56^1$	7.00	(CaseWJr)PilgrimsPatriot BringEm JustinKin	game
5-1	4-11YR-1	1	fst	28^3	59^1	$1:28^3$	$1:57^3$	Prf Hcp	15000	8x	acc	dnf					*.80	(CaseWJr)BringEm Stylized HumberTrail	accident

BLACK **LETTERKENNY LAD N** — b g 7,by Tudor Hanover, Nevele Cherie by Nevele Holiday — Alvin Jacobson, Peekskill, N.Y. — 1:51.4 M1 92 15 8 1 3 $71,209 — None in U.S.A. 91 17 1 1 1 $14,268

5 Richard Wojcio (150) Blue-White-Yellow — Tr.Raymond Fils — Last 8 starts-$39,760 — 7 1:51.4 (1) Lifetime $128,437

	6-20M1-8	1	fst	27^2	56^3	1:24	$1:51^4$	Opn	30000	6	1	3	5^4¼	4^5¼	3^4	$1:52^3$	L2.90	(ParkerH)JCsSuppy ShogunHanover LttrknyLadN	(L)traf gd pce
	6-13M1-7	1	fst	27^2	55	1:24	1:52	NW4	15000	9	6^1	5	$5^{o}3$¼	3^1	1^2	1:52	L*2.00	(ParkerH)LetterkennyLadN CaliforniaCam Spectacle	(L)charged by
	6-6M1-9	1	fst	27^3	55^3	$1:23^2$	$1:51^4$	NW13000	16000	9	1	1	1¾	1^2¼	1^1¼	$1:51^4$	L12.90	(ParkerH)LttrknyLdN ThreeFrTheRc OlFlyngFla	(L)monstrous
	5-30M1-6	1	fst	27^2	55^3	$1:25^2$	$1:53^3$	NW12500	16000	4	1	1^1	1no	1^1¼	1^1	$1:53^3$	L*1.60	(PierceR)LetterkennyLadN Camachine StylishCar	(L)game effor
	5-23M1-10	1	fst	27^1	54^2	$1:22^2$	$1:51^3$	NW4	15000	9	4^1	4	4^3¾	5^6¼	9^8¼	$1:53^1$	L4.30	(McNicholM)QuickComeback CoolFlyingFla Camaraderie	(L)tuck brec
	5-9M1-6	2	fst	30^4	$2:00^4$	$3:28^4$	3:58	Endurance	33000	2	2	3^1	1^1¼	1^1¼	3^1¾	$3:58^2$	L*2.70	(McNicholM)Improvisator Wavelength LetterkennyLadN	2 mi (L)3 moves
	5-2M1-7	1½	fst	28^1	1:27	$2:23^4$	$2:53^4$	Endurance	15000	1	2	2	1^{nk}	1^1¼	4^3¼	$2:54^2$	L*.60	(MoiseyevJ)Improvisation Ozony StylishCar	1 1/2 mi (L)prs
3-1	4-25M1-3	1⅛	fst	27^4	56^3	$1:26^2$	$2:08^4$	Endurance	15000	1	4	1^1	1^1¼	1^1¼	1^1¼	$2:08^4$	Le*.40	(MoiseyevJ)LttrknyLadN Knockyimage Improvisator	1 1/8 mi (L)ez

YELLOW **CAMACHINE** — b g 5,by Cam Fella, H H Serene by Isle Of Wight — Cass Farms, Inc., Athol, Mass. — 1:53.2 YR 92 8 3 3 1 $29,900 — 1:53.4 PPk¾ 91 32 8 7 1 $52,327

6 David Ingraham (145) Orange-Blue-White — Tr.David Ingraham — Last 8 starts-$29,900 — 5 1:53.2 Lifetime $162,147

	6-20YR-9	1	fst	27^1	55^1	$1:24^2$	$1:53^2$	Opn Hcp	25000	2	1	1	1^2	1^1	1^{nk}	$1:53^2$	12.10	(IngrahamD)Camachine CenterStrip JustinKin	speed lasted
	6-13YR-10	1	fst	27^1	57	1:26	$1:54^1$	W800¹	17500	7	5	3^1	2^{o1}	2^1	2^2¼	$1:54^3$	7.00	(IngrahamD)PilgrimsPatriot Camachine Improvisator	uncvrd 2nd best
	6-6M1-9	1	fst	27^3	55^3	$1:23^2$	$1:51^4$	NW13000	16000	10	3	2°	$5^{o}3$	4^4	5^5	$1:52^4$	L19.70	(IngrahamD)LttrknyLdN ThreeFrTheRc OlFlyngFla	(L)parked mile
	5-30M1-6	1	fst	27^2	55^3	$1:25^2$	$1:53^3$	NW12500	16000	9	5	3	2^{ono}	2^1¼	2^1	$1:53^4$	L14.90	(IngrahamD)LetterkennyLadN Camachine StylishCar	(L)parked game
	5-23M1-10	1	fst	27^4	56^3	$1:25^2$	$1:54^4$	NW6500	8000	3	3	3	2^1¾	1no	1no	$1:54^4$	L4.20	(IngrahamD)Camachine Armada PoloPlayer	(L)gme unc mile
	5-1PPk¾	1	fst	28^3	59^4	$1:28^3$	$1:57^4$	Qua		7	2	2	2	2^1¼	2¾	1:58	Lnb	(IngrahamD)Tyrannica Camachine Chemoty	(L)
	4-24PPk¾	1	fst	28^4	59^4	$1:29^4$	$1:59^2$	Qua		7	2^1	2	2	2^6	2^7¼	$2:00^4$	Lnb	(IngrahamD)FinalDestiny Camachine Tyrannica	(L)
8-1	1-25PPk¾	1						Opn	8000	2									scratched lame
	1-18PPk¾	1	fst	27^2	56^4	$1:25^4$	$1:54^4$	Opn	5000	7	3	3	2	1^1	3^3¼	$1:55^2$	L*1.90	(IngrahamD)WAThamine FinalDestiny Camachine	(L)

ORANGE **ARMBRO HERMAN** — b h 6,by Legal Notice, Armbro Penny by Tar Heel — Magnet Racing Stables, Kenmore, N.Y. — 1:53.1 YR 92 12 4 0 2 $50,000 — 1:54.1 YR 91 44 9 7 3 $113,925

7 Normand Fluet (150) Gold-Black-White — Tr.Normand Fluet — Last 8 starts-$36,250 — 6 1:53.1 Lifetime $437,852

	6-20YR-9	1	fst	27^1	55^1	$1:24^2$	$1:53^2$	Opn Hcp	25000	6	3	2	2^2	3^2	4^3¾	$1:54^1$	3.60	(FluetN)Camachine CenterStrip JustinKin	pkd tuck ever
	6-13YR-10	1	fst	27^1	56^2	$1:24^2$	1:53	Opn Hcp	25000	8	3	4	4^2¾	4^2¼	3^2	$1:53^2$	11.80	(FluetN)JustinKin CenterStrip ArmbroHerman	inside start
	6-6YR-11	1	fst	27	54^3	1:24	$1:53^1$	Opn Hcp	25000	3	1	1	1^2	1^2¾	1^3	$1:53^1$	5.20	(FluetN)ArmbroHerman ArcaneHanover CenterStrip	tie track record
	5-30YR-7	1	fst	28^1	57^1	1:25	$1:53^3$	Opn Hcp	25000	2	3	5	4^3	5^3	3^3¼	$1:54^1$	9.70	(FluetN)Cambest ArcaneHanover ArmbroHerman	up for third
	5-23YR-12	1	fst	27^1	55^4	1:25	$1:53^2$	Opn Hcp	25000	5	1	2	5^2¾	5^5	4^7¼	$1:54^4$	3.60	(FluetN)CenterStrip ThorFashion JustinKin	used shuffled
	5-16YR-3	1	fst	27^2	55^4	$1:24^4$	$1:54^4$	Opn Hcp	25000	8	5	5°	$5^{o}3$	5^3¼	6^3¼	$1:55^2$	4.40	(FluetN)ThorFashion Lionheart IdleFella	pkd gap cvr trd
	5-9YR-5	1	fst	27^1	56^3	1:26	1:55	Opn Hcp	25000	8	8	8	6^4¼	6^5¼	5^3¾	$1:55^4$	15.30	(FluetN)JstnKin BlackstickSide (dh ThorFshn SmlyFace	impr ins mid
6-1	5-2YR-10	1	fst	27^2	57^1	$1:26^2$	$1:54^2$	Opn Hcp	25000	4	1	1	1^1¼	1^1¼	1^1	$1:54^2$	4.20	(FluetN)ArmbroHerman PilgrimsPatriot BusEncore	pressed strong

GREY **JUSTIN KIN** — b h 4,by Slapstick, Denia by Silent Majority — See The Light Stable, Dix Hills, N.Y. — 1:53.0 YR 92 16 3 2 4 $71,250 — 1:53.0 ScD¾ 91 25 6 2 2 $279,470

8 Herve Filion (152) Red-Blue-White — Tr.Brett Pelling — Last 8 starts-$39,250 — 4 1:53.0 Lifetime $449,794

	6-20YR-9	1	fst	27^1	55^1	$1:24^2$	$1:53^2$	Opn Hcp	25000	7	7	7°	$6^{oo}3$¾	4^2¼	3^1¼	$1:53^3$	5.10	(FilionHer)Camachine CenterStrip JustinKin	wide start tr
	6-13YR-10	1	fst	27^1	56^2	$1:24^2$	1:53	Opn Hcp	25000	3	5	3°	2^{ono}	2no	1^{nk}	1:53	3.00	(FilionHer)JustinKin CenterStrip ArmbroHerman	track record
	6-6YR-11	1	fst	27	54^3	1:24	$1:53^1$	Opn Hcp	25000	5	6	5^1	$3^{o}2$	3^3	5^4¼	1:54	*1.50	(FilionHer)ArmbroHerman ArcaneHanover CenterStrip	wd unc no thr
	5-30YR-7	1	fst	28^1	57^1	1:25	$1:53^3$	Opn Hcp	25000	7	7	7	$6^{oo}3$¼	4^1¾	4^3¼	$1:54^4$	26.90	(MarohnJ)Cambest ArcaneHanover ArmbroHerman	4 wide wknd fe
	5-23YR-12	1	fst	27^1	55^4	1:25	$1:53^2$	Opn Hcp	25000	6	6	6	4^{oo1}¼	2^1¼	3¾	$1:53^3$	3.90	(FilionHer)CenterStrip ThorFashion JustinKin	swept faded
	5-9YR-5	1	fst	27^1	56^3	1:26	1:55	Opn Hcp	25000	6	3^1	3^1	2^{ono}	1^1¼	1^2¼	1:55	3.20	(FilionHer)JstnKin BlackstickSide (dh ThorFshn-SmlyFace	tck.chl easy
	4-25YR-5	1	fst	27^4	57	$1:25^4$	$1:55^3$	Opn Hcp	25000	7	7	4^{oo}	4^{oo1}¼	3^1¼	4^3	$1:56^1$	8.90	(FilionHer)OaklandAve TulsaBlueChip ThorFashion	wide 2x fttnd
6-1	4-18YR-4	1	sly	28^2	57^3	$1:26^3$	$1:56^1$	Opn Hcp	25000	7	5	4°	2^{o1}¼	2^1¼	3^3	$1:56^4$	2.40	(FilionHer)PilgrimsPatriot BringEm JustinKin	gd cvr in wknd

Page 15

Letterkenny is the only horse in the field of eight who didn't race at Yonkers—therefore drug-free—in his last start. All of Letterkenny's PPs were with Lasix at The Meadowlands. A reasonable conclusion is that the 7-year-old is a proven bleeder, because horses are treated with Lasix in their next starts only after bleeding in a previous race. A reasonable question then follows: Can racing without Lasix affect his performance tonight? There is absolutely no way anyone can predict before the race if it will or won't. So the correct assumption is that it may.

His PPs show four wins and two thirds in his last 8 starts. His last win was in a Non-Winners of 4, two starts back. In his most recent race, he moved up to the Open and finished a solid third despite traffic problems.

Evidently, Yonkers bettors thought so little of the regulars in Yonkers's Open Pace that they bet Letterkenny, the stranger without Lasix, down to 7-5 from the 5 post.

Even without the Lasix issue, his odds were hard to fathom. Though he was the oldest horse in the race, he was absolutely last in career earnings. His earnings the last two years ranked him seventh out of eight.

The lack of respect the Yonkers bettors gave two of their own is strange.

Three starts back, the 7 horse, Armbro Herman, tied the Yonkers track record of 1:53.1, winning by three lengths. A week later, the 8 horse, Justin Kin, broke the track record, winning by a neck in 1:53. This night, Justin Kin went off at 6-1 and Armbro Herman 13-1. Both were overlays.

Center Strip, who'd finished a close second in his last two starts, was pounded down to 2-1.

But the most startling odds belonged to Letterkenny, a 7-5 shot who was riddled with holes, one being the absence of Lasix. Justin Kin won and paid $15.20. Center Strip was second, and Armbro Herman third. Letterkenny finished last and reportedly bled copiously.

Ready for this? The same scene had been played out in the previous race when Southbound, a shipper from The Meadowlands on Lasix, was bet down to even money and finished second.

Romigs Hot Rod was a horse who was driven from extremes—extreme post positions—when he showed up as the 5 horse in a Non-

Winners of $1,500 Last 5 OR Non-Winners of 4 Races Lifetime, at Saratoga, August 20, 1992.

ONE MILE PACE
PURSE $1,900
THURSDAY, AUGUST 20, 1992
PICK THREE
&
EXACTA

FOURTH RACE

3-5 YEAR OLDS
NON-WINNERS $1500 LAST 5 STARTS
OR 4 PARI-MUTUEL RACES LIFETIME OR A RACE IN 1992
INELIGIBLE: WINNERS OF $12500 IN 1992

WARM UP-BLACK

5-2 HARD DRIVE — Program 1 — YELLOW
b g 3 Ralph Hanover-Armbro Tiffany-Most Happy Fella
Ferme Am Harwood Stable, Vaudrevil, Que.
WALLY HENNESSEY (140) bl-go-wh (145-37-30-26-.430) Tr—Pierre Paradis (.257)
Stga 1:59 1992 24 5 3 3 $9,720
BB ¾ 2:04 1991 8 3 0 0 $910
3,1:59 Lifetime $10,630

Date	Trk	Purse	Cd	Class	Dis	1/4	1/2	3/4	Time	PP	1/4	1/2	3/4	Str	Fin	Ind 1/4 Time	Ind Time	Odds	Driver	Order Of Finish (First Second Third)	Temp
8-15 92	Stga	1900	ft	NW1500L5CD	1	30	59	128 4	159 2	4	4°	2°	2°ns	4	6 8¼	32 1	201	2.70	BBelanger	Shaunson,ItsCaviar,LockStockNBar	86-0
8-7 92	Stga	1900	ft	NW1500L5CD	1	29 1	59 1	128 2	159	4	7	1°	1 1	1	1 4¼	30 3	159	5.00	WHasy	HrdDrv,Fourtwentytwo,LubcBluChp	80-0
8-1 92	Stga	2400	ft	NW2000L5CD	1	29 2	100 2	130 3	201	6	7	4°°	3°°½	4	7 8½	32	202 3	8.20	FCopolaJr	JimmyLast,LadsMan,ClascStepshot	73-0
7-14 92	YR	5500	ft	3-4YRNW3CD	1	28	58 2	127 1	156 1	3	6	7°	6°	6 3¼	6 17		158 3	21.60	BMojcio	YorMothrsBoy,ACorant,AsstWapon	84-0
7-4 92	Stga	2300	ft	NW2500L7CD	1	29 4	100 1	130 1	159 3	8	9	9	9 4½	9	8 5	29 2	200 3	53.40	BBelanger	WilsendsBrat,Triptique,Cuffie	75-0
6-26 92	Stga	2300	ft	NW2500L7CD	1	29 3	100 4	131	200	8	9	i7°°	8°°3½	9	9 11	30 2	202 1	37.60	BBelanger	TulsyRainbow,ItsCaviar,HughsPrd	88-0
6-20 92	Stga	2000	ft	NW4PMLTCD	1	29 2	100 2	129 3	200 3	6	6	2°	1°½	2	1ns	31	200 3	16.80	FCopolaJr	Hardrv,EuntsBluNcs,DosDignity	87-9

3-1 OXYMORON (NY) — Program 2 — WHITE
b g 4 Seahawk Hanover-Sweet Carrots-Tempered Yankee
Barry M. Ikler, Albany, N.Y.
KIM CRAWFORD (155) red-blk-wh (466-77-73-54-.291) Tr—Gene White (.298)
Stga 2:00 1 1992 23 2 5 3 $5,455
Stga 2:04 1991 13 1 4 3 $2,615
4,2:00 1 Lifetime $8,070

Date	Trk	Purse	Cd	Class	Dis	1/4	1/2	3/4	Time	PP	1/4	1/2	3/4	Str	Fin	Ind 1/4 Time	Ind Time	Odds	Driver	Order Of Finish (First Second Third)	Temp
8-12 92	Stga	1900	ft	NW1500L5CD	1	29 1	59 3	130	159 3	5	5	6	6°2½	4	2 1¼	29 1	159 4	4.70	KCrawford	WaltnamTwn,Oxymron,ClascStpshot	70-0
8-6 92	Stga	1800	ft	C&GNW3PMLT	1	29 4	100 2	130 1	200 1	3	1	1	1½	1	1ns	30	200 1	*1.10	DCaploJr	Oxymoron,ItalianDignity,OlRebr	80-0
7-30 92	Stga	1800	ft	NW3PMLT	1	29 1	100 1	130 3	159 4	2	3	3	2ns	1	2 2¼	29 4	200 2	*.80	DCaploJr	VideoMan,Oxymoron,Kefler	73-0
7-16 92	Stga	1800	ft	NW3PMLT	1	30 1	101 1	130 2	200	8	8	8	8 4½	7	5 5¼	29 4	201	23.70	JRandall	SnorCdam,AngusHanovr,FinalBow	77-0
7-12 92	Stga A	1500	ft	NW2PMLTCD	1	29 1	100 1	129 4	200 2	5	2	2	3 1¼	3	1 2¼	30 2	200 2	*.70	DCaploJr	Oxymoron,ParadeJty,ItalianDgnty	86-0
7-7 92	Stga	1500	ft	C&GNW2PMCD	1	29 2	101 1	131	200 4	7	6	4°	3°2½	2	2 2	29 4	201 1	6.70	DCaploJr	DirectHugo,Oxymoron,PeterMac	78-0
6-29 92	YR	3500	ft	10000CL	1	28 1	58 3	128 4	200 4	8	8	8	8	7 1½	6 3¼		201 3	12.60	BDagnalt	BossieBack,RdHotRdr,LSteToFam	74-0

10-1 RIGHT UNCLE RUBE (NY) — Program 3 — PURPLE
b g 5 Temujin-Nancy Ward-Sample Fella
B Friends Stable & Daniel J. Gallagher, NY
DAVID MARSHALL (185) ltbl-red-gld (362-38-50-51-.229) Tr—Guy Roemer (.278)
Stga 2:00 2 1992 5 1 0 0 $1,134
YR 1:59 1 1991 11 4 1 0 $6,405
4,1:59 1 Lifetime $7,864

Date	Trk	Purse	Cd	Class	Dis	1/4	1/2	3/4	Time	PP	1/4	1/2	3/4	Str	Fin	Ind 1/4 Time	Ind Time	Odds	Driver	Order Of Finish (First Second Third)	Temp
8-10 92	Stga	1500	ft	NW1000L5CD	1	28 4	59 4	130	200 2	1	1	1	1 1	1	1 1¼	30 2	200 2	5.80	PStaser	RightUncleRube,Pator,HughesPrid	77-0
8-1 92	Stga		gd	QUA	1	30 4	102 3	133	202 4	1	1	1	1		1 2¼	29 4	202 4	NB	DMarshall	RightUnclRub,Synrgy,BoldExplor	80-0
6-10 92	Stga	1900	ft	NW2000L7CD	1	29	59 3	130 2	201 3	scr	lm				scr					NvadaPlais,MonDanc,JstaplenAdam	71-0
5-21 92	Stga	2500	ft	7500CLCD	1	29 2	101 1	131 3	200 2	8	8	8	8°5¼	8	8 10 3	29 4	202 2	216.70	PStaser	HolysRUB,WilsendsBrat,Prpostrous	86-0
5-14 92	Stga	2500	ft	7500CLCD	1	28 4	59 2	129	200	4	8	8	7 4½	7	7 6	31 1	201 1	20.80	PStaser	JustaplenAdam,JonVon,ItsCaviar	61-0
5-7 92	Stga	2500	ft	7500CLCD	1	30	100 3	130 3	201	2	3	6	6 3¼	7	4 5¼	30 4	202 1	13.00	PStaser	FarLapFella,JonVon,JaredsFella	63-0
4-30 92	Stga	2300	gd	NW2100L7CD	1	28 3	59 3	129	159 3	2	4	5	4 6	3	4 7	30 4	201	13.30	DMarshall	HolysRUB,JonVon,Cuffie	58-0

9-2 CEDAR LOVE (NY) — Program 4 — BLACK
blk g 5 Holland-Love By Knight-Miracle Knight
John P. Schwed, Mayfield, N.Y.
JOHN SCHWED (160) ltblue-wh-gray (32-1-6-4-.177) Tr—John Schwed (.161)
YR 1:59 4 1992 18 2 1 2 $6,337
Stga 1:59 2 1991 39 8 5 5 $16,899
4,1:59 2 Lifetime $40,805

Date	Trk	Purse	Cd	Class	Dis	1/4	1/2	3/4	Time	PP	1/4	1/2	3/4	Str	Fin	Ind 1/4 Time	Ind Time	Odds	Driver	Order Of Finish (First Second Third)	Temp
8-13 92	Stga	2400	ft	NW2000L5CD	1	30 3	100 4	130	159 3	6	8	8	8°12	7	6 8¼	28 4	201 1	6.70	JSchwed	JonVon,TooneyBilly,SenorCedam	82-0
8-1 92	Stga	2900	ft	10000CL	1	28 2	58 2	127 3	159 1	7	7	7	6°°6	4	3 1¼	30 4	159 3	49.30	JSchwed	CrystalWall,PalmrBluChp,CdarLov	73-0
7-25 92	Stga	2900	ft	10000CL	1	28 3	59 2	129 2	158 1	5	7	7°	6°3½	5	4 6	29 2	159 2	5.80	JSchwed	CrystalWall,ANoseForTrbl,BrndonT	78-0
7-19 92	YR	3850	ft	10000CL	1	28 2	59 1	129	158 2	6	6	7°°	3°	4 4½	4 4½		159 2	3.90	JSchwed	OvrnightDlvry,CaraMio,GovnorKC	81-0
7-2 92	YR	3750	ft	10000CLCD	1	29 2	59 2	129 3	158 4	6	4	4	5	4 5¼	3 3½		159 2	12.90	JSchwed	FiddlerBlueChip,Sulsaid,CdarLov	73-0
6-17 92	YR	3750	ft	10000CLCD	1	28 3	58 1	129 3	159 2	1	4	4	4°	3 4	5 5½		200 2	1.80	JSchwed	FWFinalSay,KatrHnvr,ManhtanPrid	75-0
6-3 92	YR	3500	ft	10000CLCD	1	28 2	58 2	128 2	158 1	2	1	1	1	2 4	2 1¼		159 3	*.40	JSchwed	HonomaBrnton,CdarLov,Forthecha	75-0

8-1 ROMIGS HOT ROD — Program 5 — GREEN
ch g 4 Laetare-Sun Lady-Breton
Frances N. Lawyer & Cecil T. Walker Jr., Schenectady N.Y.
GERRY MATTISON (160) blue-or-wh (366-58-45-25-.250) Tr—Gilbert Lawyer Jr (.162)
VD ½ 2:00 1 1992 27 5 5 3 $11,029
Nfld 2:03 3 1991 14 4 1 2 $2,259
4,2:00 1 ½ Lifetime $13,288

Date	Trk	Purse	Cd	Class	Dis	1/4	1/2	3/4	Time	PP	1/4	1/2	3/4	Str	Fin	Ind 1/4 Time	Ind Time	Odds	Driver	Order Of Finish (First Second Third)	Temp
8-14 92	Stga	2000	sy	NW1500L5CD	1⅛	30 4	134 3	205 1	234 2	1	1	1	1 1	1	2 1	29 2	234 3	*1.10	GMattison	PartsGalorN,RomigsHotRod,ArtBaby	63-0
8-8 92	Stga	2400	sy	NW2000L5CD	1	30 1	102 2	132 4	203 1	8	8	8	8 5	8	7 8¼	31 1	205	15.70	GMattison	JimmyLast,MajorCollins,AvonBrz	73-0
8-1 92	Stga	2000	ft	NW1500L5	1⅛	29 4	133	203	232	3	2	2	2 1	2	2¼	29	232 1	*.90	JRandall	AvonBreeze,RomigsHotRod,Cuffie	73-0
7-18 92	Stga	2400	ft	NW2000L5CD	1	28 2	58 1	127 3	158 2	7	7	7	7 3	7	5 7¼	30 3	158 4	9.80	JRandall	Trynatopus,Rabtnahat,NvadaPlais	79-0
7-11 92	Stga	2900	ft	10000CLCD	1	28 2	58 3	127 4	158 1	7	6	4°	3°°2½	2	3 3	30 3	158 4	22.50	JRandall	CrystlWll,Fortwntytwo,RmgsHotRd	78-0
7-4 92	Stga	3500	ft	W05000LT	1	27 3	56 2	125 4	156 2	8	8	8	8 9	8	8 11	31	158 3	24.50	JRandall	VillageJoe,Paco,RalphsCaper	75-0
6-27 92	Stga	3300	sy	W04500LT	1	28 4	100	129 3	158 4	1	2	3	3 1	2	2 2	29 2	159 1	4.40	JRandall	GantKhan,RmgsHotRod,ClascStpsht	65-0

12-1 THRILLS N CHILLS (NY) — Program 6 — RED
b m 4 Seahawk Hanover-Race For Love-Race Time
Sanford J. Goldfarb, Ian Behar & Howard Tanney, NY.
STEPHEN SMITH (160) gray-red-black (10-2-0-0-.200) Tr—Michael Dukis (.222)
M 1 1:57 4 1992 15 1 1 0 $4,767
Haw 1 2:02 3 1991 13 3 1 0 $8,582
4,1:57 4 1 Lifetime $15,349

Date	Trk	Purse	Cd	Class	Dis	1/4	1/2	3/4	Time	PP	1/4	1/2	3/4	Str	Fin	Ind 1/4 Time	Ind Time	Odds	Driver	Order Of Finish (First Second Third)	Temp
8-14 92	Stga	2600	sy	10000CLCD	1	30	102 1	132 4	201 4	6	6	6°	6 3¼	5	5 10	30 1	203 4	41.00	SSmith	BoScotsPpr,JaJant,CarolynsFancy	83-0
8-5 92	Stga	1900	ft	NW1500L5CD	1	29 1	100	130 2	200 2	7	7	6	6 5	6	7 5½	30	201 2	16.40	SSmith	SnorCdam,DbdChr,Pesthdrawgal	72-0
7-7 92	YR A	3500	ft	10000CL	1	29 1	59	128 3	158 3	3	2°	1	2	2 1¼	2 2¼		159 1	3.60	SSmith	ConyIslandBaby,ThrlsNChls,BWamd	78-0
6-23 92	YR	3750	ft	10000CLCD	1	29 3	101	132	201 2	3	5	5°	3°	3 2	5 5		202 2	4.60	SSmith	StpAsdLads,BthAlmahrst,Dramsom	74-0
6-11 92	M1	6500	ft	FMnw6000L7	1	28	57 4	127 2	156	10	10i°	9°	9°°6¼	8 12½	8 20½	31 2	200	166.80	SSmith	QuotandFrsh,TestMPlea,BitmorePrd	73-0
6-5 92	M1		sy	QUA	1	29 4	59 2	129 2	158 4	2	6	6	7 12¼	7 17½	6 18	30 2	202 2	NB	RSilverman	StonebridgeScooter,Chiool,Fvrteh	80-4
5-22 92	YR		ft	QUAT-P	1	30 2	102 2	131 4	202 3	5	4	2°	1	1 3	1 5		202 3	NB	SSmith	ThrlsNChls,LifePlan,InYourFac	72-0

4-1 PORT GRAMPA (NY) — Program 9 — BLUE
b c 3 Seahawk Hanover-Wight Speed-Isle of Wight
(Lessee) Albra Stables, Yonkers, N.Y.
DANIEL CAPPELLO JR (115) blue-white (287-43-48-51-.302) Tr—Deborah Cappello (.278)
YR 1:58 3 1992 10 3 3 1 $7,782
First Starter
3,1:58 3 Lifetime $7,782

Date	Trk	Purse	Cd	Class	Dis	1/4	1/2	3/4	Time	PP	1/4	1/2	3/4	Str	Fin	Ind 1/4 Time	Ind Time	Odds	Driver	Order Of Finish (First Second Third)	Temp
8-12 92	Stga	1900	ft	NW1500L5CD	1	29 1	59 3	130	159 3	7	7	7	5°1¼	5	4 3¼	30	200 1	*1.80	DCaploJr	WaltnamTwn,Oxymron,ClascStpshot	70-0
8-1 92	Stga	2000	ft	NW4PMLTCD	1	29 2	59 3	129 3	159 2	1	3	1°	1½	2	2 1¼	30	159 3	*.40	DCaploJr	BoSctsBgFla,PrtGrampa,FnaLprdy	73-0
7-25 92	Stga	2000	ft	NW4PMLTCD	1	30 1	101 2	130 3	200 1	8i	8°	7°	6° 7	7	7 7¼	29 3	201 3	2.20	DCaploJr	FinaJopardy,SnorCdam,DCaDgnty	78-0
7-18 92	Stga		ft	QUA	1	30 1	102 1	133 3	204 4	4	4	4°	1 1	1	1 8¼	31 1	204 4	NB	DCaploJr	PortGrampa,ChcknTonght,WhtysFl	74-0
5-22 92	M1	6500	ft	nw2 cd	1	28 2	57	125 1	153 3	7	2	2	2° 1	4 5¼	5 6¼	29 2	154 4	6.50	DCaploJr	Pennant,Ringleader,Influential	85-0
5-12 92	YR A	4500	ft	3-4YRNW2CD	1	29	57 2	128 1	158 3	8	6	6°	5°°	3 2½	1½		158 3	9.80	DCaploJr	PortGrampa,LuckyCam,IndianaRed	63-0
5-3 92	MR A	7000	ft	SOPHOMORE	1	28 4	58 2	130 2	202	7	5	5°	1°°½	1½	2ns	31 3	202	*1.30	JDesimone	DeborahAr,PortGrampa,GeorgeDS	80-0

12-1 **PARADISE JEFFREY** br c 3 Slapstick-DuchessStratton-MostHappyFella | Stga 2:01 1992 8 2 3 0 $2,595
Glenn J.Angiolillo,New Canaan,Conn | First Starter
10 MICHAEL MC GIVERN (145) wh-grn (36-6-4-8-.302) Tr—Michael Mc Givern (.302) | 3,2:01 Lifetime $2,595
ORANGE

7-21^{92}	Stga		1500	ft	C&GNW2PMCD	1	30	101	130^{3}	201^{3}	4	4	2°	2°½	2	1be^{ns}	30^{4}	201^{3}	3.70	MMcGivern ParadiseJeffrey,PtrMac,SidShot	71-0
7-12^{92}	Stga	A	1500	ft	NW2PMLTCD	1	29^{1}	100^{1}	129^{4}	200^{2}	3	4	3°	2°½	2	2^{2}½	31	200^{4}	1.70	MMcGivern Oxymoron,ParadsJfry,ItalianDgnty	85-0
6-30^{92}	Stga		1500	ft	C&GNW2PMCD	1	29^{4}	100^{4}	130^{3}	201^{3}	6	6	6°	6°^{7}½	6	5^{1}½	30^{4}	202	4.50	MMcGivern OleRattler,SnorCdam,CharlGoWst	83-0
6-20^{92}	Stga		1800	ft	NW3PMLTCD	1	28^{3}	59^{3}	129^{3}	200^{2}	1x	4	4	5°[illegible]	5	4^{5}½ [illegible]	30^{1}	201^{2}	3.70	MMcGivern InvisblForc,BrdgVw,EastCoastKd	67-0
6-11^{92}	Stga		1300	ft	C&GNW1PMCD	1	29^{3}	100^{1}	130^{2}	201	2	3	1	1^{1}½	1	1^{2}½	30^{3}	201	*.70	MMcGivern ParadsJfry,AlGratLngths,Drcthgo	74-0
6-2^{92}	Stga		1300	ft	C&GNW1PMCD	1	29^{1}	100^{2}	130^{4}	200^{4}	4	5	4°	2°^{ns}	2	2^{2}	30^{2}	201^{1}	4.80	MMcGivern PrinclyMix,ParadsJfry,DrctHugo	74-0
5-25^{92}	Stga	A	1400	ft	NW1PMLTCD	1	29^{4}	100^{4}	131^{1}	202^{2}	3	4	4°	3°[illegible]	3	2^{3}	31^{3}	203	3.50	MMcGivern FinalJeopardy,ParadsJfry,Drcthgo	56-0

From the bottom up in his PPs, Romigs had drawn the 1, 8, 7, 7, 3, 8 and 1 posts. Three of the seven starts were on sloppy tracks.

A quick recap:

• June 27—Second by two lengths at 4-1 from the rail in a much tougher class (Winners of $4,500 and Over Lifetime). Spent most of the race in the pocket.

• July 4—Eighth by 11 at 24-1 in an even higher class (Winners of $5,000 and Over Lifetime). Sat eighth the whole way without a shot. The race went in 1:56.2. He's not that good or that fast.

• July 11—Dropped into a $10,000 claimer and was third by three from the 7 post at 22-1 with a bold three-wide sweep on the far turn. He tired late. The race went in 1:58.1. He checked in at 1:58.4 with a last half in :59.2.

• July 18—Back to a conditional pace (Non-Winners of $2,000 Last 5). Fifth by 2¼ from the 7 post at 9-1. Again, he had little chance coming from behind in a 1:58.2 mile.

• August 1—Drops to tonight's level and races extremely well in an unusual 1¼-mile race, finishing second by ¾ of a length as the 4-5 favorite, getting his last quarter in :29.

• August 8—Again from the 8 post, back up to NW of $2,000 Last 5. Sits last most of the way before finishing seventh by 8¾ at 15-1 on a sloppy track.

• August 14—Sloppy track back down to a NW of $1,500 Last 5. From the rail as the even-money favorite at 1¼ miles, he leads the whole way until late, finishing second by a length.

Evaluation: Romigs Hot Rod got good trips from his three races with an inside post and performed well in each. At ½-mile tracks such as Saratoga, good trips out of the 7 or 8 post are rare. Besides that, he'd been in twice over his head, caught a sloppy track three of seven times, and raced at a 1¼ mile twice. He was down to a level where he'd been second at 4-5. And he had a reasonable post made better by the scratch of the 3 horse. Out of the 4 post, he won and paid $15.80.

Here's another example. Check out Bridge View's win August 29 that showed up in his PPs the following week.

ONE MILE PACE
PURSE $2,000
SATURDAY, SEPTEMBER 5, 1992
FIRST HALF DAILY DOUBLE
&
EXACTA

FIRST RACE

3-5 YEAR OLDS
NON-WINNERS $1500 LAST 5 STARTS OR A RACE IN 1992
ALSO ELIGIBLE: NON-WINNERS $6500 LIFETIME

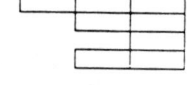

WARM UP-YELLOW

8-1 — 1 — WALDEN'S FIRST (NY) — YELLOW
b g 3 Niafirst-Tarport Louise-Thorpe Hanover — Krouner-Gould Rac Assoc,Saratoga Springs,N.Y.
GERRY MATTISON (160) blue-or-wh (410-71-48-28-.261) — Tr—Harold Goodsell (.216)
Stga 2:01^1 1992 27 3 4 5 $8,264 — 1991 13 0 1 5 $1,208 — 3,2:01^1 Lifetime $9,472

Date	Trk	Purse	Cd	Class	Dis	1/4	1/2	3/4	Time	PP	1/4	1/2	3/4	Str	Fin	Ind 1/4 Time	Ind Time	Odds	Driver	Order of Finish (First, Second, Third)	Temp
8-29^92	Stga	2000	ft	NW4PMLTCD	1	29^4	59	130	201^2	5	5	5	5°7¼	4	4¼	31^2	201^4	26.50	GMattison	FinalJeopardy,VideoMan,JthroBodin	64-0
8-25^92	Stga	1900	sy	NW1500L5CD	1	28^1	59^3	128^1	158^4	2	4	4°	2°1	3	3^1¼	31^4	201^3	9.30	GMattison	BeboroFla,HughesPrid,WaldnsFrst	75-0
8-19^92	Stga	1500	ft	NW1000L5CD	1	29^2	100^3	131	201^2	7	4	4°	3°1	3	1ns	30^1	201^2	12.00	GMattison	WaldnsFrst,BodyCopy,Pasthorwgat	72-0
8-10^92	Stga	1800	ft	NW3PMLTCD	1	28^2	59^3	129^3	159^2	3	2	2	3^1½	3	3^2½	30	200	9.30	GMattison	EastCoastKd,AngelsMgicty,WldnsFrst	77-0
8-3^92	Stga	1800	ft	NW3PMLTCD	1	29^3	100^4	130^4	159^4	3	5	5°	4°2	4	4^5	29^3	200^4	11.10	GMattison	Angerinvr,AngelsMgicty,EastCoastKd	80-0
7-23^92	Stga	1800	gd	NW3PMLT	1	28^4	100	130^2	159^3	5	6	4°	4°2½	5	5^4	30	200^4	23.50	GMattison	BoBootsBigFla,AngerHanov,VdoMan	81-0
7-16^92	Stga	1800	ft	NW3PMLT	1	30^1	101^1	130^2	200	6	5	5°	5°2½	6	6^7¼	30^3	201^2	5.30	JStarkJr	SnorCoem,AngusHanov,FinalBow	77-0
7-11^92	Stga	1800	ft	NW3PMLT	1	29^2	101^2	131^2	201^3	5	5	4°	4°1½	3	2ns	29^4	201^3	9.00	GMattison	FinalJeopardy,WaldnsFrst,ToghTrang	78-0

8-1 — 2 — BRIDGE VIEW — WHITE
b c 3 Escort-Ms Advocate-Gene Abbe — A.Wasserman, A.Scanio, L.Insalaco & J.Pappalardo,NY
JAY RANDALL (145) blue-gold-white (269-31-43-35-.247) — Tr—George Walters (.266)
Stga 2:01 1992 20 2 5 1 $4,412 — GSP 1 1:57 1991 4 1 0 1 $2,000 — 2,1:57 1 Lifetime $6,412

Date	Trk	Purse	Cd	Class	Dis	1/4	1/2	3/4	Time	PP	1/4	1/2	3/4	Str	Fin	Ind 1/4 Time	Ind Time	Odds	Driver	Order of Finish (First, Second, Third)	Temp
8-29^92	Stga	1800	ft	NW3PMLT	1	29^1	100^1	130	201^4	4	4	5	5°°4	2	1^1½	31	201^4	10.70	JRandall	BridgeView,Seafront,LouisStepr	84-0
8-22^92	Stga	1800	ft	NW3PMLT	1	29^1	100^2	129^3	159^4	1	2	2	3^1	3	2½	30^1	200	2.90	JRandall	Seafront,BrdgVw,PortMasanno	74-0
8-10^92	Stga	1800	ft	NW3PMLTCD	1	28^2	59^3	129^3	159^2	8	8	8°	5°°7½	6	7^3½	30^1	201^1	24.90	DCaploJr	EastCoastKd,AngelsMgicty,WldnsFrst	77-0
7-30^92	Stga	1800	ft	NW3PMLT	1	29^1	100^1	130^3	159^4	8	8	8°	7°°3½	6	5^3	30^1	201^3	23.40	BCross	VideoMan,Oxymoron,Keller	73-0
7-16^92	Stga	1500	ft	C&GNW2PMCD	1	30^1	101^3	131^4	201	2	1	1	1^1	1	1^1½	29^1	201	*.70	DCaploJr	BridgeView,CharlieGoWest,HFesa	77-0
7-11^92	Stga	1500	ft	C&GNW2PMCD	1	28^2	59^2	129^2	200^1	4	4	3°	2°ns	2	2ns	30^4	200^1	*1.80	DCaploJr	VideoMan,BridgeView,PeterMac	78-0
7-7^92	YR	4500	ft	3-4YRNW2CD	1	27^2	58^1	129^3	159^2	3	4	4	3	5^4½	6^4½		200^3	12.60	MCaseJr	SportsEditor,Dragonfir,Monygram	75-0
6-30^92	YR A	4500	ft	3-4YRNW2CD	1	27^1	58	127^2	158^2	3x	8	8ix°	8	8^2¼	8dist			7.90	MCaseJr	ImmenBogh - ParaGayl - Monygram -	81-0

4-1 — 3 — TROUSER MOUSE — PURPLE
blk c 3 Falcon Seelster-MaMa-Cavalcade — Westwind Hills Farm,Pattersonville,N.Y.
KIM CRAWFORD (155) red-blk-wh (544-93-87-60-.297) — Tr—David Spagnola (.354)
Stga 2:01 1992 24 3 4 4 $7,957 — QYR 2:04^1 1991 3 1 0 0 $896 — 3,2:01 Lifetime $8,853

Date	Trk	Purse	Cd	Class	Dis	1/4	1/2	3/4	Time	PP	1/4	1/2	3/4	Str	Fin	Ind 1/4 Time	Ind Time	Odds	Driver	Order of Finish (First, Second, Third)	Temp
8-31^92	Stga	1500	ft	NW1000L5CD	1	28^3	59^2	129^4	201	5	6	7	6^7½	6	1^1½	30^4	201	8.20	KCrawford	TrsrMos,CrtnThorman,JstpnAdam	67-0
8-25^92	Stga	1900	sy	NW1500L5CD	1	28^1	59^3	128^1	158^4	8	8	8i	7^16½	7	6^1½	30^4	202^2	31.70	KCrawford	BeboroFla,HughesPrid,WaldnsFrst	75-0
8-20^92	Stga	1500	ft	NW1000L5CD	1	29^4	100	129^2	159^2	2	3	3	4^3½	5	3^2½	30	200	3.60	WInsy	ClassicStepsn,NmanShan,TrsrMos	65-0
8-14^92	Stga	1300	sy	NW800L5CD	1	28^4	101	131^3	203^1	6	1°	1	2ns	2	3½	31^4	203^2	4.60	KCrawford	NemanShanu,HughesPrid,TrsrMos	63-0
8-10^92	Stga	1800	ft	NW3PMLTCD	1	28^2	59^3	129^3	159^2	5	4	4	4^3½	4	4^5	30^1	200^2	8.00	KCrawford	EastCoastKd,AngelsMgicty,WldnsFrst	77-0
8-3^92	Stga	1500	ft	NW1000L5CD	1	28	58^2	128^2	159^1	3	5°	5°	7^10½	6	6^9½	30^3	201^1	5.50	KCrawford	BrotherBri,XpressLane,JacquesLec	80-0
7-28^92	Stga	1500	ft	NW1000L5CD	1	29^1	100	129^3	159^4	7	7	7	7^9	8	8^14½	31^2	202^4	15.40	KCrawford	FrJack,LdLghtnng,JstapanAdam	74-0
7-22^92	Stga	1500	ft	NW1000L5CD	1	29^4	59^3	129^3	200	2	2	3	4^1½	3	4^5½	31^1	201	*1.30	KCrawford	LdLghtnng,ZrnbBChp,Arpperiony	72-0

3-1 — 4 — AUSSIE'S NIP — BLACK
b g 5 Armbro Aussie-Egmont Kawhai-Emory Hanover — Ronald S.Przelski & George H.Edwards,Poland,N.Y.
BRIAN CROSS (150) blue-or-white (287-28-40-42-.224) — Tr—Jody Weidman (.519)
VD M 1:58^4 1992 21 3 3 1 $5,406 — VD M 1:57 1991 42 11 2 8 $21,510 — 4,1:57 M Lifetime $41,454

Date	Trk	Purse	Cd	Class	Dis	1/4	1/2	3/4	Time	PP	1/4	1/2	3/4	Str	Fin	Ind 1/4 Time	Ind Time	Odds	Driver	Order of Finish (First, Second, Third)	Temp
8-22^92	Stga	1900	ft	NW1500L5CD	1	29^2	100^2	130^4	159^2	4	5	5°	4°2	4	4^4½	29^1	200^2	7.10	GMattison	PartiesGalore,BrandNew,WidRuld	74-0
7-29^92	VD M	2000	ft	NW1500L5CD	1	28^1	58^2	127^4	157^1	1x	7	6	6dis	6dis	6dis			*2.10	DRichards	Nlatest,FlanScooter,RdEyxon	68-0
7-24^92	VD M	1400	ft	NW800L5CD	1	27^1	57^4	126^4	157^2	7	2°	3°°	3°½	2½	2^1½	30^4	157^3	*1.20	DRichards	JimHod,AussieNip,ChristianaStor	75-0
7-21^92	VD M	1200	ft	NW800L5CD	1	27^4	59^4	129^4	158^4	4	1	1	1^2	1^3	1^2	29	158^4	1.50	DRichards	AussieNip,Jronald,Armbroindiana	61-0
7-14^92	VD M	1200	sy	NW800L5CD	1	27^4	58^3	127^4	158	5	2	1	1^1½	1^1	2½	30^2	158^1	5.60	DRichards	FreddyDallas,AussieNip,MightyGod	68-0
7-9^92	VD M	1400	ft	NW800L5CD	1	28^4	59^1	129^1	159^3	2x	9	9	9dis	9dis	9dis		204^4	3.20	JWeidman	ToderRngad,SaralynLobl,Knwodrsttu	72-0
7-4^92	VD M	1400	ft	NW800L5CD	1	27^2	58^3	129^1	158^4	3	2	3	3^1½	ix3	dnf			3.00	JWeidman	FiercerHanover,BriansBudy,Enabw	68-0
6-24^92	VD M	1400	gd	NW600L5CD	1	27^1	57^1	128	159	1	3	2	1°2½	2½	3^2½	31^4	159^4	4.60	JWeidman	SpeedOnn,WhyDont,AussieNip	62-0

5-2 — 5 — FR JACK — GREEN
b h 4 B.G's Bunny-Hiding Place-Adios Vic — Carol A.O'Leary,Millbury,Mass.
GARY KAMAL (150) wh-blue-gld (238-35-38-32-.281) — Tr—Karen Kamal (.363)
Stga 1:59^4 1992 8 2 1 1 $2,404 — Stga 2:00^1 1991 9 4 0 0 $3,634 — 4,1:59^4 Lifetime $6,038

Date	Trk	Purse	Cd	Class	Dis	1/4	1/2	3/4	Time	PP	1/4	1/2	3/4	Str	Fin	Ind 1/4 Time	Ind Time	Odds	Driver	Order of Finish (First, Second, Third)	Temp
8-29^92	Stga	2400	ft	NW2100L5CD	1	28^4	59^2	128^1	158	3	4	5	7°12½	6	5^11	29^3	200^1	8.20	GKamal	BoScrsBgFl,SlmOThSth,OlympcPwr	64-0
8-15^92	Stga	3000	ft	NW2500L5CD	1	29	58^4	129	157^3	7	7	7	6°4½	7	6^13½	30^2	200^1	18.90	GKamal	TurfyRainbow,GasoinAly,GramsChoc	68-0
8-6^92	Stga	2400	ft	NW2000L5CD	1	29^4	100^2	130	158^3	3	3	3	2°1	2	2^2½	29	159^1	2.30	GKamal	TooneyBilly,FrJack,Sabeyor	80-0
7-28^92	Stga	1500	ft	NW1000L5CD	1	29^1	100	129^3	159^4	3	4	4°	1^1	1	1^4½	30^1	159^4	2.50	GKamal	FrJack,LdLghtnng,JstapanAdam	74-0
7-21^92	Stga	1300	ft	NW750L5CD	1	28^3	59^3	130^4	201^2	6	8	8	4°°2	1	1^4½	30^1	201^2	*.90	GKamal	FrJack,Requirement,MagesChoice	71-0
7-12^92	Stga A	1300	ft	NW1000L5CD	1	29	100	130	159^1	4	4	4°	4°2½	4	3^3½	29^2	159^4	*1.50	GKamal	DirectDamage,Irse,FrJack	66-0
7-8^92	Stga	1600	ft	NW1500L5CD	1	28^2	59^3	129^2	200^1	5	6	3°	2°1	4	4^2½	31^1	200^4	5.90	GKamal	AvonBreeze,KystonTwist,Shaunson	73-0
6-27^92	Stga		ft	QUA	1	30^4	101^4	133^1	203^3	1	5	5°	4°2½	4	2^1½	30^2	204	NB	GKamal	Keller,FRJack,Sungnoshancy	82-0

6-1 — 6 — WIDE RULED — RED
b g 4 Raven Hanover-Unruled-Abercrombie — Frank J.Pectay,Ilion,N.Y.
SCOTT MONGEON (145) black-gold (50-7-6-8-.260) — Tr—Scott Mongeon (.293)
1992 18 0 2 6 $3,431 — VD M 1:59 1991 22 3 3 4 $7,314 — 3,1:59 M Lifetime $10,745

Date	Trk	Purse	Cd	Class	Dis	1/4	1/2	3/4	Time	PP	1/4	1/2	3/4	Str	Fin	Ind 1/4 Time	Ind Time	Odds	Driver	Order of Finish (First, Second, Third)	Temp
8-29^92	Stga	1900	ft	NW1500L5CD	1	28^1	58	129^3	201^3	3	2°	1°	1°½	1	5^7½	32^2	202	*1.40	DCaploJr	FrdsMarvmos,FrLpRa,SpsOtofTm	64-0
8-22^92	Stga	1900	ft	NW1500L5CD	1	29^2	100^2	130^4	159^2	3	2	2	3^1½	3	3^3½	29^1	200^1	*1.40	DCaploJr	PartiesGalore,BrandNew,WidRuld	74-0
8-15^92	Stga	2000	ft	NW4PMLTCD	1	28^3	58^3	129^3	159	5	6	6	5°°2	4	3^1½	29^1	159^1	4.10	DCaploJr	HBeSon,DirectHugo,WideRuled	68-0
8-8^92	VD M	2800	sy	WOCD-4	1	26^3	57	127^3	158^4	5	2	1	2^1½	2^2½	4^2	31^2	159^1	13.10	MScalzo	JBsVagbond,WatnOnTod,SgntHRder	62-0
8-2^92	YR	3575	ft	10000CLCD	1	28^4	57^2	128^1	158^3	1	3	3	2	2^2½	3^1½		159	*1.20	MCaseJr	SundayFella,OurAdjustor,WidRuld	79-0
7-22^92	YR	3250	ft	10000CLCD	1	28^1	100^1	131^2	201^4	7i	6	7°	4°°	4^1½	3^3		202^2	6.70	LDult	BigandTough,Fuimsjackt,WdRuld	71-0
7-11^92	VD M	2500	ft	WOCD-5	1	27^1	57^3	126^2	157	8	8	8°	8^3½	8^4½	7^8	30^2	158^3	28.60	WBailey	GasoinAly,MetroHonor,HalwMax	74-0
7-1^92	YR	3500	ft	10000CL	1	29	59^2	129^4	200^3	8	5°	2°	2	2^2½	2^2		201	2.80	MCaseJr	FithPocita,WidRuld,Fimtaneckt	81-0

10-1	**LADIES MAN**						b g 5 Abercrombie-Caroloda-TarHeel									QStga	2:02	1992 19 0 6 2			$5,191
							Jace H. Oretsky, Pla. & Deborah A. Cappello, NY.									PlmD	1:56	1991 35 4 3 1			$10,005
7	DANIEL CAPPELLO JR (115) blue-white (331-47-58-61-.301)						Tr—Deborah Cappello (.348)									4,1:56		Lifetime			$63,759
	8-28 92	Stga	1900	ft	NW1500L5CD	1	28	58	128	159	3	1	1	1	1	2	31	159	2.40	DCaploJr	FourtwentytwoLadiesMan,AugThDog 81-C
	8-20 92	Stga	2400	ft	NW2000L5CD	1	28	58	128	159	8	1	1	1	5	6	31	200	27.50	DCaploJr	HollysRJB,TonyBily,MadowMaximus 65-C
	8-15 92	Stga	3000	ft	NW2500L5CD	1	29	58	129	157	3	2	2	4x	6	7	31	200	13.80	DCaploJr	TuxyRainbow,GasonAly,GramsChoc 88-C
	8-11 92	YR	3500	ft	10000CL	1	28	58	128	159	7	5	6°	6°	5	4		159	27.00	DCaploJr	Primaiur,BobGraham,BusineMachin 86-C
BROWN	8-1 92	Stga	2400	ft	NW2000L5CD	1	29	100	130	201	4	1°	1	1	1	2	31	201	5.70	DCaploJr	JimysLast,LadiesMan,ClassSlapshot 73-C
	7-25 92	Stga	1900	ft	NW1500L5	1	28	59	128	200	2	1	1	1	1	2	31	200	3.20	DCaploJr	JacqueKarma,LadiesMan,AwsomAus 78-C
	7-18 92	Stga		ft	QUA	1	30	59	130	202	2	1	2	2	2	3	31	202	NB	DCaploJr	BestBobK,FirstFowl,LadiesMan 74-C
	5-25 92	Stga	A 2000	ft	NW2200L7CD	1	29	100	130	200	2	2	1	1	2	2	30	200	*.70	DCaploJr	GramsChoice,LadiesMan,NvadaPleb 58-C

Following two horrid PPs at Yonkers, he shipped to Saratoga. He was second by a nose, then a 5¼-length winner at odds of 3-5 in a Non-Winners of 2. Moved up to a Non-Winners of 3, he twice drew the 8 post; was eighth at the half in each race, and was soundly beaten at odds of 23-1 and 24-1.

But horses out of the 8 hole are frequently on missions impossible at ½-mile tracks. When he drew the rail in the same class, he was second at 5-2 by ¾ of a length to our old friend Seafront. The following week, Bridge View met Seafront again from the 4 post and was sent off at 10-1 despite showing three strong races at Saratoga from decent posts. He beat Seafront this time and paid $23.40. He shouldn't have been more than 4-1. In tonight's race, he was second at 9-1 to Trouser Mouse.

Strategy II — Yonkers

CHAPTER 7

Yonkers

Herve Filion, harness racing's all-time leading driver, Walter Case, Joe Marsh Jr., and Gary Mosher discussed racing on Yonkers's ½-mile track.

Filion's domination of harness racing is awesome. His 13,667 victories through September, 1992, are almost double those of Carmine Abatiello in second. Filion's near $80 million in career earnings is second to John Campbell.

Filion was born in Angers, Quebec, February 1, 1940. He won his first race driving Guy Grattan in Rigaud, Quebec, at the age of 13, then emigrated to the U.S. in 1961. He has won 16 North American driving titles, and was the youngest driver—35 then—ever inducted into Harness Racing's Hall of Fame in Goshen, N.Y. He has driven in 70,000 races with a .334 UDR through 1991. His top horses include Doorunrun Bluegrass, Grades Singing and Nansemond.

Case set a single-season record—815 and counting through early December—as 1992's leading dash winner. Case seems like he's been around forever, but he is only 31. At 27, he became the youngest driver ever to reach 3,000 wins. The native of Lewiston, Maine, has driven 600 winners or more five consecutive years.

He was the 1991 Harness Tracks of America Driver of the Year, and has an excellent career UDR of .362. He's won eight races in one night at Yonkers twice.

Marsh recorded his record 32nd straight year with 100 wins or more in 1991. The 58-year-old native of Curtice, Ohio, ranked sixth in all-time victories and 13th in career earnings heading into last year. Marsh came to Yonkers in 1975 after tremendous success in Chicago, where he won nine consecutive driving titles at Chicago's four tracks from '71-'73. He represented the U.S. in the World Driving Championships from 1973 to 1975, winning the prestigious title in '74.

Mosher, just as Case, is a young (33), talented driver born in Maine (Waterville). He entered 1992 with a streak of seven consecutive seasons of at least 200 wins and $1.5 million in earnings.

Pre-Race

How much time do you spend handicapping?

"I usually get into the paddock an hour early and sit down and watch the previous night's replays," Marsh says. "During that time, I read the program for about half an hour. I usually look for two of the best horses I have to beat in my race. Who has early speed and who doesn't? I try to make a little plan of what I might do."

Mosher says, "I probably get to the paddock half an hour before the first race. I spend 40 minutes to an hour for all the races I'm in. Just before the race, I take another quick peek just to refresh my memory. I look for late driver changes or late scratches."

Case says, "I study a lot, a couple hours, as soon as I can get the program."

Filion says, "Not that much time. There's too many things that happen in horse racing. It's tough to make a plan."

Leaving

If you've tried to leave twice and gotten hung each time, does that influence your decision to leave a third time that night?

"No, not me," Filion says. "I don't go that route. I just throw the races out. It's very rare that three races go the same way."

Mosher qualifies his answer: "Not really, but it gets you thinking maybe you should have gone home tonight. But if you have a horse who leaves, you've just got to go. Every race is different, totally different. You don't know what the other horses are going to do. You don't know what the other drivers are going to do."

For Case, the decision has ramifications: "You don't change your decision to leave. A good driver can't get intimidated. If you let yourself get intimidated by getting parked once, it'll keep happening."

Yonkers's stretch is shorter than almost every other ½-mile track. Speed dominates here, and decisions must be made quickly about leaving. How do you decide?

"You make the decision at the spur of the moment," Filion says. "You can't think about it. If you think about it, you get yourself in trouble. It's an instantaneous decision."

Case agrees: "I pretty much make that decision at the gate. Just before the wings go, I look at everybody behind the gate and see who's leaving. Before the wings fold, bingo! You make a quick decision. The turn comes up quick."

Mosher says the quality of his horse is important: "If I've got a real longshot and an outside post, I'll leave a few steps and see what the other drivers are doing. But say you've got an even money shot. The front end is where you should be and where the public thinks you should be. You're really committed when they say, 'Go.'"

Marsh says, "I watch horses scoring. I'll watch to see if a horse is being warmed up on fire. Then I watch at the gate, too, to see if the whip is up and the horse has his nose right on the gate. At Yonkers, the first few strides of the gate, you've got to go for position. If I got the 6 or 7 hole, by the time I start into the turn, I can pretty much tell if any horse is going to go on. That's when I commit myself to leaving."

Since speed is so favorable at Yonkers, what are the chances of finding a tuck after leaving?

"You've got to look for a hole," Marsh says. "You're into the turn so quick."

Case contends: "It's very, very hard to find a tuck. Horses keep up these days."

Filion says, "If you see you can get in there, you can take a tuck. But then you might have to go first-over."

It seems that every driver in every race wants the front end at Yonkers. Does that compromise the chance of going wire-to-wire?

Marsh and Case disagree. Marsh says, "It's a lot harder going wire-to-wire. Everybody's aggressive. If you can get down to the quarter in :29.1 and are lucky enough to back off the half to 1:00.2 or 1:00.4, you're okay. But these days, you might have to go :59.3 to the half. They don't give you many breathers. Sometimes, you can steal one. It's a lot harder than it used to be."

Case labels wire-to-wire attempts at Yonkers "probably the easiest thing to do. Certainly, the front end does hold up at Yonkers, but you still have to be able to rate your horse. You have to try to get a rest in the second quarter to give your horse a breather. If I make the front in :29, I like to throw in a :31 second quarter. Then I'm home free. If you've got a favorite on the front end, nobody wants to come out and attack by going first-over. They leave you alone, and you can steal the race."

Mosher says, "Yonkers is strictly a front-running track because of its real short stretch. If you've got a horse on the lead coming out of the final turn, you've got a good shot if he has any ability."

Filion cautions about wire-to-wire attempts: "You can be driving a 3-5 shot, and you look back at the half and there's three horses outside you. You have to take back or it'll be suicide. They don't pay at the half. They pay for the mile."

Do you let go and re-take?

"It happens all the time," Filion says. "It's not written, but if you're in front and somebody goes beside you, you let him go and re-take. If you don't let him go, he'll destroy you. Common sense tells you to let him go."

Marsh and Case use let go and re-take as a tactic.

Marsh: "Say I've got the 7 hole and leave and make the front. Say there's another horse whom I've looped. If he's a longshot, I'll let him go and re-take just to get rid of him."

Case: "I let the guy go if he's a longshot. I want to re-take and put him in the pocket."

Mid-Race

At 1/2-mile tracks, drivers not on the lead face a crucial decision: when to pull. Pulling on the paddock turn before the half frequently means racing as many as three turns parked out. Conversely, not pulling can be just as fruitless, because a horse can be boxed in for the rest of the mile. Nothing is more frustrating for a bettor than seeing his horse third or fourth on the rail and watching his driver not pull coming to the half. When that happens, a bettor doesn't even get the satisfaction of knowing whether or not his horse could have won if not locked in. Yet many times drivers sitting the pocket or behind the pocket elect to sit rather than pull.

The innovative open stretch—a passing lane on the inside of the leader only available in the final eighth of a mile—has made the pocket a much more attractive place to be. What's been its impact?

"I love it," Case says. "It's the greatest thing they ever did for 1/2-mile tracks. I feel everybody has a shot to win now. The guy in the 2 or 3 hole has a shot. I find myself being more patient. I just feel a lot more relaxed that I can sit in the 2 hole and have a real chance. Before, if you were in front and had the favorite in the pocket, you'd back into him (to keep him trapped inside by another horse) and he'd never get out."

Mosher concurs: "Now you don't have a guy on the front end backing up in your face if you're in the pocket. Sometimes the pocket horse pulls to the outside. I won a race today (September 29, 1992) sitting third. The pocket pulled outside and I went through on the inside. The open stretch is good for the public."

Filion says, "It's good for the industry. The open stretch gives you an opportunity to get through. You can sit in the pocket longer."

Marsh says, "When you're on the lead, you used to get a horse trapped in behind you in the pocket. Now you have to take off at the top of the stretch. If you're in the pocket, you just don't worry about being locked in. If the leader carries you to the head of the stretch, you're automatically all right."

What of ½-mile tracks without the open stretch?

Case said, "When the pace really starts to slow up, if I'm sitting fourth or third, I have to pull by the three-eighths. In this day and age, everybody is on the go. I don't want to go fourth-over. I want to go second-over.

"The pocket is a tough position. I almost hate sitting in the pocket on a ½-mile track. It used to be the garden spot. Now it's a death trap. You just don't get out. I'd rather be first-over. In the pocket, the leader will back into you to keep you locked in. There are a lot of smart drivers out there. They won't let you get out."

Filion says, "If I have a 4-5 horse in the pocket, I'll be going out of the pocket by the half. Other times, it depends on who's in front."

Marsh says, "By the time you get to the quarter pole, you get a feel of how the pace is going. If I get the sense that the leader is trying to get a breather and I'm sitting fifth, I want to go."

To Mosher, "If you're driving the favorite and you're third or fourth on the rail, you want to be pulling and giving your horse a shot."

Specifically, on ½-mile tracks without the open stretch, why would you not pull from the pocket or the 3 hole coming to the half?

"I've won 5,000 races," Marsh says. "I've watched about 20,000. I never make a mistake watching them. You could be sitting there saying, 'Why doesn't he pull?' The driver might not have the horse to pull. Maybe the horse is struggling to keep up. Say they go :58.4 or :59. They might be having trouble keeping up.

"It looks easier than it is. When you're down there on the track, you have seven other horses to consider. And your horse may be on one line (not pulling evenly on the bit). It ain't always the driver's fault. A lot of times, it's the horse not being able to pull when you want to. If you're sitting in the 2 hole going to the half, it all depends on who's in front of you. If it's a horse who might stop at the three-quarters, you want to pull. The 3 hole can be bad, especially if you're one of the contenders. You usually have to pull a little quicker than you want to, to not get trapped."

Mosher says, "You don't see too many people pull the pocket. Nine times out of 10, a driver won't pull out of the pocket on any 1/2-mile track or 5/8."

Case says, "Very rarely will the horse come out of the pocket."

Getting locked in on the rail behind the pocket horse irks Case: "I hate for a horse not to get to run any time during the race, sitting third or fourth on the rail. They just don't get out. They get out when the race is over."

What are the nuances of flushing cover?

"It's easy to flush cover," Filion says. "You like to have it, but sometimes you don't want cover because he'll back up in front of you. You don't wait too long to flush cover. You see it and feel it. A guy comes out, and you see if he has any horse."

Case says, "You want to flush cover, but only if that horse is going to be able to take you to the head of the stretch, not someone that's going to back up in your face. I wait for cover for a second, try to flush him out. But you can't sit there and wait."

Marsh offers an example: "Say you're sitting fifth or sixth and you pull at the 1/2-mile pole. You move up, go past one or two horses, and sit a bit. You want to flush the next horse out."

Another Marsh example: "If you're sixth and the favorite is second or third, you don't want to flush the horse that's fourth or fifth. You get up to the guy you want to follow and wait a bit. Just sit there. You can wait if you have a pretty good idea that he's the horse to beat. If he's the favorite, he's going to want to get out."

Mosher discusses two different scenarios: "A lot of times you'll find people will pull a horse and really shouldn't. They pull a horse trying to work out a trip. If I get away fourth or fifth, or even sixth, sometimes I don't want cover. If you're the best, you just want to grind it out first-over. When I pull out, I rush the horse up to second or between second and third. I try to keep them boxed in and have enough horse to win.

"Sometimes, I move up slower on the outside. Say I pull at the quarter, I'll move up slowly. By the half, somebody will pull. You hang out there as long as you can."

Heading For Home

When do you go three-wide?

"Usually, you're going to have to move three-wide when your cover starts to back up," Mosher says. "The best place to pull three-wide at Yonkers is the straightaway on the backside. You don't want to pull three-wide on the turn, but sometimes you can't help it."

Filion says, "Pulling three-wide depends on how strong your horse is and how scrunched up the other horses are. The race dictates that. You have to avoid getting your horse backed up by a 30-1 shot."

Marsh offers an example: "Say you're sitting third-over at Yonkers and following a horse that's keeping up. Say the horse that's first-over has been there a long time. Second-over looks tired. Then you flip out three-wide past the 5/8. If you've got horse, it's not that hard to decide."

What's the value of the whip?

"I'm not a real big whip man," Mosher says. "I don't pound on a horse too much. I like to hand-drive them as much as possible. They'll stay sweeter. You sting a horse and you'll make him sulk."

Case says, "Very rarely do I ever touch a horse with one. I hit the shaft or clunk the wheel disk. Or I growl at a horse or yell at him."

Marsh feels strongly: "I think the whip is very much over-used. A lot of horses don't need to be hit with the whip. There are a few horses that you might have to reach out and crack, but most horses can go better if you holler at them. In Norway, they won't even allow you to carry a whip."

Filion says, "A lot of times, the horse will respond to the whip. Other times, you hit a horse and he'll come back to you."

Is Yonkers different than other 1/2-mile tracks?

Case says, "Yonkers is maybe more of a speed track. At Scarborough (Maine), you could win a race from behind a little easier."

Mosher says, "Yonkers is a nice track for an aggressive driver, because if you get your horse out of the gate, you're going to get some money from the purse."

Marsh says, "When you get on a mile track, your stock has to be powerful. Half-mile tracks are more competitive. It's more up to the driver to get the right position. Maywood (Illinois) compares to

Yonkers a lot because that's a short stretch, too. When we raced at Roosevelt, that was a longer stretch. You had more time to make decisions. You have to be on the lookout all the time at Yonkers."

Best spot at Yonkers?

Filion: "Front end if you've got the best horse."

Marsh: "Second-over. That's where I want to be."

Mosher: "Right on the front."

Case: "My favorite trips are on the front or first-over. They're freedom trips—you're free to get out."

Worst spot?

Marsh: "Fourth-over or third on the rail."

Filion: "Last."

Mosher: "Sitting last or maybe the 3 hole."

Case: "There's no question. Sitting eighth at the quarter pole. It's like trying to win the lottery. Your chances are slim and none."

Track to Track

CHAPTER 8

Let's be perfectly clear: There is absolutely no claim that the numbers in this chapter are statistically significant. But they do reflect tendencies that are useful tools.

Track programs provide the percentage of winning *horses* by post position. *Harness Overlays* provides the percentage of winning *favorites* by post position. Big difference. Remember our goal: We want to identify vulnerable favorites.

With considerable help from the U.S. Trotting Association, fourteen tracks were randomly selected. The days were arbitrary: The only stipulation was that they be from 1992. A total of 11,242 races were analyzed for the number of winners, and the number of odds-on winners (odds of 1-1 or lower) by post position. The sample offered a limited supply of races on sloppy tracks, but the data is interesting and included. Races on good, heavy, slow or muddy tracks were left out.

Overall Totals

THE FAVORITES' WIN PERCENTAGES

Track (Size)	Races Sampled	All Races	Odds-On	Sloppy Track
Balmoral (5/8- and 1-mile)	650	37.2	50.6	48.9
Buffalo (1/2)	675	43.6	51.4	48.3
Hawthorne (1)	477	39.0	48.0	20.0
Hazel Park (5/8)	1,073	40.2	53.9	34.2
Los Alamitos (5/8)	301	34.9	50.9	30.0
Meadowlands (1)	882	38.3	54.2	33.8
Meadows (5/8)	949	30.9	51.5	35.7
Monticello (1/2)	1,021	40.2	52.2	37.8
Northfield (1/2)	963	44.0	59.9	38.3
Pompano Park (5/8)	613	35.6	48.9	23.1
Saginaw (1/2)	958	44.6	61.4	41.5
Saratoga (1/2)	801	41.3	52.5	46.2
Scioto Downs (5/8)	796	39.6	59.7	50.9
Yonkers (1/2)	1,083	43.8	57.0	35.5
TOTAL RACES	11,242			

The 8 post at 1/2-mile tracks

	Total	Odds-On
Buffalo	6-9	2-3
Monticello	6-22	1-4
Northfield	6-17	4-5
Saginaw	15-29	5-7
Saratoga	7-11	3-5
Yonkers	12-33	6-11
TOTAL	52-121	21-35
PERCENTAGE	43.0	60.0

Sloppy track winners by post position at 1/2-mile tracks

1	47-109
2	35-89
3	25-73
4	20-59
5	36-59
6	14-35
7	5-18
8	7-9
9	6-13
TOTAL	195-464
PERCENTAGE	42.0

The 1 post at 5/8- and 1- mile tracks

	Total	Odds-On
Balmoral	48-114	23-45
Hawthorne	25-73	14-22
Hazel Park	59-177	26-58
Los Alamitos	23-53	16-21

Sloppy track winners by post position at 5/8- and 1- mile tracks

1	19-55
2	21-62
3	15-51
4	15-43

The 1 post at 5/8- and 1- mile tracks

Meadowland	53-131	24-44
Meadows	75-187	47-87
Pompano	30-109	20-50
Scioto	48-121	26-44
TOTAL	361-965	196-37
PERCENTAGE	37.4	53.6

Sloppy track winners by post position at 5/8- and 1- mile tracks

	5	22-47
	6	14-45
	7	14-30
	8	10-23
	9	2-5
	10	3-8
TOTAL		135-369
PERCENTAGE		36.6

No surprise here. The five highest percentages of winning favorites were at 1/2-mile tracks: Saginaw (44.6), Northfield (44.0), Yonkers (43.8), Buffalo (43.6) and Saratoga (41.3). The sixth 1/2-mile track in our sample, Monticello (40.15), was edged out for sixth by Hazel Park (40.16), a 5/8-mile track. The Meadows was a decided winner for lowest percentage (30.9).

For odds-on winners, Saginaw (61.4) was first and Hawthorne (48.0) last.

Favorites on sloppy tracks were least successful at Hawthorne (20.0) and Pompano Park (23.1). Scioto Downs (50.9) was highest.

The biggest surprise: Favorites from the 8 post did incredibly well on 1/2-mile tracks (43.0); better as odds-on favorites (60.0), and even better on sloppy tracks (77.8). Apparently, the 8 post on 1/2-mile tracks is such a disadvantage that an 8 horse must show considerably more talent than the competition to be made the favorite.

Track to Track: Winning Favorites by Post Position

Balmoral Park: 5/8- and 1-mile, Crete, Illinois

1992 Stats—59 Cards—650 Races

Total				Odds-On				Sloppy Track			
1	48	114	42.1%	1	23	45	51.1%	1	3	6	50.0%
2	31	90	34.4%	2	17	39	43.6%	2	3	9	33.3%
3	34	78	43.6%	3	20	27	74.1%	3	4	6	66.7%

1992 Stats—59 Cards—650 Races (continued from page 89)

Total				**Odds-On**				**Sloppy Track**			
4	39	94	41.5%	4	14	33	42.4%	4	2	6	33.3%
5	30	86	34.9%	5	11	28	39.3%	5	5	9	55.6%
6	19	62	30.6%	6	10	23	43.5%	6	3	6	50.0%
7	23	62	37.1%	7	13	19	68.4%	7	2	2	100.0%
8	12	45	26.7%	8	6	13	46.2%	8	0	1	0.0%
9	6	19	31.6%	9	2	2	100.0%	9	2	2	100.0%
Totals	242	650	37.2%		116	229	50.7%		24	47	51.1%

No success from the 8 post here (26.7), dead last. For odds-on favorites, check out the 3 (74.1) and 7 (68.4) vs. the 2 (43.6). The 2 also did poorly on sloppy tracks (33.3).

Buffalo: ½-mile, Buffalo, New York

1992 Stats—57 Cards—675 Races

Total				**Odds-On**				**Sloppy Track**			
1	104	191	54.5%	1	51	90	56.7%	1	18	28	64.3%
2	50	128	39.1%	2	24	45	53.3%	2	5	19	26.3%
3	48	109	44.0%	3	21	41	51.2%	3	6	13	46.2%
4	38	100	38.0%	4	17	35	48.6%	4	5	14	35.7%
5	26	60	43.3%	5	8	17	47.1%	5	4	6	66.7%
6	14	50	28.0%	6	7	20	35.0%	6	0	3	0.0%
7	8	25	32.0%	7	2	5	40.0%	7	3	3	100.0%
8	7	10	70.0%	8	3	4	75.0%	8	1	1	100.0%
9	0	2	0.0%	9	0	2	0.0%	9			
Totals	295	675	43.7%		133	259	51.4%		42	87	48.3%

The 8 was much better (70.0) than the 6 (28.0) and 7 (32.0). Odds-on favorites tailed off as one would expect from the 1 post (56.7) through the 6 (35.0), but the extremely limited number of odds-on favorites from the 7 and 8 provided percentages of 40.0 and 75.0.

On sloppy tracks, the 1 (64.3) blew away the 2 (26.3), with the 5 checking in first (66.7)

Hawthorne: 1-mile, Cicero, Illinois

1992 Stats—47 Cards—477 Races

Total				Odds-On				Sloppy Track			
1 —	25 —	73	34.2%	1 —	14 —	22	63.6%	1 —	1 —	3	33.3%
2 —	35 —	76	46.1%	2 —	9 —	24	37.5%	2 —	1 —	3	33.3%
3 —	20 —	61	32.8%	3 —	7 —	21	33.3%	3 —	0 —	1	0.0%
4 —	18 —	56	32.1%	4 —	7 —	16	43.8%	4 —	0 —	1	0.0%
5 —	34 —	67	50.7%	5 —	9 —	20	45.0%	5 —	—		
6 —	21 —	61	34.4%	6 —	11 —	22	50.0%	6 —	0 —	2	0.0%
7 —	16 —	35	45.7%	7 —	8 —	9	88.9%	7 —	—		
8 —	11 —	31	35.5%	8 —	4 —	7	57.1%	8 —	—		
9 —	6 —	15	40.0%	9 —	2 —	5	40.0%	9 —	—		
10 —	0 —	2	0.0%	10 —	0 —	2	0.0%	10 —	—		
Totals —	186 —	477	39.0%		71 —	148	48.0%	55 —	2 —	10	20.0%

The 5 was a clear first (50.7) and the 1 real low (34.2). The 2 (46.1) and 7 (45.7) were a decisive second and third.

However, check out the percentages for odds-on favorites. Here the 1 is second (63.6) and the 5 fifth (45.0). The 7 (88.9) and 8 (57.3) were first and third.

Hazel Park: 5/8-mile, Hazel Park, Michigan

1992 Stats—92 Cards—1,073 Races

Total				Odds-On				Sloppy Track			
1 —	59 —	177	33.3%	1 —	26 —	58	44.8%	1 —	1 —	10	10.0%
2 —	77 —	169	45.6%	2 —	28 —	48	58.3%	2 —	8 —	21	38.1%
3 —	68 —	175	38.9%	3 —	39 —	74	52.7%	3 —	1 —	14	7.1%
4 —	57 —	127	44.9%	4 —	30 —	51	58.8%	4 —	3 —	10	30.0%
5 —	54 —	121	44.6%	5 —	28 —	49	57.1%	5 —	8 —	15	53.3%
6 —	47 —	121	38.8%	6 —	29 —	52	55.8%	6 —	8 —	19	42.1%
7 —	30 —	79	38.0%	7 —	18 —	34	52.9%	7 —	5 —	9	55.6%
8 —	27 —	69	39.1%	8 —	11 —	23	47.8%	8 —	4 —	11	36.4%
9 —	9 —	24	37.5%	9 —	2 —	5	40.0%	9 —	0 —	2	0.0%
10 —	3 —	11	27.3%	10 —	2 —	3	66.7%	10 —	—		
Totals —	431 —	1073	40.2%		213 —	397	53.7%	55 —	38 —	111	34.2%

The 2 (45.6), 4 (44.9) and 5 (44.6) were very close first, second and third.

The percentages with odds-on favorites were well-balanced. On sloppy tracks, however, the 1 and 3 were 1-10 (10.0) and 1-14 (7.1), respectively, while the 7 (55.5), 5 (53.3) and 6 (42.1) were much more successful.

Los Alamitos: ⅝-mile, Los Alamitos, California

1992 Stats—23 Cards—301 Races

Total				Odds-On				Sloppy Track			
1 —	23 —	53	43.4%	1 —	16 —	21	76.2%	1 —	1 —	2	50.0%
2 —	17 —	41	41.5%	2 —	8 —	13	61.5%	2 —	—		
3 —	14 —	43	32.6%	3 —	6 —	12	50.0%	3 —	0 —	2	0.0%
4 —	12 —	36	33.3%	4 —	6 —	17	35.3%	4 —	0 —	1	0.0%
5 —	11 —	33	33.3%	5 —	10 —	18	55.6%	5 —	0 —	2	0.0%
6 —	13 —	36	36.1%	6 —	6 —	9	66.7%	6 —	—		
7 —	3 —	23	13.0%	7 —	2 —	8	25.0%	7 —	—		
8 —	4 —	13	30.8%	8 —	1 —	4	25.0%	8 —	1 —	2	50.0%
9 —	3 —	11	27.3%	9 —	0 —	3	0.0%	9 —	—		
10 —	3 —	8	37.5%	10 —	0 —	3	0.0%	10 —	1 —	1	100.0%
11 —	1 —	3	33.3%	11 —	—			11 —	—		
12 —	1 —	1	100.0%	12 —	—			12 —	—		
Totals —	105 —	301	34.9%		55 —	108	50.9%	55 —	3 —	10	30.0%

The 1 (43.4) and 2 (41.5) were first and second, but the number that jumps out is the 7 (13.0) compared to the 6 (36.1) and 8 (30.8).

For odds-on favorites, the inside is again golden with the 1 (76.2) and 2 (61.5), while the 7, 8, 9 and 10 are a combined 3-18.

Meadowlands: 1-mile, East Rutherford, New Jersey

1992 Stats—80 Cards—882 Races

Total				Odds-On				Sloppy Track			
1 —	53 —	131	40.5%	1 —	24 —	44	54.5%	1 —	6 —	14	42.9%
2 —	45 —	131	34.4%	2 —	23 —	46	50.0%	2 —	2 —	6	33.3%
3 —	55 —	120	45.8%	3 —	23 —	42	54.8%	3 —	4 —	11	36.4%
4 —	45 —	104	43.3%	4 —	22 —	34	64.7%	4 —	5 —	9	55.6%
5 —	28 —	85	32.9%	5 —	18 —	33	54.5%	5 —	0 —	5	0.0%
6 —	28 —	79	35.4%	6 —	11 —	21	52.4%	6 —	1 —	7	14.3%

Total				Odds-On				Sloppy Track			
7 —	28 —	81	34.6%	7 —	14 —	30	46.7%	7 —	1 —	8	12.5%
8 —	27 —	73	37.0%	8 —	12 —	22	54.5%	8 —	3 —	4	75.0%
9 —	19 —	50	38.0%	9 —	9 —	16	56.3%	9 —	—		
10 —	10 —	28	35.7%	10 —	1 —	2	50.0%	10 —	1 —	4	25.0%
Totals —	338 —	882	38.3%		157 —	290	54.1%		23 —	68	33.8%

The total numbers are remarkably balanced, a reflection that the quality racing here is unsurpassed in its competitiveness. The 3 (45.8) and 5 (32.9) were high and low.

Odds-on favorites following the 4 horse (64.7) are very even, too.

Meadows: 5/8-mile, Meadow Lands, Pennsylvania

1992 Stats—72 Cards—949 Races

Total				Odds-On				Sloppy Track			
1 —	75 —	187	40.1%	1 —	47 —	87	54.0%	1 —	4 —	15	26.7%
2 —	55 —	150	36.7%	2 —	28 —	66	42.4%	2 —	6 —	12	50.0%
3 —	52 —	143	36.4%	3 —	32 —	57	56.1%	3 —	2 —	8	25.0%
4 —	53 —	131	40.5%	4 —	32 —	53	60.4%	4 —	5 —	11	45.5%
5 —	63 —	128	49.2%	5 —	37 —	65	56.9%	5 —	4 —	8	50.0%
6 —	35 —	91	38.5%	6 —	18 —	38	47.4%	6 —	0 —	5	0.0%
7 —	20 —	67	29.9%	7 —	9 —	25	36.0%	7 —	3 —	8	37.5%
8 —	11 —	39	28.2%	8 —	6 —	16	37.5%	8 —	1 —	3	33.3%
9 —	5 —	10	50.0%	9 —	2 —	3	66.7%	9 —	—		
10 —	1 —	3	33.3%	10 —	—			10 —	—		
Totals —	370 —	949	39.0%		211 —	410	51.5%		25 —	70	35.7%

The 9 (50.0), which had only 10 favorites in the sample, and the 5 (49.2) clearly stand out.

The 7 (36.0) and 8 (37.5) finished at the bottom with odds-on chalk.

Monticello: 1/2-mile, Monticello, New York

1992 Stats—88 Cards—1,021 Races

Total				Odds-On				Sloppy Track			
1 —	123 —	264	46.6%	1 —	47 —	86	54.7%	1 —	12 —	35	34.3%
2 —	84 —	204	41.2%	2 —	32 —	61	52.5%	2 —	9 —	18	50.0%

1992 Stats—88 Cards—1,021 Races (continued from page 93)

Total				Odds-On				Sloppy Track			
3 —	65 —	174	37.4%	3 —	24 —	42	57.1%	3 —	7 —	18	38.9%
4 —	48 —	147	32.7%	4 —	13 —	32	40.6%	4 —	4 —	14	28.6%
5 —	34 —	84	40.5%	5 —	11 —	19	57.9%	5 —	2 —	12	16.7%
6 —	27 —	58	46.6%	6 —	7 —	15	46.7%	6 —	6 —	11	54.5%
7 —	11 —	35	31.4%	7 —	1 —	4	25.0%	7 —	0 —	4	0.0%
8 —	6 —	22	27.3%	8 —	1 —	4	25.0%	8 —	3 —	3	100.0%
9 —	12 —	33	36.4%	9 —	3 —	3	100.0%	9 —	2 —	4	50.0%
Totals —	410 —	1021	40.2%		139 —	266	52.3%		45 —	119	37.8%

The 1 (46.59) and 6 (46.55) finish in a near dead-heat, while the 8 checks in last (27.3). However, the 8 goes 3-for-3 (100) on sloppy tracks.

The 5 (57.9) and 3 (57.1) led in odds-on favorites.

Northfield Park: ½-mile, Northfield, Ohio

1992 Stats—79 Cards—963 Races

Total				Odds-On				Sloppy Track			
1 —	108 —	230	47.0%	1 —	60 —	96	62.5%	1 —	7 —	23	30.4%
2 —	83 —	182	45.6%	2 —	42 —	70	60.0%	2 —	5 —	16	31.3%
3 —	59 —	155	38.1%	3 —	29 —	63	46.0%	3 —	2 —	9	22.2%
4 —	51 —	112	45.5%	4 —	28 —	43	65.1%	4 —	4 —	10	40.0%
5 —	45 —	88	51.1%	5 —	23 —	32	71.9%	5 —	9 —	11	81.8%
6 —	24 —	72	33.3%	6 —	13 —	24	54.2%	6 —	2 —	4	50.0%
7 —	15 —	33	45.5%	7 —	8 —	12	66.7%	7 —	0 —	1	0.0%
8 —	6 —	17	35.3%	8 —	4 —	5	80.0%	8 —	—		
9 —	33 —	74	44.6%	9 —	12 —	23	52.2%	9 —	2 —	7	28.6%
Totals —	424 —	963	44.0%		219 —	368	59.5%		31 —	81	38.3%

For those who bet favorites, betting the 5 here is not a bad way to go. The 5 finished first in total favorites (51.1), a very high second (71.9) with odds-on favorites, and first (81.8) on a sloppy track.

The 3 and 6 do poorly in all three.

Pompano Park: 5/8-mile, Pompano Park, Florida

1992 Stats—44 Cards—613 Races

Total				Odds-On				Sloppy Track			
1 —	30 —	109	27.5%	1 —	20 —	50	40.0%	1 —	2 —	6	33.3%
2 —	37 —	102	36.3%	2 —	21 —	42	50.0%	2 —	1 —	9	11.1%
3 —	32 —	79	40.5%	3 —	16 —	29	55.2%	3 —	0 —	1	0.0%
4 —	27 —	78	34.6%	4 —	15 —	29	51.7%	4 —	0 —	2	0.0%
5 —	28 —	75	37.3%	5 —	14 —	24	58.3%	5 —	2 —	5	40.0%
6 —	23 —	61	37.7%	6 —	12 —	18	66.7%	6 —	0 —	1	0.0%
7 —	20 —	55	36.4%	7 —	7 —	18	38.9%	7 —	1 —	2	50.0%
8 —	13 —	35	37.1%	8 —	4 —	13	30.8%	8 —	—		
9 —	8 —	18	44.4%	9 —	2 —	4	50.0%	9 —	—		
10 —	0 —	1	0.0%	10 —	—			10 —	—		
Totals —	218 —	613	35.6%		111 —	227	48.9%		6 —	26	23.1%

The 9 is first (44.4) and the 1 last (27.5) overall. The 6 (66.7) led with odds-on, while just about every post did poorly in a small sample of sloppy tracks, a collective 6-26 (23.1). The 2 was 1-for-9 (11.1).

Saginaw: 1/2-mile, Saginaw, Michigan

1992 Stats—78 Cards—958 Races

Total				Odds-On				Sloppy Track			
1 —	61 —	168	36.3%	1 —	31 —	59	52.5%	1 —	2 —	8	25.0%
2 —	77 —	166	46.4%	2 —	34 —	63	54.0%	2 —	7 —	13	53.8%
3 —	56 —	138	40.6%	3 —	20 —	42	47.6%	3 —	2 —	6	33.3%
4 —	63 —	134	47.0%	4 —	34 —	49	69.4%	4 —	2 —	5	40.0%
5 —	79 —	153	51.6%	5 —	36 —	49	73.5%	5 —	6 —	12	50.0%
6 —	49 —	108	45.4%	6 —	18 —	22	81.8%	6 —	2 —	7	28.6%
7 —	27 —	62	43.5%	7 —	12 —	15	80.0%	7 —	0 —	1	0.0%
8 —	15 —	29	51.7%	8 —	5 —	7	71.4%	8 —	1 —	1	100.0%
Totals —	427 —	958	44.6%		190 —	306	62.1%		22 —	53	41.5%

The numbers here were startling: the 8 first (51.7) and the 1 last (36.3) on a 1/2-mile track.

Compare the combined success of odds-on favorites from the inside 1 through 3 posts (51.8) and the 4 through 8 (71.0)!

Saratoga: ½-mile, Saratoga Springs, New York

1992 Stats—74 Cards—801 Races

Total				Odds-On				Sloppy Track			
1 —	113 —	241	46.9%	1 —	79 —	137	57.7%	1 —	13 —	27	48.1%
2 —	60 —	157	38.2%	2 —	32 —	69	46.4%	2 —	5 —	12	41.7%
3 —	45 —	116	38.8%	3 —	24 —	48	50.0%	3 —	5 —	16	31.3%
4 —	44 —	111	39.6%	4 —	28 —	48	58.3%	4 —	0 —	5	0.0%
5 —	36 —	77	46.8%	5 —	19 —	37	51.4%	5 —	7 —	8	87.5%
6 —	19 —	49	38.8%	6 —	12 —	28	42.9%	6 —	2 —	2	100.0%
7 —	4 —	24	16.7%	7 —	2 —	6	33.3%	7 —	0 —	3	0.0%
8 —	7 —	11	63.6%	8 —	3 —	5	60.0%	8 —	2 —	3	66.7%
9 —	5 —	13	38.5%	9 —	0 —	1	0.0%	9 —	2 —	2	100.0%
10 —	0 —	2	0.0%	10 —	1 —	2	50.0%	10 —	—		
Totals —	333 —	801	41.6%		200 —	381	52.5%		36 —	78	46.2%

The 5 post on this ½-mile track did almost as well as in Northfield: total (46.8), odds-on (51.4) and sloppy track (87.5).

Again, the 8 does well in total (63.6), odds-on (60.0) and sloppy track (66.7) in a small sample.

Chalk players might want to stay away from the 7 post, which was a distant last in total (16.7), just about last with odds-on (33.3) and blanked (0-3) on sloppy tracks.

Scioto Downs: ⅝-mile, Columbus, Ohio

1992 Stats—80 Cards—796 Races

Total				Odds-On				Sloppy Track			
1 —	48 —	121	39.7%	1 —	26 —	44	59.1%	1 —	7 —	8	87.5%
2 —	52 —	124	41.9%	2 —	26 —	46	56.5%	2 —	4 —	10	40.0%
3 —	36 —	109	33.0%	3 —	19 —	27	70.4%	3 —	5 —	11	45.5%
4 —	43 —	107	40.2%	4 —	17 —	31	54.8%	4 —	1 —	8	12.5%
5 —	41 —	93	44.1%	5 —	15 —	27	55.6%	5 —	4 —	6	66.7%
6 —	30 —	79	38.0%	6 —	12 —	26	46.2%	6 —	2 —	6	33.3%
7 —	23 —	64	35.9%	7 —	9 —	15	60.0%	7 —	4 —	4	100.0%
8 —	14 —	29	48.3%	8 —	10 —	11	90.9%	8 —	1 —	2	50.0%
9 —	10 —	21	47.6%	9 —	1 —	3	33.3%	9 —	1 —	1	100.0%
10 —	18 —	49	36.7%	10 —	7 —	8	87.5%	10 —	1 —	3	33.3%
Totals —	315 —	796	39.6%		142 —	238	59.7%		30 —	59	50.8%

The 8 (48.3) and 9 (47.6) ran first and second in total, while the 8 (90.9) and 10 (87.5) were awesome at odds-on.

The 1 was 7-for-8 (87.5) on sloppy tracks.

Yonkers: ½-mile, Yonkers, New York

1992 Stats—101 Cards—1,083 Races

Total				Odds-On				Sloppy Track			
1 —	126 —	289	43.6%	1 —	81 —	150	54.0%	1 —	3 —	18	16.7%
2 —	81 —	181	44.8%	2 —	47 —	83	56.6%	2 —	4 —	11	36.4%
3 —	68 —	150	45.3%	3 —	44 —	65	67.7%	3 —	3 —	11	27.3%
4 —	76 —	162	46.9%	4 —	37 —	69	53.6%	4 —	5 —	11	45.5%
5 —	54 —	121	44.6%	5 —	33 —	47	70.2%	5 —	8 —	10	80.0%
6 —	42 —	90	46.7%	6 —	19 —	37	51.4%	6 —	2 —	8	25.0%
7 —	15 —	57	26.3%	7 —	5 —	16	31.3%	7 —	2 —	6	33.3%
8 —	12 —	33	36.4%	8 —	6 —	11	54.5%	8 —	0 —	1	0.0%
Totals —	474 —	1083	43.8%		272 —	478	56.9%		27 —	76	35.5%

The biggest surprise here is the 1 finishing sixth overall (43.7), fourth at odds-on (54.0) and nearly last on sloppy tracks (16.6).

The 5 did well again here, while the 8 soundly beat the 7 in total and odds-on.

A Few for the Road

CHAPTER 9

Here's a race with several handicapping principles: 1) Bigger underlays create bigger overlays; 2) avoid horses who seldom win, and 3) the more work you put in, the better you'll do. There's a fourth point, too: Mares taking on colts and geldings in cheap races don't necessarily suffer a disadvantage.

The underlay in question is Race Power, a 12-year-old who drew the 2 post at Saratoga, May 25, 1992, in a $2,500 claimer restricted to horses who hadn't won a race in their last four starts.

ONE MILE PACE
PURSE $1,100
MONDAY, MAY 25, 1992
FIRST HALF DAILY DOUBLE
&
EXACTA

FIRST RACE

CLAIMING ALLOWANCE $2500
NON-WINNERS OF A RACE LAST 4 STARTS
INELIGIBLE: HORSES WHICH LAST RACED IN A CONDITION RACE
OR HIGHER PRICED CLAIMING RACE

WARM UP-YELLOW

12-1 **LITTLE DOC** — b g 10 MahoneTime-DocBaumEr-RockabyWay — 1992 14 0 0 1 $692
Diamond Creek Stables & Robert Siemski, N.Y. — Stga 2:04 1 — 1991 32 2 1 4 $2,921
1 PAUL DUDKA (P) (155) red-wh-blk (10-0-0-1-.033) — Tr—Gary Dudko (.114) — 4,2:00 3 — Lifetime $59,516
2,500 YELLOW

Date	Trk	Purse	Cd	Class	Dis	Leaders Time 1/4	1/2	3/4	Winners Time	PP	1/4	1/2	3/4	Str	Fin	Ind 1/4 Time	Ind Time	Odds	Driver	Order Of Finish First Second Third	Temp
5-17 92	VD	1400	ft	2500CLCD	1	27	58 1	129 3	200 3	3	5	5	5 6	5 8	5 9	31 3	202 2	7.70	PDudka	LGrandNro,KarakaKhanA,JoTxCoins	73-C
5-7 92	Stga	1300	ft	2500CLCD	1	30 2	103 2	134 2	204 3	4	3	4	5 2 1/4	5	4 2 1/4	30 1	205	15.60	PDudka	LimeBoda,LouieGilly,JollyBoy	63-C
5-1 92	Stga	1300	sy	2500CLCD	1	29	101 2	132 4	204	2	4	6°	6 5 1/4	6	6 14 1/4	33	207	23.40	PDudka	VisFromAbov,PinFlvrsA,Rightsid	58-C
4-22 92	VD	1400	ft	2500CLCD	1	28 4	100 1	130	202	5	3	4	4° 5	3 4 1/4	4 3	31 3	202 3	9.10	PDudka	BarbarosBrt,AngryAlmn,WorthyWolf	67-C
4-9 92	VD	1400	ft	2500CLCD	1	28 2	59 3	130	201	6	9	9	8° 7	7 8	5 8 1/4	31 1	202 4	17.70	PDudka	Martini,DealinDarlin,Scarlatti	48-C
4-2 92	Stga	1200	ft	2500CLCD	1	30 4	102 4	133 4	205 4	3	3	4	4° 4	3	3 4 1/4	32	206 3	16.40	PDudka	FlatironCollins,JoyBoy,LtlDoc	40-C
3-26 92	Stga	1200	sy	2500CLCD	1	29 4	102 1	134 2	205 4	7	7	7	7 10 1/4	7	6 15 1/4	33 1	209 3	41.80	PDudka	WineBest,SunRose,GrayCenturyA	52-C

5-2 — 2 — RACE POWER
b h 12 RaceTime-MissouriFreight-BulletHanover — William R.& Christine P.DeGuerre, Ballston Spa, NY
DAVID MARSHALL (185) ltbl-red-gld (71-8-8-13-.236) — Tr—Wayne Kopo (.000)
Stga 2:03 1992 8 1 1 2 $1,311 — Stga 2:01^3 1991 10 2 2 3 $3,149 — 4,1:55 1 Lifetime $114,316
2,500 WHITE

Date	Trk	Purse	Race	Q1	Q2	Q3	Fin	PP	1/4	1/2	3/4	Str	Fin	Last Q	Time	Odds	Driver	Order of finish	Temp
5-16^92	Stga	1300	ft 2500CLCD	1 30^3	101^4	131^4	202	8	9	9	9°^4	9	7^5	30^2	203	50.30	DMarshall	Fiorann,NonStopLuck,GypsyFirst	80-0
5-8^92	Stga		ft QUA	1 30	101^4	133	203	6	1	1	1^4	1	1^3	30	203	NB	DMarshall	RacePower,FlywayFlash,FinalBow	55-C
4-29^2	Stga	1300	ft 2500CLCD	1 29	100^4	132	202^4	7	2°	3°	4°^2	8	8^13	33	205^3	11.00	DMarshall	BitterHarvestN,Surimag,LiftTickt	40-C
3-26^92	Stga	1300	sy 2500CLCD	1 31	103	134^3	206^3	7	3°	5	5^2	4	3^4	32^4	207^4	6.90	DMarshall	ShadowMirage,Sureimage,RacPowr	52-C
3-14^92	Stga	1300	gd 2500CLCD	1 29	100^3	131	201^4	7	3°	1°	7°^4	8	8^16	33	205	25.30	DMarshall	FamosFla,ShdowMirag,SavnaBChp	24-C
3-8^92	Stga A	1300	sl 2500CLCD	1 29^2	101^2	132^4	203^4	5	2	3	3	2	2	31	204	3.10	DMarshall	ChmstRanbow,RacPowr,SavanaBChp	40-0
3-1^92	Stga A	1300	gd 2500CL	1 30^2	102	133	203	1	1	1	1	1	1	29^4	203	*.60	DMarshall	RacPowr,SaundnGovnor,MagcArtst	24-0

6-1 — 3 — BK'S JENNY CLAIRE
br m 4 MajesticBeau-TallahasseeTaxi-TijuanaTaxi — John A.& Karen G.Hayes & Henry H.Westbrook Jr, NY
HENRY WESTBROOK JR (160) blk-or (29-0-3-3-.092) — Tr—Henry Westbrook Jr (.124)
Stga 2:03^4 1992 16 3 3 1 $3,443 — Scar 2:02^4 1991 39 5 2 5 $9,205 — 3,2:02^4 Lifetime $14,480
3,625 PURPLE

Date	Trk	Purse	Race	Q1	Q2	Q3	Fin	PP	1/4	1/2	3/4	Str	Fin	Last Q	Time	Odds	Driver	Order of finish	Temp
5-20^92	Stga	1300	ft 2500CL	1 29^3	101	132	203^3	4	1	1	1	2	5^3	32	204	2.60	HWstbrokJ	Rightsid,WhoseYourThundr,Spoling	79-C
5-6^92	Stga	1300	ft 2500CLCD	1 30^3	102^2	132^3	203^3	6	5	3°	2°	2	2^nk	31	203^3	9.20	HWstbrokJ	WnSmPro,BKaJnyClar,WhoseYorThndr	58-C
4-29^92	Stga	1300	ft 2500CL	1 29^3	101	132^4	204	3	5	6°	5°°	4	4^3	31^2	204^3	3.30	HWstbrokJ	Fiorann,KAPenny,MakeMiaMillion	63-C
4-5^92	Stga A	1300	ft 2500CLCD	1 29	101	131^4	203	7	9	9	8°^4	8	9^6	32	204^3	14.50	HWstbrokJ	MagcArtst,OnLastBlast,ThRghtPrc	48-C
3-29^92	Stga A	1300	ft 2500CL	1 29^3	101^4	132^3	203^4	2	1	1	1^hd	1	1^nk	31	203^4	7.40	HWstbrokJ	BKaJnyClar,HoindsSng,SnyValyBoy	54-C
3-22^92	Stga A	1300	ft 2500CLCD	1 30^2	102^4	133^4	204^3	1	1	1	1^2	1	1^hd	30^4	204^3	2.90	HWstbrokJ	BKaJnyClar,ChmstRnbow,SgnHiRd	38-C
3-15^92	Stga A	1300	ft 2500CLCD	1 29^2	102^2	133^3	207	2	2	2°	1°^hd	2	2^nk	33^2	207	2.00	HWstbrokJ	KarlaKhanA,BKaJnyClar,TMScotch	21-0

12-1 — 4 — SKIPPER DIDODA
b h 5 MountainSkipper-LookinLaura-ThorpeHanover — H.Kendall Knapp,Greenfield,Mass
RAYMOND TREMBLAY (170) bl-wh-go (11-1-1-2-.202) — Tr—Raymond Tremblay (.222)
1992 5 0 1 1 $1,023 — 1991 4 0 1 0 $600 — 3,2:02^2 Lifetime $4,352
2,500 BLACK

Date	Trk	Purse	Race	Q1	Q2	Q3	Fin	PP	1/4	1/2	3/4	Str	Fin	Last Q	Time	Odds	Driver	Order of finish	Temp
5-14^92	Stga	1300	ft 2500CLCD	1 29	101	131^4	201^4	scr sk					SCT					OnLastBlast,FrtmClns,AnMarsScty	81-0
5-6^92	Stga	1300	ft 2500CLCD	1 29^2	101^2	132^3	203	7	x4°	8	8^dis	8	8^dis			18.20	RTremblay	JyfMac,CrwnLgrA,IdywdBlzd	58-C
4-22^92	PPk%	2185	ft 4000CLCD	1 28^4	58^2	128^3	159^3	5	9	9	6°°^4	4^4	3^4	31	200^2	*1.20	TSells	Windamage,ObnnsFla,SkprDidoda	77-C
4-10^92	PPk%	2500	ft 9000CL NW2	1 28^4	59	129^4	158^4	7	5	5	8^4	5^4	4^4	28^3	200	33.00	KSizer	Danngimag,DenForun,SkprKnght	77-C
3-25^92	PPk%	1700	ft 4000CLCD	1 28^2	100	130	200^3	7	8	7	8^4	7^4	4^5	30^2	201^3	5.50	HMosher	Matsbrt,HaroldWlam,FlashyDaring	72-C
3-11^92	PPk%	1700	ft 4000CLCD	1 29^2	100	129^3	159^4	9	7	7°	6°^2	2^5	2^4	30^2	200^3	8.10	PWrenn	Khantmplation,SkprDidoda,Skprstn	70-C
3-3^92	PPk%		ft QUA	1 29^3	58	127	155^4	4	1	2	2	5^2	6^24	31	200^3	NB	BRanger	CaesarsJackpot,Frazer,HalDamac	80-C

3-1 — 5 — GYPSY FIRST (NY)
b g 5 Niafirst-CandyMaker-GypsyBret — Eugene Lewis,Amsterdam NY
RICHARD PUGLIESE (115) gray-black (43-7-5-5-.266) — Tr—Cynthia Milano (.089)
1992 4 0 1 1 $751 — Stga 2:00^2 1991 31 6 5 2 $6,485 — 4,2:00^2 Lifetime $19,0[illegible]
2,500 GREEN

Date	Trk	Purse	Race	Q1	Q2	Q3	Fin	PP	1/4	1/2	3/4	Str	Fin	Last Q	Time	Odds	Driver	Order of finish	Temp
5-16^92	Stga	1300	ft 2500CLCD	1 30^3	101^4	131^4	202	3	4	4°	3°	3	3^2	30^2	202	2.80	RPugliese	Fiorann,NonStopLuck,GypsyFirst	80-C
5-8^92	Stga	1500	ft 3500CLCD	1 30	102	132^2	202	1	2	4	3	4	5^2	29^4	202	6.30	RPugliese	StrongBrz,Rving,SatrdayntFvr	61-C
5-1^92	Stga	1500	ft 3500CL	1 29^4	101	132^3	203	3	4	4°	1°°	3	4^5	31^3	204	9.70	RPugliese	Wainbrg,Rving,SaturdayntFvr	56-C
4-16^92	VD%	1600	sy 3000CL	1 28^2	59	130^4	200^4	4	6°	4	3°^2	3^2	2^3	30	201^2	6.80	RPugliese	StveGotPlnty,GypsyFrst,WrthChck	38-C
4-3^92	Stga		ft QUA	1 30	102^4	133^4	206	6	5	5	5^5	5	6^2	31^3	206^2	NB	RPugliese	Popyack,DainDarin,BoScotsBgFla	32-C
11-27^91	Stga	1200	ft 2500CLCD	1 29^4	102	134	205	3	5°	6°	3°°	1	1	31^2	205^2	*1.90	RPugliese	GypsyFirst,Ermaland,MagicArtist	35-C
11-14^91	Stga	1200	ft 2500CLCD	1 29^4	102	132^2	203^4	7	7	6°	6°^3	6	4^6	32	205	2.60	RPugliese	VideoAngus,ShawnyRom,BroadwayPs	38-C

8-1 — 6 — SPOOLING ‡
b m 5 B G'sBunny-RaceyJane-RaceTime — Brenda DeMartino, Saratoga Springs NY
GERRY MATTISON (160) blue-or-wh (67-11-13-6-.302) — Tr—David De Martino (.133)
1992 10 0 1 2 $1,085 — Phld 2:01 1991 24 2 1 3 $6,3[illegible] — 4,2:01 Lifetime $16,555
3,000 RED

Date	Trk	Purse	Race	Q1	Q2	Q3	Fin	PP	1/4	1/2	3/4	Str	Fin	Last Q	Time	Odds	Driver	Order of finish	Temp
5-20^92	Stga	‡1300	ft 2500CL	1 29^3	101	132	203^3	1	2	2	3^1	4	3^1	31^2	203^4	*1.00	RPugliese	Rightsid,WhoseYourThundr,Spoling	79-C
5-13^92	Stga	‡1300	ft 2500CLCD	1 29	100	130^4	202	8	8	8	7°^3	6	4^3	31^2	202^4	39.90	RPugliese	ThGratHry,WhoseYorThndr,WnSmPro	79-C
5-6^92	Stga	‡1500	ft FMNW1500L7	1 29	100^4	131^4	203	8	1	1	1^ns	6	8^11	33^3	205^2	15.70	RPugliese	CilWthAXs,BoenArond,DamysFly	56-C
4-29^92	Stga	‡1500	ft FMNW1500L7	1 29^3	101^3	132	204^2	9	4	2°	1°^nk	2	3	32^3	204^3	7.10	RPugliese	HiLoGoddess,DamysFly,Spoling	63-C
4-2^92	Stga	‡1500	ft NW1500L7CD	1 30^2	101^4	132^4	204^4	7	1	2	3	3	2	32	205	9.10	RPugliese	WhoseYourThunder,Spooling,Srybel	40-C
3-5^92	Stga	‡1500	gd NW1500L7CD	1 29	100^2	132^2	204^4	4	1	1	1	1	4	32^3	205	*2.30	RPugliese	BrandNwJwl,DamysFly,Rightsid	45-C
2-28^92	Stga	‡1900	sy F&MNW3PMCD	1 30	101^4	133	205	6	6	5°	7°^6	8	6^7	32^2	206^3	24.10	DDMartno	Hawdagoin,HotRail,Rightside	42-C

10-1 — 7 — FULLA D'OR
br h 5 WarmBreeze-FullasCousin-JollyRoger — Gene A.White,Melrose NY
DANIEL CAPPELLO JR (115) blue-white (30-6-4-5-.330) — Tr—Gene White (.257)
VD% 2:01 1992 9 1 1 2 $1,41[illegible] — 1991 24 0 4 4 $2,302 — 5,2:01% Lifetime $6,76[illegible]
2,500 BROWN

Date	Trk	Purse	Race	Q1	Q2	Q3	Fin	PP	1/4	1/2	3/4	Str	Fin	Last Q	Time	Odds	Driver	Order of finish	Temp
5-20^92	Stga	1300	ft 2500CLCD	1 30	100^2	130	201	2	3	3	4^5	4	3^4	30^4	202	13.70	DCaploJr	LightBluFla,MagicArtist,FulaDor	79-C
5-9^92	Stga	1300	ft 2500CLCD	1 28^4	100^3	131	202^2	3	6	6	7^4	7	6^2	30^4	202^4	16.80	JRandall	Ufinthfastlan,RbiConrad,Rghtsd	70-C
5-2^92	VD%	1600	sy 3000CL	1 27	58^4	128^3	159	4	8	8	7°^1	7^1	5^5	30	200	20.30	GGibson	MisquamicutMagic,WnsBet,GmAdago	63-C
4-22^92	VD%	1600	ft 3000CL	1 28^2	59	129^3	200	6	8	8°	x8°^7	8^7	8^17	31	202^2	3.10	KCrawford	JBsTxan,MohawkShyLyn,HyatBitmor	67-C
4-15^92	VD%	1400	ft 3000CL	1 27^4	59	130	201	4	4	3°	2°	1^1	1^1	30^3	201	50.80	KCrawford	FullaDor,WineBest,JBsTexan	46-C
4-3^92	Stga	1300	ft 2500CLCD	1 29^4	102	133^3	204	1	3	5	5^7	5	3^3	30^3	204^3	41.80	JRandall	StveGotPlnty,AnMarscoty,FulaDor	37-C
3-26^92	Stga	1300	sy 2500CLCD	1 30^3	103	135	207^2	9	4	5	3^4	3	2^3	32	208	12.10	JRandall	IdealSocietyA,FulaDor,ChrTrck	52-C

4-1 — 8 — MOVE FREELY
br g 8 Abercrombie-DancingWheels-StrikingImage — Colen A.Mosher,Irasburg Vt
JOHN STARK JR (145) red-wh-lblu (56-20-6-8-.464) — Tr—Craig Mosher (.219)
Stga 2:02 1992 14 4 1 3 $3,563 — Stga 1:59^2 1991 37 9 8 6 $16,332 — 5,1:59 Lifetime $60,642
2,500 GRAY

Date	Trk	Purse	Race	Q1	Q2	Q3	Fin	PP	1/4	1/2	3/4	Str	Fin	Last Q	Time	Odds	Driver	Order of finish	Temp
5-14^92	Stga	1300	ft 2500CLCD	1 29	59^2	129^3	200^2	1	1	1	1	2	3^1	32	201^3	1.60	JStarkJr	IdylwoodBlizzard,Remmen,MovFrly	61-0
5-7^92	Stga	1300	ft 2500CLCD	1 29^3	101	131	202	2	2	2	2	2	4^2	31^2	202^3	1.90	JStarkJr	ViewFromAbove,Fiorann,Sureimage	63-C
4-29^92	Stga	1300	ft 2500CLCD	1 29^3	100	130	201^3	2	1	1	1^2	1	2^2	31^4	202	*.80	JStarkJr	CrownLagerA,MoveFreely,SaltyB	63-C
4-23^92	VD%	1600	ft 3000CL	1 27^3	57^3	128	158^4	8	3°	1	1	1^2	5^3	31^2	159^2	*2.50	KCrawford	WineBet,DaxsLilTurk,TailgatParty	59-C
4-5^92	Stga A	1300	ft 2500CLCD	1 29	101	131^4	203	8	7	7°	6°^3	6	6^4	31^3	204	3.40	KCrawford	MagcArtst,OnLastBlast,ThRghtPrc	48-C
3-29^92	Stga A	1500	ft 3500CL	1 28^3	59^4	130^2	202^2	8	8°	7°	7^2	7	7^4	33^2	205	5.90	KCrawford	FamousFella,Temble,Riveting	54-C
3-21^92	Stga	1300	ft 2500CLCD	1 30	101^4	131^4	202^3	2	1	1	1^2	1	1^5	30^4	202^3	*.20	KCrawford	MoveFreely,Sondanced,ChrysBaby	28-C

By definition, how strong can a favorite be in this race since it took four losing efforts to fit the condition?

Race Power had won $114,316 lifetime with a mark of 1:55.1 as a 4-year-old a long time ago. This obviously classy horse, however, was well past his prime. We document this by looking at his record for the last two years. In 18 starts, he was 3-3-5 with earnings of $4,460. These are not powerful numbers.

Race Power had finished eighth by 13¾ lengths at this level, April 2. He didn't race again until a qualifier, May 8, when he won by three lengths.

In his one and only return race, May 16, Race Power drew the 8 post, was sent off at 50-1 in the same class, and finished seventh by five lengths, 2½ lengths behind the 5 horse tonight, Gypsy First, who went off at 5-2. Now, today, there was a significant post change, Race Power from the 8 to the 2 and Gypsy First from the 3 to the 5. Gypsy First would go off 2-1. But that isn't the greatest concern. Here's what is: A 12-year-old with just one race back, a stroll from the 8 post at 50-1 after missing six weeks (five if you include the qualifier), would go off at even money. At Saratoga, $2,500 is the bottom claiming level. Though Race Power had legitimate bad luck in post position draws—three 7's and an 8 in his last four starts—his health, sharpness and extremely limited success the past two years were legitimate knocks.

As Race Power dropped to 1-1, the search for overlays had long begun.

Avoiding horses who rarely won eliminated the 1, Little Doc (2-for-46 the last two years), the 4, Skipper Didoda (0-9), the 6, Spooling (2-for-34), and the 7, Fulla D'Or (1-33).

This leaves us with the 3, BK's Jenny Claire, the 5, Gypsy First, and the 8, Move Freely.

Gypsy First was an obvious contender. He'd been competitive, without winning, in $3,000 and $3,500 claimers; had won six of 31 starts last year; and, in his fourth '92 start, when he dropped from $3,500 to $2,500, was third by 1¼ lengths, beating Race Power in a 2:02 race whose last half went in a very fast—for this level—1:00.1. He held his own in the last half while racing on the outside. He is the horse to beat. His 2-1 odds were reasonable. An overlay? Not at 2-1.

Move Freely was plainly the class of the field, winning just under $20,000 the last two years with a record of 13-9-9 in 51 starts. This 8-year-old knows just one way to win: on the lead. But would he leave from the 8 hole? In three previous races from the 8 post, he'd left just once, forging his way to the lead in a :57.3 half at Vernon Downs, a speedier ¾-mile track near Syracuse, New York. He didn't leave in his other two races from the 8 post and was no factor in either. The 8 post is such a disadvantage that drivers can't gun their horses to the lead every time. It takes a lot out of a horse.

Another consideration that would affect his tactics was the early speed of his rivals inside him. Race Power, BK's Jenny Claire and Spooling were candidates to make the front, but none of them always raced on the lead. Tempering their drivers' enthusiasm for leaving was the fact that if Move Freely left, he'd run any other frontrunner into the ground to make the top. He'd been doing so his entire career at Saratoga, but that's an item not in the program. Once again, the more information you have, the better.

Of Move Freely's seven PPs, he'd gone off at odds of: 1-5, 5-1, 3-1, 5-2, 4-5, 9-5 and 8-5. All but the race at 5-1 odds were at tonight's level. He was 10-1 here.

An overlay? You bet. If he left and made the lead in reasonable fractions, he could win. With three other potential leavers inside of him, it was a calculated guess, one aided by the way he scored. A definite negative was that he'd lost his last three starts from posts 2, 2 and 1. Moving outside to the 8 post wasn't going to make it easier.

However, Move Freely's propensity for leaving was another knock on the heavy favorite, Race Power, whose two wins—including the qualifier—were both wire-to-wire off opening quarters of :30.2 and :30 and first halves of 1:02.1 and 1:01.4. Move Freely, albeit from the rail, made the top in fractions of :29 and :59.2 his last start. Move Freely's bid for the lead, if he made one, would preclude any chance of Race Power going wire-to-wire, his m.o. in victory.

This takes us to the 3, BK's Jenny Claire, one of only two mares in the field. Spooling was the other.

BK's two-year record was 8-5-6 in 55 starts with earnings of $12,648. Only Move Freely earned more.

We'll start at the bottom of BK's PPs. She proved she fit well at this level, winning twice and losing by a nose from inside posts in three races. Her next start was a no-factor ninth, beaten by 6¾ lengths from the 7 post.

She didn't get another start for 24 days, from April 5 to April 29. She finished a so-so fourth by three lengths at 3-1 when she was forced to go three-wide around the final turn. Remember our belief that horses off a layoff need a tightener? Applied here, her mediocre fourth was understandable. Accordingly, she should have improved in her next start, and she did. Again racing from off the pace out of the 6 hole, she went first-over and finished second by a neck at 9-1.

She then skipped a week, returning on May 20th to finish a tiring fifth on a wire-to-wire attempt from the 4 post. Her owner/trainer/driver Henry "Bucky" Westbrook, Jr., wheeled her right back here on four days rest instead of the usual six. We conclude that if her physical problems caused her to miss weeks in her previous PPs, she certainly didn't seem to still have them. Her appearance off a shorter-than-normal rest week suggested she was sound now.

Since she previously improved sharply in her second start off a layoff, she could do so again here.

Her versatility racing on or off the lead was a definite advantage here. Sent off at 5-2 the previous week from the 4 post, she drifted up to 6-1 at post time. Westbrook gave a flawless drive, taking back at the start, getting an ideal second-over trip and winning by four lengths to pay $14.60. Race Power was fourth. Fulla D'Or, off at 48-1, rallied to finish second, providing a $394.60 exacta. Ouch! That's why we wheel horses, sometimes. Unfortunately, this wasn't one of them. Catching a $44 Daily Double eased the pain.

The fifth race at Saratoga, July 19, 1991, matched a field of 8 New York Sire Stakes 2-year-old pacing fillies.

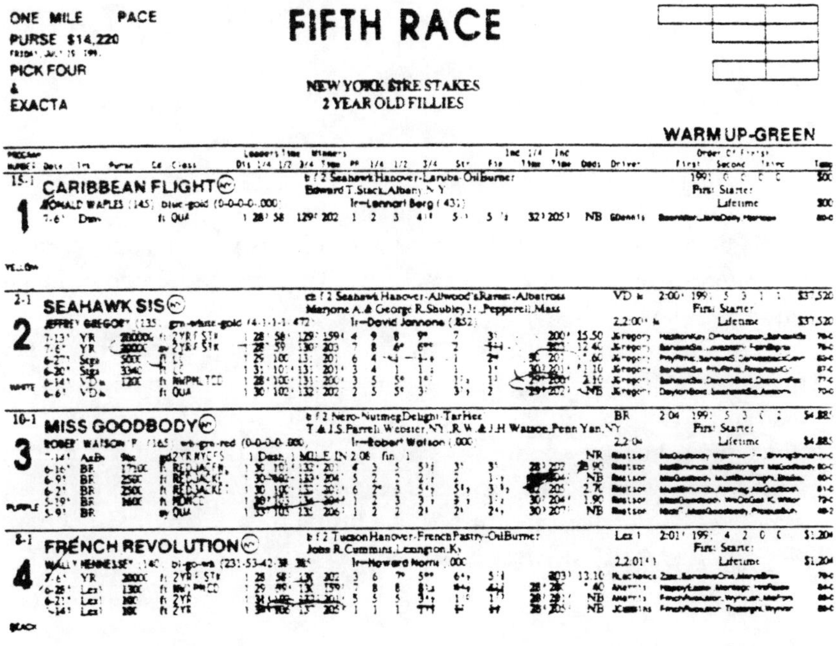
ONE MILE PACE
PURSE $14,220
PICK FOUR
&
EXACTA

FIFTH RACE
NEW YORK SIRE STAKES
2 YEAR OLD FILLIES

WARM UP-GREEN

15-1 CARIBBEAN FLIGHT
1
b f 2 Seahawk Hanover-Laruba-OilBurner
Edward T. Stack, Albany, N.Y.
Tr—Lennart Berg (.431)
RONALD WAPLES (145) blue-gold (0-0-0-0-.000)
First Starter
Lifetime
YELLOW

2-1 SEAHAWK SIS
2
ch f 2 Seahawk Hanover-Allwood'sRamm-Albatross
Marjorie A. & George R. Saubley Jr., Pepperell, Mass
Tr—David Jannone (.852)
JEFFREY GREGORY (135) grn-white-gold
VD 2:00 1991 5 3 1 1 $37,520
First Starter
Lifetime $37,520
WHITE

10-1 MISS GOODBODY
3
b f 2 Nero-NutmegDelight-TarHee
T & J.S. Parrell, Webster, NY, R.W. & J.H. Watson, Penn Yan, NY
Tr—Robert Watson (.000)
ROBERT WATSON (165) wh-grn-red (0-0-0-0-.000)
BR 2:04 1991 5 3 0 2 $4,885
First Starter
Lifetime $4,885
PURPLE

8-1 FRENCH REVOLUTION
4
b f 2 Tucson Hanover-FrenchPastry-OilBurner
John R. Cummins, Lexington, Ky
Tr—Howard Norris (.000)
WALLY HENNESSEY (140)
Lex 1 2:01 1991 4 2 0 0 $1,204
First Starter
Lifetime $1,204
BLACK

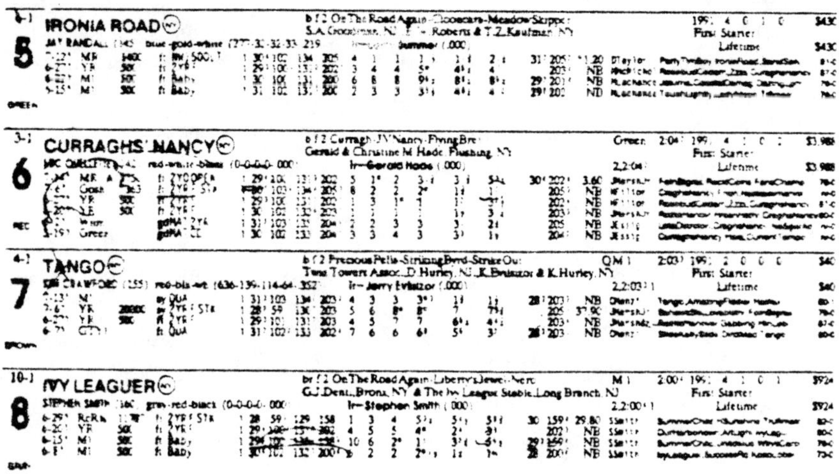
6-1 IRONIA ROAD
5
b f 2 On The Road Again-Cloonecars-Meadow Skipper
S.A. Goodman, NJ; L.L. Roberts & T.Z. Kaufman, NY
First Starter
Lifetime $430
GREEN

3-1 CURRAGHS' NANCY
6
b f 2 Curragh-JV Nancy-Flying Bret
Gerald & Christine M Hade, Flushing, NY
Tr—Gerald Hade (.000)
First Starter
Lifetime $3,988
RED

4-1 TANGO
7
b f 2 Precious Fella-Striking Byrd-Strike Out
Twin Towers Assoc., D Hurley, NJ; K Bruzzor & K Hurley, NY
Tr—Jerry Evbazor (.000)
First Starter
Lifetime $40
BROWN

10-1 IVY LEAGUER
8
br f 2 On The Road Again-Liberty's Jewel-Nero
G.J. Dent, Bronx, NY & The Ivy League Stable, Long Branch, NJ
Tr—Stephen Smith (.000)
First Starter
Lifetime $924

A quick look at this race would lead you to believe the 2 horse, Seahawk Sis, was an obvious standout. This is why it pays to get a program before you get to the track. A little research here found a gigantic overlay.

Seahawk Sis had three wins, one second and one third in her five starts. After breaking her maiden at Vernon Downs, she finished first and a close second by a neck in a Late-Closer series at Saratoga. She followed that by winning a $20,000 New York Sire Stakes race at Yonkers on a sloppy track. In her last start, a $200,000 Sire Stakes race at Yonkers, she rallied to finish third, losing by five lengths. The race went in 1:59.4. Inside post here; can't lose, right?

Wrong.

Let's take an extensive look at the 3 horse, Miss Goodbody. After winning her career debut in 2:04.4 at Buffalo Raceway, she then raced three consecutive weeks in a Late Closer there called the Red Jacket. She finished third by $18\frac{1}{2}$; won in 2:04.2 by a length and a half, then finished third by five in 2:02.1. She then missed nearly a month before racing at a fair denoted AxBy.

Buffalo Raceway, like Yonkers and Saratoga, is a $\frac{1}{2}$-mile track. It's never a bad idea when handicapping 2-year-old stakes races on a $\frac{1}{2}$-mile track to pay attention to horses who have raced well, or at the very least competed, on one. Many 2-year-olds have difficulty negotiating the tighter and additional turns of a $\frac{1}{2}$-mile track.

Miss Goodbody had no problem with that. In fact, she put in a race at Buffalo superior to those of Seahawk Sis.

In her last start at Buffalo, her PP line shows she raced evenly throughout, sitting third, fifth and third. But racing evenly in the second half was quite an accomplishment in a 2:01.1 race. Miss Goodbody got her final quarter in :28.3, an outstanding final quarter for any horse on a $\frac{1}{2}$-mile track, let alone a 2-year-old filly. She raced her final half in :59.2.

Seahawk Sis got her final quarter in :30 and her final half in 1:00.2 in her last race, but the final time (1:59.4) was much faster—the equivalent of seven lengths—than Miss Goodbody's (2:01.1). And Seahawk Sis's final time of 2:00.4 was better than Miss Goodbody's 2:02.1. You can also say that Miss Goodbody sucked along in her race, that is, got carried to a faster mile by just following the winner in front of her.

But time out.

The comparative time of Yonkers 2:02.1 is $\frac{2}{5}$ of a second faster than Buffalo. Taking that into consideration makes Miss Goodbody's effort even more impressive in comparison. In no way, shape, or form had Seahawk Sis shown a final quarter in the neighborhood of :28.3 in her four starts on a $\frac{1}{2}$-mile track. Seahawk Sis's fastest closing quarter was :29.2 in her maiden win at Vernon, a $\frac{3}{4}$-mile track rated $2\frac{3}{5}$ seconds faster than Buffalo.

This doesn't mean Miss Goodbody was going to blow away Seahawk Sis, but it did mean that she had a reasonable chance to win the race. Her 2:08 effort at the fair was a tune-up for this race. The time wasn't important because Miss Goodbody had previously raced a final quarter in :28.3 and a final half in :59.2 at Buffalo. A repeat performance would be good enough to win tonight. It was.

Seahawk Sis went off at 2-5; Miss Goodbody 7-1. If your handicapping discovers a legitimate contender at 7-1, go for it. Over-bet Seahawk Sis created a $16.40 win for Miss Goodbody.

ONE MILE PACE
PURSE $3,200
FRIDAY, JULY 10, 1992
FIRST HALF MID DOUBLE & EXACTA

SEVENTH RACE

FILLIES & MARES
PREFERENCE TO HIGHER MONEY WINNERS LAST 5 STARTS
(POST POSITION 1 ASSIGNED)
何嘉仁美語學校
HESS LANGUAGE SCHOOL

WARM UP-BROWN

10-1 — 1 — SUNDANCE NANCY (NY) — br m 7 SundanceSkipper-GazellesNesbit-ArmbroNesbit — Robert B.Talbert,Granville N.Y. — QStga 2:01 1992 0 0 0 0 $00; 1989 4 0 2 2 $8,025
KIM CRAWFORD (155) red-blk-wh (287-48-51-33-.304) Tr—Robert Talbert (.299) — 3,1:56 1 — Lifetime $22,645 — YELLOW

Date	Trk	Purse	Cd	Class	Dis	1/4	1/2	3/4	Time	PP	1/4	1/2	3/4	Str	Fin	Ind 1/4 Time	Ind Time	Odds	Driver	First, Second, Third	Temp
7-1	Stga		ft	QUA	1	30	100	131	201	7	5°	1	1	1	1	30	201	NB	KCrawford	SndancNancy,TheRghtPrc,FnnShan	75-0
6-27	Stga		ft	QUA	1	30	101	133	203	2x	7	7	6°°	5	3	30	204	NB	KCrawford	Keller,FRJack,SundanceNancy	62-0
2-7	M1	12500	ft	F-Mnw3LC	1	28	58	128	157	5	8	6°	3°	3	2	28	157	6.90	MLachance	NuzaEmrald,SundancNancy,SlvrSu	30-
1-24	M1	10000	ft	F-Mnw2LC	1	29	58	129	158	11	8	8°°	4°°	3	3	29	159	4.10	MLachance	SlvrSu,MisMarpol,SundancNancy	50-0
1-17	M1	10000	ft	F-Mnw2LC	1	30	58	129	159	1	3	4	9	8	2	28	159	*1.30	MLachance	Fanastick,SndancNancy,HalwHapy	42-0
1-10	M1	10000	ft	F-Mnw2LC	1	29	58	128	159	10	10°	9°	8°	7	3	30	200	3.30	MLachance	Jontelle,Mchenry,SundanceNancy	34-
12-30	GSP1	5000	ft	F-Mnw6750	1	30	59	128	158	6	8	8°	7°	6	2	28	158	2.30	MLachance	MeRarHanovr,SndancNancy,GoHonyGo	3-

8-1 — 2 — BONNIE CASTLE DOT (NY) — b f 3 OnTheRoadAgain-Precious Dot-Precious Fella — Catherine J.& John E.Randall Sr.,Valatie,N.Y. — Stga 1:59 1992 10 2 4 1 $4,438; Stga 2:05 1991 5 2 1 0 $2,120
JAY RANDALL (145) blue-gold-white (156-19-21-17-.233) Tr—Jay Randall (.291) — 3,1:59 — Lifetime $6,558 — WHITE

Date	Trk	Purse	Cd	Class	Dis	1/4	1/2	3/4	Time	PP	1/4	1/2	3/4	Str	Fin	Ind 1/4 Time	Ind Time	Odds	Driver	First, Second, Third	Temp
7-3	Stga	3200	sy	F&MHC	1	29	101	131	200	2	2	2	4	5	4	30	201	4.00	JRandall	MmngFntsy,AshCanWyn,FrmThAshs	80-0
6-23	Stga	1900	ft	FMNW2000L7	1	27	59	129	159	4	3	2°°	1	1	1	30	159	*2.10	JRandall	BonCstlDot,YngBtotrobi,MsRanbow	69-0
6-17	Stga	1800	ft	F&MNW3PMCD	1	28	100	130	200	4	1	1	1	1	1	29	200	3.90	JRandall	BonCstlDot,WlowyBary,ShalThFrn	79-0
6-5	Stga	1800	sy	F&MNW3PMLT	1	29	100	131	203	3	4	3°	3°	2	2	31	203	*1.60	JRandall	MeStrmMstr,BnCstlDot,CrsCrkTcan	61-0
5-29	Stga	1800	ft	F&MNW3PMLT	1	30	101	131	202	6	1	1	1	1	2	31	202	15.00	JRandall	CasomGrl,BonCstlDot,HapyLdyJar	71-0
5-22	Stga	1900	ft	F&MNW3PMLT	1	28	59	130	201	5	5	5°	4°	4	4	32	202	7.30	JRandall	LDeGrmmy,CrsCrkTcan,MeStrmMstr	81-0
5-15	Stga	1900	ft	NW3PMLT	1	29	101	130	202	3	3	4	ix4°	4	4	32	203	14.50	JRandall	Abycmmp - Prewnhy - BonCstlDot -	7-0

5-2 — 3 — CEIL WITH A KISS (NY) — br m 5 PreciousFella-Ceil'sByeBye-ByeByeSam — Joel J.Flanders & Sandra L.McTygue,Saratoga Springs NY. — PPk 1:59 1992 19 7 4 2 $9,318; Stga 2:01 1991 41 1 6 8 $7,018
JOHN STARK JR (145) red-wh-lblu (203-50-24-31-.363) Tr—David Bez (.750) — 5,1:59 — Lifetime $27,545 — PURPLE

Date	Trk	Purse	Cd	Class	Dis	1/4	1/2	3/4	Time	PP	1/4	1/2	3/4	Str	Fin	Ind 1/4 Time	Ind Time	Odds	Driver	First, Second, Third	Temp
6-26	Stga	2600	ft	10000CLCD	1	28	58	128	159	5	5	5ix°	6	6	6			*.90	JStarkJr	AncntFir,JsJant,DiamondHuntrA	66-0
6-12	Stga	2600	ft	10000CL	1	29	100	131	200	5	1	2	2°	2	1	28	200	2.50	JStarkJr	ClWthAKs,JsJant,PrtTompnata	81-0
6-2	Stga	1900	ft	6000CLOP	1	29	59	129	159	1	3	3	3	2	1	29	159	*.90	JStarkJr	ClWthAKs,Tnptiqu,LadyLilian	74-0
5-27	Stga	1900	gd	6000CLOP	1	29	101	131	201	2	3	3°	2°	1	1	29	201	*.60	JStarkJr	CeilWthAKs,MsRainbow,Tnptiqu	51-0
5-13	Stga	1500	ft	4000CLOPz	1	30	102	132	202	1	2	2	3	2	1	29	202	*1.40	BWalker	ClWthAKs,NorthsongRos,HLosGods	79-0
5-6	Stga	1500	ft	4000CLOP	1	29	100	131	203	5	3	3°	3°°	1	1	31	203	5.80	BWalker	ClWthAKs,BosnArond,DamysFly	56-0
4-16	PPk	2100	ft	4000CLFM	1	29	100	129	200	6	1°	2	3	3	6	31	201	4.00	STrites	MandysMagic,CharmFantasy,TmGranTo	72-0

10-1 — 4 — MS RAINBOW (NY) — b m 4 StormDamage-TambatrosRainbow-Albatross — Cambridge Valley Stb Inc, Schuylerville NY. — Stga 1:59 1992 15 4 5 3 $7,773; QStga 2:06 1991 2 0 1 0 $420
DAVID MARSHALL (185) ltbl-red-gld (215-23-28-27-.221) Tr—David Marshall (.238) — 4,1:59 — Lifetime $8,193 — BLACK

Date	Trk	Purse	Cd	Class	Dis	1/4	1/2	3/4	Time	PP	1/4	1/2	3/4	Str	Fin	Ind 1/4 Time	Ind Time	Odds	Driver	First, Second, Third	Temp
6-30	Stga	1900	ft	FMNW2000L7	1	28	59	129	159	1	1	1	1	1	1	30	159	*.70	DMarshall	MsRanbow,ValablScttr,YongBtotrobi	83-0
6-23	Stga	1900	ft	FMNW2000L7	1	27	59	129	159	7	7	6°	5°	5	3	31	200	5.80	DMarshall	BonCstlDot,YngBtotrobi,MsRanbow	69-0
6-16	Stga	1900	ft	FMNW2000L7	1	29	59	129	159	4	4	3°	1°	1	2	30	159	1.50	DMarshall	Tnptique,MsRainbow,Tropical	74-0
6-9	Stga	1900	ft	FMNW2000L7	1	28	59	130	200	5	5	6°	3°°	2	2	29	200	4.20	DMarshall	RaceMeTara,MsRainbow,Tnptique	72-0
6-2	Stga	1900	ft	FMNW2000L7	1	29	59	129	159	8	5	5	5	5	4	29	200	63.40	DMarshall	ClWthAKs,Tnptiqu,LadyLilian	74-0
5-27	Stga	1900	gd	FMNW2000L7	1	29	101	131	201	3	5	5	5°	4	2	29	201	7.50	DMarshall	CeilWthAKs,MsRainbow,Tnptiqu	51-0
5-20	Stga	2000	ft	FMNW2000L7	1	30	103	135	204	2	2	3	3	3	2	29	204	*1.30	DMarshall	RaceMeTara,MsRainbow,Tropical	79-0

12-1 — 5 — ANCIENT FIRE (NY) — blk m 5 AncientMariner-SatinFire-Chuckeen — Charles W.Pulver & Neil B.Gold,Chatham N.Y. — Stga 1:59 1992 18 2 2 2 $6,584; Stga 2:01 1991 27 1 2 3 $7,577
CHARLES PULVER (185) blk-white-green (22-5-1-3-.298) Tr—Charles Pulver (.273) — 5,1:59 — Lifetime $29,722 — GREEN

Date	Trk	Purse	Cd	Class	Dis	1/4	1/2	3/4	Time	PP	1/4	1/2	3/4	Str	Fin	Ind 1/4 Time	Ind Time	Odds	Driver	First, Second, Third	Temp
7-3	Stga	3200	sy	F&MHC	1	29	101	131	200	3	4	6	7	7	7	31	203	29.30	CPulver	MmngFntsy,AshCanWyn,FrmThAshs	80-0
6-26	Stga	2600	ft	10000CLCD	1	28	58	128	159	1	1	1	1	1	1	31	159	24.00	CPulver	AncintFir,JsJant,DiamondHuntrA	66-0
6-19	Stga	2600	ft	10000CLCD	1	29	59	128	159	4x	7	7	7	7	7	31	201	30.50	CPulver	JJsJeanette,PortTomponata,HChs	71-0
6-12	Stga	2600	ft	10000CL	1	29	100	131	200	4	5	5	6°	6	5	29	201	28.80	CPulver	ClWthAKs,JsJant,PrtTompnata	81-0
5-29	Stga	2600	ft	10000CLCD	1	28	59	129	159	3	4ix	8	8	8	7	30	204	43.00	CPulver	JJsJant,KystonChbis,YngBtotrobi	71-0
5-22	Stga	2700	ft	10000CLCD	1	28	100	130	200	6	7°	6°	6°°	6	6	30	201	14.50	JStarkJr	KystonChbis,YngBtotrobi,JsJant	81-0
5-12	YR A	3750	ft	10000CL	1	28	59	129	200	5	5	4°	4°	4	2		200	10.50	RWolcio	HToBlugras,AncntFr,AnothrChrstr	63-0

4-1 — 6 — JOVITA LOBELL — b m 5 Troublemaker-JazzSinger-Albatross — Robert Metzner,Albany,N.Y. — Stga 1:59 1992 21 5 3 3 $12,875; Stga 1:59 1991 34 6 5 4 $14,387
FRANK COPPOLA JR (150) ltbl-wh-br (337-55-50-56-.301) Tr—Carl La Bombard (.381) — 3,1:56 1 — Lifetime $55,375 — RED

Date	Trk	Purse	Cd	Class	Dis	1/4	1/2	3/4	Time	PP	1/4	1/2	3/4	Str	Fin	Ind 1/4 Time	Ind Time	Odds	Driver	First, Second, Third	Temp
6-26	Stga	3200	ft	F&M	1	28	59	128	158	6	6	6	5°°	6	6	30	159	2.60	FCopolaJr	AshCanWyn,MomngFantsy,OvrNAbov	66-0
6-19	Stga	3200	ft	F&M	1	29	100	130	200	6	1	1	1	1	1	29	200	4.80	FCopolaJr	JovitaLobel,JDsAlain,LadyLilian	71-0
6-12	Stga	3200	ft	F&M	1	28	59	129	159	2	1	1	1	1	1	29	159	3.20	FCopolaJr	JovtaLobl,LadyLlan,MomngFntasy	81-0
6-5	Stga	3200	sy	F&MHC	1	29	100	131	201	3	4	5	7	7	7	30	202	11.80	DMarshall	SpnshDncr,MomngFantsy,LauazHot	61-0
5-29	Stga	3200	ft	F&M	1	29	100	129	159	5	5	6	5	5	5	29	200	17.70	DMarshall	OctrComonwr,MmngFntsy,SpnshDnc	71-0
5-22	Stga	3200	ft	F&M	1	28	57	128	159	8	8	i8	6°	6	4	30	200	18.80	DMarshall	Maxpoe,SpanshDancr,MomngFantsy	81-0
5-15	Stga	2900	ft	F&M	1	29	100	130	159	8	7	7°	7°	4	3	29	200	4.80	FCopolaJr	MmngFantasy,LadyLlan,JovtaLo	7-0

3-1 — 7 — ASH CAN WYN — b m 5 BretHanover-LadyHanover-Albatross — R.O.Bowman,Gloversville NY.& L.M.Kraeger,Saratoga NY. — VD 1:56 1992 14 6 4 1 $12,941; Stga 1:58 1991 32 4 6 6 $24,263
JOHN LESLIE (190) red-black-white (36-1-4-7-.154) Tr—John Leslie (.193) — 5,1:56 — Lifetime $53,067 — BROWN

Date	Trk	Purse	Cd	Class	Dis	1/4	1/2	3/4	Time	PP	1/4	1/2	3/4	Str	Fin	Ind 1/4 Time	Ind Time	Odds	Driver	First, Second, Third	Temp
7-3	Stga	3200	sy	F&MHC	1	29	101	131	200	7	7	7°	5°	3	2	29	201	2.40	JLeslie	MmngFantsy,AshCanWyn,FrmThAshs	80-0
6-26	Stga	3200	ft	F&M	1	28	59	128	158	3	3	3°	3°	1	1	29	158	3.60	JLeslie	AshCanWyn,MomngFantsy,OvrNAbov	66-0
6-19	Stga	3200	ft	F&M	1	29	100	130	200	4	5	5°	4°	4	4	29	200	*1.20	JLeslie	JovitaLobel,JDsAlain,LadyLilian	71-0
6-9	M1	11000	ft	FMnw8500L7	1	28	57	127	155	1	4	2°	2°	3	7	29	156	7.80	JLeslie	JabrMouth,BryMs,LawdyLawdyLady	75-0
5-26	M1	11000	sy	FMnw8500L7	1	28	57	126	155	7	8	9°	8°	9	6	28	156	11.40	JLeslie	ArmbroJillian,BryMs,BuiltoSuit	50-0
5-10	VD	3500	ft	F&MCD-1	1	28	58	126	156	5	3°	3°	3°	3	1	29	156	*1.50	JLeslie	AshCanWyn,ClassySis,ManarAnel	72-0
5-3	VD	3500	ft	F&MCD-1	1	28	59	127	156	3	4	4°	3	2	1	29	156	*1.50	JLeslie	AshCanWyn,ClassySis,ManarAnel	59-0

6-1 **MORNING FANTASY** br m 4 MorningBreeze-TripleH.Conna-TripleH.Pride | Stga 1:59^{3} 1992 9 2 3 3 $6,726

8 WENDELL DONAWAY (150) pur-gld (30-3-5-6-.259) | Roger T.Slobody,West Brookfield,Mass. | Stga 1:59^{4} 1991 24 7 5 0 $12,928

GRAY | Tr—Wendell Donaway (.239) | 4,1:59^{3} Lifetime $20,304

7-3^{92}	Stga	3200	sy	F&M HC	1	29^{2}	101^{1}	131^{1}	200	5	5	3°	1°½	1	1^{1}½	29^{3}	200^{4}	3.60	WDonaway	MrnngFantsy,AshCanWyn,FrmThAshs	80-0
6-26^{92}	Stga	3200	ft	F&M	1	28	59^{4}	128^{4}	158	2	2°	2°	1°1	2	2^{1}½	30	158^{2}	*1.80	WDonaway	AshCanWyn,MorningFantsy,OvrNAbov	98-0
6-19^{92}	Stga	3200	ft	F&M	1	29	100^{3}	130^{2}	200	5	6	6	6^{5}½	6	5^{4}½	29^{2}	200^{4}	5.60	WDonaway	[illegible],JDeAlain,LadyLilian	7-0
6-12^{92}	Stga	3200	ft	F&M	1	28^{3}	59^{2}	129^{3}	159^{2}	6	3	3°	3°^{2}	2	3^{4}½	30^{1}	200^{1}	*2.40	WDonaway	[illegible],LadyLilian,MorningFntasy	8-0
6-5^{92}	Stga	3200	sy	F&M HC	1	29^{4}	100^{4}	131^{1}	201^{3}	6	6	6°	4°^{2}½	4	2ns	29^{4}	201^{3}	3.70	WDonaway	SpnshDncr,MorningFantsy,LaJazHot	6-0
5-29^{92}	Stga	3200	ft	F&M	1	29^{3}	100^{3}	129^{4}	159^{1}	1	1	1	1^{2}	1	2^{1}½	29^{4}	159^{3}	1.70	WDonaway	QckComomr,MrnngFntsy,SpnshDncr	7-0
5-22^{92}	Stga	3200	ft	F&M	1	28	57^{4}	128^{4}	159	7	7	i7°	5^{3}½	5	3^{3}½	30^{1}	159^{3}	8.90	WDonaway	Maxpos,SpanishDancr,MorningFantsy	8-0

The appearance of Morning Fantasy in Saratoga's seventh race, July 10, 1992, brought together so many elements of handicapping that they should be measured collectively. We've got class, form, avoiding horses off layoffs, horses nobody believes, and the one dearest to our hearts: Underlays create overlays. The bigger the underlay, the bigger the overlay.

Let's go to work.

The $3,200 Fillies and Mares Handicap Pace produced a field of eight. This handicap race assigned only one position: the 1. The horse given the rail was Sundance Nancy. She's an interesting study.

If we avoid horses off three weeks, what do we do with this 7-year-old mare? Her last race was February 7. Of 1989!

In case you missed it, 1989!

Showing competitive lines in Non-Winners of 2 and 3 races at The Meadowlands from '89, she hadn't raced in 1990 or 1991.

She was given two qualifiers for her return: breaking, recovering and finishing third in 2:04, then a sparkling win by 11 lengths in 2:01.3 from the 7 post. A qualifier.

Need a race? She probably needed half a dozen.

She wasn't a super horse before her layoff, accumulating $22,645 in lifetime earnings.

Maybe it was because of that single qualifier, or maybe it was the post position and the services of top driver Kim Crawford; but this mare, listed at a generous 10-1 on the morning line, took money early and consistently. She went off at 7-2. That means a significant amount of money which could have been played on other contenders was bet on her. Her presence literally raised the odds on every other horse in the race. She broke on the first turn. Case closed.

What of the others?

In post position order:

2 Bonnie Castle Dot—A promising 3-year-old taking on older horses. She won two straight, then finished fourth to Morning Fantasy on a sloppy track in her last start. At 3-1, she was a fair price.

3 Ceil With A Kiss—Reformed claimer had won five straight, moving up from a $4,000 claimer to $10,000, when she suffered an interference break in her last start. Facing better horses tonight, she is another underlay at 5-2. Odds of 5-1 would have been reasonable. Pass.

4 Ms Rainbow—Starting at the bottom PP, we discover she lost twice to Ceil With A Kiss and once to Bonnie Castle Dot. She moves up off a wire-to-wire score from the rail. She's 18-1 and deserves it. Pass.

5 Ancient Fire—Won a $10,000 claimer two starts back, giving her credentials similar to those of Ceil With A Kiss. She was seventh by 11 1/4 lengths to Morning Fantasy in the slop last time. She's 41-1. Pass.

6 Jovita Lobell—The 5-year-old mare won twice in this company before finishing a poor sixth by 7 1/2 to Ash Can Wyn and Morning Fantasy. She then missed a week. She shows no other race off more than a week in her PPs. At 5-1, she's a legitimate contender.

7 Ash Can Wyn—This classy 5-year-old mare had a solid record last season (4-6-6 in 32 starts with $24,263 in earnings), and was doing just as well this year with a 6-4-1 mark in 14 starts and earnings of $12,941. It's interesting to note Jovita Lobell had won $12,875 this year, but did so in 21 starts, seven more than this mare. Ash Can Wyn had two starts at Vernon Downs, winning both; two at The Meadowlands finishing sixth and seventh, and three starts at Saratoga:

- Fourth by 4 1/4 from the 4 post, losing to Jovita Lobell.
- First by 1 3/4 from the 3 hole, beating Morning Fantasy.
- Second by 3 1/2 from the 7 post on a sloppy track last week behind Morning Fantasy.

Ash Can Wyn is 3-1. At the very least, she's the horse to beat. Her 1991-92 earnings beat every rival in this field by $10,000 or more.

8 Morning Fantasy—The 4-year-old mare had a solid record last year—7-5-0 in 24 starts with earnings of $12,928—and this year: 2-3-3 and earnings of $6,726 in nine starts.

Many horses don't reach their peak until their 4-year-old season, and she was definitely a candidate. Her seven PPs were all competitive in this class. Two starts back, she ran a game second, losing by 1 3/4 lengths to Ash Can Wyn from the 2 post. Ash Can Wyn had the 3. Morning Fantasy went a long first-over trip. We decipher this by her PP of that race, showing she was parked while third, then second, then first. The race went in 1:58.2 and was a strong performance by

Morning Fantasy, who was the 9-5 favorite. Ash Can Wyn was 7-2.

This takes us to Morning Fantasy's last race. It was on a sloppy track, and it was super. She went off at 7-2 from the 5 post, while Ash Can Wyn went off at 2-1 from post 7. Morning Fantasy was awesome with a similar first-over move. This time, she drew off to win by $3\frac{1}{2}$, getting her final quarter in :29.4 and final half in :59 for a 2:00.4 mile on the sloppy oval.

Quite possibly, this was the best race of her career, certainly of her Saratoga career. Yet she had traded decisions with both Jovita Lobell and Ash Can Wyn.

Jovita Lobell, Ash Can Wyn and Morning Fantasy each seemed solid. But on the tote board, Morning Fantasy was dismissed at 17-1. Here's a mare who obviously registers positively on class—she won this race last week—and form: two strong efforts in her last two starts.

Think about this: On June 26, Jovita Lobell, Ash Can Wyn and Morning Fantasy went off at odds of 5-2, 7-2 and 9-5 from the 6, 3 and 2 posts, respectively. While Jovita Lobell missed the race July 3rd, Ash Can Wyn and Morning Fantasy went off at 2-1 and 7-2, respectively, from the 7 and 5 posts.

Now they're 5-1, 3-1 and 17-1 from adjoining post positions, thanks in part to the money wagered on Sundance Nancy (who would remain winless through October).

A suicidal speed duel on the front end produced a :56.3 first half and set the race up for a closer. Morning Fantasy got the job done. Bonnie Castle Dot was second and Ash Can Wyn a courageous third after disputing the early fractions. Morning Fantasy returned $37.20. She combined with Song Guy, a 3-1 winner in the next race, for a middle double of $212.60. Is this a great country or what?

Don't Ask

With some overlays, don't stop and ask questions.

ONE MILE PACE
PURSE $3,000
SATURDAY, AUGUST 22, 1992
TRIPLE
&
EXACTA

SIXTH RACE

CLAIMING ALLOWANCE $10000

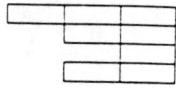

WARM UP-RED

PROGRAM NUMBER

6-1 **RIVLEA FRANK C** — ch g 7 CoralRidge-SpaceHaven-MeadowWar — Walter J.Bassett,South Windsor,Conn.
YR 1:56^4 1992 20 4 2 5 $12,286 / PPk 1:57^4 1991 35 8 3 5 $13,866 / 7,1:56^4 Lifetime $45,912

1 GREGORY ANNALORO (130) red-wh (10-1-4-1-.356) — Tr—Bruce Nichols (.000) — 10,000 YELLOW

Date	Trk	Purse	Cd	Class	Dis	1/4	1/2	3/4	Time	PP	1/4	1/2	3/4	Str	Fin	Ind 1/4 Time	Ind Time	Odds	Driver	Order Of Finish (First, Second, Third)	Temp
7-29^92	YR	3750	sy	10000CLCD	1	28^2	58	128^3	159^2	4	6	5°	7°°	7^1¼	7^11½		201^4	4.40	TWing	HmeWhsta,OvrnghtDlvry,Shnnstorm	74-0
7-19^92	YR	4125	ft	10000CLCD	1	28	58^1	127^2	157^4	5	6	6	3°°	2^nk	3^1¼		158^1	*1.10	LOult	QByrd,SteadyNubbin,RivleaFrankC	81-0
7-6^92	YR	4250	ft	10000CLCD	1	29	59^3	129^4	159^2	3	3	5	5	3^4	3^4		200^1	3.40	DIngraham	Autobot,DCR,RivleaFrankC	74-0
6-24^92	YR	4750	ft	12500CLz	1	28	58	127^4	157^1	2	2	1	1ix	8^10½	8^dis			3.80	LOult	Nthicam,Eminent+,Montrachet+	67-0
6-12^92	YR	4000	ft	10000CLCD	1	28^3	58^3	127^2	156^4	1	1	1	1	1^½	1^1		156^4	*1.10	WCaseJr	RivleaFrankC,Marzec,WellOnter	70-0
5-31^92	MR A	2800	sy	10000CL	1	29^2	100^4	132^3	202^2	1	2	2	2^2	2^1½	3^1½	29^4	202^4	6.10	JDesilone	PrmComand,Hathnay,RivleaFrankC	52-1

9-2 **TOPPER D** (NY) — b g 5 Temujin-GaleKnight-MamiesKnight — Karen M.Gasbarro,Franklin Mass.
Stga 1:58^4 1992 22 3 5 5 $11,202 / YR 1:59^1 1991 27 4 3 5 $16,071 / 3,1:58^3 Lifetime $44,896

2 BRUCE MATTISON (165) bl-or-wh (267-25-37-24-.201) — Tr—Stephen Thompson (.242) — 10,000 WHITE

Date	Trk	Purse	Cd	Class	Dis	1/4	1/2	3/4	Time	PP	1/4	1/2	3/4	Str	Fin	Ind 1/4 Time	Ind Time	Odds	Driver	Order Of Finish (First, Second, Third)	Temp
8-8^92	Stga	3000	sy	10000CL	1	30^4	103^2	133^1	203^4	8	5	4°	4°^1½	4	2^1½	30^2	204^1	8.30	RPugliese	PalmerBlueChip,TopperD,Jacsulo	73-0
8-1^92	Stga	2900	ft	10000CL	1	28^1	100	129^3	159	8	6	5°	6°^1	6	6^2½	29^2	159^3	25.20	RPugliese	LordWaratahN,GypsyHlBrnt,BrndonT	73-0
7-11^92	Stga	2900	ft	10000CLCDz	1	28^4	59^2	129^2	158^1	6	6	4°	3°^1	3	4^4¼	29^2	159	19.50	SHongeon	PausesBigGy,RomoBoy,PalmrBluChp	76-0
7-4^92	Stga	2900	ft	10000CL	1	29	59^1	128	157^2	4	6	4°	4°^2	4	5^2½	29^2	157^4	6.00	SHongeon	SongOrator,RomoBoy,PausesBigGuy	75-0
6-27^92	Stga	2900	sy	10000CL	1	28^1	58	128^4	158^4	1	1	1	1½	1	1^1½	30	158^4	*1.30	SHongeon	TopperD,CrystalWall,Tundra	60-0
6-20^92	Stga	3000	ft	10000CL	1¼	31	132^4	203^1	233^1	6	6	5°	3°°^1	2	2^nk	29^4	233^1	20.80	SHongeon	PalmerBlueChip,TopperD,Cashwrd	97-0

5-2 **GYPSY FIRST** (NY) — b g 5 Niafirst-CandyMaker-GypsyBret — Jerry Smith & Clayton Miller, Taberg, N.Y.
VD 1:56^4 1992 16 4 3 4 $8,200 / Stga 2:00^2 1991 31 6 5 2 $6,485 / 5,1:56^4 Lifetime $26,526

3 JAY RANDALL (145) blue-gold-white (237-28-37-27-.243) — Tr—Richard Ruffles (.346) — 10,000 PURPLE

Date	Trk	Purse	Cd	Class	Dis	1/4	1/2	3/4	Time	PP	1/4	1/2	3/4	Str	Fin	Ind 1/4 Time	Ind Time	Odds	Driver	Order Of Finish (First, Second, Third)	Temp
8-15^92	Stga	3200	ft	NW2500L5CD	1	29	59^2	129^1	158^3	3	1	2	2^1½	2	1^nk	29^1	158^3	14.70	JRandall	GypsyFirst,VillageJuno,LarrySmar	68-0
8-3^92	Stga	2600	ft	NW2300L5CD	1	29^2	59^3	129	158^1	2	1	2	4^1½	5	6^5½	29^4	159^2	3.80	GMattison	SgnalHlHrb,BoSctsBgFla,TryHanow	73-0
7-25^92	VD	3000	ft	WOCD-3	1	26^1	55^4	126	155^4	3	3	3	4^2½	5^4½	6^5½	30^4	157^2	3.40	DRichards	JBFeoa,SunsetJody,Niastrator	71-0
7-18^92	VD	3000	sy	WOCD-3	1	26^3	55	124^2	153^4	3	4	4	4°^1½	4^1½	3^10	30^3	155^4	2.80	CConnorJr	HolyTerror,Niastrator,GypsyFirst	77-0
7-11^92	VD	3500	ft	WOCD-2	1	27^1	57^2	125^1	155	1	4	5	4^4½	3^2½	2^nk	28^3	155	10.70	CConnorJr	HMarlene,GypsyFirst,WhirlRockFla	74-0
7-4^92	VD	3500	ft	WOCD-2	1	26^4	56	125^2	153^4	1	5	5	4^4½	4^1½	5^5½	30^3	156^4	5.00	HOkusaJr	LonTogsWarior,DemondAn,Michael	58-0

3-1 **LORD WARATAH N** — br g 8 Waratah(F)-Jokeda-Bye Bye Song(F) — Jeffrey R.Franklin,Plainville,Mass.
YR 1:58^2 1992 19 4 4 4 $16,578 / M 1 1:54^3 1991 38 9 7 5 $49,072 / 7,1:54^3 1 Lifetime $105,243

4 GARY KAMAL (150) wh-blue-gld (206-31-36-29-.294) — Tr—Karen Kamal (.455) — 10,000 BLACK

Date	Trk	Purse	Cd	Class	Dis	1/4	1/2	3/4	Time	PP	1/4	1/2	3/4	Str	Fin	Ind 1/4 Time	Ind Time	Odds	Driver	Order Of Finish (First, Second, Third)	Temp
8-15^92	Stga	3000	ft	10000CL	1	30	101^3	131	200^2	3	3	3°	2°^½	2	2^1	29^1	200^3	*1.70	GKamal	SaBngand,LordWaratahN,BrandNew	68-0
8-8^92	Stga	3000	sy	10000CL	1	30^4	103^2	133^1	203^4	2x	8	8	8^dis	8	8^dis			*1.40	GKamal	PalmerBlueChip,TopperD,Jacsulo	73-0
8-1^92	Stga	2900	ft	10000CL	1	28^1	100	129^3	159	5	4	3°	2°^½	2	1^nk	29^1	159	3.40	GKamal	LordWaratahN,GypsyHlBrnt,BrndonT	73-0
7-25^92	Stga	2400	ft	NW2000L5CD	1	29^2	100^1	129^3	159^2	4	4	3°	2°^1	2	2^ns	29^3	159^2	2.90	GKamal	GypsyHlBrt,LrdWrtahN,CovRdExprs	76-0
7-18^92	Stga	2400	ft	NW2000L5CD	1	28^1	58^2	127^2	158^2	7	5	3°	2°^1½	2	2^2	31	158^4	7.60	GKamal	MeadowMaxima,LordWarthN,MjorCoins	79-0
7-11^92	Stga	2900	ft	10000CLCD	1	28^4	59^2	129^2	158^1	7	7	6°	5°^2	5	6^3½	30^1	200	14.40	GKamal	PausesBigGy,RomoBoy,PalmrBluChp	76-0

12-1 **LITTLE OFF** — br g 6 KeystoneAndy-TopItOff-ChrisTime — Todd D Johnston,Ballston Spa N.Y.
YR 1:57^4 1992 24 6 2 3 $11,009 / Stga 2:02 1991 23 2 4 3 $4,411 / 6,1:57^4 Lifetime $30,948

5 RICHARD PUGLIESE (115) gray-black (200-25-34-24-.259) — Tr—Todd Johnston (.364) — 10,000 GREEN

Date	Trk	Purse	Cd	Class	Dis	1/4	1/2	3/4	Time	PP	1/4	1/2	3/4	Str	Fin	Ind 1/4 Time	Ind Time	Odds	Driver	Order Of Finish (First, Second, Third)	Temp
8-12^92	YR	4500	ft	12500CL	1	27^2	56^3	126^4	156^3	4	2°	2°	3	4^5	7^10		158^3	16.70	JStarkJr	QByrd,RightOnCourse,JammaLobell	74-0
8-5^92	YR	4500	ft	12500CL	1	29^4	59^2	127^4	157	8	7	6°	7	5^5½	5^5¼		158	21.80	LOult	IronstonArtist,QByrd,ChargandSnd	74-0
7-27^92	YR	3750	ft	10000CLCD	1	27^3	57	127	157^4	2	1	1	1	1^½	1^1		157^4	3.00	LOult	LittleOff,NightLeader,Dykstra	76-0
7-17^92	YR	3750	ft	10000CLCD	1	29	57^4	128^2	200^2	8	3°	2°	1°	2^1	1½		200^2	5.20	LOult	LittleOff,SpdyJons,BnansRoorA	58-0
7-3^92	YR	3750	gd	10000CLCD	1	29^1	100^2	131	201^2	5	3	4	5	5^3½	3½		201^3	6.20	WCaseJr	ComposerChmnes,Dykstra,LittleOf	51-0
6-24^92	YR	3500	ft	10000CLCD	1	30	102	131^4	201^4	2	1	1	1	1^½	1^2		201^4	*.50	WCaseJr	LittlOf,HilariousGlw,PrmPlugThr	37-0

10-1 **TRYNSTOPUS** — b h 4 RalphHanover-FoggyAnna-Hunter'sStar — Ferme Am Harwood Stable,Vaudrevil,Que.
Stga 1:58^2 1992 10 2 4 1 $5,476 / BB 1:58 1991 29 3 9 3 $19,489 / 3,1:58 Lifetime $34,165

6 KIM CRAWFORD (155) red-blk-wh (480-81-76-54-.294) — Tr—Pierre Paradis (.251) — 12,500 RED

Date	Trk	Purse	Cd	Class	Dis	1/4	1/2	3/4	Time	PP	1/4	1/2	3/4	Str	Fin	Ind 1/4 Time	Ind Time	Odds	Driver	Order Of Finish (First, Second, Third)	Temp
8-15^92	Stga	3000	ft	10000CL	1	28	57^1	127	158	1	1	3	3^1½	3	2^nk	30^4	158	2.60	BBelanger	CrystlWall,Trynstopus,PalmrBlChp	68-0
8-1^92	Stga	4200	ft	WO5000LTCD	1	28^2	100^2	130^2	159^1	5	6	7°	5°^2½	5	4^2½	28^4	159^3	11.00	BBelanger	SavThTigr,VillageJuno,WhirlRockFla	73-0
7-25^92	Stga	2900	ft	NW2500L5CD	1	29^1	100^4	130^2	159^2	1	2	2	3^1	2	1^nk	28^4	159^2	7.90	PBeaulieu	Trynstopus,DinnaFred,TheRemedy	76-0
7-18^92	Stga	2400	ft	NW2000L5CD	1	28^2	58	127^3	158^2	1	2	4	4^1	4	1½	30^3	158^2	7.70	BBelanger	Trynstopus,Rabtrane,NvadaPlaza	79-0
7-7^92	Stga	1750	ft	NW1500L5CD	1	28^3	58^1	128^4	200^2	6	i6	6°	4°°^5	2	2^nk	30^3	200^2	*2.10	WHnsy	FieryDancr,Trynstopus,VoiceLovr	76-0
6-26^92	Stga	2050	ft	NW2000L7CD	1	29	59^2	129^2	159^4	8	8°	8°	8°^4½	9	7^5½	30^3	200^4	33.90	BBelanger	LuboBluChip,Exhibitor,FeryDancr	68-0

12-1 **C FRED** — br h 5 Conquered-ScarletKnox-KnoxHanover — Harry Nieberg,Brooklyn,N.Y.
YR 1:58 1992 23 4 4 5 $14,982 / YR 1:59 1991 17 4 1 0 $4,060 / 5,1:58 Lifetime $23,799

7 JACK RICE (134) wh-blu-red (0-0-0-0-.000) — Tr—Jack Rice (.000) — 10,000 BROWN

Date	Trk	Purse	Cd	Class	Dis	1/4	1/2	3/4	Time	PP	1/4	1/2	3/4	Str	Fin	Ind 1/4 Time	Ind Time	Odds	Driver	Order Of Finish (First, Second, Third)	Temp
8-12^92	YR	4500	ft	NW4000L8CD	1	29^2	100^2	129^4	159	2	3	2°	2°	3^3½	3^1½		200^2	*1.10	JRice	LJoeyAussie,OverEdge,CFred	74-0
7-31^92	YR	4500	sy	NW4000L8CD	1	28^3	58^3	129^1	200^3	6	3°°	1	1	1½	3^1½		201	*1.10	RWojcio	ShadowChase,LJoeyAussie,CFred	69-0
7-22^92	YR	4500	ft	NW4000L8CD	1	29^2	100	129^2	158	2	1	1	1	1^2	1^3½		158	2.00	JRice	CFred,ProciousGodGuy,DinosaurDan	71-0
7-14^92	MR	1400	ft	NW750L6CD	1	29^2	59	129^1	158^1	3	1°	1	1^1½	1½	1^2	29	158^1	*.50	JRice	CFred,PuissandCalls,DionysonDart	84-0
7-7^92	MR	2200	ft	MW2000L6CD	1	30	101^3	132^3	201^4	6	8	8°	9^7½	8^9½	6^4½	28^3	202^3	6.20	JRice	WsCrack,ChampagnSpctrm,SwftApolo	71-0
6-28^92	MR A	2300	ft	NW2300L6CD	1	29^1	100	129^4	159^2	8	8	8°	8°°^6½	8^9	7^8½	30	201^1	13.80	JRice	GVFirbes,IdealCharmr,NationalHro	75-0

10-1 **JON VON** — b g 8 LookadatVon-ViedonVickie-AdiosVic — Scott F.Leickert,Queensbury N.Y.
Stga 1:58^3 1992 28 6 8 3 $17,385 / MR 1:57^2 1991 44 12 10 4 $26,376 / 7,1:57^2 Lifetime $101,312

8 JOHN STARK JR (145) red-wh-lblu (279-61-34-42-.337) — Tr—Scott Leickert (.550) — 10,000 GRAY

Date	Trk	Purse	Cd	Class	Dis	1/4	1/2	3/4	Time	PP	1/4	1/2	3/4	Str	Fin	Ind 1/4 Time	Ind Time	Odds	Driver	Order Of Finish (First, Second, Third)	Temp
8-13^92	Stga	2400	ft	7500CLOP	1	30^3	100^4	130	159^3	1	1	1	1^1½	1	1^ns	29^3	159^3	1.50	JStarkJr	JonVon,TooneyBilly,SenorCedam	62-0
7-31^92	Stga	2400	gd	NW2000L5CD	1	28^3	58^3	128^2	158^3	5	7°	4°	3°^1	2	1^1½	30	158^3	3.80	JStarkJr	JonVon,GramsChoice,LousGift	64-0
7-23^92	Stga	1800	sy	5000CLHC	1	30^1	101^4	132^1	201^4	7	7°	6°	4°°^½	2	1^2	29^2	201^4	7.10	JStarkJr	JonVon,Hahn,IdylwoodBlizzard	61-0
7-16^92	Stga	1500	ft	3500CLz	1	27^4	57^2	128^2	200^4	6	2°	2°	3^1½	6	7^18½	35^4	204^2	12.40	BMattison	YoungBrandyWine,MoonRockA,Tnbl	77-0
7-9^92	Stga	1500	ft	3500CL	1	28^3	58	127^1	157^3	1	1	1	1^3½	1	4^7½	31^4	159	5.20	BMattison	SeaBngend,MoonRockA,Tembie	79-0
7-2^92	Stga	1500	ft	3500CLz	1	29^1	100	130^2	200	5	1°	1	1^1	1	2^7½	30^1	200^3	4.10	CMosher	SeaBngend,JonVon,MoonRockA	78-0

4-1 **GYPSY HILL BRENT** — b g 7 Bonded Yankee-LovelyBaroness-BaronHanover — The I-87 Connection, Voorheesville N.Y.
Stga 1:59^2 1992 23 2 6 5 $9,140 / YR 1:59^3 1991 39 7 10 3 $23,935 / 5,1:57^4 Lifetime $64,521

9 FRANK COPPOLA JR (150) ltbl-wh-br (529-87-78-83-.299) — Tr—David Spagnola (.339) — 10,000 BLUE

Date	Trk	Purse	Cd	Class	Dis	1/4	1/2	3/4	Time	PP	1/4	1/2	3/4	Str	Fin	Ind 1/4 Time	Ind Time	Odds	Driver	Order Of Finish (First, Second, Third)	Temp
8-15^92	Stga	3000	ft	10000CL	1	28	57^1	127	158	5	5	5°	4°^2	4	4^nk	30^3	158	4.50	FCopolaJr	CrystlWall,Trynstopus,PalmrBlChp	68-0
8-8^92	Stga	3000	ft	10000CL	1	29^3	100^2	130^2	159^4	6	6	6°	3°^1	3	2^nk	29^1	159^4	12.70	JRandall	LnySmar,GypsyHlBrnt,CrystalWall	73-0
8-1^92	Stga	2900	ft	10000CL	1	28^1	100	129^3	159	6	5	4°	4°^2	4	2^nk	29	159	20.90	FCopolaJr	LordWaratahN,GypsyHlBrnt,BrndonT	73-0
7-25^92	Stga	2400	ft	NW2000L5CD	1	29^2	100^1	129^3	159^2	1	2	2	3^1	3	1^ns	29^3	159^2	7.50	FCopolaJr	GypsyHlBrt,LrdWrtahN,CovRdExprs	76-0
7-21^92	Stga	2050	ft	NW1500L5CD	1	28^4	100	130^2	201^1	6	4	4°	4°^1½	4	2^nk	30^3	201^1	3.00	JRandall	YoungSadt,GypsyHlBrnt,DCsDgnty	71-0
7-11^92	Stga	2900	ft	10000CLCD	1	28^2	58^3	127^4	158^1	8	8	7°	7^5	8	7^7	30^4	159^3	30.50	FCopolaJr	CrystlWll,Fortentytwo,RmgerlotRd	76-0

TRACKMAN'S SELECTIONS 3-4-9

NO.9 SCORES FROM SECOND TIER

CHECK YOUR TICKETS AT TIME OF PURCHASE. SARATOGA RACEWAY CANNOT BE RESPONSIBLE FOR ERRORS DISCOVERED AFTER YOU LEAVE THE WINDOW.

The morning line of 10-1 on the 6 horse, Trynstopus, in a $10,000 claimer at Saratoga, August 22, was hard to comprehend.

From his PPs:

- June 26—Seventh by 5¼ from the 8 hole in a Non-Winners (NW) of $2,000 Last 7 starts at 33-1.
- July 7—In a NW of $1,500 Last 5, second by a head from the 6 post as the 2-1 favorite despite being interfered with before the first quarter.
- July 18— Wins a NW of $2,000 Last 5 by ¾ of a length in 1:58.2 from the rail at 7-1.
- July 25—Again from the rail, again at 7-1, another win by a head in a NW of $2,500 Last 5, in 1:59.2 off a final quarter in :28.4.
- August 1—Big step up to Winners Over $5,000 Lifetime. From the 5 post at 11-1, he has the misfortune of being seventh through a slow 1:00.2. The final half goes in :58.4, and he rallies to finish fourth by 2¼ in 1:59.3, his last quarter in :28.4, his last half in :58.1.
- August 15—In a $10,000 claimer from the rail at 5-2, he takes the lead in a :28 first quarter, surrenders the top spot, and comes on to lose by a head in a 1:58 mile.

Tonight, he's in the same company with the benefit of a driver switch rom capable Bert Belanger to Kim Crawford, annually the track's No. or 2 driver.

A note: Trynstopus is in the same company even though his claiming price is listed as $12,500. The $2,500 difference comes from a 25 percent allowance for 4-year-old horses in claiming races. In his top PP, his race is listed as a $10,000 claimer, but his claiming price was the same: $12,500.

His odds? 7-1. He paid $17 to win and combined with the 5-2 favorite, Gypsy First, for a $113.40 exacta. That was Trynstopus's third win in his last five starts, each at 7-1.

Just One More

ONE MILE PACE
PURSE $1,300
SATURDAY, OCTOBER 3, 1992
PICK THREE (RACES 3-5)
&
EXACTA

THIRD RACE

CLAIMING ALLOWANCE $2500
PREFERENCE TO WINNERS OF A RACE LAST 4 STARTS

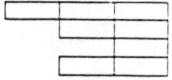

WARM UP-PURPLE

Column key: PROGRAM NUMBER · Date · Trk · Purse · Cd · Class · Leaders Time (Dis, 1/4, 1/2, 3/4) · Winners Time · PP · 1/4 · 1/2 · 3/4 · Str · Fin · Ind 1/4 Time · Ind Time · Odds · Driver · Order Of Finish (First, Second, Third) · Temp

3-1 SMASHING BG — b h 4 B.G'sBunny-SmashingJane-MostHappyFella — RJ.Adsit Jr.,Burlington Vt.& E.L.Adsit,Stillwater NY.

1 FRANK COPPOLA JR (150) ltbl-wh-br (726-129-101-106-.304) Tr—Eric Adsit (.270)

3,125 YELLOW

Stga 1:59^3 1992 19 3 1 4 $4,6[illegible] · Phld 2:02^2 1991 18 1 3 4 $5,642 · 4,1:59^3 Lifetime $12,[illegible]99

Date	Trk	Purse	Cd	Class	Dis	1/4	1/2	3/4	Time	PP	1/4	1/2	3/4	Str	Fin	Ind 1/4 Time	Ind Time	Odds	Driver	Order Of Finish	Temp
9-25^92	Stga	1300	ft	2500CL	1	29	100	130^2	201^2	3	4	5°	5°°^2½	3	3^1½	30^2	201^2	5.80	FCoppolaJr	WnthropsKd,Prasworthy,SmashngBG	58-0
9-18^92	Stga	1300	ft	2500CL	1	29^4	100^1	130^1	202^1	3	3	3	4^5½	4	6^12½	33	204^3	*1.40	FCoppolaJr	RacePower,SavenaBluChip,JollyBoy	77-0
9-4^92	Stga	1300	ft	2500CL	1	29^1	101^1	131^2	202^4	scr sk					SCT					HollandsSong,Irase,JackWagon	74-0
8-20^92	Stga	1500	ft	3500CL	1	29^1	100^3	130^2	200^1	6	4	3°	2^4½	6	8^9½ p^7	31^3	202	6.00	FCoppolaJr	IdylwoodBlizzard,Hahn,StrongBrz	88-0
8-12^92	Stga	1300	ft	2500CL	1	28^2	59^1	129	200^1	9	5	4°	2^1½	2	1^2½	31	200^1	*1.50	FCoppolaJr	SmashingBG,Chezz,Obsidian	70-0
8-6^92	Stga	1100	ft	2500CL	1	28^4	100^1	129^3	200	7	1	1	2^1	4	4^3½	31^4	201^3	*1.50	FCoppolaJr	LimSoda,[illegible]	80-0
7-24^92	Stga	1450	ft	2500CL	1	28^4	100	130	201^1	6	6	6°	6°°^1½	5	2^1½	31	201^3	1.90	FCoppolaJr	LightBIFls,SmashngBG(Dh)CragoMag	74-0

9-2 WINTHROP'S KID — b h 8 WinthropLobell-Kreizer's Kids-SteadyStar — Frank J.Salino Jr. & John J.Curtis III, NY.

2 JAY RANDALL (145) blue-gold-white (338-39-54-43-.247) Tr—Frank Salino Jr (.303)

2,500 WHITE

Stga 2:01^2 1992 24 5 3 2 $4,930 · QStga 2:04^1 1991 9 0 1 1 $818 · 8,2:01^2 Lifetime $17,960

Date	Trk	Purse	Cd	Class	Dis	1/4	1/2	3/4	Time	PP	1/4	1/2	3/4	Str	Fin	Ind 1/4 Time	Ind Time	Odds	Driver	Order Of Finish	Temp
9-25^92	Stga	1300	ft	2500CL	1	29	100	130^2	201^2	1	2	2	2^1	2	1^1½	30^4	201^2	*1.60	JRandall	WnthropsKd,Prasworthy,SmashngBG	58-0
9-18^92	Stga	1100	ft	2500CL	1	29	100	131	201	5	3°	4	5°°^2	4	4^2½	31^1	202^3	2.80	JRandall	Donaway,Prasworthy,MrGarySalwey	77-0
9-11^92	Stga	1300	ft	2500CL	1	30	101^1	131^4	201^4	6	7	6°	6°^3½	6	7^5	30^2	202^4	9.20	GKamal	SavnaBluChp,WnSmPro,HolandsSong	86-0
9-5^92	Stga	1300	ft	2500CL	1	28^4	58^4	129^2	200^4	1	4	3	3°^1½	2	2^ns	31^1	200^4	2.50	JRandall	ChrstanGB,WnthropsKd,JolyFrost	78-0
8-28^92	Stga	1300	ft	2500CL	1	28^3	59^1	130^2	202	10	7	7	6°^4	5	3½	30^4	202	22.90	JRandall	WinSumPro,CindrKat,WnthropsKd	81-0
8-22^92	Stga	1300	ft	2500CL	1	28^1	58^4	129	200^2	scr sk					SCT					WinSumPro,CraigoMagee,AvngrHil	74-0
8-11^92	Stga	1300	ft	2500CL	1	28^2	59^4	131^1	201^3	x1	9	9	9^16½	9	9^16½	30	204^4	3.00	JRandall	JolyFrst,WhoseYorThngr,HolndsSng	75-0

4-1 CASINO EMPRESS (NY) — b m 6 Niatross-NativeEmpress-Adios Vic — Charles E.& Joan C.Henderson,Lebanon,Conn.

3 JOHN CROSS (120) bl-or-wh (22-2-0-4-.152) Tr—John Cross (.108)

3,000 PURPLE

Stga 2:00^3 1992 9 3 0 1 $1,792 · VD 1:59^4 1991 24 2 1 3 $3,562 · 5,1:59^4 Lifetime $7,413

Date	Trk	Purse	Cd	Class	Dis	1/4	1/2	3/4	Time	PP	1/4	1/2	3/4	Str	Fin	Ind 1/4 Time	Ind Time	Odds	Driver	Order Of Finish	Temp
9-25^92	Stga	1300	ft	2500CL	1	28^1	58^1	128^3	200	6	6	6°	5°^3½	4	3^2½	31	200^2	3.20	JCross	RacePower,TimlyPlay,CasinoEmprs	58-0
9-17^92	Stga	1200	ft	2500CLCD	1	29	59^2	129^1	200^3	4	7	7°	6°^3½	6	1^ns	30^4	200^3	25.30	JCross	CasinoEmpress,LeeshaLou,HotRail	80-0
9-11^92	Stga	1100	ft	2500CL	1	29^3	100^4	130^2	202	1	2	3	3^1	3	1½	31^2	202	*2.10	JCross	CasinoEmpress,Prasworthy,BilMot	88-0
9-5^92	Stga	1300	ft	2500CL	1	28^4	58^4	129^2	200^4	7	8	8	8^5½	8	8^7½	31^3	202^1	80.20	JCross	ChrstanGB,WnthropsKd,JolyFrost	78-0
8-28^92	Stga	1300	ft	2500CL	1	28^3	59^1	130^2	202	1	1	3	4^1½	4	5^4½	32^4	203^2	8.20	JCross	WinSumPro,CindrKat,WnthropsKd	81-0
8-14^92	Stga	1300	sy	2500CL	1	29^3	102	132^2	203^1	6	8	8	7°^5½	7	5^7½	31^1	204^3	18.30	JCross	JoyfMac,PseForm,YongBrandyWn	63-0
8-8^92	Skow	750	ft	NW500CD	1	31	102	132^1	202^4	8	8°	7	6^4½	6	6^4	30^3	203^3	22.30	SMacKnz	SumPilot,MollysView,MightyFrankl	74-0

5-2 RACE POWER — b h 12 RaceTime-MissouriPreight-BulletHanover — William R.& Christine P.DeGuerre, Ballston Spa, NY.

4 KIM CRAWFORD (155) red-blk-wh (658-114-107-78-.303) Tr—Wayne Kopa (.346)

2,500 BLACK

Stga 2:00 1992 23 5 5 3 $5,411 · Stga 2:01^3 1991 10 2 2 3 $3,149 · 4,1:55 1 Lifetime $118,416

Date	Trk	Purse	Cd	Class	Dis	1/4	1/2	3/4	Time	PP	1/4	1/2	3/4	Str	Fin	Ind 1/4 Time	Ind Time	Odds	Driver	Order Of Finish	Temp
9-25^92	Stga	1300	ft	2500CL	1	28^1	58^1	128^3	200	5	2	2	2°^1	1	1^1½	31^1	200	3.10	KCrawford	RacePower,TimlyPlay,CasinoEmprs	58-0
9-18^92	Stga	1300	ft	2500CL	1	29^4	100^1	130^3	202^1	1	1	1	1^1½	1	1^5	31^3	202^1	4.80	KCrawford	RacePower,SavenaBluChip,JollyBoy	77-0
9-11^92	Stga	1300	ft	2500CL	1	30	101^1	131^4	201^4	3	4	5	7^4½	7	5^3½	30	202^3	16.30	KCrawford	SavnaBluChp,WnSmPro,HolandsSong	86-0
9-5^92	Stga	1300	ft	2500CL	1	28^4	58^4	129^2	200^4	4	1	1	2^1	4	7^6	32^2	202	9.40	KCrawford	ChrstanGB,WnthropsKd,JolyFrost	78-0
8-28^92	Stga	1300	ft	2500CL	1	28^3	59^1	130^2	202	4	4	1°	2°½	6	6^5½	33^1	203^4	*1.80	KCrawford	WinSumPro,CindrKat,WnthropsKd	81-0
8-20^92	Stga	1200	ft	2500CL	1¼	31	132	202	233^4	1	1	1	1^4	1	1^1	31^4	233^4	*1.10	KCrawford	RacePowr,SignalHilLoma,MaryFlyr	88-0
8-11^92	Stga	1200	ft	2500CL	1¼	29^2	132^1	202^3	233^2	1	1	1	1^2	2	2^4	31^3	234^1	*.90	KCrawford	BelieveMe,RacePower,PwtDore	75-0

12-1 IDEAL SOCIETY A — b g 10 RomeoHanover-MissHancove-Hancove(F) — Mary LaBombard, Ballston Spa, N.Y.

5 GLENN RAIA (135) red-white-gold (92-5-8-13-.150) Tr—Glenn Raia (.214)

2,500 GREEN

QStga 2:05^2 1992 10 2 2 0 $2,173 · Stga 2:03 1991 32 3 3 7 $5,058 · 7,1:58^4 Lifetime $90,273

Date	Trk	Purse	Cd	Class	Dis	1/4	1/2	3/4	Time	PP	1/4	1/2	3/4	Str	Fin	Ind 1/4 Time	Ind Time	Odds	Driver	Order Of Finish	Temp
9-25^92	Stga		ft	QUA	1	30^2	101^2	133	205^2	5	2	2°	2°½	1	1^ns	32^2	205^2	NB	GRaia	IdealSocityA,StormProcton,LftOvr	50-0
3-26^92	Stga	1300	sy	2500CLCD	1	30^3	103	135^1	207^2	1	1	1	1^2	1	1^3½	32^1	207^2	2.70	GRaia	IdealSocietyA,FulaDor,OwlTrick	52-0
3-19^92	Stga	1300	ft	2500CLCD	1	30^1	102^2	134^2	205^1	1	2	2	3^1	2	2½	30^4	205^2	21.40	FRaiaII	ShesGotPlnty,IdealSocityA,PnAvnsA	33-0
3-12^92	Stga	1200	gd	2500CLCD	1	30^2	103^1	134	206^1	1	1	1	1^3	1	1½	32^1	206^1	*1.30	FRaiaII	IdealSocityA,LastCandy,BrianaLob	27-0
3-7^92	Stga	1300	gd	2500CLCD	1	29^3	101^2	133^4	204^4	8	8	8	8^4½	8	7^12½	32^3	207^1	62.90	GRaia	MagicArtst,ChrysteBaby,HolandsSng	36-0
3-1^92	Stga A	1300	gd	2500CL	1	29	100^4	132^2	203^4	6	7	7°	6°°^5½	6	4^2½	30^3	204^1	37.50	FRaiaII	JustFly,LimeSoda,OneLastBlast	24-0
2-22^92	Stga	1300	sy	2500CLCD	1	31	102^4	133^4	206^3	1	4	4°	4°^3	4	5^1½	33^4	208^1	3.50	GRaia	MesMeMlon,MagicArtst,WngingTCing	37-0

10-1 TIGRESS TONI — b m 6 Domitian-FlyingToni-FlyingBret — Bert T.& Albert J.Doolen,Frankfort,N.Y.

6 BRIAN CROSS (150) blue-or-white (362-46-46-54-.247) Tr—Al Doolen (.319)

3,000 RED

VD 1:59^1 1992 29 3 5 7 $5,616 · VD 1:56^4 1991 31 5 2 6 $7,118 · 5,1:56^4 Lifetime $31,799

Date	Trk	Purse	Cd	Class	Dis	1/4	1/2	3/4	Time	PP	1/4	1/2	3/4	Str	Fin	Ind 1/4 Time	Ind Time	Odds	Driver	Order Of Finish	Temp
9-30^92	Stga	1300	ft	2500CL	1	31^3	103^3	134^3	204^2	8	8	8°	8^5½	7	6^5½	29^4	205^3	6.60	BCross	ChrlFlan,StrmProctn,StrmptnArw	48-0
9-23^92	Stga	1300	ft	2500CL	1	30	101	132	203^1	2	2	2	2°½	1	1½	31^1	203^1	1.60	BCross	TigressToni,AvonTrumpet,MaryFlyr	56-0
9-7^92	VD A	1500	ft	3000CLCD	1	26^4	56^3	128	201^2	9	6	7	5°°^4½	4^2½	3^nk	32^2	201^2	*1.10	DickabonJ	WiggerWan,Comdenswthm,TigrsToni	77-0
9-3^92	VD	1400	gd	2500CLCD	1	28^1	59	128^4	159^4	5	1	1°	1^2½	1^4½	1^1½	31	159^4	1.90	DickabonJ	TigrsToni,Joyousrtest,CandoCoins	73-0
8-27^92	VD	1200	ft	2500CLCD	1	27^1	57^2	128^3	159^4	5	1°	1	1^3	1^2	3^2	31^3	200^1	*2.00	DickabonJ	BigTimGuy,DespradoColins,TgrsTon	80-0
8-18^92	VD	1500	ft	3000CLCD	1	27^3	58	127^3	158^2	4	5	2°	2^ns	4^5	5^3½	32^2	200	7.00	DickabonI	WineBest,BudBundy,RebelConrad	64-0
8-12^92	VD	1400	ft	2500CLCD	1	27^4	59	129^2	200^1	2	1	1	1^1½	1½	3½	30^4	200^1	2.40	CLawton	EagleShadow,Pfizel,TigressToni	88-0

8-1 P J MARKOS (NY) — br h 5 PraisedDignity-ScarletMarkos-FloridaPro — Euripides J.,Evangelos J.& Peter J.Markos,Ipswich,Mass.

7 PASCAL BEAULIEU (180) red-white (34-5-4-3-.242) Tr—Pierre Paradis (.260)

2,500 BROWN

Stga 2:01^4 1992 13 1 2 2 $1,927 · Stga 2:00^4 1991 34 3 6 3 $6,501 · 4,2:00^4 Lifetime $12,919

Date	Trk	Purse	Cd	Class	Dis	1/4	1/2	3/4	Time	PP	1/4	1/2	3/4	Str	Fin	Ind 1/4 Time	Ind Time	Odds	Driver	Order Of Finish	Temp
9-25^92	Stga	1300	ft	2500CL	1	28^1	58^1	128^3	200	7	7	7	7°^4½	5	4^2½	30^4	200^2	33.40	PBeaulieu	RacePower,TimlyPlay,CasinoEmprs	58-0
9-16^92	Stga	1100	ft	2500CL	1	29^1	59^3	130^3	201^4	1	1	1	1^1	1	1½	31^1	201^4	*1.10	PBeaulieu	PJMarkos,Nerdust,CharlieFoxtrot	81-0
9-7^92	Stga A	1300	ft	2500CL	1	30	100^4	131^1	202	10	5	5	7^3½	4	4^2	30^3	202^2	12.60	PBeaulieu	HotRail,AvonTrmpet,IronstonBrz	71-0
8-10^92	Stga	1100	ft	2500CL	1	29^4	101^1	131^2	202^3	6	8	7°	6°^3	5	4^3	31^1	203^1	7.20	BBelanger	CraigoMagee,BdScotsFancy,BilMot	77-0
8-5^92	Stga	1100	ft	2500CL	1	29^1	100^2	130^4	202^1	2	1	1	1^ns	3	5^1½	34	204^4	*1.00	BBelanger	SadBadDad,ThrPartHarmony,SnoxyK	72-0
7-29^92	Stga	1100	ft	2500CL	1	29	59^4	130^4	202^2	5	2	2	4^2	6	7^14	34	205^1	3.20	BBelanger	WheataSampson,GrayBndt,SadBadDad	86-0
7-22^92	Stga	1250	ft	2500CL	1	30^2	101^4	132	202^1	1	1	1	1^1	1	3^nk	30^1	202^1	*1.70	BBelanger	KeystoneMoores,RacPowr,PJMarkos	72-0

10-1 SKIP'S ON TIME — b g 6 TrentonTime-SkipperSue-SirCarlton — Richard F.Ruffles,West Edmeston NY.

8 JOHN STARK JR (145) red-wh-lblu (326-70-43-49-.338) Tr—Richard Ruffles (.305)

2,500 GRAY

VD 1:59^3 1992 27 6 3 7 $7,042 · Har 2:02^3 1991 30 2 3 7 $3,817 · 6,1:59^3 Lifetime $17,888

Date	Trk	Purse	Cd	Class	Dis	1/4	1/2	3/4	Time	PP	1/4	1/2	3/4	Str	Fin	Ind 1/4 Time	Ind Time	Odds	Driver	Order Of Finish	Temp
9-19^92	Stga	1300	ft	2500CL	1	30	100^4	132	202^3	8	8	8°	6°°^1½	4	3^4	31	203^2	9.20	JRandall	BelieveMe,Ermaland,SkipsOnTime	85-0
9-12^92	Stga	1300	ft	2500CL	1	29	100^3	131^3	202^4	6i	7	7	7°^2½	6	3^3½	31^1	203^2	23.50	JRandall	JolyFrost,ChristianGB,SkpsOnTm	80-0
9-2^92	VD	1500	ft	3000CLCD	1	26^3	58^3	128^4	159	1	5	6	7°^5½	5^4½	3^2½	29^2	159^2	12.90	DickabonJ	Chrissipr,SirBrandmr,SkipsOnTm	89-0
8-25^92	VD	1400	ft	2500CL	1¼	29	57^4	129^4	216	2	2	1°	2	5^10½	7^11½		218^1	*1.60	DickabonJ	NBshotsa,BourbonhileHapy,BdBndy	81-0
8-14^92	VD	1200	ft	2500CL	¾	28^2	57^4		128^2	2	3	2°		1½	1^ns		128^2	*1.40	DickabonJ	SkpsOnTm,KarsitaKhanA,UndrThTabl	89-0
8-7^92	VD	1500	ft	3000CL	1	27	58^3	129^1	159^1	9	4	3°	2°^1	2^2	3^2½	30^1	159^3	22.50	DickabonJ	Adedol,MementoHll,SkipsOnTime	80-0
7-31^92	VD	1200	gd	2500CL	¾	29^2	58^2		128^4	8	8	7°°		7^1½	4^5½		130	13.00	CConnorJr	Adedol,Gordy,WiggerWann	72-0

Winthrop's Kid and Smashing Big had the 2 and 1 posts, respectively, in a $2,500 claimer at Saratoga, October 3, 1992. They'd faced each other the previous week. From the rail, Winthrop's Kid won by 1¼ lengths as the 8-5 favorite. From the 3 post, Smashing Big was third by 1¼, getting nosed out for second.

Their post position shift tonight was certainly a plus for Smashing Big, but not the earth-shattering one that the odds suggested. Smashing Big went off at 7-5 and again finished third. Winthrop's Kid went off at 8-1, won again, and paid $19.60.

Don't ask. Just smile and collect.

Exotics

CHAPTER 10

Betting horses used to be a simple procedure: win, place, show and one Daily Double a night. No more. Now tracks have several Doubles; dozens of exactas, quiniellas and triples; and difficult multiple wagers such as a Pick 3 or Pick 4.

The proliferation of exotic and multiple wagers has created a new handicapping tool: watching monitors displaying potential payoffs in such bets.

A simple example: the Daily Double. In the Double, the tote board shows the odds for the first race. A monitor showing potential Double payoffs can be used to analyze betting in the second race, even though there are no actual win odds. Check the projected Daily Double payoffs on the monitor; see which horses in the second race are being bet heavily, and bet accordingly. Using the 5 horse in the first race as an example, a 5-1 Double will pay $25, while a 5-2 returns $50, and a 5-3 $100. The 1 horse in the second race should be shorter odds than the 2, and both should be lower odds than the 3.

Herein lies a slight edge. After the first race, jot down the potential Double payoffs shown on the toteboard or TV monitors for horses 1 through 8 (or 1 through 10). Occasionally, horses have been played significantly more or less in the Double than the second race win odds indicate. In our example, say the combinations of 5-2 and 5-6 were each paying $50 in the Double. But the win odds just before post time show the 2 at 2-1 and the 6 at 3-1. You can deduce that a win bet on the 6 has more value than the 2 because of the identical Double payoffs. For our concerns, betting the 6 to win has more value than the 2 if our handicapping indicated they were close in ability.

The Golden Rule

Never bet an overlay in exotics without playing anything to win on him. There's no greater sense of stupidity at the race track—trust me on this one—than handicapping a $20 winner and not cashing a cent because you played him exclusively in exactas and triples. Shave a small bit off your investment that race—or spend a couple extra dollars—and bet the horse to win. You can't waste high-paying overlays. Get some kind of return on a win ticket. Boxing horses in exactas is much preferable to using a horse just one way—either first or second. It'll hurt if you only bet a 5-1 horse by using him on top of exactas, and he gets nipped at the wire by a 40-1 shot for a $300 exacta you didn't have.

Wheeling

We mentioned creative ways to bet favorites at the beginning of the book. Wheeling is one of them. Wheeling is also a way to use $1 or $2 bets for leverage in exotic and/or multiple bets such as a Pick 3.

Let's say your handicapping pinpointed a solid choice. You hope for odds of 5-1, but the horse is the favorite at 2-1. The options: skip the race (never a bad move if your horse is an underlay); bet another contender, or bet the fave in exactas.

Of the other 7 horses in the race, you think one of them has an outside chance of winning. But he's bet down, too. Perhaps it's time to wheel the favorite in the exacta.

Wheeling simply means covering all possible combinations. In an exacta race, a wheel of favorite-ALL means you hit the exacta if the fave wins regardless of who finishes second. If the fave wins and the second choice in the wagering finishes second, you'll get an underlay, exactly what we're trying to avoid. You will hit the exacta, but lose money. However, if the favorite wins and one of the longshots finishes second, you'll likely get a generous return.

Horses can be wheeled for first or second in exacta races. If you wheel a horse for second and a longshot wins, you'll get value. Again, the down side is when the the second choice wins and your favorite finishes second. Again, you'll hit the exacta and get back less money than you wagered.

Accept that. A wheel is a speculative bet.

Wheel overlays? Absolutely. Here we touch upon the idea of using $1 bets for leverage. If a horse you like is, say, 4-1 in an 8-horse field, and you plan on investing $15 on the race, you can bet $8 to win on the horse and use the other $7 for a $1 wheel. If you'd like to cover yourself in case he loses, wheel him for second. You'll still collect the win bet. Another option is to wheel him first and second for $14. This is not the same as blowing a win bet, because if the horse wins, you will collect money. Betting him in exactas with just two or three other horses without a win bet is taboo because your horse may win and yet you may collect nothing.

Multiples: It Only Takes One

Want to take a shot at a Pick 3 or Pick 4? Go for it! We'll teach you about just saying no; leveraging using $1 or $2 bets, and saving your bet when you're live heading into the last race of a Pick 4 to guarantee at least a partial reward for your good handicapping in the previous three races.

The Pick 4 is a great inducement for getting your program and handicapping before you head to the track. It also forces you to focus on your gambling strategy for the night, specifically the four races of a Pick 4.

The payoffs can be outlandish when a favorite or two lose. A Pick 4 at Saratoga last September consisted of horses individually paying win prices of $3.20, $2.80, $13.20 and $10. That's horses at odds of 3-5, 2-5, 5-1 and 4-1. A $200 payoff would be generous. This paid $513.

There's another advantage to playing a Pick 4: You don't have to play each individual race. Of course, there's also a chance you'll have good-paying winners and miss them because you've only played them in Pick 4s. That point is as valid now as it was a page or two back. It's tough having a solid winner in only a Pick 4 and then losing. However, hitting just one Pick 4 with such a winner will more than compensate. If you like a horse a lot in one of the four races, go right ahead and bet him to win if you can afford it.

Just Say No

The first step in playing a Pick 4 is identifying the contenders by eliminating the pretenders. While it's difficult to handicap a winner of four consecutive races, it's reasonable to find horses that you perceive have no chance in each race. You have to get rid of them. You have to just say 'No.'

The easiest horses to toss out are those who have been beaten soundly by other horses in tonight's race one or more times with no apparent excuse. Some horses' PPs are so bad they almost jump out of the program at you. Another negative is horses who rarely win, the ones with a record of 1-for-40 the last two years. The more horses you want to eliminate, the harder it becomes to separate them. But separate them you must.

If there are eight horses in each of the four races, there are 4,096 combinations. If there are 10 horse fields, the number of combinations jumps to 10,000. To bet them all would cost $20,000 for $2 bets or $10,000 for $1 ones. Our mission is to shear each field in the four races to make the Pick 4 bet-able.

Winning the first of the four races will give us action in one, two, or, we hope, three of the next races.

As we weed out horses with no chance, you'll get a various number of horses you deem live in the four races. You can use four horses in the first race, two in the next, three next, then two. That's $48 of action using $1 bets or $96 using $2 ones.

Another strategy is to key the Pick 4 with a standout in one of the four races. If you think the 1 horse in the second race of the Pick 4 is a cinch, you can use 4, 4 and 3 horses in the other races. The cost again is $48 for $1 bets.

What if you do that and get antsy about your cinch? Okay, you've thought about it and you want to save with a second horse in the cinch's race. Using him with all the other combinations would mean a total investment of $96 for $1 bets. But you only want to spend $60. Here's what you do. Take the second horse from the cinch's race and use him on a separate ticket with only your top two choices in the other 3 races. The cost? Just $8 more, raising your $48 initial investment to $56.

Go for it! It's not impossible, and one big score can carry you a long way even if you only bet $1 combinations.

The first three races of the Pick 4 at Saratoga, July 19, 1991, were divisions of the New York Sire Stakes Pace for 2-year-old fillies. Usually, there is a dominant 2-year-old in one or more of the divisions, which makes them poor betting races. But if they weren't enticing win or exotic wagers, they could be played in the Pick 4.

Handicapping before the races sorted out contenders in the three divisions, and also the difficult final race of the Pick 4, a $2,500 claimer with nine horses. Next was deciding how much to invest. We went with $60. Instead of betting 30 $2 combinations, we chose 60 $1 plays. It's a question of strategy. Greed suggests $2 tickets, but using $1 tickets gives you the kind of leverage mentioned earlier. We're seeking overlays. Using $1 tickets allows you to use the third or fourth contender in one race that your handicapping suggests may be wide open. Hitting just one can create unbelievably juicy payoffs because favorites are so over-bet, especially at ½-mile tracks. The down side is that you could hit a Pick 4 with all the favorites and get a return so chintzy that you lose money. But that's okay. Let all your friends at the track giggle when you spend $50 with $1 bets and get a Pick 4 paying $40 for $2. That gets you back $20, a $30 loss which is difficult to explain to the spouse: "Yes, honey, I hit the Pick 4. I correctly picked winners of four consecutive races and lost $30."

Or you can simply miss the Pick 4 completely. But just remember: It only takes one.

Our handicapping identified the contenders in the Pick 4 races that night at Saratoga to be, by race: the 5-6-8, the 1-4-8, the 2-3, and the 1-2-3-6-10. Of those 13 contenders, we'd left question marks by the 4 in the second race and the 10 in the fourth one (a late scratch had reduced the field to nine). Including those two on all our tickets would have cost $90, $30 more than we were going to spend. A simple solution was to save with the two horses we were least sure about.

ONE MILE PACE
PURSE $14,220
FRIDAY, JULY 19, 1991
PICK FOUR (RACES 3-6)
&
EXACTA

THIRD RACE

NEW YORK SIRE STAKES
2 YEAR OLD FILLIES

5	14.00	7.40	3.20
2		4.80	2.60
3			3.40
Ex	5-2		62.00

WARM UP-PURPLE

Columns: PROGRAM NUMBER · Date · Trk · Purse · Cd · Class · Leaders Time Dis 1/4 1/2 3/4 · Winners Time · PP · 1/4 · 1/2 · 3/4 · Str · Fin · Ind 1/4 Time · Ind Time · Odds · Driver · Order Of Finish First Second Third · Temp

12-1 ON THE WILD SIDE (NY) — b f 2 Storm Damage-Happy Time Gal-Most Happy Fella — John M. Blomgren, Wayland, Mass. — 1991 5 0 1 0 $220 — First Starter
1 RAYMOND TREMBLAY (170) bl-wh-go (109-12-14-16-.230) Tr—Allison Mac Donald (.000) — Lifetime $220 — YELLOW

Date	Trk	Purse	Cd	Class	Dis	1/4	1/2	3/4	Time	PP	1/4	1/2	3/4	Str	Fin	Ind 1/4	Ind Time	Odds	Driver	Order of Finish	Temp
7-13 91	Stga	1200	sl	NW1PMLTCD	1	31 1	103 4	135 2	206 2	4	4	4	6°4	5	4 10	32 1	208 2	10.90	RTremblay	StopMakingSns,BrysOnSwp,RockOn	67-0
7-5 91	Bang	600	ft	NW1PMLFT	1	31	102 4	135 2	208	2	6	5°	5°	4	4	32 4	208 3	9.30	HMosher	CindysTootsie,RajenAbel,Pockets	69-0
6-28 91	Bang	200	ft	2YR	1	33 3	107 2	138 2	209 3	1	2	2°	2	2	2	31 1	209 4	NB	HMosher	GeishuFlash,OnThWildSd,MarcsW1B	84-0
6-21 91	Bang	200	ft	2YR	1	31 4	103 3	133 1	208	1	5	5	4	4	4	33 1	209 4	NB	HMosher	CindysTotal,GeishFlash,BarryBmp	70-0
6-14 91	Bang	200	ft	LE2YR	1	31 4	102 3	134 2	205 2	2	7	6°	5	6	6	34 3	212 3	NB	AMacDonal	OutForBlod,RcWhepromony,GnSpicr	68-0

4-1 CADILLACING (NY) — b f 2 On The Road Again-Albaquel-Albatross — Richard S. Staley, Los Angeles, Calif. — 1991 0 0 0 0 $00 — First Starter
2 DOUGLAS ACKERMAN (175) blu-gra (0-0-0-0-.000) Tr—Douglas Ackerman (.000) — Lifetime $00 — WHITE

Date	Trk	Purse	Cd	Class	Dis	1/4	1/2	3/4	Time	PP	1/4	1/2	3/4	Str	Fin	Ind 1/4	Ind Time	Odds	Driver	Order of Finish	Temp
7-10 91	M1		ft	QUA	1	29 3	100 3	131 3	159 4	7	2	2	3	3	4	28 4	200 3	NB	DAckerman	SeaniChang,TwoReens,SmokyEvening	75-0
7-3 91	M1		ft	QUA	1	30 4	101	131	200 2	4	6	6	5°	5	5	29	201 2	NB	DAckerman	TyMeUp,PartyTonight,IndianReoer	70-0

6-1 HOT AT NIGHT (NY) — b f 2 Tucson Hanover-Bh Belle-Precious Fella — J.G. Ince, E.J. Dziengel Jr., NY & Lawlor Racing Stable, NJ — 1991 2 0 0 0 $300 — First Starter
3 KIM CRAWFORD (155) red-blk-wh (636-139-114-64-.352) Tr—Edward Dziengel Jr (.000) — Lifetime $300 — PURPLE

Date	Trk	Purse	Cd	Class	Dis	1/4	1/2	3/4	Time	PP	1/4	1/2	3/4	Str	Fin	Ind 1/4	Ind Time	Odds	Driver	Order of Finish	Temp
7-14 91	MR A	3750	ft	2YOOPEN	1	29 4	100	131 3	202	3	5	5	4	4	4	30 1	202 4	34.70	DDzngl	FoinBigras,RocksCoins,FanaChamp	78-0
7-6 91	Gosh	7363	ft	2YRF STK	1	30	103 4	134 4	205 3	x2	3	3	[illegible]	7	6		209	NB	DDzngl	CraghsNancy,Fnon,Nastassimanns	~-0
6-28 91	MR		ft	2YRBABY	1	31 4	105	137	207 4	3	3	1	1	1	2	30 4	207 4	NB	DDzngl	Catamaran,HotAtNight,MostApricav	74-0

12-1 DUCHESS FERGIE (NY) — b f 2 Niatross-Wish Me Wings-Most Happy Fella — J.S. Some, Paramus, N.J. & M. Barnett, Englewood Cliffs, N.J. — 1991 3 0 0 0 $125 — First Starter
4 FRANK COPPOLA JR (150) ltbl-wh-br (642-130-100-96-.339) Tr—Richard Roadarmel (.000) — Lifetime $125 — BLACK

Date	Trk	Purse	Cd	Class	Dis	1/4	1/2	3/4	Time	PP	1/4	1/2	3/4	Str	Fin	Ind 1/4	Ind Time	Odds	Driver	Order of Finish	Temp
7-13 91	PcD⅝	1300	ft	NW1PMLTCD	1	29 4	100 4	131	201 4	1	4	5	7	6	5	30 4	203 1	22.90	GWasilluk	KasAnKy,BlatantlyBald,PrettyMai	77-0
7-5 91	PcD⅝	1200	ft	MDNCDFM	1	30 1	102	131 2	202 4	3	4	4	4	4	5	31 4	203 4	9.30	DKing	FoxyFirstLady,DonaDamel,ImAClassicTo	70-0
6-19 91	PcD⅝		gd	QUA	1	31 4	103 3	135	204 4	5	1	1	3	3	3	30 2	205 4	NB	DKing	FoxyFuss,ChampagnSantaF,DchsFrg	88-2
6-14 91	PcD⅝	100	ft	2YRF BABY	1	30 1	100 4	131 4	201 2	1	6	6	6	6 10	6	31 1	204 3	NB	GWasilluk	GRdAlmmri,CanWTlkDrct,FoxyFrstLdy	84-0

3-1 CUT 'N DRIED (NY) — b f 2 Storm Damage-Sweet Lavender-Niatross — Rocco F. & Ermilinda Manzi, Vernon, NY. — VD⅝ 2:02 1991 2 1 0 0 $760 — First Starter
5 DANIEL CAPPELLO JR (115) blue-white (246-43-38-38-.312) Tr—Rocco Manzi (.444) — 2,2:02⅝ Lifetime $760 — GREEN

Date	Trk	Purse	Cd	Class	Dis	1/4	1/2	3/4	Time	PP	1/4	1/2	3/4	Str	Fin	Ind 1/4	Ind Time	Odds	Driver	Order of Finish	Temp
6-30 91	VD⅝	2000	ft	COLEMUFLR	1	28 4	59 3	129	158 1	2	2	2	3	3	4	30 2	200	NB	BAllen	Hmstngr,Tmeofthenc,BoncastNorth	78-0
6-23 91	VD⅝	1200	ft	NWPMLTCD	1	28 2	59 3	131 4	202 1	2	2°	1	1	1	1	30 2	202 1	*1.00	BAllen	CutnDrd,TrthWarer,BrnestaCarona	80-0
6-13 91	VD⅝		ft	QUA	1	30	102 3	132 1	203 1	4	2	2	2°	2	1	30 3	203 1	NB	BAllen	CutnDrd,ClassicFriction,Niafast	80-0

5-2 WITSENDS MISSY (NY) — b f 2 On The Road Again-Lap Dog-Keystone Ore — David G. & Georgina D. Rahal, Saddle River, NJ. — QGTY1 2:02 1991 3 0 1 0 $5,300 — First Starter
6 REJEAN DAIGNEAULT (143) lblu-red-wh (0-0-0-0-.000) Tr—Rejean Daigneault (.000) — Q2,2:02 1 Lifetime $5,300 — RED

Date	Trk	Purse	Cd	Class	Dis	1/4	1/2	3/4	Time	PP	1/4	1/2	3/4	Str	Fin	Ind 1/4	Ind Time	Odds	Driver	Order of Finish	Temp
7-6 91	YR	20000	sy	2YRF STK	1	29 2	101 1	131 3	203 3	2	1	1	1	1	2		203 3	7.70	RDegnalt	TwoRoses,WitsendsMissy,GloriaW	79-0
6-23 91	M1 A	27500	ft	2yrF Stk	1	28	56 3	126 1	156	9	4°	2°	2°	6	6 10	31 3	158	81.90	JPavlaJr	HazlionKay,ChnaPrncs,WhysCaro	68-0
6-16 91	M1 A	6000	ft	2yrF	1	28 1	57 1	127	157 2	9	9	9	7	7	5	30 1	158 2	16.00	CManzi	Springazz,MisPegy,BuiltFiction	85-0
6-7 91	GTY1		ft	QUA	1	31	102	132 2	202	5	4	4	3	2	1	29 1	202	NB	CManzi	WitsendsMissy,Porsain,FlyBims	80-0
5-31 91	GTY1		ft	QUA	1	31 1	103	134 4	204 2	7	6	6	7	6	4	28 4	205	NB	CManzi	RozlanHanover,SeaLov,Marrouw	80-0

8-1 AMAZING FIDDLER (NY) — b f 2 Nero-Amazing Gigi-Laverne Hanover — The J & L Dubow Stable, NY. & Alan L. Small, NJ. — 1991 2 0 0 0 $00 — First Starter
7 WALLY HENNESSEY (140) bl-go-wh (231-53-42-38-.385) Tr—Alan Small (.000) — Lifetime $00 — BROWN

Date	Trk	Purse	Cd	Class	Dis	1/4	1/2	3/4	Time	PP	1/4	1/2	3/4	Str	Fin	Ind 1/4	Ind Time	Odds	Driver	Order of Finish	Temp
7-13 91	M1		sy	QUA	1	31 3	103 1	134 2	203 3	3	1	1	1	2	2	29 1	203 3	NB	JCampbell	Tango,AmazingFiddler,Halifax	80-1
6-27 91	YR	500	ft	2YRF	1	29 3	101	131 2	203	7	7	6°	6°°	7	7		204 2	NB	WCaseJr	RozlanHanover,Gabbing,HlnLobi	87-0
6-20 91	YR	500	ft	2YRF	1	30	102 1	132 4	203 2	5	4	4°	x7	7	6			NB	WCaseJr	RozlanHanover,HrcanHeatv,CraghsNancy	80-0

10-1 MOMENTUM YOUNG (NY) — b f 2 Storm Damage-Momentum Almahurst-Falcon Almahurst — Black Bag Stable, Miller Place, N.Y. — 1991 4 0 2 1 $784 — First Starter
8 FRANK POPFINGER JR (160) blue-gold (0-0-0-0-.000) Tr—Frank Popfinger Jr (.000) — Lifetime $784 — GRAY

Date	Trk	Purse	Cd	Class	Dis	1/4	1/2	3/4	Time	PP	1/4	1/2	3/4	Str	Fin	Ind 1/4	Ind Time	Odds	Driver	Order of Finish	Temp
7-12 91	VD⅝	1200	ft	NWPMLTCD	1	27 4	59	129	158 2	3	5	5°	3°	3	2	29 4	159 1	4.50	FPopfngrJ	Dieman,MomntmYong,NicholasCoins	82-0
7-4 91	VD⅝	1200	ft	2YRMDNCD	1	29 2	101 1	131 1	159 1	6	2	2	2	2	2	28 3	200 1	6.30	BAllen	HolyTerror,MomntumYoung,GoCatGo	80-0
6-27 91	YR	500	ft	2YRF	1	28 3	100	129 4	200 2	4	3	3	5	5	4		206 3	NB	FPopfngrJ	ArtLight,OurHarbortown,BrynnM	87-0
6-21 91	VD⅝	1200	ft	NWPMLTCD	1	29 1	101 2	131	200 2	6	7	7°	6°	5	3	30 1	202 1	9.00	PTuttle	PoseVean,ShnahBGod,MomntmYong	80-0
6-13 91	VD⅝		ft	QUA	1	31 1	102 3	133	203 4	1	5	5	3°	1	2	30 2	204	NB	FPopfngrJ	Manso,MomntumYoung,SplashGordon	80-0
6-6 91	VD⅝		ft	QUA	1	30 1	102 4	134 2	205	x7	7	7	7	7	7	30 2	206	NB	PTuttle	Lpg,JoshCollins,Timeofthenc	70-0

ONE MILE PACE
PURSE $1,300
FRIDAY, JULY 19, 1991
TRIPLE
EXACTA
PICK FOUR

SIXTH RACE

10 | 37.20 | 16.80 | 5.60
6 | 16.00 | 5.00
5 | 16.20
EX 10-6 192.80
TRI 2,262.00

CLAIMING ALLOWANCE $2500
WINNERS OF 1 BUT NOT 2 RACES IN 1991

WARM UP-RED

Column key: PROGRAM NUMBER, Date, Trk, Purse, Cd, Class, Leaders Time (Dis, 1/4, 1/2, 3/4), Winners Time, PP, 1/4, 1/2, 3/4, Str, Fin, Ind 1/4 Time, Ind Time, Odds, Driver, Order Of Finish (First, Second, Third), Temp

3-1 — 1 — BROADWAY PAUL

b h 5 Tyler'sBrother-HotLips-Adios Vic
Jeanne E.Jones,S Glens Falls,N.Y.
JOSEPH DE CARLO (150) blk-wh (57-7-2-5-.172) Tr—Joseph De Carlo (.194)
QStga 2:04 1991 8 1 2 2 $1,658
Stga 2:03 1990 17 1 1 3 $2,350
4,2:03 Lifetime $11,052
Claim price: 2,500

Date	Trk	Purse	Cd	Class	Dis	1/4	1/2	3/4	Time	PP	1/4	1/2	3/4	Str	Fin	Ind 1/4	Ind Time	Odds	Driver	Order Of Finish	Temp
7-12	Stga	1100	ft	2500CLCD	1	30	101	132	202	9	4	4°	5°°	3	2	30	202	10.00	JDeCarlo	TMScotch,BroadwayPaul,SocaJoen	82-0
7-5	Stga	1100	ft	2500CLCD	1	29	101	131	203	1	1	1	1	1	2	32	203	*2.20	DMarshall	JoyfMac,BroadwayPaul,ShrmpScamp	65-C
6-26	Stga	1100	ft	2500CLCD	1	29	101	132	204	8	3	3	2°	2	1	31	204	4.30	JDeCarlo	BroadwayPaul,BogieLobell,KayVee	83-0
6-18	Stga	1100	ft	2500CLCD	1	29	101	132	204	8	8		7°°	4	4	31	204	10.90	JDeCarlo	GryCntryA,BrthnyLv,StdysKngKhn	78-0
6-7	Stga	1100	ft	2500CLCD	1	29	101	131	210	1	3	1°	2°°	1	4	39	210	2.90	JDeCarlo	ShmptnAnw,KysnMcrs,ImgonBrz	79-C

4-1 — 2 — JIFFY'S HITTER (NY)

b g 6 HotHitter-JiffyBunny-B.G'sBunny
Gordon K.Petteys,Greenwich N.Y.
DAVID MARSHALL (185) ltbl-red-gld (481-53-65-67-.232) Tr—Linda Flynn (.306)
Stga 2:02 1991 7 1 3 1 $1,370
Stga 2:00 1990 18 2 2 1 $3,396
4,1:59 Lifetime $24,909
Claim price: 2,500

Date	Trk	Purse	Cd	Class	Dis	1/4	1/2	3/4	Time	PP	1/4	1/2	3/4	Str	Fin	Ind 1/4	Ind Time	Odds	Driver	Order Of Finish	Temp
7-12	Stga	1100	ft	2500CLCD	1	30	101	132	202	6	8	9	8	8	6	30	203	5.10	DMarshall	TMScotch,BroadwayPaul,SocaJoen	82-C
7-4	Stga A	1000	ft	AMATEUR	1	30	102	133	204	8	8	8	7°	7	7	31	205	4.60	JPainter	HoindsSong,PoetvRh,KyssonPncy	81-C
6-25	Stga	1200	ft	2500CLCD	1	29	100	130	202	7	7	7	5	6	2	31	203	12.90	DMarshall	GypsyFirst,JiffyHitter,Joggin	81-C
6-13	Stga	1000	ft	AMATEUR	1	31	102	132	203	4	7	6°	4°	3	3	31	204	NB	JPainter	HamptonBoy,UnbeatblStar,Ymm	70-C
6-6	Stga	800	ft	AMATEUR	1	30	102	132	204	6	6	6°	5°	4	2	30	204	NB	JPainter	AGoFella,JiffyHitter,RBsReward	70-C

5-2 — 3 — IN TRANSIT

b h 6 RalphHanover-HurricaneWave-ShadowWave
Trip S Stable,Windsor Locks,Conn.
PERRY SIMSER (154) gold-green (102-20-14-14-.318) Tr—Perry Simser (.397)
Stga 2:01 1991 5 1 1 1 $1,054
Stga 2:01 1990 16 3 2 2 $4,180
4,1:59 Lifetime $34,037
Claim price: 2,500

Date	Trk	Purse	Cd	Class	Dis	1/4	1/2	3/4	Time	PP	1/4	1/2	3/4	Str	Fin	Ind 1/4	Ind Time	Odds	Driver	Order Of Finish	Temp
7-11	Stga	1200	ft	2500CLCD	1	29	100	130	200	5	5	4°	4°°	2	2	30	201	2.30	PSimser	GypsyFirst,InTransit,Noisy	89-0
7-6	Stga	1100	ft	2500CLCD	1	28	59	130	201	4	5	5	3°	2	1	31	201	*1.20	PSimser	InTransit,BackPackr,FloronCoins	80-C
6-25	Stga	1200	ft	2500CLCD	1	29	100	130	202	4	6	6	7°°	4	6	32	203	3.70	PSimser	GypsyFirst,JiffyHitter,Joggin	81-C
6-13	Stga	1200	ft	2500CLCD	1	30	101	131	202	2	3	4	4	4	3	31	203	2.40	PSimser	LillTicket,PrtctStv,InTransit	70-0
6-4	Stga	1200	ft	2500CLCD	1	29	101	132	202	3	4	3°	2°	3	5	30	203	6.40	PSimser	FlemngLght,YongBrndyWn,Tggs	91-0

6-1 — 4 — MASTER NOEL

b h 11 HonestMaster(F)-BrowngateMissy-TudorHanover
Thomas J.Kronk & Susan L.Agnew,Ballston Spa,N.Y.
FRANK COPPOLA JR (150) ltbl-wh-br (642-130-100-96-.339) Tr—Thomas Kronk (.274)
Stga 2:06 1991 17 1 3 4 $2,509
1990 21 2 4 4 $3,739
5,1:57 Lifetime $92,028
Claim price: 2,500

Date	Trk	Purse	Cd	Class	Dis	1/4	1/2	3/4	Time	PP	1/4	1/2	3/4	Str	Fin	Ind 1/4	Ind Time	Odds	Driver	Order Of Finish	Temp
7-11	Stga	1100	ft	2500CLCD	1	30	101	132	203	4	5	5°	3°°	2	2	31	203	6.40	FCoppolaJr	PrtctStv,MastrNoi,WhrsChan	89-C
7-5	Stga	1100	ft	2500CLCD	1	30	101	133	204	5	8	9°	7°°	6	4	30	204	17.30	JRandall	Joggin,JulesVerne,LindenThnier	65-0
6-21	Stga	1100	ft	2500CLCD	1	29	101	131	202	7	8	8°	7°°	7	6	31	203	52.20	JRandall	TarrtonStacy,JmuamChcn,Carabest	72-0
6-14	Stga	1100	ft	2500CLCD	1	30	102	132	202	2	4	4	3°	3	3	31	203	6.30	FCoppolaJr	JetsCompatible,JustFly,MastrNoi	77-C
5-6	Stga	1100	ft	2500CLCD	1	29	59	129	201	3	5	5°	5	6	4	32	203	4.00	FCoppolaJr	MayFifty,KashsaF,TarrtonStacy	79-C

12-1 — 5 — DODGE BOY

b g 4 Insomniac-JensGirl-George VanAllen
Anne G.Haley,Cuttingsville,Vt.
NELSON HALEY (150) red-green-white (0-0-0-0-.000) Tr—Nelson Haley (.000)
Bang 2:03 1991 7 1 1 0 $636
Stga 2:06 1990 15 1 0 3 $1,721
4,2:03 Lifetime $2,357
Claim price: 3,125

Date	Trk	Purse	Cd	Class	Dis	1/4	1/2	3/4	Time	PP	1/4	1/2	3/4	Str	Fin	Ind 1/4	Ind Time	Odds	Driver	Order Of Finish	Temp
7-4	Bang	A750	ft	NW400L4STS	1	28	59	129	201	8	7	7	7	6	6	30	202	36.30	NHaley	StingStone,WelysOrem,BabyOmore	80-0
6-28	Bang	750	sy	NW301L5CD	1	29	100	130	202	5i	6	5°	4	6	6	32	203	42.80	NHaley	MeadowTim,Donybroong,ShaonLobl	84-0
6-22	Bang	700	ft	NW2PMLFT	1	30	101	132	203	1	1	1	1	1	1	30	203	3.90	RGodbloodJ	DodgBoy,ModCzn,KawarthaMandalay	80-0
6-15	Bang	600	gd	NW301CD	1	30	102	135	207	6	7	8	5	3	2	31	207	22.50	NHaley	AnothrAcount,DodgBoy,ChpsEscon	80-2
6-8	Bang	1000	ft	NW2PMLFTLC	1	30	102	133	204	7	6	6	5°°	4	4	31	205	84.30	NHaley	BetchesBoBoy,Jonsomorsu,DorsEmo	72-C

8-1 — 6 — GRAY BANDIT

gr g 6 DistantThunder-SharonPrincess-CKAdios
James & John DiSalvatore Jr.,Schenectady NY.
GARY KAMAL (150) wh-blue-gld (385-55-44-63-.261) Tr—Karen Kamal (.343)
Stga 2:04 1991 17 1 2 2 $3,429
Stga 2:00 1990 37 4 5 11 $13,013
5,2:00 Lifetime $38,258
Claim price: 2,500

Date	Trk	Purse	Cd	Class	Dis	1/4	1/2	3/4	Time	PP	1/4	1/2	3/4	Str	Fin	Ind 1/4	Ind Time	Odds	Driver	Order Of Finish	Temp
7-13	Stga	1400	sl	3000CL	1	30	102	133	205	7	3°	2°	2°	5	7	33	207	5.60	GKamal	SavanaBluChp,BrianaLobl,PnPvrsA	67-0
7-5	Stga	1800	ft	4000CL	1	28	58	129	201	8	5	5	5	6	5	31	202	22.50	GKamal	SaturdaynitFvr,PJManoe,MackSmt	65-C
6-14	Stga	1800	ft	4000CL	1	29	100	131	202	5	3	3	4	4	4	31	203	1.90	GKamal	GaryOceson,CasualFlash,LimSoda	77-0
6-4	Stga	1800	ft	4000CL	1	29	59	130	200	2	4	4°	2°°	2	4	31	201	5.50	GKamal	LghtBluFla,SheGotPnty,MackSmt	81-0
5-27	Stga A	1600	ft	4000CL	1	29	100	130	200	8	8	8	8	8	3	30	201	15.60	GKamal	MangmOcson,BrinaLobl,GrayBandt	78-0

15-1 — 7 — STANDY'S KING KHAN Scr

b g 7 GenghisKhan-J.M.Swift-AdiosRonnie
Dean R.Brown Jr.,Ludlow,Vt.
JAMES BROWN (190) red-gold (13-1-0-4-.179) Tr—James Brown (.179)
PcD ⅞ 2:05 1991 19 1 0 4 $1,930
PcD ⅞ 2:01 1990 30 3 5 5 $10,504
4,1:58 ⅞ Lifetime $68,649
Claim price: 2,500

Date	Trk	Purse	Cd	Class	Dis	1/4	1/2	3/4	Time	PP	1/4	1/2	3/4	Str	Fin	Ind 1/4	Ind Time	Odds	Driver	Order Of Finish	Temp
7-13	Stga	1100	sl	2500CLCD	1	31	102	134	206	3	1	1		2	6	33	207	11.90	JBrown	BackPackr,CandiTrch,Xystonigio	67-0
7-6	Stga	1100	ft	2500CLCD	1	29	102	132	203	4	3	4	6	3	5	31	204	6.10	JBrown	Noisy,BogieLobell,FancyFree	80-0
6-27	Stga	1100	ft	2500CLCD	1	30	101	132	202	6	4	4	3	3	3	30	203	11.90	JBrown	NotAFoly,PlotMad,StandysKngKhan	83-0
6-18	Stga	1100	ft	2500CLCD	1	29	101	132	204	6	4	4°	4	3	3	31	204	5.10	JBrown	GryCntryA,BrthnyLv,StdysKngKhn	78-0
6-7	Stga	1100	ft	2500CLCD	1	29	101	131	210	7	1	1	1	4	5	40	211	10.70	JBrown	ShmptnAnw,KysnMcrs,ImgonBrz	79-C

10-1 — 8 — NOISY

b g 5 Royce-CricketAlmahurst-Kawartha Eagle
Donald W.DeLuca, Steven X.Kouray & Jordan L.Myers, NY
JORDAN MYERS (180) gray-grn-brown (82-5-14-12-.205) Tr—Jordan Myers (.200)
Stga 2:03 1991 20 1 3 3 $3,648
Stga 1:59 1990 35 8 2 0 $10,587
4,1:59 Lifetime $17,365
Claim price: 2,500

Date	Trk	Purse	Cd	Class	Dis	1/4	1/2	3/4	Time	PP	1/4	1/2	3/4	Str	Fin	Ind 1/4	Ind Time	Odds	Driver	Order Of Finish	Temp
7-11	Stga	1200	ft	2500CLCD	1	29	100	130	200	2	3	3	2°	3	3	30	201	7.10	JMyers	GypsyFirst,InTransit,Noisy	89-0
7-6	Stga	1100	ft	2500CLCD	1	29	102	132	203	6	6	5°	4°	2	1	30	203	*2.60	JMyers	Noisy,BogieLobell,FancyFree	80-0
6-25	Stga	1800	ft	4000CL	1	28	59	130	200	4	7	7°	7°	8	7	31	202	3.90	MInsy	HollysRJB,MoonRockA,LimeSoda	81-C
6-14	Stga	1800	ft	4000CL	1	29	100	131	202	1	1	1	2	5	7	32	204	*1.40	JMyers	GaryOceson,CasualFlash,LimSoda	77-0
5-31	Stga	1600	ft	4000CL	1	29	100	130	201	5	6	6	6	5	4	30	201	10.40	JMyers	DownwmLloyd,JollyBoy,ComeOnLiz	79-C

12-1 — 9 — TWIN BETS (NY)

b m 8 Conquered-TrickyNewport-Overtrick
William J.Blake Jr.,Gansevoort NY.
WILLIAM BLAKE JR (170) green-wh-gold (40-4-2-7-.186) Tr—William Blake Jr (.237)
Stga 2:03 1991 16 1 1 2 $1,794
Stga 2:04 1990 25 3 3 4 $3,986
5,2:02 Lifetime $26,610
Claim price: 3,000

Date	Trk	Purse	Cd	Class	Dis	1/4	1/2	3/4	Time	PP	1/4	1/2	3/4	Str	Fin	Ind 1/4	Ind Time	Odds	Driver	Order Of Finish	Temp
7-13	Stga	1100	sl	2500CLCD	1	31	102	134	206	6	6	7	8	8	4	32	207	26.40	WBlakeJr	BackPackr,CandiTrch,Xystonigio	67-0
7-5	Stga	1100	ft	2500CLCD	1	30	101	133	204	7	5°	5	9	8	7	32	206	30.50	WBlakeJr	Joggin,JulesVerne,LindenThnier	65-0
6-28	Stga	1100	ft	2500CLCD	1	30	101	131	203	8	4°	4	5	5	6	32	204	29.50	WBlakeJr	TrfTrumpet,Badgmanor,Jutsvm	82-0
6-18	Stga	1100	ft	2500CLCD	1	29	101	132	203	4	3°	5°	8	7	7	31	204	30.50	WBlakeJr	SgnsHilLma,FlemgLght,ShmpScmp	78-C
6-11	Stga	1100	gd	2500CLCD	1	29	101	133	210	4	6°	5	7	7	7	37	212	24.70	WBlakeJr	LeishaLou,Setara,Flckrng	64-C

8-1 — 10 — SPEED ARTIST

b m 9 Nansemond-ArtisticYankee-Columbia George
C.P.Siligato, L.R & J.F.LaBarge, NY
JOHN SCHWED (160) ltblue-wh-gray (111-16-13-16-.257) Tr—Carl Siligato (.133)
Stga 2:02 1991 6 1 0 0 $703
Altmt 2:09 1990 16 1 2 1 $1,980
5,1:59 ⅞ Lifetime $19,590
Claim price: 3,000

Date	Trk	Purse	Cd	Class	Dis	1/4	1/2	3/4	Time	PP	1/4	1/2	3/4	Str	Fin	Ind 1/4	Ind Time	Odds	Driver	Order Of Finish	Temp
7-12	Stga	1100	ft	2500CLCD	1	30	101	132	202	8	2	2°	2°	2	4	31	203	40.60	JSchwed	TMScotch,BroadwayPaul,SocaJoen	82-0
7-4	Stga A	1200	ft	2500CLCD	1	29	100	130	209	7	7	7°	6	6	7	38	210	11.90	JSchwed	AvonTrumpet,GypsyFirst,Ermaland	81-0
6-28	Stga	1800	ft	4000CL	1	28	58	129	201	5	5	5	5	6	7	32	202	40.40	JSchwed	SatrdaynitFvr,CasalFlash,MackSmt	82-C
6-12	Stga	1700	ft	4000CLCD	1	29	101	131	201	8	8	8	7°°	8	8	32	204	58.30	JSchwed	StormEClare,AnothrPlog,ComOnLiz	84-0
6-5	Stga	1100	ft	2500CLCD	1	29	101	132	202	3	3	1°	1	1	1	30	202	2.70	JSchwed	SpdArtst,Pogwimag,WhatsSampson	84-C

ONE MILE PACE
PURSE $14,220
FRIDAY, JULY 19, 1991
PICK FOUR
&
EXACTA

FIFTH RACE

NEW YORK SIRE STAKES
2 YEAR OLD FILLIES

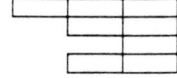

WARM UP-GREEN

PROGRAM NUMBER	Date	Trk	Purse	Cd	Class	Dis	Leaders Time 1/4	1/2	3/4	Winners Time	PP	1/4	1/2	3/4	Str	Fin	Ind 1/4 Time	Ind Time	Odds	Driver	Order Of Finish First Second Third	Temp

15-1 CARIBBEAN FLIGHT (NY) — b f 2 Seahawk Hanover-Laruba-Oil Burner — Edward J. Stack, Albany, NY
1 — RONALD WAPLES (145) blue-gold (0-0-0-0-.000) — Tr—Lennart Berg (.431)
1991 0 0 0 0 $00 — First Starter — Lifetime $00
YELLOW

Date	Trk	Purse	Cd	Class	Dis	1/4	1/2	3/4	Time	PP	1/4	1/2	3/4	Str	Fin	Ind 1/4	Ind Time	Odds	Driver	Order Of Finish	Temp
7-6^1	Dmv		ft	QUA	1	28^7	58	129^7	202	1	2	3	4^1	5^1	5^7	32^3	205^3	NB	GDennis	Sconidlen,JaneDolly,Hjerlope	80-0

2-1 SEAHAWK SIS (NY) — ch f 2 Seahawk Hanover-Allwood's Rarest-Albatross — Marjorie A. & George R. Shubley Jr., Pepperell, Mass.
2 — JEFFREY GREGORY (135) grn-white-gold (4-1-1-1-.472) — Tr—David Jannone (.852)
VD 2:00^4 1991 5 3 1 1 $37,520 — First Starter — 2,2:00^4 Lifetime $37,520
WHITE

Date	Trk	Purse	Cd	Class	Dis	1/4	1/2	3/4	Time	PP	1/4	1/2	3/4	Str	Fin	Ind 1/4	Ind Time	Odds	Driver	Order Of Finish	Temp
7-13^1	YR	200000	ft	2YRF STK	1	28^1	58^4	129^7	159^4	4	9	8	9°	7	3^5		200^4	15.50	JGregory	HazlonKay,OrHarborlown,SahawkSs	70-0
7-6^1	YR	20000	sy	2YRF STK	1	28^7	59	130^7	203	7	8	6°	6°°	2	1^1		203^1	12.40	JGregory	SahawkSis,Lovebirthr,FoinBigras	79-0
6-27^1	Siga	5000	ft	LC	1	29	100	131	201	6	4	1	1	1	2^hd	30	201	*.60	JGregory	PrtyRthis,SahawkS,CanvasbackCoyn	83-0
6-20^1	Siga	3340	ft	LC	1	31^1	101^4	131	201^4	3	4	1	1	1	1^4	30^3	201^4	*1.10	JGregory	SahawkSis,PrtyRthis,AmericablGr	87-0
6-14^1	VD	1200	ft	NWPMLTCD	1	28^4	100^4	131^2	200^4	3	5	5°	1^07	1^7	1^3	29^7	200^4	2.10	JGregory	SahawkSis,DaytonBold,DecountRat	77-0
6-6^1	VD		ft	QUA	1	30^7	102^4	132^3	202^7	2	5	5°	3^7	3^7	2^1	29^7	202^3	NB	JGregory	DaytonBold,SeahawkSis,Awsomi	70-0

10-1 MISS GOODBODY (NY) — b f 2 Nero-Nutmeg Delight-Tar Heel — T. & J.S. Farrell, Webster, NY., R.W. & J.H. Watson, Penn Yan, NY.
3 — ROBERT WATSON (P) (165) wh-grn-red (0-0-0-0-.000) — Tr—Robert Watson (.000)
BR 2:04^7 1991 5 3 0 2 $4,885 — First Starter — 2,2:04^7 Lifetime $4,885
PURPLE

Date	Trk	Purse	Cd	Class	Dis	1/4	1/2	3/4	Time	PP	1/4	1/2	3/4	Str	Fin	Ind 1/4	Ind Time	Odds	Driver	Order Of Finish	Temp
7-14^1	AxBy	966	gd	2YRNYCFS	1 Dash, 1 MILE IN 2:08 fin 1													NR	RWatson	MsGodbody,WarmionTm,ShnngSnnahrv-0	
6-16^1	BR	17100	ft	REDJACFNL	1	30	101^4	132^4	201	4	3	5	5^3	3^5	3^5	28^3	202	28.90	RWatson	MstBirwncbl,MstBMonight,MsGodbody	80-C
6-9^1	BR	2500	ft	REDJACKET	1	30	102	133^4	204^7	5	2	2	2	2	1		204	NB	RWatson	MisGodbody,MustBMonight,BlaBau	80-C
6-2^1	BR	2500	ft	REDJACKET	1	30	100^4	132^3	201^4	6	2°	3	5^4	5^1	3^1	32	205^7	2.70	RWatson	MustBirwncbl,Alsimag,MsGodbody	81-0
5-19^1	BR	1600	ft	MONCD	1	30^7	103^7	134	204^4	1	2	3	3	3	1^7	30^7	204^4	1.90	RWatson	MissGoodbody,WeDoGail,KLWilton	72-0
5-9^1	BR		sy	QUA	1	33^7	103^7	135	206^3	1	2	2	2^1	2^1	2^4	30^3	207^7	NB	RWatson	NicolT,MissGoodbody,PrciousBufy	48-2

8-1 FRENCH REVOLUTION (NY) — b f 2 Tucson Hanover-French Pastry-Oil Burner — John R. Cummins, Lexington, Ky
4 — WALLY HENNESSEY (140) bl-go-wh (231-53-42-38-.385) — Tr—Howard Norris (.000)
Lex 1 2:01^4 1991 4 2 0 0 $1,204 — First Starter — 2,2:01^4 1 Lifetime $1,204
BLACK

Date	Trk	Purse	Cd	Class	Dis	1/4	1/2	3/4	Time	PP	1/4	1/2	3/4	Str	Fin	Ind 1/4	Ind Time	Odds	Driver	Order Of Finish	Temp
7-6^1	YR	20000	ft	2YRF STK	1	28	58^7	130	202	3	6	7°	5°°	6^4	5^7		203^3	13.10	MLachance	Zzzs,SensitiveOne,MaryeBrew	79-0
6-28^1	Lex1	1300	ft	NW1PMCD	1	29	59^4	130	159^7	7	8	8	8^1	4^4	4^2	28^4	200	*.40	AHarris	HappyEaster,Montego,HrsRaide	84-0
6-21^1	Lex1	100	ft	2YR	1	31	102	132	201	5	5	5	3^4	1^10	1^13	28^7	201^4	NB	AHarris	FrnchRvolution,Wynrush,MisPprs	85-0
6-14^1	Lex1	100	ft	2YR	1	34	106	137	205	1	1	1	1	1	1	28^4	205^4	NB	JCummins	FrnchRvolution,Thatsright,Wynrsh	83-0

6-1 IRONIA ROAD (NY) — b f 2 On The Road Again-Clooncara-Meadow Skipper — S.A. Goodman, NJ., E.W. Roberts & T.Z. Kaufman, NY.
5 — JAY RANDALL (145) blue-gold-white (277-32-32-33-.219) — Tr—Larry Summer (.000)
1991 4 0 1 0 $430 — First Starter — Lifetime $430
GREEN

Date	Trk	Purse	Cd	Class	Dis	1/4	1/2	3/4	Time	PP	1/4	1/2	3/4	Str	Fin	Ind 1/4	Ind Time	Odds	Driver	Order Of Finish	Temp
7-12^1	MR	1400	ft	NW1500LT	1	30^4	102	134	205	4	1	1	1	1^1	2^1	31^7	205^7	*1.20	DTaylor	PartyTimBoy,IroniaRoad,SandSply	81-0
6-27^1	YR	500	ft	2YRF	1	29^3	100^3	131^7	202^7	3	4	4	5°	4^4	4^7		203^4	NB	MNicholl	RosebudCedam,Zzzs,CurghsNancy	87-0
6-22^1	M1	500	ft	Baby	1	30	100	131	200^3	6	8	8	9^6	8^1	8^6	29^7	201^4	NB	MLachance	Jatuma,CoastalDamag,DazingLght	78-C
5-15^1	M1	500	ft	Baby	1	31	102	131^3	200	2	3	3	3^5	4^1	4^10	29^7	202	NB	MLachance	TouchLightly,LadyNison,Trfmax	78-0

3-1 CURRAGHS' NANCY (NY) — b f 2 Curragh-JV Nancy-Flying Bret — Gerald & Christine M. Hade, Flushing, NY
6 — LUC OUELLETTE (142) red-white-black (0-0-0-0-.000) — Tr—Gerald Hode (.000)
Green 2:04^7 1991 4 1 0 2 $3,988 — First Starter — 2,2:04^7 Lifetime $3,988
RED

Date	Trk	Purse	Cd	Class	Dis	1/4	1/2	3/4	Time	PP	1/4	1/2	3/4	Str	Fin	Ind 1/4	Ind Time	Odds	Driver	Order Of Finish	Temp
7-14^1	MR A	3750	ft	2YOOPEN	1	29^4	100	131^3	202	5	1°	2	3^1	3^1	5^2	30^4	202^4	3.60	JMarshJr	FoinBigras,RocidCoins,FansChamp	78-0
7-6^1	Gosh	7363	ft	2YRF STK	1	30	103^4	134^4	205^3	8	2	2	2°	1^1	1		205^3	NB	HFillion	CraghsNancy,Fnqn,Nastassmanns	n-0
6-27^1	YR	500	ft	2YRF	1	29^3	100^3	131^7	202^7	1	3	1°	1	1^7	3^7		202^4	NB	HFillion	RosebudCedam,Zzzs,CuraghsNancy	87-0
6-20^1	YR	500	ft	2YRF	1	30	102	132^4	203	1	1	1	1	1	3^1		203^3	NB	JMarshJr	RoztaHanovr,HrcanHeltv,CraghsNancy	80-0
6-2^1	Wilm		gd	MAT 2YR	1	31^7	103^7	135	204^4	2	2	3	3	3^1	2^1		205	NB	JEssig	LotaDetrction,CraghsNancy,NoSgarAd	n-0
5-19^1	Green		gd	MAT CD	1	30	102	133	204^7	3	3	4	3	3^3	1^1		204^7	NB	JEssig	CurraghsNancy,Hera,CurrentTempo	n-0

4-1 TANGO (NY) — b f 2 Precious Pella-Striking Byrd-Strike Out — Twin Towers Assoc., D. Hurley, NJ., K. Evilsizor & K. Hurley, NY.
7 — KIM CRAWFORD (155) red-blk-wh (636-139-114-64-.352) — Tr—Jerry Evilsizor (.000)
QM 1 2:03^3 1991 2 0 0 0 $40 — First Starter — 2,2:03^3 1 Lifetime $40
BROWN

Date	Trk	Purse	Cd	Class	Dis	1/4	1/2	3/4	Time	PP	1/4	1/2	3/4	Str	Fin	Ind 1/4	Ind Time	Odds	Driver	Order Of Finish	Temp
7-13^1	M1		sy	QUA	1	31^3	103	134^7	203^3	4	3	3	3°^3	1^1	1^1	28^3	203^3	NB	DManzi	Tango,AmazingFiddler,Halifax	80-1
7-6^1	YR	20000	sy	2YRF STK	1	28^7	59	130^7	203	5	6	8°	8°	7	7^3		205	37.90	JMarshJr	SahawkSis,Lovebirthr,FoinBigras	79-C
6-27^1	YR	500	ft	2YRF	1	29^3	101	131^7	203	4	5	7	7	6^1	4^4		203^4	NB	JMarshJr	RosebudCedam,Gabbing,HinLobi	87-C
6-7^1	GTY1		ft	QUA	1	31^7	102^7	133	202^4	7	6	6	6^1	5^6	3^7	28^3	203	NB	DManzi	SlideKellySlide,DirctMad,Tango	80-C

10-1 IVY LEAGUER (NY) — br f 2 On The Road Again-Liberty's Jewel-Nero — G.J. Denti, Bronx, NY & The Ivy League Stable, Long Branch, NJ
8 — STEPHEN SMITH (160) gray-red-black (0-0-0-0-.000) — Tr—Stephen Smith (.000)
M 1 2:00^4 1991 4 1 0 1 $924 — First Starter — 2,2:00^4 1 Lifetime $924
GRAY

Date	Trk	Purse	Cd	Class	Dis	1/4	1/2	3/4	Time	PP	1/4	1/2	3/4	Str	Fin	Ind 1/4	Ind Time	Odds	Driver	Order Of Finish	Temp
6-29^1	RcR	11787	ft	2YRF STK	1	28	59^3	129	158	1	3	4	5^3	5^4	5^8	30	159^4	29.80	SSmith	SummerChild,HSunshine,Trufmax	82-0
6-20^1	YR	500	ft	2YRF	1	29^4	100	131	202	4	5	5	4°	2^4	3^3		202^3	NB	SSmith	OurHarborlown,ArtLight,IvyLagur	80-0
6-15^1	M1	500	ft	Baby	1	29	100	130	158	10	6	2°	1	3^7	5^5	29^3	159^4	NB	SSmith	SummerChild,UnitdMus,WitysCaro	78-0
6-8^1	M1	500	ft	Baby	1	30	102	132^3	200^4	6	2	2	2°	1^1	1^hd	28	200^4	NB	SSmith	IvyLeaguer,SuccessRd,KokoLobell	73-0

ONE MILE PACE
PURSE $14,220
FRIDAY, JULY 19, 1991
PICK FOUR
&
EXACTA

FOURTH RACE

NEW YORK SIRE STAKES
2 YEAR OLD FILLIES

1	3.40	2.80	2.60
4		6.80	6.40
2			3.40
Ex	1-4	16.20	

100 2

WARM UP-BLACK

Program Number | Date | Trk | Purse | Cd | Class | Leaders Time: Dis 1/4 1/2 3/4 | Winners Time | PP | 1/4 | 1/2 | 3/4 | Str | Fin | Ind 1/4 Time | Ind Time | Odds | Driver | Order Of Finish: First Second Third | Temp

5-2 1 COASTAL DAMAGE (NY) — YELLOW
b f 2 StormDamage-Jef'sMaui-WindshieldWiper
Waples Stable Inc, Campbellville, Ont.
RONALD WAPLES (145) blue-gold (0-0-0-0-.000) Tr—Gerald Nelson (.000)
1991 2 0 1 0 $125 First Starter Lifetime $125

Date	Trk	Purse	Cd	Class	Dis	1/4	1/2	3/4	Time	PP	1/4	1/2	3/4	Str	Fin	Ind 1/4 Time	Ind Time	Odds	Driver	Order Of Finish	Temp
7-10 91	M1		ft	QUA	1	29	59	127	156	8	4	5	6	5	4	28	157	NB	RWaples	Ironridge,Alazar,TooSharp	75-0
7-3 91	M1	6000	ft	2yrF	1	29	59	131	159	7	5°	6°	2°	8	8	31	202	6.30	JMoiseyev	TochLghtly,StngNoucar,PrayForan	78-0
6-22 91	M1	500	ft	Baby	1	30	100	131	200	3	6	7	8	4	2	28	200	NB	RWaples	Jatuma,CoastalDamag,Dazzinglght	76-0
6-14 91	YR		ft	QUA	1	30	101	131	202	8	8	8	6	7	7		204	NB	RWaples	SwtChf,Incrediblnow,antShDwn	71-0

12-1 2 REGROUP (NY) — WHITE
b f 2 Niatross-Trudy'sPrecious-PreciousFella
Warren J. Chernin, North Brunswick, NJ.
DONALD WIEST (165) or-wh (0-0-0-0-.000) Tr—Donald Wiest (.000)
1991 1 0 0 0 $00 First Starter Lifetime $00

Date	Trk	Purse	Cd	Class	Dis	1/4	1/2	3/4	Time	PP	1/4	1/2	3/4	Str	Fin	Ind 1/4 Time	Ind Time	Odds	Driver	Order Of Finish	Temp
7-14 91	RcR	2000	ft	2YRMAIDEN	1	29	100	132	201	2	3	4°	4	4	8		203	62.40	DWiest	RadiantFF,YankSchonr,MyCnamonGn	78-0
7-6 91	RcRx		ft	QUA	1	29	100	130	202	2	1	1	1	3	8	36	206	NB	DWiest	BooBooDoo,WatMain,MarylandLady	84-0

10-1 3 FABERGIE (NY) — PURPLE
b f 2 StormDamage-SunrayPrsca-ColumbiaGeorge
Prestige Stable, Hinsdale, Ill.
KIM CRAWFORD (155) red-blk-wh (636-139-114-64-.352) Tr—Wayne Nickells (.000)
1991 0 0 0 0 $00 First Starter Lifetime $00

Date	Trk	Purse	Cd	Class	Dis	1/4	1/2	3/4	Time	PP	1/4	1/2	3/4	Str	Fin	Ind 1/4 Time	Ind Time	Odds	Driver	Order Of Finish	Temp
7-10 91	M1		ft	QUA	1	30	100	130	158	8	7	6°	6	6	6	29	201	NB	WNickells	KnowHow,JustRacin,SpicyScooter	75-0
7-6 91	M1		ft	QUA	1	28	59	128	158	x9x	10	10	10	10	10			NB	WNickells	Pensive,Sovereignty,GvsBunny	75-0

9-2 4 HELEN LOBELL (NY) — BLACK
b f 2 PraisedDignity-HansaLobell-Jamuga
Nova Meadows Inc, Sterling, Va. & John L. Baxter, Clarksburg, NJ.
JOHN BAXTER (150) blu-wh (0-0-0-0-.000) Tr—John Baxter (.000)
1991 5 0 0 1 $85 First Starter Lifetime $85

Date	Trk	Purse	Cd	Class	Dis	1/4	1/2	3/4	Time	PP	1/4	1/2	3/4	Str	Fin	Ind 1/4 Time	Ind Time	Odds	Driver	Order Of Finish	Temp
7-6 91	YR	20000	sy	2YRF STK	1	28	59	130	203	2	1°	2	4	8	8		205	21.40	JBaxter	SahawkSis,Lovablstvr,FoinBigns	79-0
6-27 91	YR	500	ft	2YRF	1	29	101	131	203	2	3	3°	2	2	3		203	NB	JBaxter	RazzleHanover,Gaboing,HlnLobl	87-0
6-15 91	M1	500	ft	Baby	1	31	101	132	202	x9x	10	10	10	7	6	30	204	NB	JBaxter	DirectMelody,CoranLobel,Capri	78-0
6-9 91	M1 A	20162	ft	2yrF Stk	1	29	58	127	156	x8x	12	12	12	12	12			84.50	JBaxter	ChinaPrncs,HazltonKay,SeyorLovld	80-0
5-31 91	GTY1		ft	QUA	1	30	102	132	200	5	2	2	2	2	2	28	201	NB	JBaxter	Scandalizer,HelenLobel,FiftySims	80-0
5-25 91	M1	500	ft	Baby	1	29	101	132	200	4	3	x7	7	7	6	28	201	NB	JBaxter	BlvFcson,AmbroKran,BroanKarmon	83-0

4-1 5 NASTASIA ALMAHURST (NY) — GREEN
b f 2 PraisedDignity-Nastassia-TylerB
D.R. Firmstone, Penn Yan, NY. & K.E. Ball, Oakfield, NY.
KENNETH BALL (135) brown-gold (1-0-0-0-.000) Tr—Kenneth Ball (.000)
1991 3 0 0 2 $1,156 First Starter Lifetime $1,156

Date	Trk	Purse	Cd	Class	Dis	1/4	1/2	3/4	Time	PP	1/4	1/2	3/4	Str	Fin	Ind 1/4 Time	Ind Time	Odds	Driver	Order Of Finish	Temp
7-6 91	Gosh	7363	ft	2YRF STK	1	30	103	134	205	6	4	4	6	4	3		206	NB	KBall	CragheNancy,Fnqn,Nastasiamanns	N-0
6-26 91	BR	1600	ft	MONF-MCD	1	30	102	135	206	2	2	2	3	3	3	30	206	3.90	KBall	QSAbsdon,CncyBamb,Nastasiamanns	84-0
6-16 91	BR	1600	ft	MONCD	1	30	102	133	203	4	5	5	6	6	5	31	205	18.60	KBall	SirMagicalElite,FirAlack,BCoins	80-0
6-6 91	BR		ft	QUA	1	31	102	134	205	3	2	3	3	4	4	31	206	NB	KBall	GathouseBnty,Socrtted,BCoins	80-0
5-30 91	BR		ft	QUA	1	32	103	137	210	4	5	5	6	5	3	31	210	NB	KBall	ChsaaEnrgy,MontnAsh,Nataslmnt	78-0

10-1 6 YOUNG NICBETH (NY) — RED
b f 2 Niatross-TD'sBeauty-BretHanover
S. Goldfarb, Contact High Stbl, J. Manni Jr., J. Guilfoyle
STEPHEN SMITH (160) gray-red-black (0-0-0-0-.000) Tr—Stephen Smith (.000)
1991 1 0 0 0 $40 First Starter Lifetime $40

Date	Trk	Purse	Cd	Class	Dis	1/4	1/2	3/4	Time	PP	1/4	1/2	3/4	Str	Fin	Ind 1/4 Time	Ind Time	Odds	Driver	Order Of Finish	Temp
6-20 91	YR	500	ft	2YRF	1	30	102	132	203	6	5	5	4	4	4		204	NB	SSmith	RazzleHanover,HrcanHathr,CragheNancy	80-0

8-1 7 A T'S SUSAN (NY) — BROWN
ch f 2 SeahawkHanover-MyPaula-Nero
Antonios Tsougarakis, Clarksburg, NJ.
DONALD DANCER (130) blu-go (3-1-1-0-.519) Tr—Robert Riddle (.000)
1991 1 0 0 0 $25 First Starter Lifetime $25

Date	Trk	Purse	Cd	Class	Dis	1/4	1/2	3/4	Time	PP	1/4	1/2	3/4	Str	Fin	Ind 1/4 Time	Ind Time	Odds	Driver	Order Of Finish	Temp
7-12 91	YR		ft	QUA	1	31	101	133	204	7	5	5	4°	3	3		204	NB	RMojcio	Stingetti,SubCompact,ATsSusan	N-0
6-20 91	YR	500	ft	2YRF	1	30	102	132	203	7	7	6	5	5	5		204	NB	RMojcio	RazzleHanover,HrcanHathr,CragheNancy	80-0

3-1 8 SUZY SEAHAWK (NY) — GRAY
b f 2 SeahawkHanover-MostHappySuzy-MostHappyFella
M.R. Cohen, Huntington Sta., NY. & V. Cohen, Wantagh, NY.
WALLY HENNESSEY (140) bl-go-wh (231-53-42-38-.385) Tr—Nicholas Sodano (.000)
1991 0 0 0 0 $00 First Starter Lifetime $00

Date	Trk	Purse	Cd	Class	Dis	1/4	1/2	3/4	Time	PP	1/4	1/2	3/4	Str	Fin	Ind 1/4 Time	Ind Time	Odds	Driver	Order Of Finish	Temp
7-13 91	M1		sy	QUA	1	30	101	132	200	2	2	2	2	3	3	28	200	NB	JCampbell	Pensive,DazzlingLght,SuzySeahawk	80-1
7-6 91	M1		ft	QUA	1	28	59	128	158	10	9	9°	7	7	5	30	200	NB	MLachance	Pensive,Sovereignty,GvsBunny	73-0

Here's how it worked. For our main ticket, we used the 5-6-8 with the 1-8 with the 2-3 with the 1-2-3-6. The 24 combinations cost $48. We spent $12 more on two separate tickets using the two question mark horses with only our best selections in each race. To save with the 4, we bet the 5-6 with the 4 with the 2-3 with the 2-3. That cost $8. To save with the 10, we bet the 5-6 with the 1 with the 2-3 with the 10. That cost $4. The total investment was $60.

We thought we were on our way to a good night with the Daily Double when one of the three horses we used in the first race won and paid $22. We had used five horses in the second race (the 15 $2 combinations cost $30), and we expected to cash, very possibly for more than $100. Wrong. Every now and then, racing has a way of knocking you silly for being so presumptuous. An 8-1 shot we didn't have beat a 6-1 shot we did. The winning horse was 1-for-34 lifetime. Ouch.

But the Pick 4 started well. Our 5, 6 and 8 in the first race of the Pick 4 went off 6-1, 4-5 and 13-1. The 5, Cut 'N Dried, won by 1¾ lengths and paid $14. Getting the 4-5 shot out of the Pick 4 was a definite plus.

We had the 1-8 on our main ticket and the 4 on our saver in the next race. They went off at odds of 3-5, 5-1 and 12-1. We thought we'd blown our chance for a decent payoff when the 3-5 favorite, Coastal Damage, beat our 12-1 saver, Helen Lobell, by just half a length. Regardless, we were still alive heading into Race 3 with our main ticket and the saver using the 10 in the final race.

This is the fun part. Saratoga's computers allow you to see Pick 4 payoffs after just two races. We anxiously waited for the payoffs with our two horses in Race 3: the 2, Seahawk Sis, and the 3, Miss Goodbody. If the names ring a bell give yourself a star. Their merits were analyzed in the last chapter.

With Seahawk Sis, our five live $1 Pick 4 tickets were paying: $98, $115, $31, $197 and $492. Not bad except for one. However, the $1 payoffs with Miss Goodbody were: $1,970, $1,313, $1,970, $1,970 and $1,970. My heart skipped a beat. And on a note of pure avarice, these were the payoffs with Coastal Damage ($3.40) winning the second race. What would our live saver tickets be paying if 12-1 Helen Lobell won? It wouldn't have mattered, because the saving ticket with her didn't win.

Miss Goodbody did, easily, by 2¼ lengths. She paid $16.20. Showtime!

We were now live with five of the nine horses in the finale to the Pick 4. Now was the time to save, and with the huge payoffs, it wasn't a difficult decision. Had Seahawk Sis won and left us facing payoffs as low as $31, betting any more to save would have been foolish.

The luxury of Miss Goodbody's payoffs meant we could save by betting the other four horses enough to make a substantial return. If one of our five live tickets won, how much would it matter if the return was $50-$100 less? Not much. And we didn't have to bet much to cover ourselves. The four horses we didn't have went off at 14-1, 27-1, 19-1 and 47-1. We bet $10 win and a $2 exacta wheel on the lower two of the four, and a $1 exacta wheel with the other two for a total cost of $68. The estimated returns were somewhere from $250-$400 depending on the exacta payoff. The peace of mind was well worth it.

The 10 horse, Speed Artist, won by a nose at 17-1 over the 6 horse, Gray Bandit, the 7-2 second choice. The Pick 4 payoff was the same with both. Picking up $1,970 from a $1 Pick 4 saver bet felt awfully sweet.

Also Eligibles

CHAPTER 11

The Claim Game

Claimers race at all levels, cheap to incredibly expensive. What's most important when handicapping them is to identify how they have performed at the level they're racing at tonight. There's an old adage about handicapping: Never ask a horse to do something he's never done. In other words, don't ask a horse who can win a $6,000 claimer to win at $10,000. That's true with one vital codicil: if he has shown he can't win at that higher level. If a horse loses three races at $10,000 badly, drops down to $6,000 and wins easily twice, and then moves back to $10,000, his current form from the two wins won't be enough to compensate for his class because he has shown—at least from his available PPs—that he doesn't have the class to win at $10,000.

This is anything but black and white. Some horses may still be improving, even at the age of 5, and thus haven't defined their class. Or a horse may be claimed, and then perform dramatically better for his new trainer and/or driver.

Plus, don't forget that we only get a look at a horse's six to eight PPs. In previous PPs not in the program, he might have shown that he's won at a higher level or lost at a lower one. Yet again, familiarity is an asset. Going to the track on Saturday night for a couple months may give you a look at important races not in his current PPs. Remember, take any edge you can.

General Knight showed up in a claiming race for $70,000 at The Meadowlands, May 30, 1992. He drew the 8 post.

9 MEADOWLANDS
PACE
ONE MILE
WARM UP COLOR-PURPLE
PURSE $22,000
ASK FOR HORSE BY PROGRAM NUMBER

EXACTA AND SECOND HALF OF LATE DOUBLE
CLAIMING HANDICAP $40000 - $75000
POST POSITIONS DRAWN TO PRICE

128th RACING DAY SATURDAY,MAY 30, 1992

Column heads: Date, Track Race #, Purse, Tk, Cd, Tmp, Class; Leaders Time Winners: Dist, 1/4, 1/2, 3/4, Time; P.P., 1/4, 1/2, 3/4, Str, Finish, Lst 1/4, Time, Odds, Driver; Order of Finish: First Second Third; Temp Allow

30-1 NILAN (L) br g, 5, by Albatross—Trutara Hanover by Tar Heel
Pasquale Cecio Jr., Greenwich, Conn.
$72,072 - 4, 1:531 (1) Driver-EDDIE DAVIS 167 (wht-red) (618-54-52-64-.169)
BREEDER-HANOVER SHOE FARMS INC,PA.
Tr.-Marschia Gardner (.245)
M1 1:542 1992 17 3 2 4 $26,880
M1 1:531 1991 32 5 5 5 $30,947
1 ♦ 40,000 RED

Date	Track Race #	Purse	Tk	Class	Dist	1/4	1/2	3/4	Time	PP	1/4	1/2	3/4	Str	Finish	Lst 1/4	Time	Odds	Driver	Order of Finish	Temp
5-23	M1 9	22000	ft	40000CLHC	1	28	561	1243	152	1	32¼	33¼	42¼	55¼	53¼	272	1523	42.50L	EDavis	RamsyHanovr,PckUpYorFt,DgntyofMan	85-0
5-16	M1 10	15000	ft	nw4 cd	1	274	563	1251	1524	8	88¼	x1019	1024	10dis	1031P9	29	159	27.40L	EDavis	ColFlyingFla,HnryLtsgo,NoTwstr	54-0
5-9	M1 7	22000	ft	40000CLHC	1	273	544	124	1514	1	1½	32½	53½	43½	54½	28	1523	15.60L	EDavis	RmsyHnvr,PckUpYrFt,GnrlKnght	60-0
5-2	M1 7	20000	ft	40000CLHC	1	274	544	1224	152	1	31¾	42½	53½	43½	32½	29	1522	53.80L	EDavis	GnralKnght,RamsyHanovr,Nilan	75-0
4-24	M1 11	14000	sy	Z30000CLHC	1	274	562	1253	1541	1	31¾	11½	1½	31½	104½	301	1554	*1.60L	JMoiseyev	PlgrmsPunch,NoRansom,KngCharls	68-0
4-10	M1 11	14000	ft	30000CLHC	1	282	562	1254	154	1	1o1	11½	11½	11½	2½	282	1541	*1.60L	JMoiseyev	Krenshaw,Nilan,TownAngel	52-0
4-3	M1 1	14000	ft	30000CLHC	1	274	553	1254	155	5	2o½	11½	11½	11½	2½	292	1551	*2.70L	JMoiseyev	Dictionary,Nilan,DaBen	34-2

15-1 PIANIST b g, 5, by French Chef—Enid Gray by Lieutenant Gray
Pianist Stable, Campbell Hall, N.Y.
$145,870 - 4, 1:532 (1) Driver-RAY SCHNITTKER 145 (br-go-wht) (60-4-9-9-.200)
BREEDER-CLEARVIEW STABLES,CONN.
Tr.-Warren Schnitker (.203)
M1 1:543 1992 19 2 3 2 $42,350
M1 1:532 1991 32 5 5 5 $54,625
2 ♦ 40,000 BLUE

Date	Track Race #	Purse	Tk	Class	Dist	1/4	1/2	3/4	Time	PP	1/4	1/2	3/4	Str	Finish	Lst 1/4	Time	Odds	Driver	Order of Finish	Temp
5-23	M1 9	22000	ft	40000CLHC	1	28	561	1243	152	2	44	54½	64½	45	42½	271	1523	13.40	RSchnittker	RamsyHanovr,PckUpYorFt,DgntyofMan	85-0
5-16	M1 6	22000	ft	40000CLHC	1	27	544	1234	1514	2	32½	54½	53½	53½	3½	273	152	52.20	RSchnittker	RameyHanover,SandKey,Pianist	54-0
5-9	M1 7	22000	ft	40000CLHC	1	273	544	124	1514	2	54	75	94	910	9o½	283	1534	18.10	JDoherty	RmsyHnvr,PckUpYrFt,GnrlKnght	60-0
5-2	M1 11	12000	ft	nw9000L7cd	1	29	584	1261	1534	8	9o9½	8o4	5o3½	34	2ns	284	1534	5.60	JDoherty	DrawingBoard,Pianist,SanAndre	75-0
4-25	M1 4	11000	ft	nw8500L7cd	1	274	574	1271	1544	2	21½	21½	21½	1½	11½	272	1544	*.90	BWebster	Pianist,JpsRebel,DrawingBoard	42-0
4-11	M1 11	16000	ft	nw13500L7	1	284	564	1254	1534	3	55	65½	85½	54½	54	273	1543	17.40	RSchnittker	LtnnyLadN,ScotshStag,SandKy	45-0
4-3	M1 3	11000	ft	nw8500L7cd	1	292	1001	1294	1572	3	32½	42½	53½	76½	42½	272	1574	4.80	RPierce	AMond,OrangSovrgn,SamyAlmahrst	34-2

7-2 DIGNITY OF MAN (L) b h, 5, by Praised Dignity—Leslie Hanover by Best of All
Royal Stable,Lincroft,N.J.
$250,579 - 5, 1:522 (1) Driver-JOHN CAMPBELL 155 (wht-mar-blue) (1146-195-142-141-.280)
BREEDER-LANA LOBELL FMS OF NJ INC,etc.
Tr.-Rosemary Smutz St.-R.Flis (.241)
M1 1:522 1992 17 5 0 2 $61,150
M1 1:531 1991 13 4 3 1 $57,985
3 ▼ 55,000 WHITE

Date	Track Race #	Purse	Tk	Class	Dist	1/4	1/2	3/4	Time	PP	1/4	1/2	3/4	Str	Finish	Lst 1/4	Time	Odds	Driver	Order of Finish	Temp
5-23	M1 9	22000	ft	60000CLHC	1	28	561	1243	152	4	55½	4o4½	3o1½	33½	32	273	1522	2.40L	JoCampbell	RamsyHanovr,PckUpYorFt,DgntyofMan	85-0
5-16	M1 6	22000	ft	70000CLHC	1	27	544	1234	1514	7	77½	8o5½	6o4	64½	41	272	152	3.40L	JoCampbell	RameyHanover,SandKey,Pianist	54-0
5-9	M1 12	16000	ft	nw13500L7	1	274	553	1234	1522	3	67	6o4½	5o4½	32	11½	274	1522	*.90L	JoCampbell	DgntyofMan,SandKy,ShognHanovr	60-0
5-2	M1 9	17000	ft	nw13750L7	1	274	561	1243	1523	2	34½	32½	2o1½	21½	11½	274	1523	3.60L	JoCampbell	DgntyofMan,SmartAly,JpsRebel	75-0
4-25	M1 6	30000	ft	Opn	1	28	551	124	1521	1	55	65½	52½	56	89½	293	1541	67.70L	WFahy	NuclearFlsh,PrncEbny,Echlon	42-0
3-28	M1 5	22000	ft	60000CLHC	1	272	57	1262	1534	1	33½	54½	53½	54½	49½	284	1554	22.10	CManzi	Bookmaker,GnralKnght,JsPurky	32-2
3-21	Fhld 6A	11000	ft	WO15000CD	1	274	563	1254	1562	1	4	4	52½	64½	67½	312	1574	2.40	JMoiseyev	MontanHidaway,Camlid,WghtwarCanyon	35-1

10-1 SAND KEY (L) br g, 5, by Artie's Dream—Penny Royal by Airliner
The Alycon Stable,Dresher,Pa.
$155,520 - 4, 1:512 (1) Driver-RON PIERCE 138 (red-wht-blu) (843-104-107-130-.245)
BREEDER-CARMINE ABBATIELLO SB INC,N.J.
Tr.-Jerry Evilsizor (.260)
M1 1:554 1992 15 2 4 2 $31,740
M1 1:512 1991 35 4 5 5 $62,900
4 ♦ 60,000 GREEN

Date	Track Race #	Purse	Tk	Class	Dist	1/4	1/2	3/4	Time	PP	1/4	1/2	3/4	Str	Finish	Lst 1/4	Time	Odds	Driver	Order of Finish	Temp
5-23	M1 9	22000	ft	60000CLHC	1	28	561	1243	152	5	66½	64	5o3½	76½	84	282	1533	4.30L	RPierce	RamsyHanovr,PckUpYorFt,DgntyofMan	85-0
5-16	M1 6	22000	ft	60000CLHC	1	27	544	1234	1514	4	21½	43½	4o2½	32½	2ns	273	1514	12.10L	RPierce	RameyHanover,SandKey,Pianist	54-0
5-9	M1 12	16000	ft	nw13500L7	1	274	553	1234	1522	1	43½	1½	21½	43	21½	283	1523	6.60L	RPierce	DgntyofMan,SandKy,ShognHanovr	60-0
5-2	M1 7	20000	ft	60000CLHC	1	274	544	1224	152	4	1½	21½	42½	54	87½	301	1532	14.20L	JSchwind	GnralKnght,RamsyHanovr,Nilan	75-0
4-25	M1 7	20000	ft	CL HC	1	274	553	1241	1531	scr	sick									JsPurky,PckUpYorFt,RamsyHanovr	42-0
4-18	M1 4	20000	ft	NW15500L6	1	283	57	1244	1523	2	43½	42½	54	52½	3½	271	1524	24.20L	JSchwind	LtnnyLadN,BostonBluChp,SandKy	42-0
4-11	M1 11	16000	ft	nw13500L7	1	284	564	1254	1534	7	7o7½	7o6½	6o4½	44	33	274	1542	3.40L	JoCampbell	LtnnyLadN,ScotshStag,SandKy	45-0

6-1 PICK UP YOUR FEET b h, 6, by Abercrombie—Sinuous by Bye Bye Byrd
M.Mintz,R.P.Frantz & R.Ross Inc., N.J., N.Y., Pa.
$296,552 - 4, 1:524 (1) Driver-MIKE LACHANCE 149 (red-blk-wht) (1035-123-160-114-.241)
BREEDER-ALINE WHITE,QUE.
Tr.-Russell Frantz (.214)
M1 1:542 1992 17 2 5 4 $35,765
1991 5 0 0 0 $3,800
5 ▲ 60,000 BLACK

Date	Track Race #	Purse	Tk	Class	Dist	1/4	1/2	3/4	Time	PP	1/4	1/2	3/4	Str	Finish	Lst 1/4	Time	Odds	Driver	Order of Finish	Temp
5-23	M1 9	22000	ft	55000CLHC	1	28	561	1243	152	3	21½	21½	21½	22	21	272	1521	8.40	MLachance	RamsyHanovr,PckUpYorFt,DgntyofMan	85-0
5-16	M1 6	22000	ft	70000CLHC	1	27	544	1234	1514	6	4o2½	2½	31½	21½	62½	28	1521	6.50	MLachance	RameyHanover,SandKey,Pianist	54-0
5-9	M1 7	22000	ft	65000CLHC	1	273	544	124	1514	6	2o1½	21	31½	21½	21½	274	152	3.70	MLachance	RmsyHnvr,PckUpYrFt,GnrlKnght	60-0
5-2	M1 7	20000	ft	65000CLHC	1	274	544	1224	152	6	4o2½	3o1½	2ons	31½	54½	30	1524	3.90	MLachance	GnralKnght,RamsyHanovr,Nilan	75-0
4-25	M1 7	20000	ft	NW14500CD	1	274	553	1241	1531	2	42½	4o1½	1½	11	2hd	29	1531	5.70	WODonnell	JsPurky,PckUpYorFt,RamsyHanovr	42-0
4-18	M1 4	20000	ft	nw15500L6	1	283	57	1244	1523	1	31½	3o1½	2o1½	22	41	274	1524	15.60	CManzi	LtnnyLadN,BostonBluChp,SandKy	42-0
4-11	M1 7	20000	ft	nw16500L7	1	29	554	1243	1541	1	4o1½	1ohd	2ohd	21½	69½	312	156	3.00	RPierce	BostonBluChp,Townation,OSoBrav	45-0

20-1 THREE FOR THE ROAD ch h, 5, by On The Road Again—Dozen Roses by Bret Hanover
John Karikas,Bronx,N.Y.
$54,000 - 4, 1:53 (1) Driver-RAY REMMEN 170 (wht-grn-go) (214-30-32-26-.264)
BREEDER-JOHN KARIKAS,N.Y.
Tr.-Larry Remmen St.-R.Remmen (.279)
M1 1:531 1992 9 3 1 0 $16,200
M1 1:53 1991 17 3 1 5 $24,350
6 ▼ 60,000 YELLOW

Date	Track Race #	Purse	Tk	Class	Dist	1/4	1/2	3/4	Time	PP	1/4	1/2	3/4	Str	Finish	Lst 1/4	Time	Odds	Driver	Order of Finish	Temp
5-23	M1 9	22000	ft	75000CLHC	1	28	561	1243	152	9	910½	99½	86½	66½	64	27	1524	24.80	RRemmen	RamsyHanovr,PckUpYorFt,DgntyofMan	85-0
5-16	M1 10	15000	ft	nw4 cd	1	274	563	1251	1524	3	54½	4o3½	3o2	2½	43	274	1532	4.50	RRemmen	ColFlyingFla,HnryLtsgo,NoTwstr	54-0
5-9	M1 8	15000	ft	nw4 cd	1	273	55	1234	1524	10	9o8½	8o9½	9o8	65½	2½	273	153	2.50	JoCampbell	PradwnBy,ThrForThRoad,JdgRyan	60-0
5-1	M1 8	9000	ft	nw7500L7cd	1	282	562	1251	1531	3	7o5½	5o3½	3oo1	12½	13½	274	1531	*1.20	RRemmen	ThrForThRd,UndrWranty,HotWalkr	55-0
4-25	M1 1	8000	ft	nw5000L7cd	1	282	57	1262	1543	8	88	85½	8oo4½	1hd	13½	272	1543	2.00	JoCampbell	ThrForThRoad,FarChpN,BadSt	42-0
4-18	M1 2	8000	ft	nw5000L7cd	1	281	58	1264	1552	6	8o9½	6o4½	6o4	32	1ns	274	1552	*1.50	RRemmen	ThrForThRd,FrChpN,ImprovsHnvr	42-0
4-11	M1 8	15000	ft	nw4 cd	1	293	572	1264	1551	1	32½	44½	54	56½	54	284	1562	21.90	RRemmen	Cameradene,JudgeRyan,BondStr	45-0

15-1 JESSEE PURKEY‡ b g, 6, by Walton Hanover—Tia Hanover by Tyler B
R.Press,M.Rosenblum,M.Tullo & R.Spetz, N.Y., N.J.
$397,210 - 6, 1:531 (1) Driver-JOE PAVIA JR 135 (mar-go-wh) (67-3-11-3-.151)
BREEDER-BILLIE J.JESSEE,PA.
Tr.-Robert Bongiorno (.274)
M1 1:531 1992 20 6 0 2 $81,240
Mea⅝ 1:532 1991 34 10 4 8 $106,669
7 ▲ 70,000 PINK

Date	Track Race #	Purse	Tk	Class	Dist	1/4	1/2	3/4	Time	PP	1/4	1/2	3/4	Str	Finish	Lst 1/4	Time	Odds	Driver	Order of Finish	Temp
5-23	M1 9‡	22000	ft	Z65000CLHC	1	28	561	1243	152	7	89½	8o8¾	9o6½	9x9½	9x8¾	274	1534	11.80	ABier	RamsyHanovr,PckUpYorFt,DgntyofMan	85-0
5-16	M1 6‡	22000	ft	65000CLHC	1	27	544	1234	1514	5	65½	76½	7o5½	76½	51¾	272	1521	11.70	ABier	RameyHanover,SandKey,Pianist	54-0
5-9	M1 7‡	22000	ft	70000CLHC	1	273	544	124	1514	7	65½	5o3½	2o1	54½	78½	291	1532	7.60	ABier	RmsyHnvr,PckUpYrFt,GnrlKnght	60-0
5-2	M1 7‡	20000	ft	70000CLHC	1	274	544	1224	152	8	10o10	98½	9o6½	85½	64	29	1531	8.50	ABier	GnralKnght,RamsyHanovr,Nilan	75-0
4-25	M1 7‡	20000	ft	70000CLHC	1	274	553	1241	1531	6	76	75	5o3½	33	1hd	282	1531	15.10	ABier	JsPurky,PckUpYorFt,RamsyHanovr	42-0
4-18	M1 4‡	20000	ft	75000CLHC	1	283	57	1244	1523	10	910	97	9o8½	97½	95½	271	1534	13.30	ABier	LtnnyLadN,BostonBluChp,SandKy	42-0
4-11	M1 9‡	25000	ft	w 15000 L1	1	284	574	1262	1533	4	67	4o3½	3o1½	32½	65½	28	1543	5.60	ABier	Coplan,GnralKnight,JakandElwod	45-0

6-1 GENERAL KNIGHT b h, 5, by Panorama—Cream and Crimson by Happy Motoring
David H. Brooks, Old Westbury, N.Y.
$330,084 - 5, 1:52 (1) Driver-MICKEY MC NICHOL 160 (blu-blk-wht) (677-70-68-64-.191)
BREEDER-KENTUCKIANA FARMS,KY.
Tr.-A.(Tony) Monica (.253)
M1 1:52 1992 19 2 5 2 $52,550
M1 1:523 1991 32 4 7 3 $148,810
8 ▲ 70,000 GRAY

Date	Track Race #	Purse	Tk	Class	Dist	1/4	1/2	3/4	Time	PP	1/4	1/2	3/4	Str	Finish	Lst 1/4	Time	Odds	Driver	Order of Finish	Temp
5-23	Fhld 11A	20000	ft	PREFINVHC	1	274	564	125	154	2	4	5	53½	53½	51¾	284	1542	7.30	RPierce	Perpetuity,Cambest,SteelyGlow	89-0
5-16	Fhld 11A	20000	sy	PREFINVHC	1	281	58	127	1551	3	5	6	4o3	42½	34½	282	156	2.80	RPierce	ArcanHanovr,StlyGlow,GnralKnght	50-0
5-9	M1 7	22000	ft	75000CLHC	1	273	544	124	1514	9	7o7½	6o4½	4o2½	33	32	274	1521	3.50	RPierce	RamsyHanovr,PckUpYorFt,GnralKnght	60-0
5-2	M1 7	20000	ft	75000CLHC	1	274	544	1224	152	9	2o½	11½	1ns	11	1½	291	152	10.30	RPierce	GnralKnght,RamsyHanovr,Nilan	75-0
4-25	M1 7	20000	ft	60000CLHC2	1	274	553	1241	1531	4	3o1½	2hd	x8x7	8dis	8dis			4.20	JParkerJr	JsPurky,PckUpYorFt,RamsyHanovr	42-0
4-18	M1 4	20000	ft	70000CLHC	1	283	57	1244	1523	9	1o½	21½	32½	42½	52	274	153	3.70	MLachance	LtnnyLadN,BostonBluChp,SandKy	42-0
4-11	M1 9	25000	ft	w 15000 L1	1	284	574	1262	1533	6	11½	11½	11½	11½	2½	272	1534	9.10	CManzi	Coplan,GnralKnight,JakandElwod	45-0

5-2 **RAMSEY HANOVER** b h, 5, by Tyler B--Rhodena Hanover by Strike Out Tr.-Richard Norman St.-Bt Pelling (.394)
Michael Schwartz & Arthur C.Bowen, Calif M1 1:51 4 1992 15 5 2 2 $59,840
$247,041 - 5, 1:51 4 (1) Driver-JACK MOISEYEV 165 (blk-wh-go) (1151-223-137-129-.297) BREEDER-HANOVER SHOE FARMS INC,PA Lex1 1:52 4 1991 17 12 3 1 $174,492
9◆ 75,000 PURPLE

5-23	M1 9	22000	ft	75000CLHC	1 28	56 1	124 3	152	8	1o1½	1 1½	1 1½	1 2	1 1	27 2	152	*1.40	JMoiseyev	RamsyHanovr,PckUpYorF1,DgntyofMan	85-0
5-16	M1 6	22000	ft	75000CLHC	1 27	54 4	123 4	151 4	8	5o4½	1o½	1 1	1 1½	1ns	28	151 4	*.70	JMoiseyev	RamseyHanover,SandKey,Pianist	54-0
5-9	M1 7	22000	ft	75000CLHC	1 27 3	54 4	124	151 4	8	4o3	1o1	1 1	1 1½	1 1¼	27 4	151 4	*1.90	JMoiseyev	RmsyHnvr,PckUpYrF1,GnrlKnght	60-0
5-2	M1 7	20000	ft	75000CLHC	1 27 4	54 4	122 4	152	10	5 3½	5o3	3o1½	2 1	2¾	29 1	152 1	*2.10	JMoiseyev	GnralKnight,RamsyHanovr,Nian	75-0
4-25	M1 7	20000	ft	75000CLHC	1 27 4	55 3	124 1	153 1	8	5o3½	1ono	2½	2 1	3 1½	29 1	153 2	6.30	JMoiseyev	JsPurky,PckUpYorF1,RamsyHanovr	42-0
4-11	M1 7	20000	ft	75000CLHC	1 29	55 4	124 3	154 1	7	2o½	2hd	1hd	1 1½	5 7	31	155 3	*1.90	JMoiseyev	BostonBluChip,Townaton,OSoBrav	45-0
3-28	LA½ 2	10000	gd	PREF	1 28 2	57	125 3	154 2	6	1	2	3	2 2	1¾		154 2	9.00L	RCroghan	RamsyHanovr,TrTyrant,SmothLordN	-0

4-1 **SPECTACLE** b g, 5, by Albatross--Reveille Time by Race Time Tr.-Richard Macomber (.318)
Mountain Top Farm,C.Macomber,E.Hauck Sr. & J.Franzese,Fla,Pa M1 1:51 2 1992 11 3 1 3 $20,561
$110,107 - 5, 1:51 2 (1) Driver-CATELLO MANZI 165 (wht-l blu-blu) (924-112-111-114-.229) BREEDER-THOMSON G STABLES,PA M1 1:52 1 1991 36 9 4 7 $77,180
10▲ 75,000 Blue-Rd

5-23	M1 4	18000	ft	nw12750L7	1 28 1	55 2	124 1	152 2	9	10 9½	9 8	7 5½	3 2	2¾	27 1	152 3	7.50	JoCampbell	JJsRebel,Spctacl,PatsFlagship	85-0
5-16	M1 9	13000	ft	nw10500L7	1 27 4	55 1	123	151 2	1	4 3½	4 4½	2o4	2 2½	1ns	27 3	151 2	*.90	JoCampbell	Spectacle,OurieATan,JunesBaby	54-0
5-9	M1 10	12000	ft	nw9100L7cd	1 28 2	56 1	125	153 4	6	7o6½	7o7½	6o5	3 2½	2nkP1	27 4	153 4	3.10	JoCampbell	Twnton(DQ),Spctacl,PasngChampn	60-0
4-17	PPk⅝ 8	3600	ft	NW2000L6CD	1 28 1	58	126 2	154 4	3	4	3 4½	2o1	2hd	1 2½	28 1	154 4	*.80	WHennessey	Spctacl,EarlyHonor,LicnsToRac	74-0
4-11	PPk⅝ 2	5500	gd	NW3900L6CD	1 28	59 4	128 4	157 2	1	5	4o2	2o1	3 3	5 1¼	28 3	157 3	4.30	RMacomber	PoloPlayer,Narrator,Ragtime	76-0
4-4	PPk⅝ 11	4200	ft	NW2500L6CD	1 28 2	58 3	127 1	156 2	5	6	5o3½	4o2½	4 4	6 2½	29 1	156 4	3.00	RMacomber	InterLog,KnowHow,JimLambert	72-0
3-28	PPk⅝ 6	3900	ft	NW2500L6	1 28 2	58	126 2	155 1	8	3o	1 1½	2 1	4 2½	3 2¾	29	155 3	2.10	RMacomber	PrnsNwSong,Illuminator,Spctacl	75-0

General Knight had been claimed on April 25 at a $60,000 price. He broke that night and finished a distant eighth.

His new owners gave him two races in a $75,000 claimer. He drew the 9 post in each, finishing first by 3/4 of a length in what *Sports Eye* termed a "brave effort," then was third by two lengths.

In those two races, Ramsey Hanover—the 9 horse tonight—was second by 3/4 to the General from the 10 post, then beat him by 2 lengths from the 8 post. Ramsey Hanover had also beaten him the night General Knight was claimed.

General Knight got a slight advantage tonight in post position draw.

Each had raced twice since their last meeting. Ramsey Hanover won both of his starts at the same claiming level. Tonight, off three straight wins, he'd go off a deserving favorite at even money. He'd beaten 7 of his 9 opponents, and some, such as General Knight, more than once.

While Ramsey Hanover was building his winning streak, General Knight raced twice at Freehold's 1/2-mile track. He finished third by 4 1/2 and fifth by 1 3/4, hardly inspirational. But checking out his opponents was interesting. In the first start at Freehold, he was beaten by Arcane Hanover. The next week, he was beaten by Perpetuity as Cambest finished second.

Since *Sports Eye* carried Yonkers's and The Meadowlands' entries in the same issue, we notice—if we're sharp—that both Arcane Hanover and Cambest were entered against each other in the Open Handicap at Yonkers.

Arcane had won two legs of the prestigious George Morton Levy Series. In 1991-92, he'd won 26 races and earned $447,240 from 56 starts.

Cambest was just working himself back into shape with a first, third and second in his only '92 starts, all at Freehold. However, he'd won 15 of 40 starts and $655,530 in 1990-91 while racing against the likes of 1991 Horse of the Year Precious Bunny, Three Wizards and Artsplace—a shoo-in for 1992 Horse of the Year—in races such as the Little Brown Jug and Breeders' Crown. This was an extremely talented colt.

Knowing that General Knight was competitive with these two horses changes the evaluation of his two Freehold defeats.

But the question you always try to answer with claimers remains: 'Has he won or raced well at this level?'

The General certainly had in his last two Meadowlands races. In fact, he'd won and finished third in those races from the 9 post both times. In fact, the PPs reveal that he had beaten six of his rivals tonight, including Ramsey Hanover, the even-money favorite.

General Knight might not be quite as good as Ramsey Hanover, but he was competitive with him and had beaten him. General Knight drifted up in price to 9-1 and won. Ramsey Hanover was out of the money.

What's the Score?

The fundamental message of this book is to take any edge you can; the more information, the better. You can get an advantage by watching a horse warm up in his training mile an hour or so before his race; his demeanor in the post parade, and the way he subsequently scores—his final preparation before the start.

If it's a warm summer night and you're up to a little work, watch horses as they go their final warm-up mile between races.

Identifying horses is easy. Every horse has a saddle cloth color-coded to identify what race he will be in—i.e. the 5th race is green; the 6th is yellow. The number on the cloth indicates his post. Frequently, many horses from the same race warm up in the gap between the same two races.

This doesn't have to be drudgery. You don't have to monitor every horse's training miles. But, if you see a horse breaking all over the place, make a note in your program. Horses making breaks in their warm-ups, especially trotters, are worth avoiding at post time. At the same time, note if a horse looks super sharp in his training mile.

The training mile doesn't guarantee how a horse will do in his race. Many drivers or trainers take a good strong hold during a training mile so the horse doesn't exert himself too much.

Horses should be alert in the post parade and not washy (sweat around the neck which looks white).

Watching scoring can provide an edge. Drivers who will be leaving frequently score their horses faster than their rivals. Sometimes, they don't show that burst of speed initially in front of the grandstand after the post parade, but rather on the straightaway on the backstretch. If you've handicapped a horse to leave, and he appears sluggish scoring, beware.

Also beware that you don't spend too much time watching horses score and forgetting that post time is in two minutes. There's no crueler punishment in racing than handicapping a winning overlay and getting shut out at the windows.

Playing the Favorite—If You Must

Brandon T showed up in a field of seven in the third race at Saratoga, July 2, 1992, making a precipitous drop from a $10,000 claimer to $5,000. He'd won at $10,000 in three of his eight PPs, finished second by a nose in a $15,000 claimer, and won by four lengths at 3-5 when he was dropped from $10,000 to $7,500. In his last start, on a sloppy track at $10,000, he was third by half a length in a race that went in 2:00.3 on a sloppy track! If that wasn't enough, he also was adding the innovative quick-hitch sulky, an equipment change that generated considerable success last summer.

ONE MILE PACE
PURSE $1,800
THURSDAY, JULY 2, 1992
PICK THREE (RACES 3 - 5)
&
EXACTA

THIRD RACE

CLAIMING ALLOWANCE $5000

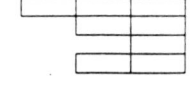

WARM UP-PURPLE

Columns: PROGRAM NUMBER · Date · Trk · Purse · Cd · Class · Leaders Time (Dis 1/4 1/2 3/4) · Winners Time · PP · 1/4 · 1/2 · 3/4 · Str · Fin · Ind 1/4 Time · Ind Time · Odds · Driver · Order Of Finish (First Second Third) · Temp

8-1
1 **CHRISTIAN GB** — b g 8 Ted's Choice(F)-Jamies Express-Jessee Hanover — Scott L. Krouner, Saratoga N.Y.
DAVID MARSHALL (185) ltbl-red-gld (183-20-26-24-.232) Tr—Matthew Medeiros (.319)
PPk ⅝ 1:59^{1} 1992 20 1 3 3 $3,514
Bang 2:00^{3} 1991 31 1 4 4 $5,153
6,1:57 ⅝ Lifetime $18,312
5,000 YELLOW

Date	Trk	Purse	Cd Class	Dis	1/4	1/2	3/4	Time	PP	1/4	1/2	3/4	Str	Fin	Ind 1/4 Time	Ind Time	Odds	Driver	Order Of Finish	Temp
6-26^{92}	Stga	1900	ft 5000CL	1	29	130^{2}	200^{4}	231^{4}	3	4	6	6^{3½}	6	3^{5½}	31^{3}	233^{1}	14.00	DMarshall	MajorCollins,DVFela,ChristianGB	66-0
6-17^{92}	Stga	1900	ft NW2000L7CD	1	29^{1}	100	128^{4}	159^{3}	3	3	2°	2°^{½}	4	6^{3¾}	31^{1}	200^{1}	8.60	DCaploJr	SmashingBG,MoonDance,XpressLane	79-0
6-10^{92}	Stga	1500	ft 3500CL	1	29	100	129^{2}	159^{1}	2	2	3	3^{1½}	3	2^{4½}	30^{2}	200	*1.80	DCaploJr	GypsyFirst,ChristianGB,HdnAcorn	71-0
5-30^{92}	PPk⅝	1700	ft 4000CL	1	28^{2}	57^{4}	126^{3}	156^{4}	8	9	9	8°^{7½}	8^{9¾}	4^{8¾}	30^{1}	158^{2}	56.30	CRichards	Nickerson,CSouperStar,Crashland	80-0
5-23^{92}	PPk⅝	1700	ft 4000CL	1	28	58^{2}	128	157^{3}	7	2°	2	5^{4¾}	5^{6}	5^{8¾}	30^{2}	159^{1}	30.00	CRichards	BtrYt,Dodad,Crashland(Dh)NoDrams	75-0
5-14^{92}	PPk⅝	1700	ft 4000CLCD	1	29^{1}	58^{1}	128^{1}	159^{1}	2	1	1	1^{2}	1^{2¾}	1^{3}	31	159^{1}	4.70	CRichards	ChristianGb,Maradona,LongTimGon	78-0
4-30^{92}	PPk⅝	2185	ft 4000CLCD	1	28^{1}	59	128^{4}	200^{2}	8	1°	3	4	4^{2½}	6^{2}		200^{4}	35.20	CRichards	JJKolb,Maradona,NielsenLobell	71-0
4-23^{92}	PPk⅝	2185	ft 4000CLCD	1	28^{3}	58^{2}	128	158^{2}	6	1°	4	4^{2½}	4^{4}	4^{2½}	31^{2}	159^{4}	39.90	CRichards	KnorsPrmpNirpn,LostMang,VctoryChocs	78-0

10-1
2 **STRIKING BREEZE** — b g 6 Lightning Strikes-Deborah's Woe-Melvin's Woe — John J. Dwyer, Germantown, NY
GERRY MATTISON (160) blue-or-wh (203-35-27-17-.274) Tr—Jane Ordway (.254)
Stga 2:02 1992 14 2 1 2 $2,674
Stga 1:59^{3} 1991 31 2 9 0 $7,070
5,1:59^{3} Lifetime $16,044
5,000 WHITE

Date	Trk	Purse	Cd Class	Dis	1/4	1/2	3/4	Time	PP	1/4	1/2	3/4	Str	Fin	Ind 1/4 Time	Ind Time	Odds	Driver	Order Of Finish	Temp
6-26^{92}	Stga	1900	ft 5000CL	1	29	130^{2}	200^{4}	231^{4}	5	1°	4	4^{2¾}	5	6^{11¾}	32^{4}	234	20.00	JStarkJr	MajorCollins,DVFela,ChristianGB	66-0
6-19^{92}	Stga	1800	ft 5000CL	1	30	101^{1}	131^{1}	200^{2}	8	8	8	8^{8¾}	8	8^{10½}	29^{3}	202^{2}	12.50	JStarkJr	idywodBlizard,DVFla,MajorCoins	71-0
6-5^{92}	Stga	1800	sy 5000CL	1	29^{2}	100^{4}	132	202	8	9	7°	4°^{2¾}	4	3^{3½}	30^{2}	202^{4}	9.30	JStarkJr	Wainbrg,MajorCollins,StrikingBrz	61-0
5-29^{92}	Stga	1800	ft 5000CL	1	28^{4}	58^{3}	129^{4}	201	6	1	2	3^{1½}	4	7^{4¾}	31^{4}	201^{4}	11.30	JStarkJr	JaredsFella,PacinPapy,AutoVancN	71-0
5-22^{92}	Stga	1900	ft 5000CL	1	29^{4}	101	131	201	3	5	4°	4°°^{1½}	3	3^{2½}	30	201^{2}	3.20	JStarkJr	Riveting,MoonRockA,StrikingBrz	61-0
5-15^{92}	Stga	1900	ft 5000CL	1	29	59	129^{1}	200^{2}	7	3°	2°	3°^{1}	7	7^{3½}	31^{3}	201	24.70	JStarkJr	PcnPpy,Winbrg,Prpetra(Dh)SnoUd	71-0
5-8^{92}	Stga	1500	ft 3500CLCD	1	30^{1}	102	132^{2}	202	4	4	2°	2°^{hd}	2	1^{ns}	29^{3}	202	15.00	JStarkJr	StrikingBrz,Rvtng,SatrdayntFvr	61-0
5-1^{92}	Stga	1500	ft 3500CL	1	29^{4}	101^{1}	132^{3}	203	6	6	6	7°^{3}	6	5^{6½}	31	204^{1}	36.30	KCrawford	Wainbrg,Rvtng,SaturdayntFvr	58-0

4-1
3 **MAJOR COLLINS** (NY) — b g 4 Elitist-Lieutenants Rose-Lieutenant Gray — (Lessee) Richard A. Bowman, Norton Hill NY.
RICHARD PUGLIESE (115) gray-black (103-17-11-17-.279) Tr—Susan Kenney (.222)
1992 18 1 3 2 $3,860
YR 1:59^{3} 1991 32 3 1 4 $9,535
3,1:59^{3} Lifetime $30,469
6,250 PURPLE

Date	Trk	Purse	Cd Class	Dis	1/4	1/2	3/4	Time	PP	1/4	1/2	3/4	Str	Fin	Ind 1/4 Time	Ind Time	Odds	Driver	Order Of Finish	Temp
6-26^{92}	Stga	1900	ft 5000CL	1	29	130^{2}	200^{4}	231^{4}	4	5	3°	1°^{½}	1	1^{3}	31	231^{4}	14.00	RPugliese	MajorCollins,DVFela,ChristianGB	66-0
6-19^{92}	Stga	1800	ft 5000CL	1	30	101^{1}	131^{1}	200^{2}	2	3	5	5^{3½}	5	3^{2¾}	29	200^{4}	26.00	RPugliese	idywodBlizard,DVFla,MajorCoins	71-0
6-12^{92}	Stga	1800	ft 5000CL	1	29^{2}	100	130^{3}	159^{3}	6	8	7°	6°^{3¾}	7	6^{7¾}	29^{4}	201	10.80	RPugliese	idywodBlizard,DVFla,Prpostrous	81-0
6-5^{92}	Stga	1800	sy 5000CL	1	29^{2}	100^{4}	132	202	2	3	2°	3^{1½}	2	2^{1}	29^{4}	202^{1}	10.20	RBeachy	Wainbrg,MajorCollins,StrikingBrz	61-0
5-25^{92}	Phld	A 3000	ft 4000CL	1	29	59^{1}	129^{1}	159^{4}	3	6	7	6°^{4½}	6^{3½}	3^{1¾}	30	200	19.10	ABeachy	StrawbryVndor,Ruckus,MajorCoins	54-0
5-20^{92}	Phld	A 3000	ft 4000CLCD	1	29^{1}	100	129^{4}	200	1	2	3	3^{1½}	3^{1½}	3^{2½} pl7	30^{3}	200^{3}	7.00	ABeachy	ToghPolcy,MajorCoins+,Sintargt	70-0
5-10^{92}	Phld	A 3000	gd 4000CL	1	29^{3}	100^{3}	130^{2}	200^{3}	8	9°	9	9°^{6¾}	9^{7½}	8^{9¾}	30^{4}	202^{2}	98.30	ABeachy	Ralphosars,JasonChoc,StormnGos	57-1
4-30^{92}	Phld	A 3000	ft 4000CL	1	28^{4}	59^{4}	130^{2}	200	8	8°	9	9^{5½}	9^{7½}	8^{7}	30^{1}	201^{3}	118.90	ABeachy	MachoBrz,LordsRegN,EnviroDrct	61-0

5-2
4 **BRANDON T** — blk g 6 Trutar Hanover-Princess Brandy-Golden Go — Dyce Martin & Elizabeth Mary Spallutc, Cortland, N.Y.
JOHN STARK JR (145) red-wh-lblu (176-47-21-29-.388) Tr—Scott Leickert (.647)
Stga 1:58 1992 20 7 1 3 $11,521
LouD 1:57^{4} 1991 34 4 5 6 $8,690
5,1:57^{4} Lifetime $30,163
5,000 BLACK

Date	Trk	Purse	Cd Class	Dis	1/4	1/2	3/4	Time	PP	1/4	1/2	3/4	Str	Fin	Ind 1/4 Time	Ind Time	Odds	Driver	Order Of Finish	Temp
6-27^{92}	Stga	2900	sy 10000CL	1	29^{2}	100	130	200^{3}	2	3	2°	3°^{1}	3	3^{¾}	30^{2}	200^{3}	2.30	JStarkJr	RomeoBoy,PalmrBluChip,BrandonT	63-0
6-20^{92}	Stga	3000	ft 10000CL	1	31	132^{4}	203^{1}	233^{1}	1	1	2	4^{1¾}	5	6^{4}	30^{3}	234	*1.50	GMattison	PalmerBlueChip,TopperD,CashwGd	67-0
6-13^{92}	Stga	2900	ft 10000CL	1	29^{3}	59^{4}	129^{2}	159^{1}	4	1	1	1^{3}	1	1^{2½}	29^{4}	159^{1}	*1.00	DCaploJr	BrandonT,TopperD,FirstPromise	82-0
6-3^{92}	Stga	2400	ft 7500CLHC	1	29^{1}	100^{3}	130	159^{1}	5	1	1	1^{1}	1	1^{4}	29^{1}	159^{1}	*.70	JStarkJr	BrandonT,PacinPappy,WtandsBrat	77-0
5-25^{92}	Stga	A 3000	ft 10000CLHC	1	28^{3}	59^{2}	128^{4}	159^{1}	7	4	4°	5°^{2½}	6	5^{2½}	31^{2}	200^{3}	*1.20	JStarkJr	HollysRJB,PaulasBigGuy,AugThDog	58-0
5-16^{92}	Stga	3500	ft 15000CLOP	1	28	57^{4}	128^{4}	158^{4}	1	2	2	2°^{1}	2	2^{ns}	29^{4}	158^{4}	*.50	JStarkJr	TruckinHome,BrandonT,RalphsCapr	60-0
5-9^{92}	Stga	3000	ft 10000CL	1	28^{3}	58^{3}	128	158	1	1	1	1^{2¾}	1	1^{5}	30	158	*.90	JStarkJr	BrandonT,OffTheBench,EastfldDl	70-0
5-2^{92}	Stga	3000	sy 10000CL	1	29	101	132^{2}	202^{3}	1	2	1	1^{1½}	1	1^{2½}	30^{1}	202^{3}	*.30	JStarkJr	BrandonT,FarLapFella,TroubleiAm	60-0

3-1
5 **WALLENBERG** — br g 7 Genghis Khan-J.D. Valley-Harold J. — Checkmate Knight Rc Stb, Scotia, N.Y.
DOUGLAS MAURA (175) black-blue (11-4-3-0-.515) Tr—Douglas Maura (.515)
Stga 2:01^{4} 1992 15 6 3 0 $6,202
Stga 2:03^{4} 1991 12 2 1 0 $1,838
4,1:57^{4} ⅝ Lifetime $16,240
5,000 GREEN

Date	Trk	Purse	Cd Class	Dis	1/4	1/2	3/4	Time	PP	1/4	1/2	3/4	Str	Fin	Ind 1/4 Time	Ind Time	Odds	Driver	Order Of Finish	Temp
6-26^{92}	Stga	1900	ft 5000CL	1	29	130^{2}	200^{4}	231^{4}	1	2	1	2^{½}	3	5^{8}	32^{3}	233^{2}	4.20	DMaura	MajorCollins,DVFela,ChristianGB	66-0
6-19^{92}	Stga	1800	ft 5000CL	1	30	101^{1}	131^{1}	200^{2}	4	5°	2°	2°^{½}	2	6^{5½}	30^{1}	201^{2}	8.50	DMaura	idywodBlizard,DVFla,MajorCoins	71-0
6-5^{92}	Stga	1800	sy 5000CL	1	29^{2}	100^{4}	132	202	3	1°	1	1^{½}	1	1^{1}	30	202	*1.40	DMaura	Wainbrg,MajorColins,StrikingBrz	61-0
5-29^{92}	Stga	1800	ft 5000CL	1	28^{4}	58^{3}	129^{4}	201	scr sk					scr					JaredsFella,PacinPapy,AutoVancN	71-0
5-22^{92}	Stga	1900	ft 5000CL	1	29^{4}	101	131	201	8	9°	8°	7°°^{2½}	7	7^{1½}	31	202^{3}	8.50	DMaura	Riveting,MoonRockA,StrikingBrz	81-0
5-15^{92}	Stga	1900	ft 5000CL	1	29	59	129^{1}	200^{2}	3	6	6	5°°^{2}	4	2^{ns}	30^{4}	200^{2}	3.30	DMaura	PcnPpy,Winbrg,Prpetra(Dh)SnoUd	71-0
5-8^{92}	Stga	2000	ft 5000CLHC	1	29^{2}	100^{3}	131^{1}	201^{4}	4	6	6°	2°°^{1}	1	1^{ns}	30^{2}	201^{4}	2.90	DMaura	Wallenberg,WtandsBrat,SonoUd	61-0
5-1^{92}	Stga	1500	ft 3500CL	1	29^{4}	101^{1}	132^{3}	203	5	5	5°	2°°^{ns}	1	1^{2½}	30^{2}	203	4.20	DMaura	Wainbrg,Rvting,SaturdayntFvr	58-0

6-1 **MINSTREL HILL** — br h 8 FalconAlmahurst-MissyHill-SilentMajority — 1992 1 0 0 0 $152
Deborah A.& Daniel J.Cappello & William F.Davignon, NY. Stga 2:00 1991 16 5 3 3 $9,792
6 DANIEL CAPPELLO JR (115) blue-white (128-24-17-24-.324) Tr—Deborah Cappello (.278) 5,1:57^4 Lifetime $104,233
5,000 RED

Date	Trk	Purse	Cd	Class	Dis	1/4	1/2	3/4	Time	PP	1/4	1/2	3/4	Str	Fin	Ind 1/4 Time	Ind Time	Odds	Driver	Order Of Finish	Temp
6-26^{92}	Stga	1900	ft	5000CL	1	29	130^2	200^4	231^4	6	6	7	5°^{3}½	4	4^{1}½	31^4	233^1	18.30	DCaploJr	MajorCollins,DVFela,ChristianGB	66-0
6-17^{92}	Stga		ft	QUA	1	29^4	58^4	128^2	158^4	1	4	4	4^{2}¾	4	4^{3}	30^3	203^2	NB	DCaploJr	CaesJckpot,ZrchBChp,BrtsHoind	65-0
6-10^{92}	Stga		ft	QUA	1	31^3	102	132^4	203^2	1	3	4	4^1	5	5^{3}½	31	205^2	NB	DCaploJr	XpressLane,EarlPts,HotUtlTcki	66-0
6-22^{91}	Stga	3200	ft	10000CL	1	29	101	130^1	159^2	2	2	2	3^1	3	2^{1}½	29^3	200	12.50	DCaploJr	SixPackSam,MinstrelHil,Niachanc	65-0
6-15^{91}	Stga	3200	ft	10000CL	1	29	59^3	129^3	159^1	2	2	2	2^1	2	4^{1}½	30^3	200^2	4.50	DCaploJr	PlutsFortun,StormySmr,SixPackSam	84-0
6-8^{91}	Stga		ft	QUA	1	31^2	102^2	133^4	204^1	2	1	1	1^{2}½	1	1^{1}½	30^2	204^1	NB	DCaploJr	MinstrelHill,NightRoma,LuckyCam	70-0
5-10^{91}	Stga	3300	ft	15000CL	1	29^2	100^4	130^3	159^4	4	5	5	5°^{2}½	5	6^{3}½	29^2	200^2	8.50	DCaploJr	Fourtwentytwo,Synergy,AwesomAus	70-0
5-3^{91}	Stga	3300	ft	15000CL	1	28^3	100^4	130^3	200^1	2	3	4	5^2	5	3^{3}½	30	201	5.10	DCaploJr	GypsyHillBrent,Synrgy,MinstrlHil	50-0

12-1 **GETTY** — b h 5 Royce-Gorgeous-ColumbiaGeorge — 1992 4 0 2 0 $2,187
Stas Racing Stable & Anthony J.Pellegrino, NY YR 1:58^3 1991 31 4 3 3 $14,157
7 JOHN STASKOWSKI (125) red-white (0-0-0-0-.000) Tr—Michael Staskowski (.111) 3,1:56 1 Lifetime $32,903
5,000 BROWN

Date	Trk	Purse	Cd	Class	Dis	1/4	1/2	3/4	Time	PP	1/4	1/2	3/4	Str	Fin	Ind 1/4 Time	Ind Time	Odds	Driver	Order Of Finish	Temp
6-27^{92}	Stga		ft	QUA	1	30^4	101^4	133^1	203^3	7	6	6	7°^{3}½	6	5^{3}½	30^2	204^1	NB	JStaskows	Keller,FRJack,SundanceNancy	62-0
5-30^{92}	Stga		ft	QUA	1	30^3	101	131	201^4	x5	pu				dnf			NB	JStaskows	SgnalHlHrb,PoconoWolf,DancMHom	60-0
2-3^{92}	YR	4000	ft	10000CL	1	28^3	59^2	130^2	200^3	3	5	6°	4°°	4^{3}½	8^{6}½		201^4	15.00	RDagnalt	BisEncor,Yalcombacknow,RghtOnCon	30-0
1-28^{92}	YR A	4000	ft	10000CL	1	28	58^4	129^2	200^4	6	6	3°°	3°	2^1	2^{nk}		200^4	*1.40	WCaseJr	ImDunrovin,Getty,Autobot	35-0
1-10^{92}	YR	4750	ft	NW4000L8CD	1	28^2	59^2	129^4	200^3	2	4	3°	2°	3^{2}½	2^{ns}		200^3	10.60	WCaseJr	BabeRuth,Getty,ViewFromAbove	44-0
1-3^{92}	YR	4750	ft	NW4000L8CD	1	30^2	102^1	132^3	203	3x	8	8	8	8^{15}	8^{20}		207	7.70	GMosher	ItsThRitz,NomojsBigras,WzardofRs	41-0
12-20^{91}	YR	4000	ft	10000CL	1	28^2	59^2	130^3	201^1	8	3	3°	2°	3^{1}½	6^{3}½		201^4	2.30	WCaseJr	MillersDon,Paladium,KlsLtlKp	31-0
12-10^{91}	YR	4000	ft	10000CL	1	29	59^1	129^3	200^4	4	8	7	7°°	4^{4}½	3^{2}½		201^1	7.60	GMattison	CoveRoadike,AutoVanceN,Getty	44-0

ONE MILE PACE
PURSE $2,500
THURSDAY, JULY 2, 1992
PICK THREE
&
EXACTA

FOURTH RACE

THE MILLER HIGH LIFE PACING SERIES - 2ND LEG
2 YEAR OLDS

WARM UP-BLACK

8-1 **CURROBBIE** (NY) — b g 2 Curragh-BerneidaTurner-ArmbroPerry — 1992 4 0 1 2 $98
John J.,Norma L.& Ronald R.Richmond,Gansevoort,NY. First Starter
1 BRUCE MATTISON (165) bl-or-wh (144-12-25-9-.201) Tr—David Allen (.106) Lifetime $98
YELLOW

Program Number Date	Trk	Purse	Cd	Class	Dis	Leaders Time 1/4	1/2	3/4	Winners Time	PP	1/4	1/2	3/4	Str	Fin	Ind 1/4 Time	Ind Time	Odds	Driver	Order Of Finish First Second Third	Temp
6-25^{92}	Stga	2500	ft	LC	1	29^2	100^4	131^4	201^1	5	6	6	7°^{3}½	6	6^{11}½	31	203^2	56.00	BMattison	ShedrowRomeo,OlympusHeights,Win	67-0
6-20^{92}	Stga		ft	2YRQUA	1	31^1	104	134^3	205^3	1	2	2	2°½	2	2^{ns}	31	205^3	NB	BMattison	RomanticBeau,Currobbie,Spedskin	64-0
6-13^{92}	Stga	200	ft	BABY	1	31^2	104	134^3	204^3	4	3	3°	2°^{1}	3	4^{3}½	30^4	205^3	NB	BMattison	OlympusHeights,HarysFam,Curobi	70-0
6-6^{92}	Stga	200	sl	BABY	1	32^2	103^2	136^2	208^2	3	1	2	1^5	3	3^{4}½	33^3	210	NB	BMattison	ShedrowRomeo,BigMorgan,Curobie	60-0
5-30^{92}	Stga	200	ft	BABY	1	31^4	104	135^1	207	4	4	1°	1^{1}½	1	2^{ns}	31^4	207	NB	BMattison	MarineForecast,Curobi,BigMorgan	60-0

3-1 **WIN** — b c 2 MorningBreeze-WhiteOriginal-MountainSkipper — 1992 3 0 0 1 $300
Roger T.Slobody, West Brookfield, Mass. First Starter
2 WENDELL DONAWAY (150) pur-gld (26-2-5-6-.261) Tr—Wendell Donaway (.227) Lifetime $300
WHITE

Date	Trk	Purse	Cd	Class	Dis	1/4	1/2	3/4	Time	PP	1/4	1/2	3/4	Str	Fin	Ind 1/4 Time	Ind Time	Odds	Driver	Order Of Finish	Temp
6-25^{92}	Stga	2500	ft	LC	1	29^2	100^4	131^4	201^1	4	5	5	5^{2}½	3	3^{5}½	30	202^1	39.60	WDonaway	ShedrowRomeo,OlympusHeights,Win	67-0
6-18^{92}	Stga	1300	ft	C&GNW1PMCD	1	30^4	102^1	132^1	203^1	1x	2°	1	2^{3}½	4	[illegible]	33^1	206	5.10	WDonaway	MaideFla,MarinForcast,BigMorgan	76-0
6-11^{92}	Stga	1300	ft	C&GNW1PMCD	1	29^3	100^1	130^2	201	8	8	8	8^{11}½	8	[illegible]	32	204^3	25.00	WDonaway	ParadeJty,AlGratLngths,DrctHgo	74-0
5-30^{92}	Stga		ft	QUA	1	31^4	103^1	133^4	204^2	4	7	5°	3^{1}½	3	3^{1}¾	29^4	206^4	NB	WDonaway	CharlaJewel,ShiningSharlu,Win	60-0

10-1 **FORREST JUNGLE** — br c 2 ForrestSkipper-StormyMorning-StormDamage
D.MacTavish Jr,L.Oakwood,Fla,B.Cappione,NY.& W.MacKimmie,Que — 1992 1 0 0 0 $00 — First Starter — Lifetime $00
3 PERRY SIMSER (154) gold-green (61-10-10-10-.310) — Tr—Perry Simser (.386)
PURPLE

Date	Trk	Purse	Cd	Class	Dis	1/4	1/2	3/4	Time	PP	1/4	1/2	3/4	Str	Fin	Ind 1/4 Time	Ind Time	Odds	Driver	First, Second, Third	Temp
6-25^{92}	Stga	2500	ft	LC	1	30^{1}	102^{3}	133^{3}	202^{3}	6	6	7i	7°^{5}	x7	7$^{15\frac{1}{4}}$	31^{1}	206^{7}	64.60	PSimser	ThatBadBoy,MeNext,MarinForcast	67-0
6-10^{92}	PcD⅝		ft	QUA	1	30^{2}	101^{3}	131^{3}	202^{1}	6	7i	6	6$^{11\frac{1}{4}}$	6$^{14\frac{1}{2}}$	6^{16}	29^{4}	205	NB	GDaisleyJr	BrntaLow,LazyDaz,DiaguisDlimit	66-0
6-3^{92}	PcD⅝		ft	QUA	1	31	101^{2}	132	202^{1}	5	6	6	5$^{7\frac{1}{2}}$	5$^{6\frac{1}{2}}$	5^{10}	30^{4}	204^{1}	NB	GDaisley	GlaRebel,HitchHanover,ArmbroUf	66-0

5-2 **MARINE FORECAST** (NY) — b c 2 StormDamage-CandyBlueChip-MostHappyFella — Stga 2:07 — 1992 4 1 1 2 $749
Arlene L.& Jules J.Siegel,Somerville,N.J. — First Starter
4 NEAL SHAPIRO (150) white-blue-red (11-5-2-0-.556) — Tr—Neal Shapiro (.526) — 2,2:07 — Lifetime $749
BLACK

Date	Trk	Purse	Cd	Class	Dis	1/4	1/2	3/4	Time	PP	1/4	1/2	3/4	Str	Fin	Ind 1/4 Time	Ind Time	Odds	Driver	First, Second, Third	Temp
6-25^{92}	Stga	2500	ft	LC	1	30^{1}	102^{3}	133^{3}	202^{3}	7	7	6i°	3°$^{3\frac{1}{4}}$	3	3$^{1\frac{1}{4}}$	29^{4}	204	8.20	WInsy	ThatBadBoy,MeNext,MarinForcast	67-0
6-18^{92}	Stga	1300	ft	C&GNW1PMCD	1	30^{4}	102^{1}	132^{1}	203^{1}	4	5	4°	3°$^{3\frac{1}{4}}$	2	2^{7}	30^{4}	203^{3}	1.20	WInsy	MaidaFla,MarinForcast,BigMorgan	76-0
6-13^{92}	Stga	200	ft	BABY	1	28^{4}	100^{1}	130^{1}	200^{3}	7	6°	5	4°^{17}	3	5$^{13\frac{1}{2}}$	31	204^{3}	NB	NShapiro	ShdrowRomo,MixdFam,MarinForcast	70-0
6-6^{92}	Stga	200	sl	BABY	1	32^{2}	103^{2}	136^{2}	208^{2}	scr jg					scr					ShadrowRomeo,BigMorgan,Curobie	60-0
5-30^{92}	Stga	200	ft	BABY	1	31^{4}	104	135^{1}	207	5	5	4°	5$^{4\frac{1}{2}}$	3	1ns	31	207	NB	NShapiro	MarineForecast,Curobi,BigMorgan	60-0

4-1 **LORD LONICA** — b c 2 IcarusLobell-LonelyHeart-Overtrick — Stga 2:05 — 1992 3 1 1 0 $700
222 Stable,Kings Park,N.Y. — First Starter
5 KEVIN GOULD (140) gold-grn-white (21-2-1-3-.169) — Tr—Kevin Gould (.215) — 2,2:05 — Lifetime $700
GREEN

Date	Trk	Purse	Cd	Class	Dis	1/4	1/2	3/4	Time	PP	1/4	1/2	3/4	Str	Fin	Ind 1/4 Time	Ind Time	Odds	Driver	First, Second, Third	Temp
6-25^{92}	Stga	2500	ft	LC	1	30^{1}	102^{3}	133^{3}	202^{3}	2	2	2x	8dis	8	8dis			13.40	KGould	ThatBadBoy,MeNext,MarinForcast	67-0
6-16^{92}	Stga	1300	ft	C&GNW1PMCD	1	30^{3}	103^{3}	134^{7}	205	4	1	1	1^{3}	1	1$^{3\frac{3}{4}}$	30^{3}	205	*1.00	KGould	LordLonica,HapyPapou,SmonsWsdom	74-0
6-6^{92}	Stga	200	sl	BABY	1	31	105^{3}	136^{4}	206	2	2	2	2$^{1\frac{1}{2}}$	2	2$^{1\frac{1}{2}}$	29	206^{1}	NB	KGould	MixedFame,LordLonica,SunsetMufl	60-0

6-1 **ROADWORTHY** (NY) — b g 2 OnTheRoadAgain-LadyLynnJ-Albatross — 1992 1 0 0 0 $125
John A.Navelli,Rome,N.Y. — First Starter
6 KIM CRAWFORD (155) red-blk-wh (254-41-45-31-.301) — Tr—David Jannone (.528) — Lifetime $125
RED

Date	Trk	Purse	Cd	Class	Dis	1/4	1/2	3/4	Time	PP	1/4	1/2	3/4	Str	Fin	Ind 1/4 Time	Ind Time	Odds	Driver	First, Second, Third	Temp
6-25^{92}	Stga	2500	ft	LC	1	30^{1}	102^{3}	133^{3}	202^{3}	3	4	5i	6^{5}	6	5$^{8\frac{3}{4}}$	29^{4}	204^{7}	e1.40	KCrawford	ThatBadBoy,MeNext,MarinForcast	67-0
6-18^{92}	VD⅝		ft	QUA	1	29^{4}	103^{3}	135^{2}	204^{7}	4	7	6	6$^{6\frac{1}{2}}$	6$^{8\frac{3}{4}}$	6$^{9\frac{3}{4}}$	29^{3}	206^{1}	NB	JGregory	MrShomalo,LaTrosKash,PolshdSlvr	78-0

ONE MILE PACE
PURSE $1,300
THURSDAY, JULY 2, 1992
PICK THREE
&
EXACTA

FIFTH RACE

COLTS & GELDINGS
5 YEAR OLDS & UNDER
NON-WINNERS 1 PARI-MUTUEL RACE LIFETIME
INELIGIBLE: WINNERS OF 3 RACES LIFETIME

WARM UP-GREEN

4-1 **YOUNG LUXURY** — b g 3 SmartestRemark-LuxuryHanover-BigTowner — 1992 8 0 1 0 $939
Jay L.Randall, John Perrone & Joseph S.Emanuelo, NY. — First Starter
1 JAY RANDALL (145) blue-gold-white (144-17-20-16-.232) — Tr—Jay Randall (.271) — Lifetime $939
YELLOW

Program Number / Date	Trk	Purse	Cd	Class	Leaders Time Dis	1/4	1/2	3/4	Winners Time	PP	1/4	1/2	3/4	Str	Fin	Ind 1/4 Time	Ind Time	Odds	Driver	Order Of Finish First, Second, Third	Temp
6-23^{92}	Stga	1300	ft	C&GNW1PMCD	1	29^{3}	101	131^{1}	202	1	2	1	2$\frac{1}{2}$	3	4$^{4\frac{1}{2}}$	31^{7}	202^{4}	*1.80	JRandall	SnorCdam,LouSkpr,BoncstlHawk	69-0
6-13^{92}	Stga	1300	ft	C&GNW1PMCD	1	30^{7}	102^{1}	133^{4}	204^{7}	2	2	2	2$^{1\frac{1}{2}}$	2	2$^{1\frac{3}{4}}$	3[illegible]	204^{3}	10.50	JRandall	CharliGoWst,YongLxry,TrashMastr	82-0
6-6^{92}	Stga	1300	ft	C&GNW1PMCD	1	30^{1}	100^{7}	131^{1}	201^{4}	4	5	4°	3°^{7}	7	8$^{15\frac{1}{4}}$	33^{7}	205	8.30	JRandall	JacsuJo,ChariGoWst,MohawkShyRon	73-0
5-30^{92}	Stga	1300	ft	C&GNW1PMCD	1	29^{4}	101^{3}	132	202^{4}	5	6	4°	4°$^{7\frac{1}{2}}$	4	[illegible]	3[illegible]	203^{1}	6.80	JRandall	DeputyRalph,JacsuJo,NickyJoeFla	65-0
5-23^{92}	Stga	1400	ft	C&GNW1PMLT	1	30^{1}	102^{7}	133^{3}	202^{4}	6	6	5°	4°^{7}	4	4^{4}	2[illegible]	203^{3}	16.40	JRandall	GoldCardMorgan,Nrduel,DptyRalph	68-0
5-14^{92}	Stga	1400	ft	C&GNW1PMCD	1	30^{4}	102^{4}	133^{3}	203^{3}	4	4	4	4$^{7\frac{1}{2}}$	4	4$^{4\frac{1}{2}}$	30^{7}	204^{4}	3.40	JRandall	DbdeCheer,Nerduel,DeputyRalph	61-0
5-7^{92}	Stga	1400	ft	C&GNW1PMCD	1	30^{7}	102^{7}	133^{3}	204	6	7	7°	4°$^{3\frac{1}{2}}$	4	4$^{1\frac{1}{2}}$	30	204^{1}	7.60	JRandall	WaldnaFirst,FinalJopardy,PlrMac	63-0

10-1 **BRYJESS PULVERIZER** (NY) — b c 2 EmpireLarry-SatinFire-Chickeen — 1992 4 0 0 0 $00
Neil B.Gold & Charles W.Pulver,Chatham,N.Y. — First Starter
2 CHARLES PULVER (185) blk-white-green (19-5-1-2-.327) — Tr—Charles Pulver (.296) — Lifetime $00
WHITE

Date	Trk	Purse	Cd	Class	Dis	1/4	1/2	3/4	Time	PP	1/4	1/2	3/4	Str	Fin	Ind 1/4 Time	Ind Time	Odds	Driver	First, Second, Third	Temp
6-23^{92}	Stga	1300	ft	C&GNW1PMCD	1	29^{3}	101	131^{1}	202	7	8	7°	6°$^{5\frac{1}{2}}$	8	8$^{10\frac{1}{2}}$	31^{3}	204	40.80	CPulver	SnorCdam,LouSkpr,BoncstlHawk	69-0
6-13^{92}	Stga	1300	ft	C&GNW1PMCD	1	30^{7}	102^{1}	133^{4}	204^{7}	8	8	7°	6°°$^{4\frac{1}{2}}$	7	7^{5}	30^{4}	205^{7}	50.20	CPulver	CharliGoWst,YongLxry,TrashMastr	82-0
6-6^{92}	Stga	1300	ft	C&GNW1PMCD	1	30^{1}	100^{7}	131^{1}	201^{4}	3	4	5	5$^{3\frac{1}{2}}$	4	4$^{7\frac{3}{4}}$	31^{3}	203^{7}	51.20	CPulver	JacsuJo,ChariGoWst,MohawkShyRon	73-0
5-30^{92}	Stga	200	ft	BABY	1	30^{4}	103^{7}	134^{3}	202^{4}	4	6	6	7$^{15\frac{1}{2}}$	7	6$^{7\frac{3}{4}}$	29^{4}	207^{3}	NB	JRandall	CmeMgcTrk,BtysUmbria,Olympsnghts	60-0

6-1 **SPEEDSKIN** — b g 2 Redskin-PineHillNell-GoodTime — 1992 0 0 0 0 $00
John C.& Paulette Painter,Gloversville,N.Y. — First Starter
3 BERT BELANGER (140) bl-wh-go (122-15-11-12-.206) — Tr—Bert Belanger (.286) — Lifetime $00

Date	Trk	Purse	Cd	Class	Dis	1/4	1/2	3/4	Time	PP	1/4	1/2	3/4	Str	Fin	Ind 1/4 Time	Ind Time	Odds	Driver	First, Second, Third	Temp
6-20^{92}	Stga		ft	2YRQUA	1	31	104	134^{3}	205^{3}	4	3	3	4$^{5\frac{1}{2}}$	4	3^{5}	31	206^{3}	NB	BBelanger	RomanticBeau,Currobbie,Speedskin	64-0

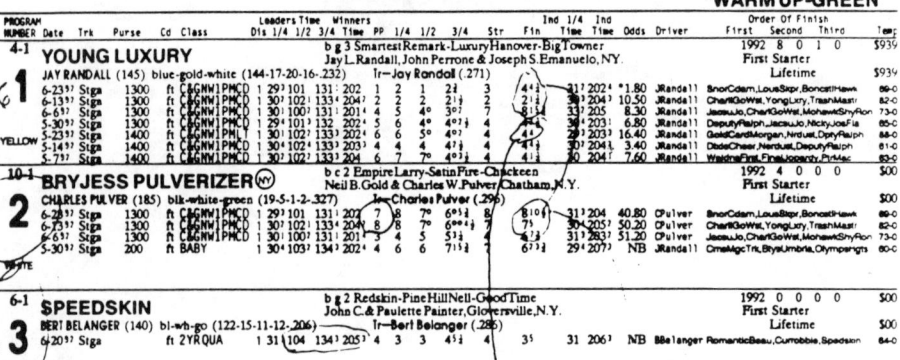

PURPLE

5-2 **HOLD ON TIGHT** — br g 3 Escort-SugarPlumSarah-FlyingBret — 1992 11 0 1 2 $969
Robert E.Lussier,Fair Haven,Vt. — First Starter
4 BRUCE MATTISON (165) bl-or-wh (144-12-25-9-.281) Tr—Robert Lussier (.146) — Lifetime $969
BLACK

6-18^{92}	Stga		1300	ft	C&GNW1PMCD	1	29^{1}	58^{4}	129^{4}	200^{4}	2	4	4	$3^{\circ 1}$	2	$3^{1\frac12}$	31	201	29.30	BBelanger	NclarFshn,AtGrtLngths,HldOnTght	78-0
6-11^{92}	Stga		1300	ft	C&GNW1PMCD	1	29^{3}	100^{1}	130^{2}	201	4	5	5	$5^{\circ 4\frac12}$	5	$4^{11\frac12}$	32	203^{2}	15.50	BBelanger	ParadsJfry,AtGratLngths,DrctHgo	74-C
6-2^{92}	Stga		1300	ft	C&GNW1PMCD	1	29^{1}	100^{2}	130^{4}	200^{4}	6	6	6°	$4^{\circ 4}$	4	[illegible]	30^{4}	202^{2}	17.30	BBelanger	PrinclyMix,ParadisJfry,DrctHugo	74-0
5-23^{92}	Stga		1400	ft	C&GNW1PMLT	1	30^{1}	102^{2}	133^{3}	202^{4}	8	8	7°	$5^{\circ 4}$	5	$5^{5\frac12}$	29^{2}	203^{4}	26.70	BBelanger	GoldCardMorgan,Nrdust,DptyRalph	88-0
5-14^{92}	Stga		1400	ft	C&GNW1PMCD	1	30^{4}	102^{4}	133^{3}	203^{3}	1	2	2	$2^{\circ \frac12}$	3	[illegible]	31	204^{3}	*1.20	BBelanger	DbdeCheer,Nerdust,DeputyRalph	61-0
5-1^{92}	VD(m)		1200	gd	NWPMLTCD	1	28^{2}	100^{4}	130^{4}	201^{1}	7	1	1	2^{2}	$2^{2\frac12}$	$2^{2\frac12}$	30^{2}	201^{3}	4.60	DHckabonJ	Baruck,HoldOnTight,DiscountRate	51-0
4-25^{92}	VD(m)		1200	ft	NWPMLTCD	1	27^{4}	59^{1}	128^{4}	158^{4}	1	4	4	$5^{3\frac12}$	$5^{7\frac12}$	3^{1}	31	200^{2}	39.00	DHckabonJ	DaytonBold,Baruck,HoldOnTight	59-C

8-1 **HELLO TUX** (NY) — b c 3 TucsonHanover-HelloDruid-SayHello — QStga 2:04^{2} 1992 8 0 0 1 $557
Cardinal Ranch,Saratoga Springs,N.Y. — 1991 1 0 0 0 $00
5 DAVID MARSHALL (185) ltbl-red-gld (183-20-26-24-.232) Tr—Richard Butler (.083) — Q3,2:04^{2} Lifetime $557
GREEN

6-23^{92}	Stga		1300	ft	C&GNW1PMCD	1	29^{3}	101	131^{1}	202	2	4	6	$7^{5\frac12}$	5	5^{7}	31	203^{2}	9.10	DMarshall	SnorCdam,LousSkpr,BoncstlHawk	89-0
6-17^{92}	Stga			ft	QUA	1	29^{2}	101^{1}	132^{1}	204^{2}	4	4	4	$4^{\circ 1\frac12}$	4	[illegible]	32	204^{2}	NB	DMarshall	HelloTux,DVCinflight,ItTkesTime	65-0
4-2^{92}	Stga		1200	ft	NW1PMLTCD	1	29^{4}	101^{4}	133	203^{4}	8	5	5	5^{4}	5	$4^{8\frac12}$	31^{3}	205^{2}	17.20	DMarshall	WndyNtchRhir,PrdsDan,BonCstlChp	40-0
3-26^{92}	Stga		1200	sy	NW1PMLTCD	1	32	106^{1}	138	208^{3}	2	2	2	$2^{2\frac12}$	2	$4^{8\frac12}$	31^{4}	210^{1}	6.50	DMarshall	BeboroFla,ParadeDan,RobnsBatman	52-C
3-19^{92}	Stga		1200	ft	NW1PMLTCD	1	31^{1}	102^{3}	134^{3}	205	5	6	6	$5^{4\frac12}$	4	5^{6}	30^{4}	206^{1}	12.10	DMarshall	PaulesPride,BeeboroFela,Baruck	33-0
2-23^{92}	Stga	A	1200	gd	NW1PMLTCD	1	29^{4}	102^{4}	134^{3}	203^{4}	8	5°	5	$6^{4\frac12}$	6	7^{18}	32	207^{2}	56.00	DMarshall	RushMHom,WaldnsFrst,FrdlsMshmos	34-C
2-9^{92}	Stga	A	1200	gd	NW1PMLTCD	1	30^{3}	103^{2}	136	208^{3}	8	5	5	$6^{\circ 2\frac12}$	5	4^{2}	33^{3}	210	20.10	DMarshall	ItalianDignity,WaldnsFrst,Twnkl	24-C

3-1 **LOUIS SKIPPER** — br h 5 SkippersSun-LusettaHanover-TarHeel — 1992 2 0 1 0 $325
Coming Through Stable, Pittsfield, Ma. — 1991 22 0 1 1 $2.615
6 ANTHONY GIOVANNELLI (136) blk-gra (12-4-2-0-.426) Tr—Kenneth Clairmont (.000) — Lifetime $4.511
RED

6-23^{92}	Stga		1300	ft	C&GNW1PMCD	1	29^{3}	101	131^{1}	202	5	7	5°	$3^{\circ 1\frac12}$	2	2^{3}	31	202^{3}	2.20	AGovanl	SnorCdam,LousSkpr,BoncstlHawk	89-0
6-17^{92}	Stga			ft	QUA	1	29^{4}	101^{2}	132^{2}	202^{2}	2	2	2	$3^{1\frac12}$	2	[illegible]	30^{1}	202^{4}	NB	AGovanl	BustByBy,LouisSkpr,BaloonyBlChp	65-0
6-13^{92}	Stga			ft	QUA HD	1	30^{1}	101^{1}	132^{2}	204^{1}	3	5	5	$5^{\circ 12}$	5	$5^{15\frac12}$	32^{3}	207^{2}	NB	JBarchi	SnorCdam,MadGShgbrk,FlatbdFord	70-0
3-6^{92}	Phld			ft	QUA T-P HD	1	30^{3}	101^{2}	131^{2}	201	6	5°	5	$6^{15\frac12}$	$6^{16\frac12}$	$7^{28\frac12}$	32	206^{3}	NB	SRufo	Cleverlator,TWan,CTV	48-1
3-3^{92}	Phld	A	2800	ft	MDNCD	1	29^{4}	100^{2}	131^{3}	202^{1}	8	8	8	$7x^{\circ 12\frac12}$	8^{17}	$8^{27\frac12}$	32^{3}	206^{3}	41.10	CCitoJr	DigDeep,PastryChef,QuillasSting	38-0
2-8^{92}	M1			ft	QUA	1	29^{2}	100^{4}	131	159^{3}	3	7	7	$6^{13\frac12}$	$6^{16\frac12}$	$6^{19\frac12}$	29^{4}	203^{2}	NB	FCarlucci	Tmtros,ThOthrGuy,LndwodCnturon	33-2
1-21^{92}	M1			ft	QUA	1	29^{2}	101^{2}	131^{4}	200^{2}	7	8	8	$8^{18\frac12}$	$8^{22\frac12}$	8^{30}	31	206^{2}	NB	FCarlucci	BuckysGirl,SwngngMandy,RoyctaTp	28-2

12-1 **THE OLD DUFFAH** — b c 3 MorningBreeze-WhiteIce-FlyFlyByrd — 1992 6 0 0 1 $449
(Lessee)Linda L.Laudig, Chatham, N.Y. — QStga 2:07 1991 2 0 0 0 $00
7 KEVIN GOULD (140) gold-grn-white (21-2-1-3-.169) Tr—Linda Laudig (.042) — Q2,2:07 Lifetime $449
BROWN

6-23^{92}	Stga		1300	ft	C&GNW1PMCD	1	29^{3}	101	131^{1}	202	4	6	8	$8^{6\frac12}$	6	$7^{10\frac12}$	31^{2}	204	11.00	JMongonJr	SnorCdam,LousSkpr,BoncstlHawk	89-0
6-11^{92}	Stga		1300	ft	C&GNW1PMCD	1	29^{3}	100^{1}	130^{2}	201	3	1	2	$4^{3\frac12}$	4	$5^{11\frac12}$	33	204^{1}	17.10	KGould	ParadsJfry,AtGratLngths,DrctHgo	74-0
6-2^{92}	Stga		1300	ft	C&GNW1PMCD	1	29^{1}	100^{2}	130^{4}	200^{4}	3	3	3	$5^{4\frac12}$	5	$4^{7\frac12}$	30^{3}	202^{1}	17.30	KGould	PrinclyMix,ParadisJfry,DrctHugo	74-0
5-25^{92}	Stga	A	1400	ft	NW1PMLTCD	1	29^{4}	100^{4}	131^{1}	202^{2}	7	7	5°	$5^{3\frac12}$	5	$4^{11\frac12}$	32^{3}	204^{3}	14.50	BMattison	FinalJopardy,ParadsJfry,DrctHgo	56-0
5-16^{92}	Stga		1400	ft	C&GNW1PMCD	1	29^{3}	101	131^{2}	202^{2}	5	6	5°	$4^{\circ 1\frac12}$	4	$3^{3\frac12}$	31^{2}	203	20.20	KGould	PeterMac,FinalJoprdy,ThOldDufah	80-C
5-9^{92}	Stga		1400	ft	C&GNW1PMCD	1	31	103	133^{4}	203^{3}	6	6	5i°	$6^{17\frac12}$	6	$6^{17\frac12}$	29^{4}	206	16.50	KGould	HHFella,DirectHugo,BrigidsBoy	70-C
5-1^{92}	Stga			ft	QUA	1	30^{4}	102^{1}	134	205^{1}	3	3	3	6^{2}	6	4^{2}	31^{1}	205^{3}	NB	KGould	SignalHillBilly,InW,MizMin	48-C

12-1 **OFF SET** — b g 3 JayTime-VitaAnBye-Bye Bye Andy — QStga 2:07^{3} 1992 6 0 0 0 $130
David Horenstein,Albany,N.Y. — 1991 0 0 0 0 $00
8 GERRY MATTISON (160) blue-or-wh (203-35-27-17-.274) Tr—Sean Campbell (.000) — Q3,2:07^{3} Lifetime $130
GRAY

6-20^{92}	Stga			ft	QUA	1	31^{1}	103^{3}	134^{1}	204^{3}	4	3	3	3^{3}	4	$4^{6\frac12}$	31	205^{4}	NB	WHnsy	RdEyExprs,LandmrkLiz,TrousrMous	64-C
6-18^{92}	Stga		1300	ft	C&GNW1PMCD	1	30^{4}	102^{1}	132^{1}	203^{1}	8	8	8°	$8^{13\frac12}$	8	$8^{23\frac12}$	33^{1}	208	121.10	DHornstn	MaidsFla,MarinForcast,BigMorgan	78-C
6-11^{92}	Stga		1300	ft	C&GNW1PMCD	1	29^{3}	100^{1}	130^{2}	201	1	4	6	$7^{6\frac12}$	7	$8^{18\frac12}$	33	204^{3}	47.30	DHornstn	ParadsJfry,AtGratLngths,DrctHgo	74-0
5-28^{92}	Stga		1300	ft	C&GNW1PMCD	1	30^{3}	101^{3}	133	203^{4}	5	3°	1°	$4^{\circ 2}$	6	7^{10}	32^{2}	205^{4}	35.90	DHornstn	FaxThis,AtGratLngths,JacsJlyBan	62-0
5-21^{92}	Stga		1400	ft	C&GNW1PMCD	1	29^{2}	59^{4}	131	200^{3}	6	7	7	6^{9}	6	$6^{11\frac12}$	30	202^{4}	179.70	DHornstn	RolandLobell,PrnclyMix,FaxThis	85-0
4-30^{92}	Stga		1400	gd	C&GNW1PMCD	1	29^{3}	101^{4}	131^{4}	202^{2}	1	4	4	$5^{7\frac12}$	5	$5^{10\frac12}$	31^{2}	204^{3}	95.60	DHornstn	Castiron,RolandLobl,WaldnsFirst	58-0
4-20^{92}	Stga			ft	QUA	1	30^{4}	102	133^{1}	205^{3}	5	4	4	$4^{\circ 6\frac12}$	3	4^{5}	32^{1}	206^{3}	NB	DHornstn	Nerdust,AlleWonga,NowinaHaribal	50-0

There was no intelligent win bet because he went off at 2-5. But what of the Pick 3, which began with the third race?

A scratch left only a field of five in the fourth race, a Late Closer Series for 2-year-olds. A field of seven maidens would compete in the fifth. If either the fourth or the fifth race showed a strong favorite we liked, there was no reason to play Pick 3s. However, the favorite in both races looked vulnerable.

In the fourth, the 4 horse, Marine Forecast, was a reasonable favorite, but would go off at an unreasonable price: 4-5. In the fifth, the two morning-line favorites, Hold On Tight and Louis Skipper, had lifetime records of 0-for-11 and 0-for-24, respectively.

The horse we liked the most in the fifth was the 2, Bryjess Pulverizer, 10-1 on the morning line.

We went with two $2 tickets, both using Brandon T exclusively in the third: a) with all five horses in the fourth and just the 2 in the sixth (costing $10); and b) with the 4, 5 and 6 in the fourth and the 1, 3, 4 and 6 in the fifth (costing $24). Total bet: $34.

This Pick 3 had the potential of being hit and paying less than what we bet. We just had to live with that possibility.

But that didn't happen this night.

Brandon T ($2.80) won the third and Lord Lonica won the fourth, paying $14.20 to win.

That left us live in the Pick 3 with five horses, whose payoffs were: 1—$106; 2—$215; 3—$263.20; 4—$71, and 6—$78.

The 1 horse won at 3-1, giving us a $106 return. The 4 was second and the 2 a fairly-close third.

That said, let's add a touch of reality. Usually playing such heavy favorites is dumb. I have hundreds of examples, but we're near the end of the book and we don't have a lot of space. Trust me.

Late Changes

Scratches may force you to re-think an entire race. If you'd identified two speed horses and tossed out both expecting a speed duel, what happens if one is scratched? Doesn't that mean the remaining one is the lone speed? Or will another driver leave with a different horse for the same reason?

What happens when you liked the 7 horse, but dismissed him because of his post, and he gets scratched into the 6 hole?

We don't want to keep you up nights thinking about this, but it does happen.

Equipment changes provide important information. Thoroughbred tracks note a change in blinkers—off or on—right in the entries. Harness tracks are lax in not doing the same with their horses' equipment. Bettors must rely on an equipment board somewhere in the grandstand and clubhouse, and/or announcements.

By far, the most important equipment change in 1992 was the quick-hitch sulky. Most horses improved dramatically using it for the first time.

Chicago, Chicago

Chicago offers a unique handicapping challenge. The Windy City offers harness racing at $1/2$, $5/8$, $7/8$ and 1-mile tracks. "I believe it's unique," Ron Marsh, one of Chicago's top drivers, says. "Every three or four months we go to a different racetrack. Not only do the horses have to be versatile, but the trainers and drivers, too."

And handicappers.

Here's the deal: Maywood is a $1/2$-mile track. Balmoral has a $5/8$-mile track for night racing inside a 1-mile oval used only in the daylight. Racing at Hawthorne is on a 1-mile track, and Sportsman's is believed to be the only $7/8$-mile facility in the country.

"We have it all. As a professional handicapper, I love it," Mike Paradise says. Paradise is a busy man. Besides serving as Sportsman's Park's Director of Public Relations, he is a handicapper for the *Chicago Tribune* and co-host of Chicago Harness Racing on Sports Channel Chicago.

His handicapping abilities were tested—along with everyone else's—in the spring of 1991 when Sportsman's Park unveiled its new race course. The $5/8$ oval was increased to $7/8$ of a mile. A field of 10 with one trailer became fields of 10 across the front. An ordinary stretch became the longest in North America, 1,436 feet—that's more than the final quarter of a mile on a straightaway. "It was pretty weird," Marsh says. "For the first two weeks, everybody was feeling it out. The strategy at first was to stay near the front."

That changed. "One of the best winning moves was to leave, wait, and then make a strong move to the lead on the backside," says Marsh, whose father drives at Yonkers. "Wait until after a quarter to make a move. That strategy won a lot of races."

Favorites didn't. "The percentage of favorites went down drastically," Paradise says. "People got a real quick feel of it."

Horses also. "You've got horses for courses, for sure," Ron Marsh says. "You've got horses that do better at Maywood. Others do better at Hawthorne. The horses who do better at bigger tracks do well at Sportsman's."

The way horses performed at Sportsman's first 7/8-mile meeting was intriguing. "I don't think there's any question that this track is the most honest track (without a bias) for anyone," Paradise says. "Post positions didn't play as big a part. The rail is not that big an advantage."

He's right. The 1 post checked in sixth of the 10 posts in win percentage at 10.3. From the 2 through 10, the percentages were: 11.4, 11.2, 11.7, a high of 15.0 from the 5 post, 13.7, 9.1, 9.2, 9.2 and 6.7. The parity of the 2 through 4 posts, and that of the 7 through 9, reflect the vibrant competitiveness of the remodeled track.

But that all changes when racing periodically shuffles off to another Chicago track. "The biggest thing when you talk about Chicago handicapping is that it's night and day difference when you go from Sportsman's to Maywood," Paradise says. Marsh agrees: "When we move from Sportsman's to Maywood, it's a big, big change. All the horses were pacing fantastic closing quarters at Sportsman's. Then they go to Maywood, and it's hard to handicap."

Paradise frequently looks to drivers: "I believe that because of the uniqueness of the staggered starting gate at Sportsman's, driver strategy takes a big part, not as much as at a 1/2-mile, but more than at 1-mile tracks."

Some pointers from Paradise:

- "The best time to gamble and make money is early in a new meeting. If you know your horses, you can do well. When you wait to get a line on these horses, so does everyone else. Then your $14 winner is paying $5 or $6."
- "If you see early action on a horse, everyone thinks the horse is hot. You can't be distracted by early money on a horse."
- "Avoid cheap speed horses at Maywood."
- "When they come from Maywood to Sportsman's, drivers look at the long, long stretch and they wait. You can get guys who can steal a race on the front end."

- "I strongly believe in horses for courses."

From Marsh:

- "You always want to watch horses dropping down."
- "Look for aggressive drivers."

A Final Word

Enjoy!